England’s Seaside Heritage from the Air

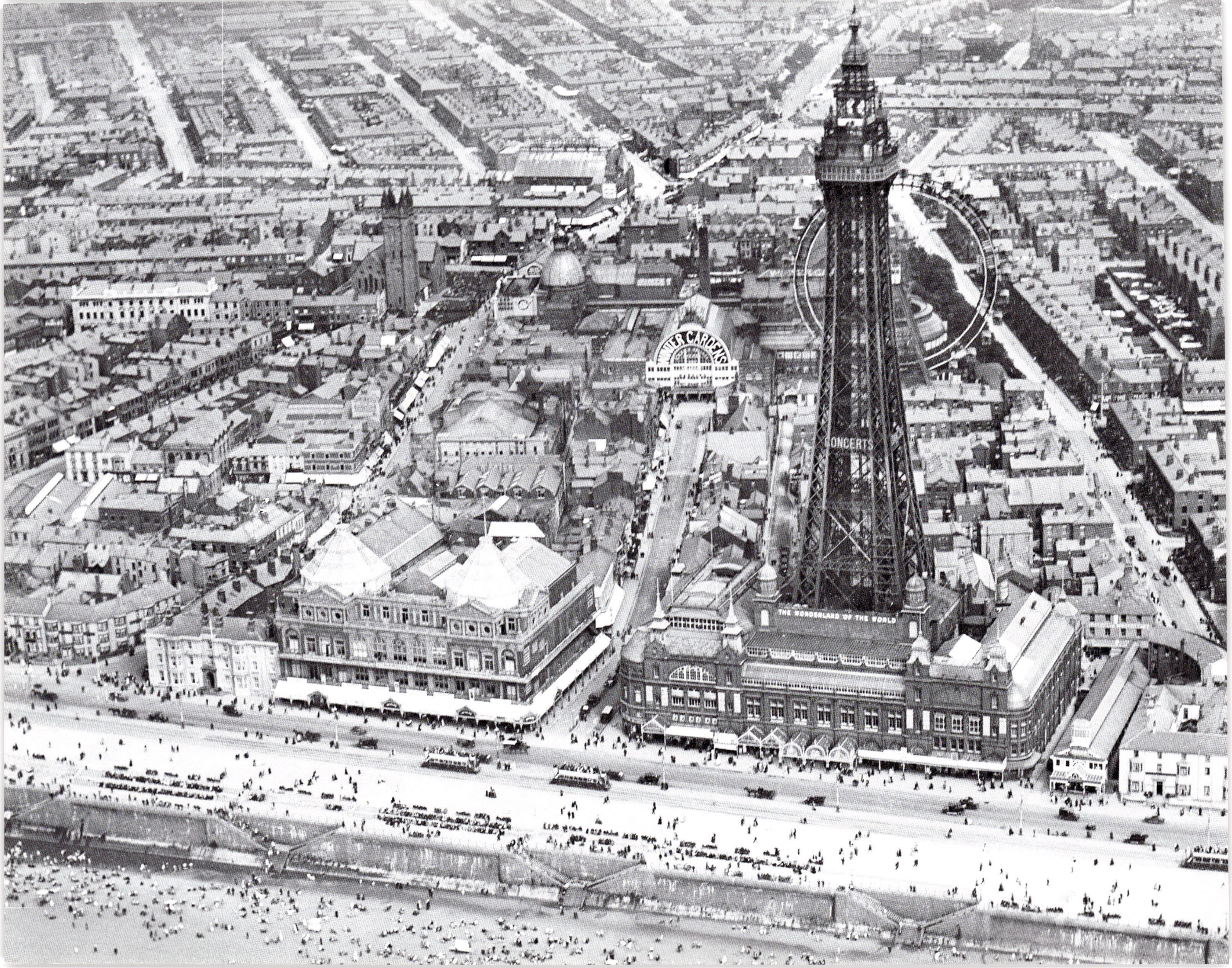
CONCERTS
THE WONDERLAND OF THE WORLD

England's Seaside Heritage from the Air

Allan Brodie

Historic England

Published by Liverpool University Press on behalf of Historic England, The Engine House, Fire Fly Avenue, Swindon SN2 2EH
www.HistoricEngland.org.uk

Historic England is a Government service championing England's heritage and giving expert, constructive advice, and the English Heritage Trust is a charity caring for the National Heritage Collection of more than 400 historic properties and their collections.

First published 2021

ISBN 978-1-80085-964-7

British Library Cataloguing in Publication data
A CIP catalogue record for this book is available from the British Library.

Historic England holds an unparalleled archive of 12 million photographs, drawings, reports and publications on England's places. It is one of the largest archives in the UK, the biggest dedicated to the historic environment, and a priceless resource for anyone interested in England's buildings, archaeology, landscape and social history. Viewed collectively, its photographic collections document the changing face of England from the 1850s to the present day. It is a treasure trove that helps us understand and interpret the past, informs the present and assists with future management and appreciation of the historic environment. For more information about images from the Archive, contact Archives Services Team, Historic England, The Engine House, Fire Fly Avenue, Swindon SN2 2EH; telephone (01793) 414600.

Typeset in Source Sans Pro 9/12pt

Edited by Sarah Enticknap
Page layout by Carnegie Book Production
Printed by Gomer Press.

Frontispiece: Blackpool Tower and the Winter Gardens, Blackpool, Lancashire July 1920 EPW002059

Contents

Preface

Aerofilms Ltd was created in 1919, and almost immediately set off to the seaside. Some of the earliest photographs taken by this new company were at resorts in the south-east of England in the early months of 1920, and the company regularly returned to the seaside during the subsequent decades.

The period covered in this book ranges primarily from 1920 to 1953 and shows seaside resorts at somewhere close to the peak of their popularity, which has been variously put at anywhere between the 1950s and the mid-1970s. The interwar years so vividly captured in these images saw a substantial expansion of resorts and frequently a recasting of the facilities being provided for visitors. By this date, some resorts had been welcoming holidaymakers for two centuries, and at many resorts, larger and more modern entertainment facilities were appearing, along with new arrivals in the form of outdoor bathing pools and amusement parks. A growing number of motor vehicles are obvious over the decades, but this was a period where the train was still the dominant means of going to the seaside and aerial photographs illustrate clearly how railway lines and stations shaped the fabric of many seaside resorts.

The Aerofilms collection of more than one million photographs was acquired by the responsible national heritage bodies for England, Scotland and Wales in 2007, and in the subsequent decade around a tenth of the collection representing the earlier decades were digitised and can be viewed on the Britain from Above website at www.britainfromabove.org.uk/en.

In their first full year of operation, Aerofilms logged 2,332 aerial photographs in the registers. Today, when a telephone can contain a camera, photography may seem to be a straightforward skill, but for the pioneering photographers of Aerofilms, life was much more complicated. The images were captured one at a time on glass negatives measuring 5 inches by 4 inches in bulky cameras. Therefore, it is no surprise that there are errors in some of the negatives, such as a bit of flare from the sun or the edge of the wing. However, this often adds to the authenticity of the image and offers great insights into the conditions under which these heroic photographers worked.

Introduction

School history once taught that the Victorians invented the train and duly went to the seaside; in fact, the roots of the modern seaside holiday lie a century earlier. By the early 18th century, the wealthiest in English society were regularly visiting spas to drink mineral water in the belief that this would improve their health and cure their often self-inflicted medical conditions. Some doctors and scientists were also recognising that the sea could have a similar curative effect and began promoting the virtues of bathing in cold seawater. While the operators of a spa could control access to its mineral waters, enterprising doctors and businesspeople came up with the bathing machine and strongly recommended that this should be used under the supervision of a qualified medical practitioner or bathing guide. Most scientific evaluations of seawater found that it was most effective when it was cold and so a day at the Georgian seaside would begin with a bath in a bathhouse or more often a dip in the sea before the sun had warmed the water. This left the remainder of the day free to undo any of the good that might have been accomplished, in assembly rooms, at circulating libraries, drinking in coffee houses and visiting the theatre.

The earliest seaside resorts were working ports; they already enjoyed some entertainment facilities and had accommodation for visitors who would lodge in rooms in the houses of the working population. Ports were on regular coaching routes and, perhaps most importantly, already had easy access to the sea. Some of these first seaside resorts, such as Brighton or Margate, are no longer ports; others, such as Scarborough and Weymouth, have managed to continue as working ports and seaside resorts. However, other early seaside resorts, such as Liverpool, Portsmouth and Southampton, are now firmly ports, access to the sea for leisure purposes being pushed outwards as their economies became dominated by commerce.

By the late 18th century, the desire to spend time at the seaside was spreading down through society, and Margate was welcoming shopkeepers and tradespeople from London who would arrive at its harbour on sailing vessels that had previously carried cargo. Margate was the first seaside resort to experience a form of mass tourism, particularly once steamers began to ply the route between central London and the Kent resort in 1815. It was the first resort to witness substantial expansion beyond its original historic footprint from the 1760s onwards, with the erection of Cecil Square and Hawley Square. By the early 19th century, huge urban extensions to seaside resorts were being constructed, for instance, to the east and west of Brighton and at St Leonards beside Hastings, and on some stretches of coastline entirely new resorts were being established. Southport, founded at the end of the 18th century, and Bournemouth, established during the 1810s, have grown into popular seaside resorts, but Hayling Island, which was the location for an ambitious development in the 1820s, did not enjoy similar success.

During the course of the 18th century, the small number of brave sea bathers gradually became hundreds and perhaps a few thousand visitors each year to the most popular resorts. With the creation of a national railway system by the mid-19th century, the busiest seaside resorts welcomed hundreds of thousands of holidaymakers, and in the case of a resort such as Blackpool, millions came each year. In many counties, industrialisation led to an erosion of the traditional local holidays and festivities; however, in Lancashire and Yorkshire they survived into the 19th and 20th century, though by then the week or fortnight holiday was usually being taken at seaside resorts such as Blackpool.

Railways not only changed the way that people travelled to the seaside, but also transformed resorts, shaping and zoning subsequent housing and industrial developments. Prestigious housing would be located where a sea view could be enjoyed, while working people's homes and industrial businesses might be concentrated along the tracks or around the railway station. The increase in the number of visitors made redundant the small-scale, intimate facilities enjoyed by wealthy Georgian sea bathers and in their place came large, sometimes industrial-scale venues and attractions.

The new technology of the Industrial Revolution embodied by the train also had an impact on the fabric of seaside resorts. Wooden jetties by the mid-19th century were being superseded by seaside piers on iron piles designed to cater for the growing number and size of steamers. Seaside piers were also becoming fashionable places to promenade as well as places of entertainment. Winter gardens, sometimes vast new glasshouses inspired by the Crystal Palace, appeared at many seaside resorts, and novel forms of transport, such as cliff lifts, cliff railways and electric trains, also proved popular with holidaymakers. Cinemas and amusement parks would become popular attractions at seaside resorts once electricity was available.

The First World War interrupted the development of seaside resorts, but the interwar years saw many adding

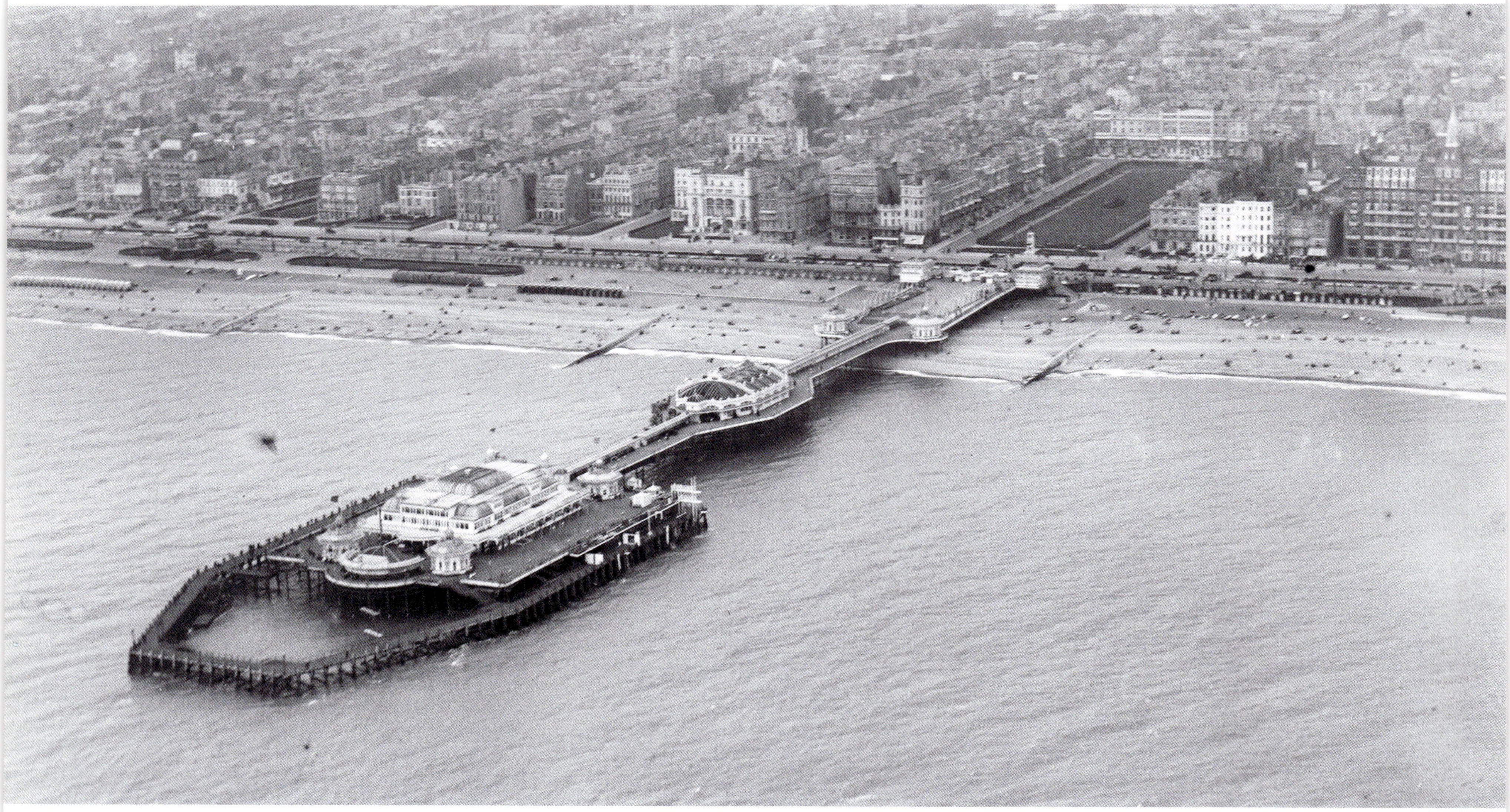

West Pier, Brighton, East Sussex April 1920 EPW000516

new seafront facilities, most notably the open-air pool or lido. Few now survive, but the Aerofilms collection contains many images that capture the scale of these new facilities. Holiday camps appeared in large numbers between the wars, providing affordable accommodation as well as a range of entertainment facilities, and the scale of these sites is often best appreciated from the air. Aerial photographs of the interwar years also show that a growing number of people were coming to the seaside by car, charabanc or bus; however, the major shift away from the railway would only take place after the Second World War.

The most important event for seaside resorts between the wars was probably the 1938 Holidays with Pay Act, which for the first time granted statutory annual leave to a large part of the country's population. The Second World War inevitably interrupted its implementation, but when peace returned, growing numbers of people could begin to enjoy a week or a fortnight at the seaside. Increasing numbers of holidaymakers came by car and this contributed to the outward expansion of resorts and the creation of new resorts and settlements on previously undeveloped stretches of coastline. This process had begun between the wars with the creation of some plotlands, such as at Peacehaven and Jaywick, but a growing number of chalets and caravan settlements appeared in the 1950s and 1960s.

Almost the latest photographs featured in this collection date from 1953, a momentous year in the history of England's seaside resorts. A storm surge in the North Sea devastated several resorts on the east coast of England and killed 307 people, some of whom died in their beds. The result of this event was captured by Aerofilms, which reacted quickly to this disaster. The impact of the surge was exacerbated by the lack of investment in the coastal protection at many resorts and led to a national re-evaluation of the height to which sea defences should be built. By the early 21st century, however, climate change and rising sea levels have led to further consideration and new investment to protect England's colourful and valuable seaside heritage.

The images selected in this book begin by telling the story of seaside resorts from their origins in the 18th century before looking at how people travelled to the seaside and moved around at seaside resorts. Initially restricted to coaches and stagecoaches, holidaymakers in the 19th century could also travel to their destination on board steamers and later on trains. Both forms of transport have left their mark on seaside resorts, through the provision of piers and jetties on seafronts and perhaps more profoundly due to the impact of railway lines and stations on the plan and character of the towns. The coastal location and geographical form of some seaside resorts prompted investors to construct cliff lifts and cliff railways to allow visitors to travel effortlessly between their lodgings on the clifftops and the beach and sea below. The first visitors to seaside resorts came in search of improved health, and over the course of the 19th and 20th centuries a variety of facilities were created for this. These range from small bathing pools to large swimming pools, and are well illustrated in the Aerofilms collection.

Today there is a greater emphasis on having fun while at the seaside, and to this end a number of themes are explored in these aerial photographs. Topics covered include activities on the beach and the range of entertainments available at the seaside, including amusement parks and funfairs, the joy of the seaside pier and the pleasure of a stroll around seafront gardens. To make full use of the pleasures of the seaside resort, most people would want to stay for more than one day, and a range of options for accommodation developed during the 19th and 20th centuries, from the grandest of grand hotels, through lodging rooms in residents' houses to the holiday camps and caravan sites of the 20th century. Aerial photography proves to be a particularly effective way of capturing the form and scale of some of these expansive sites.

Hitherto, most of the content has focused on man-made interventions and creations, but the seaside resort is often a place where people can be found to be in stark contrast with the power of nature. The sea, once regarded as a place where monsters lived, still has the power to sink ships and destroy sea defences and even whole islands. However, the sea is also a place where man has worked for millennia harvesting its riches, and unfortunately it has also been a place where rival nations have come into conflict. The easy access to the sea found at seaside resorts inevitably also made them ideal places for invading forces and, therefore, since the 16th century, more or less substantial military defences have been constructed at many. Seaside resorts have also been the location for many significant historical events, and the presence of the sea seems to arouse something spiritual in anyone who sits and contemplates it. Therefore, it is no surprise that the seafront of many seaside resorts has proved an ideal place for commemorating historical figures, brave seafarers and events that have shaped the history of these islands.

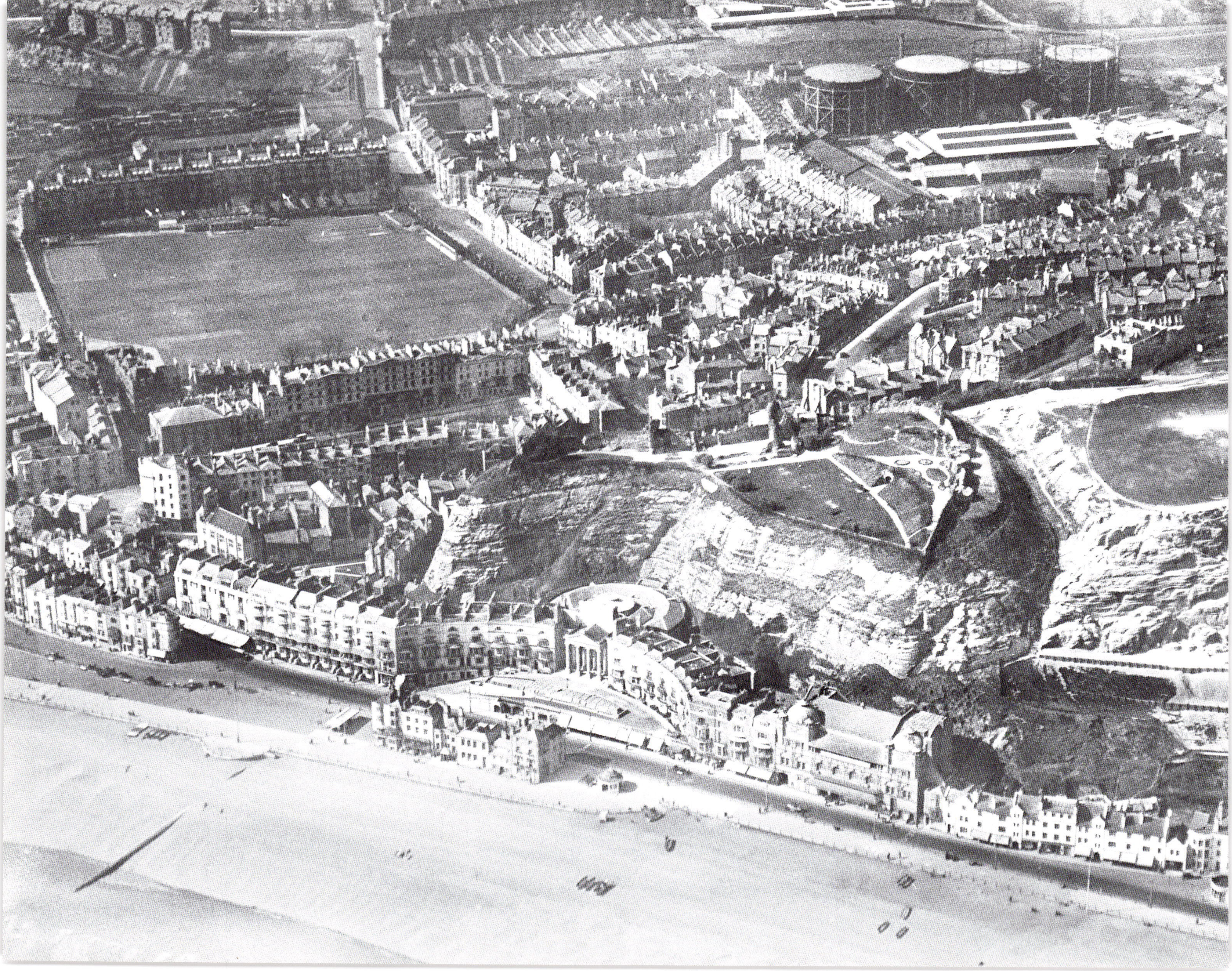

Pelham Crescent, the castle and environs, Hastings, East Sussex
24 April 1929

Hastings is arguably the most famous seaside town in England, not for its beach or fish and chips, but for an event that did not take place there. On 28 September 1066, William the Conqueror arrived at Pevensey, seized control of the Roman fort there and marched to Hastings to await the arrival of King Harold's forces. A hastily constructed castle at Hastings is depicted in the Bayeux Tapestry and is likely to have been a timber tower around which earth was banked. The site of this castle is unknown and may not necessarily have been on the site of the medieval castle on the clifftop seen in this photograph. When the Normans did clash with, and defeat, the Anglo-Saxons on 14 October, it was not at Hastings, but a few miles inland at Battle.

In front of the clifftop ruins of the castle can be seen Pelham Crescent, constructed between 1824 and 1828 by Thomas Pelham, Earl of Chichester. It is unusual on the seafront of seaside resorts because of the prominence of a large church at its centre, and this has a large bazaar of shops in front. To the right of Pelham Crescent can be seen the former Palace of Varieties, constructed by Ernest Runtz in 1897–9 as a music hall. This building later became a cinema, a bingo hall and an amusement arcade (*see* p 173).

This 1929 photograph also shows Beach Terrace in front of Pelham Crescent. It appears to be a mixture of 18th- and 19th-century buildings in a haphazard arrangement and it was demolished during the early 1930s reconfiguration of the seafront. The site is now a car park. Behind Pelham Crescent in the distance is a cricket ground that is now the site of a large shopping centre. Between it and the castle is Wellington Square, which was laid out in 1819–23. Houses were built around three sides of the square, the seaward fourth side being left undeveloped to allow occupants of the houses views of the sea.

EPW026212

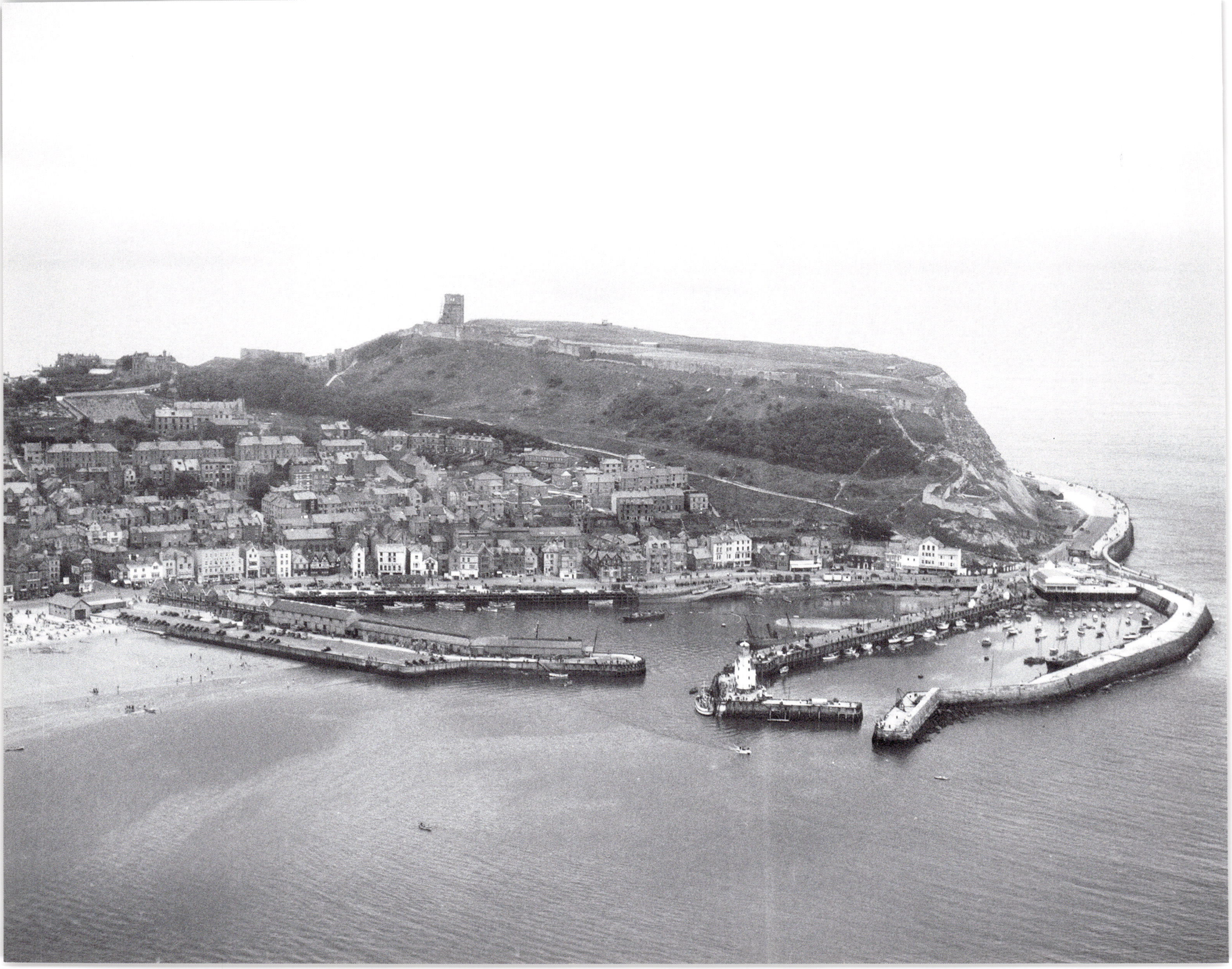

The Old and East Harbours and Scarborough Castle, Scarborough, North Yorkshire
23 June 1948

The story of the seaside dates back to the Tudor and Stuart period. Leland's *Itineraries* (*c* 1540) records a patient sent to a coastal village for the sake of his health; sea bathing was used for some conditions by the end of the 16th century and Henry Manship refers to doctors in Cambridge in 1619 who sent patients to Great Yarmouth 'to take the air of the sea'. At Scarborough seawater was drunk as a cure to supplement the spring water being imbibed at the spa, and by 1667 Dr Robert Wittie, in his book on Scarborough Spa, noted that bathing in seawater had cured his gout. By *c* 1700 Sir John Floyer, the leading advocate of cold-water bathing, was proclaiming that the sea could act as a huge 'Cold Bath' to cure many ills.

Scientists and medical writers were becoming enthusiastic about sea bathing, and there are indications from personal documents that ordinary people were taking to the sea by the start of the 18th century. In the meticulous journal of the Lancashire landowner Nicholas Blundell (1669–1773), his family sought medical treatment by visiting doctors and various spas, making a pilgrimage to Holywell in north Wales and bathing in the sea close to their home at Little Crosby, near Liverpool. Blundell's first recorded dip in the sea occurred on 5 August 1708 because the weather was particularly hot; a year later, Blundell's children bathed in the sea to cure what appears to have been some skin disease. Other early references suggest that bathing might take place on a suitable stretch of coastline, but by the early 18th century some accounts of sea bathing make it clear that if a visitor wanted lodgings or entertainment, they would head for a coastal port.

During the 1730s and 1740s there are references to sea bathing and associated leisure activities at not only Scarborough, but also Brighton, Margate and Weymouth. One perhaps surprising early seaside resort is Liverpool; there appears to have been an active 'sea bathing' scene on the shores of the Mersey approximately where the Liver Building stands today. However, during the course of the 19th century, the growth of the port forced sea bathing further afield and eventually Liverpudlians took to the sea at New Brighton across the river or further up the Lancashire coast at Southport.

EAW016694

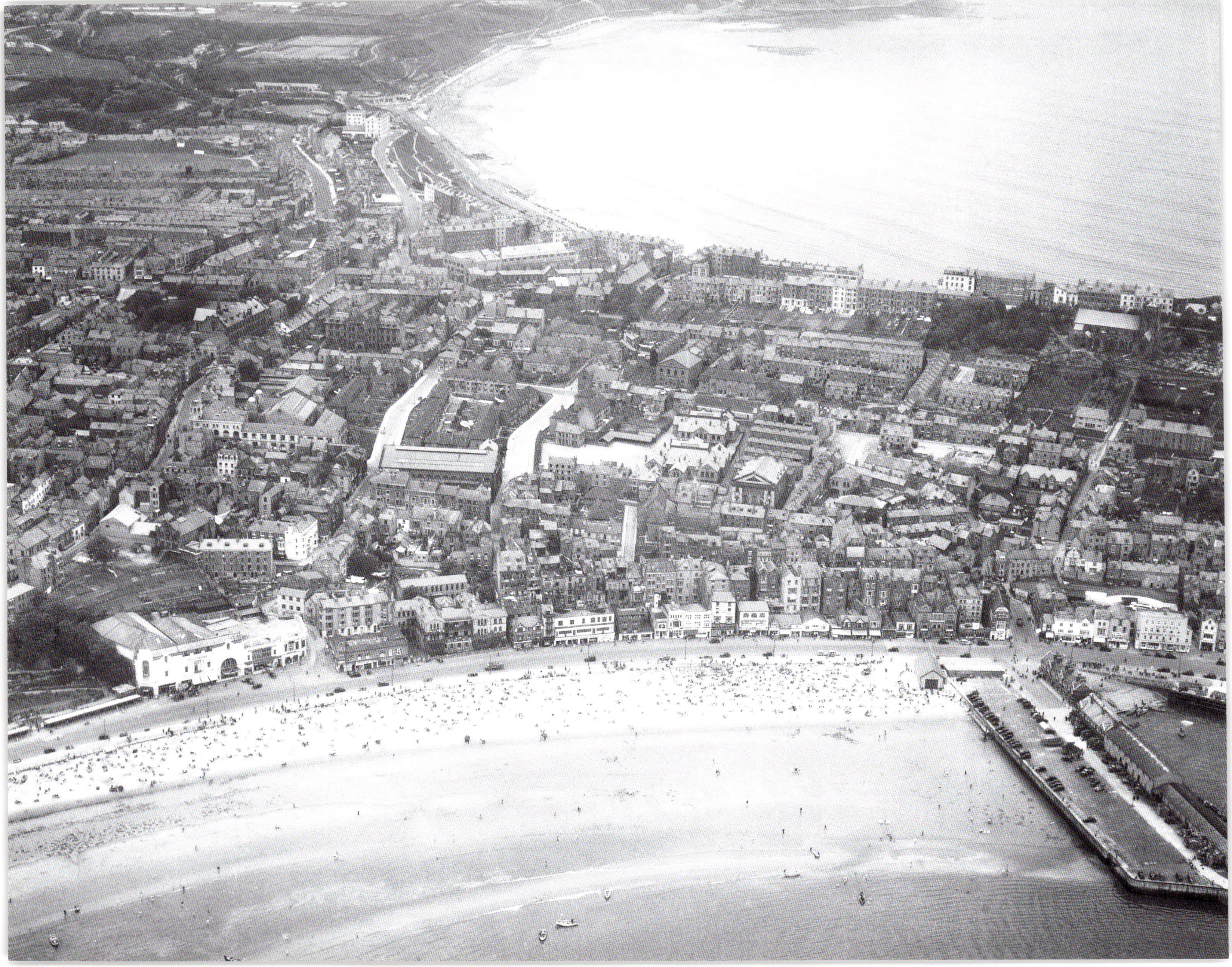

Foreshore Road, the town and North Bay, Scarborough, North Yorkshire

23 June 1948

This second photograph of Scarborough was taken on the same day as the image on p 3 and shows a cross-section through the historic town between South Bay in the foreground and North Bay in the background. The Norman castle and medieval parish lie beyond the right edge of this image, but the dense street pattern and small houses occupying the area of the walled medieval town are obvious in the centre of the image. These are in contrast to the large Georgian and Victorian houses along the top of the hillside that enjoy views looking out over both bays. The two bays were originally only connected by roads passing over the hill; however, the creation of Marine Drive at the end of the 19th century around the coast allowed them to communicate at sea level for the first time.

In the foreground can be seen the beach of South Bay. Between the St Nicholas Gardens on the left and the harbour on the right, the variety of activity on a seafront is well illustrated. The leftmost, white building is a cinema and the Arcadia; Will Catlin's troupe of pierrots played on the beach at Scarborough, but by 1906, as he was finding the rent to be too high, he bought some land near the seashore on which to erect a stage with a canvas top. He later moved into the Arcadia, which had opened in 1903 and subsequently became the Futurist Cinema. Beside it, in 1859 an exotic Turkish Bath was constructed, and around 1900 this became an 'Indian village'; it was later taken over for use as an amusement arcade. Along the remainder of the seafront are houses of various dates, the ground floors of which had been used to provide entertainments and sustenance for holidaymakers. At the right-hand side of the image, beside the arm of the harbour, can be seen the small lifeboat house, which has today been replaced by a much larger structure.

EAW016689

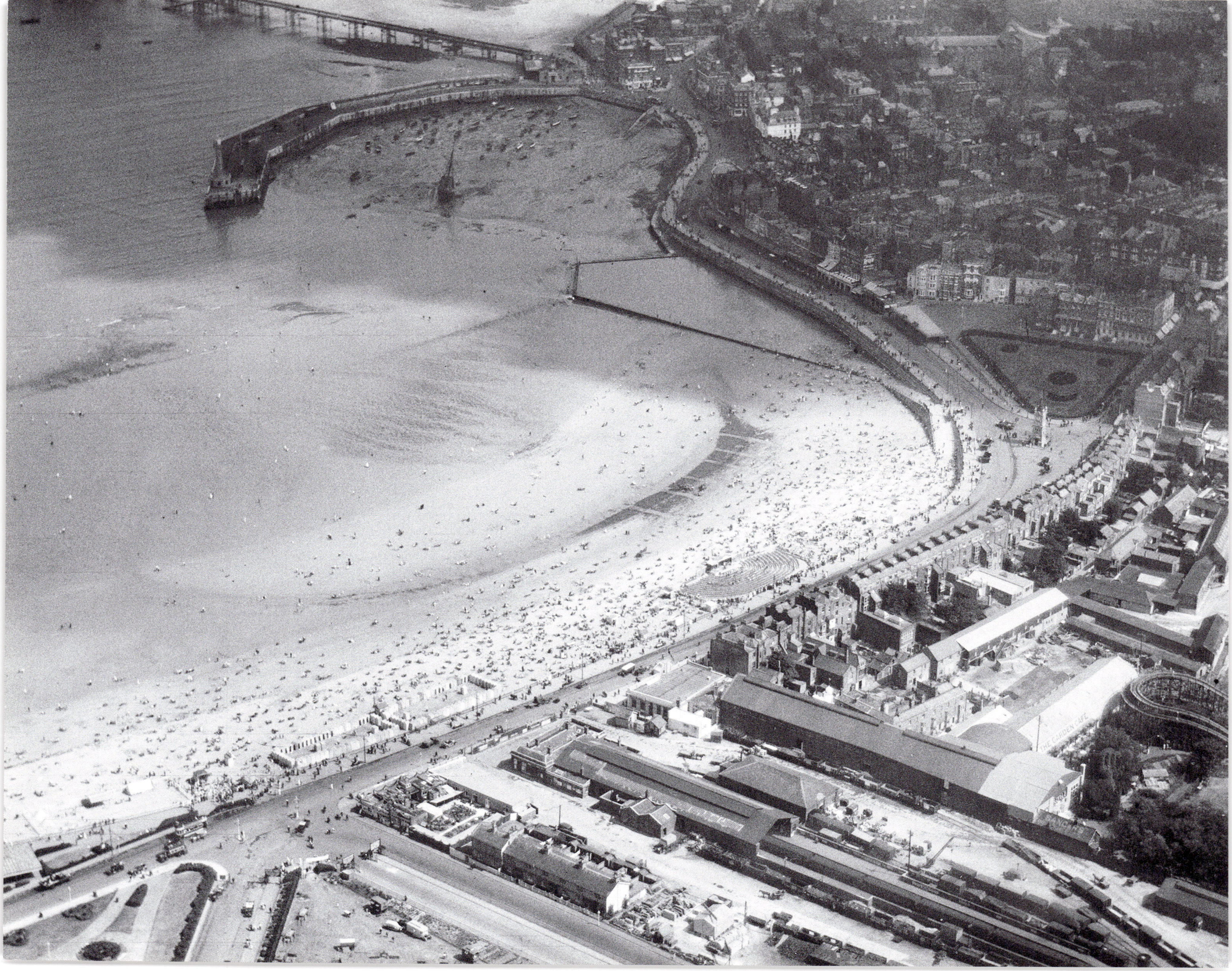

The station and Marine Terrace, Margate, Kent
1923

This photograph shows some of the key features in the history of Margate as a seaside resort. At the beginning of the 18th century it was a small, struggling fishing port with a modest harbour that served the trade in agricultural products and goods between London and the Isle of Thanet. By the 1730s, there is evidence of a seafront bathhouse standing within the area of the harbour, and in the course of the 18th century Margate became a popular destination for Londoners. Enjoying a visit to Margate was not limited to the wealthy and local people, as it was at most resorts, as the town's location at the end of the River Thames allowed London's tradespeople and shopkeepers to shut up shop for a few days and head along the river on one of the sailing boats. These were initially for transporting cargo, but increasingly were used for passengers.

Margate's current harbour was built in 1810–15, in time for the first steamers that ran along the river, dramatically increasing the number of people who could visit the resort. Around the same period, Margate and its historic town, seen at the top of the photograph, were linked along the seafront to the area to the west where the Royal Sea Bathing Hospital had been established in the 1790s. Although Margate had the new harbour, the increasing size of vessels visiting the port meant that a timber jetty was needed to land passengers at low tide, and this was replaced in the 1850s by Eugenius Birch's first iron pier, which can be seen extending seawards from the harbour arm.

The advantage that Margate had enjoyed over other resorts because of its location on the Thames was lost with the coming of railways, as Londoners could then choose from a wide range of resorts. Margate acquired two railway stations, in 1846 and 1863, and something of this complicated railway infrastructure can be seen at the bottom of the photograph.

The seaside holiday was transformed in the 19th century as a result of technology, not only allowing new forms of transport, but also new forms of entertainment. Margate was home to Dreamland, the former site of a circus menagerie in the late 19th century, transformed in 1920 into one of England's leading amusement parks. The Scenic Railway of 1920, an early form of roller coaster, can be seen on the right-hand side of the picture and still survives today in the modern heritage amusement park (*see* p 147).

EPW009161

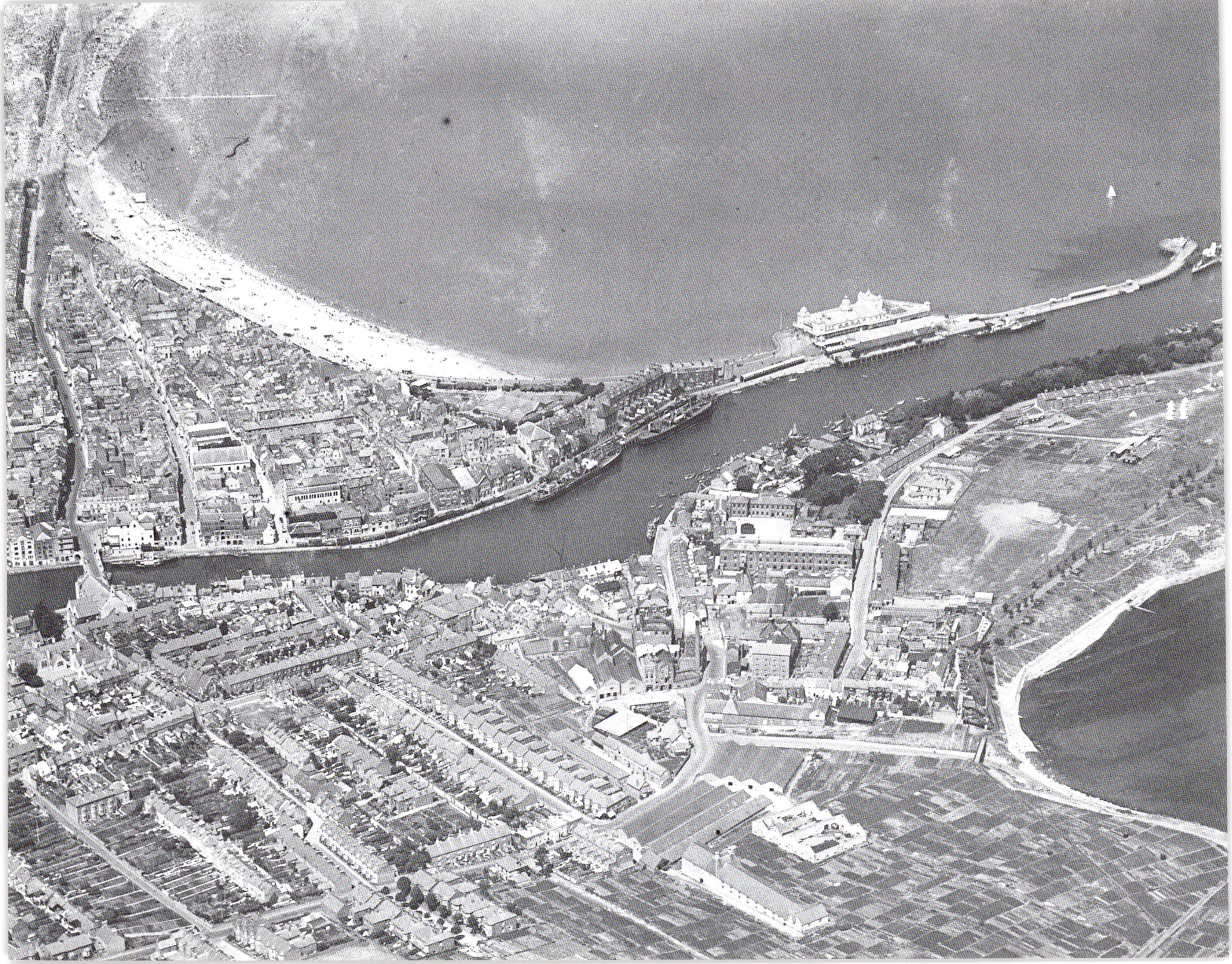

The town and harbour, Weymouth, Dorset
June 1925

In the Middle Ages, what is modern-day Weymouth consisted of two towns, Weymouth to the south of the harbour (bottom of the photograph) and Melcombe Regis to the north. The harbour is reputed to be where the Black Death arrived in England in June 1348. This vital economic facility was a source of constant dispute until the two towns became one legal entity in the late 16th century and the first bridge was built to link the two.

When the first sea bathers came to Weymouth in the 1740s, Melcombe Regis, a medieval new town, was a small triangular settlement (seen at the top of the photograph) that largely turned its back on its beach, which had been used for dumping rubbish rather than for bathing in the sea. Nevertheless, by the 1770s, bathing machines were taking people into the sea and there was a bathhouse on the quayside in the harbour. Ralph Allen, who had made his fortune from supplying stone for the reconstruction of Bath, first came to Weymouth in 1750 and built a house on the quayside. His presence encouraged the arrival of various aristocrats, making Weymouth a prestigious destination, and in 1789 George III made his first visit to the resort to improve his health.

Weymouth had been the haunt of the wealthy, but the arrival of the railway in the mid-19th century, with its station built on reclaimed land to the west of the town (seen in the top left), opened the resort up to a wider market. At the turn of the 20th century, the town was a popular destination for factory outings from the Great Western Railway Works in Swindon, when thousands of workers arrived on trains to enjoy a few days at the seaside (*see* p 21). This view also shows the Weymouth Quay railway station, which opened in 1889 to serve cross-channel ferries using Weymouth Harbour, one of which might be seen at the end of the pier. This route was connected to the main railway network via a harbour tramway that carried passenger trains around the centre of the town until the 1980s.

The 19th century also saw the enlargement and extension seawards of the harbour and the construction of the Nothe Fort, seen here on the far right of the photograph. This photograph shows a number of tents in neat rows inland from the fort, an indication of the presence of troops.

EPW013673

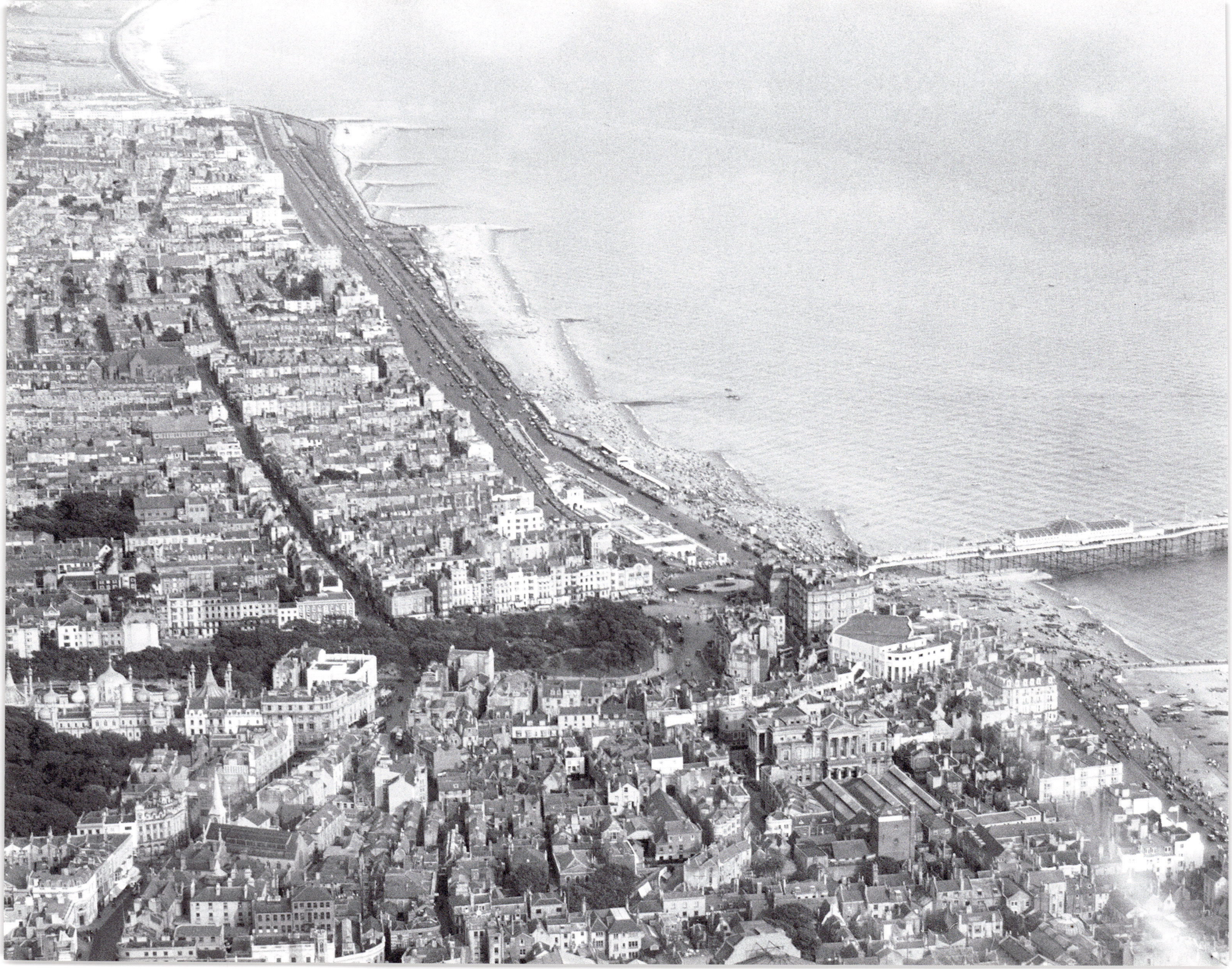

The town centre and the seafront, Brighton, East Sussex
August 1932

Like Margate, early 18th-century Brighton was struggling economically and the new fad for sea bathing came to its rescue. The historic town was located to the south of where the Palace Pier would later be constructed and is now the attractive shopping and leisure area in the centre of the city known as the Lanes. This area is densely packed with narrow, winding streets, and some timber-framed and pebble-walled houses of the old town survive, with the green open area to the north, the Steine, or Old Steine. This was once an area used by fishermen for drying their nets, but with the coming of aristocratic sea bathers it increasingly became a fashionable promenade. Therefore, when the Prince Regent was seeking to buy a house, he purchased a farmhouse in this area. By 1822 it had become transformed into the Royal Pavilion, which can be seen in the centre left of the photograph. To the left, beyond the edge of the photograph, lies the monumental Royal Stables and Riding House, a large domed building built in 1803–8 by William Porden for the Prince Regent's horses.

Brighton grew rapidly throughout the 19th century, and much of this urban development can be seen spreading northwards from the Steine. As well as being a popular place to live, the resort became a popular place to visit. The railway arrived in 1840, with the line to London importantly opening in the following year. The Chain Pier was built in 1823, a short distance to the north of where the Palace Pier can be seen in the photograph. This suspension-bridge structure survived until a devastating storm in 1896 and was replaced with the Palace Pier, which opened in 1899 at the end of the Steine.

Today, Brighton is a popular place to live, visit and to commute to London. This factor, and its exciting metropolitan atmosphere, has earned it the title of London-by-the-Sea or London-on-Sea.

EPW039534

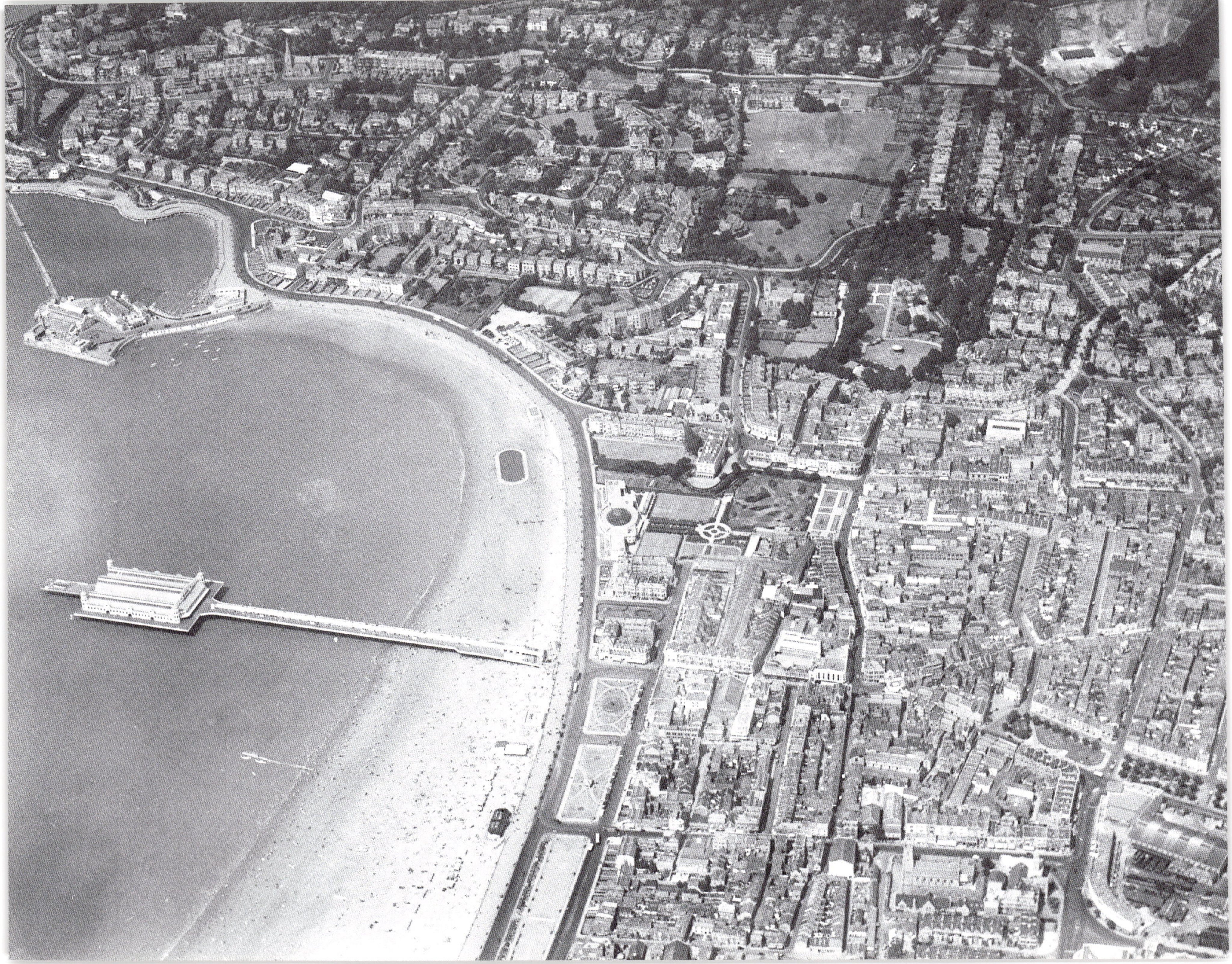

The Grand Pier and the town, Weston-super-Mare, Somerset
July 1935

The earliest seaside resorts were located at ports where there were pre-existing accommodation and entertainment facilities, an existing clientele, and at least a basic form of transport infrastructure in the sense of regular coaching services. Ports also had access to the sea and it is clear at early resorts that even aristocratic bathers were content to take to the water in, or near, a harbour, as readily as from a nice sandy beach. Therefore, on parts of the coast where there had been a lot of development, resorts could easily be formed, and such was the case at Scarborough, Margate, Brighton and Hastings. Elsewhere there was a desire, and need, to establish facilities for sea bathing on undeveloped stretches of the coast, leading to the creation of resorts such as Blackpool, Southport and Weston-super-Mare.

The first visitors to Weston arrived in the late 18th century and found a village of around 100 people scattered in the area around the foot of Worlebury Hill. The first hotel opened in 1810 and an Enclosure Act was passed in 1810 to stimulate the development of the settlement. By 1841, the year the railway arrived, the population had risen to 2,100, and in the subsequent decades distinctive areas of development would become recognisable.

In the bottom right-hand corner of this photograph can be seen the site of the original railway station, which by 1935 had become the goods station and yard. In this area can be seen streets of dense, working-class housing, whereas on the hillside at the top of the photograph are the larger terraces and, from the 1860s onwards, villas and semi-detached houses. The seafront was also a favoured location for wealthier residents and visitors, and larger houses can be seen there.

This photograph also shows Weston's Grand Pier in the centre; Birnbeck Pier lies beyond the top right of the photograph (*see* p 53 and p 129). Weston's wide tidal range meant that for most of any day, the sea was a long way from the beach, hence the creation of the enclosed Marine Lake beside Knightstone Island in the late 1920s (*see* p 81).

EPW048457

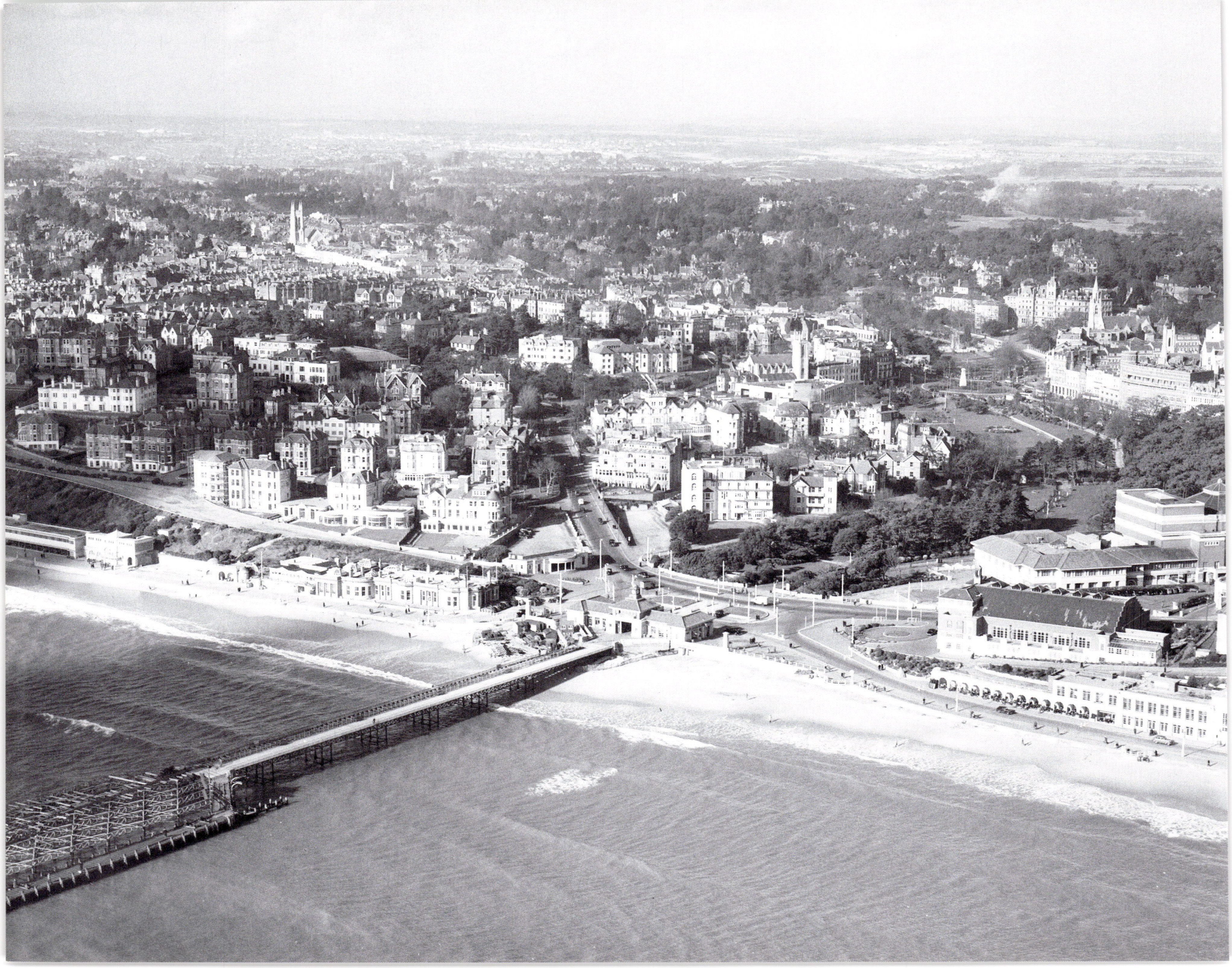

Pier Approach, the Pleasure Gardens and the town, Bournemouth, Dorset
7 February 1951

Like Weston-super-Mare, Bournemouth was a speculative development that began with modest investments. Lewis Tregonwell first built a house on this uninhabited stretch of coast in 1811–12, at a spot where there was a gap in the cliffs down to the beach as a result of the River Bourne. His house is now part of the Royal Exeter Hotel, which can be seen on the right-hand side of the main road rising up behind the pier. This was followed by an inn and a handful of cottages to accommodate people in search of improved health.

In 1825 Bournemouth was described as a 'new-built watering-place' with excellent bathing, but it suffered at this date from limited accommodation. However, an 1837 guidebook recorded that the politician and landowner Sir George William Tapps-Gervis (1795–1842) was carrying out a series of improvements: 'villas, crescents, streets and baths, in all varied styles of architecture are rearing their heads as if by magic'. This development was wholly separate from the activity taking place on the west side of the River Bourne (to the left of the pier), where Tregonwell had established his 'neat marine villa', the inn and several detached houses 'in the cottage style'. Development on either side of the river flanked the route through the gap in the cliffs to the seafront where the baths, reading room and later the pier were constructed.

Bournemouth Pier is the third pier to be erected in the town. The first was a landing jetty that lasted from 1855 to 1857 before being swept away by storms. A second timber jetty designed by George Rennie opened on 17 September 1861, but it suffered damage from marine worms known as *Teredo navalis*. It was in the process of being rebuilt when a succession of heavy storms destroyed it in 1876. The third structure was an iron pier designed by Eugenius Birch (1818–84). It opened on 11 August 1880 and was altered and extended in the subsequent two decades. To prevent use by the enemy it was breached on 5 July 1940 and partially reopened in August 1946, though it was only fully restored in 1953. Evidence of this repair programme can be seen at the left-hand side of the photograph.

EAW034624

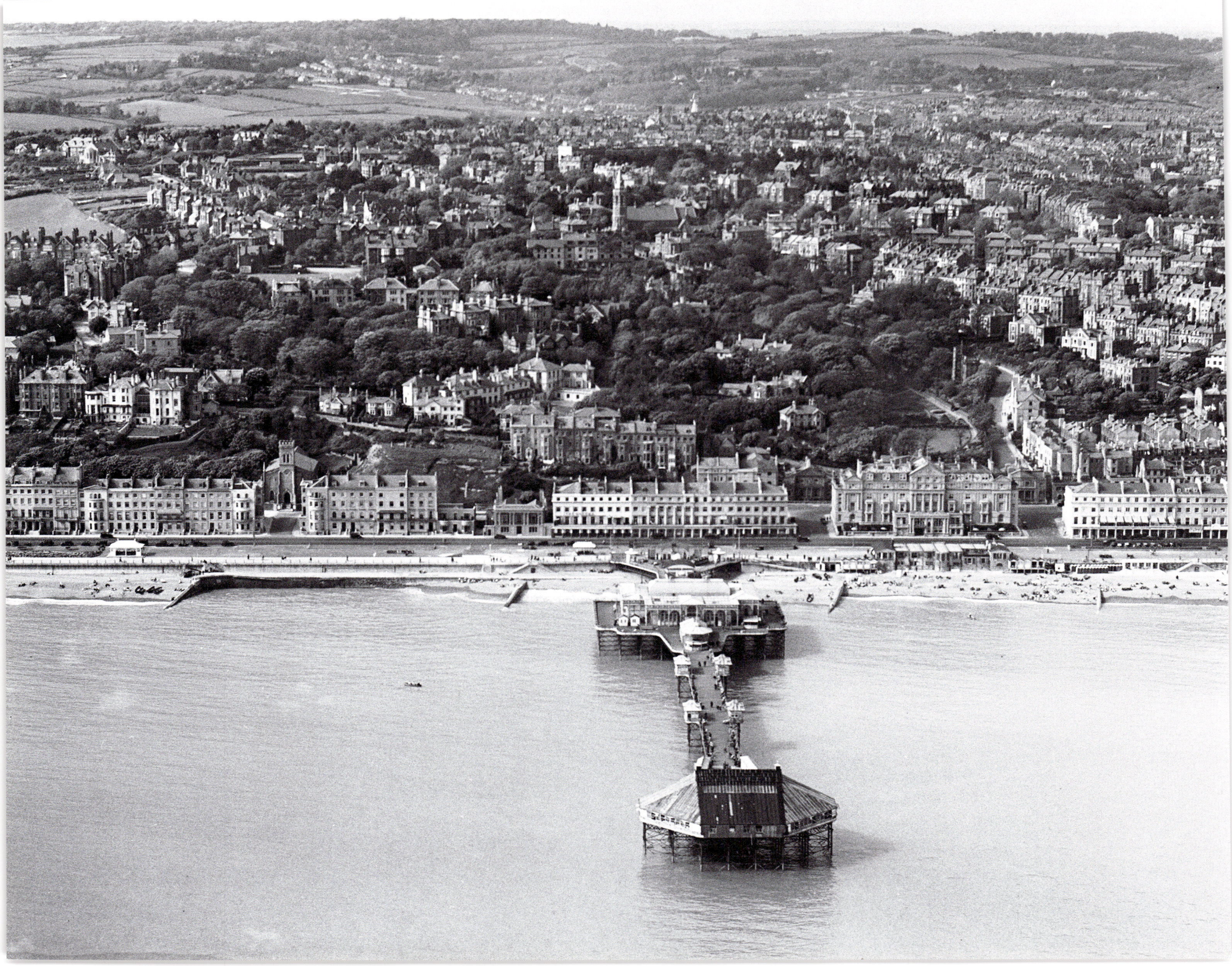

The Palace Pier and town, St Leonards, East Sussex
25 May 1931

By the early 19th century, the taste for a seaside holiday was proving sufficiently strong to allow a few entrepreneurs to invest in new grandiose schemes; some proved to be great successes, but others, at least in hindsight, seemed to have been doomed to fail. Investors were seeking to attract the growing number of prosperous middle-class visitors and residents to their developments, and to achieve this they provided houses that sought to echo the epitomes of fashionable architecture: Bath and central London developments such as Regent's Park and Eaton Square.

Large schemes at Brighton and Hastings were the leading projects in the 1820s and influenced a number of ambitious developments in subsequent years. In 1823, Thomas Read Kemp embarked on the construction of a large estate on his land to the east of Brighton and most of the development was completed over the next two decades. At the other end of Brighton, Brunswick Town was built from 1824 on land owned by the Scutt family (*see* p 171 and p 207).

A short distance to the west of Hastings another scheme with a direct link to Regent's Park began in the late 1820s. In February 1828 James Burton purchased part of a farm for the construction of the new town a short distance to the west of Hastings. He had worked as a builder on some of John Nash's terraces around Regent's Park and his son Decimus Burton had designed a number of the other buildings. St Leonards consisted of grand terraces along the seafront flanking a hotel (to the right of the pier), with an elegant but low building in front housing baths, a bank and a library, which had disappeared before this photograph was taken. Behind there was an assembly room and on the hillside a park was formed surrounded by villas. The settlement also included a parish church to the west (demolished in 1944) and two lower-status inland streets were created to meet the needs of the new settlement's inhabitants, Mercatoria to house merchants and Lavatoria for laundry services. Like Brunswick Town at Brighton, St Leonards was legally a separate administrative entity. An Improvement Act in 1832 appointed 75 commissioners to be responsible for its construction and management until its amalgamation with the Hastings Town Council in 1885.

St Leonards Palace Pier was constructed in 1891 by Richard St George Moore (1858–1926), with an ornate pavilion capable of holding 700 people. It was effectively rebuilt in 1933. When it was put up for auction in 1938 it had an enormous deck area, measuring more than four times that of the largest pier in Blackpool. In 1936 alone, it entertained one million visitors. It was demolished in 1951.

EPW035337

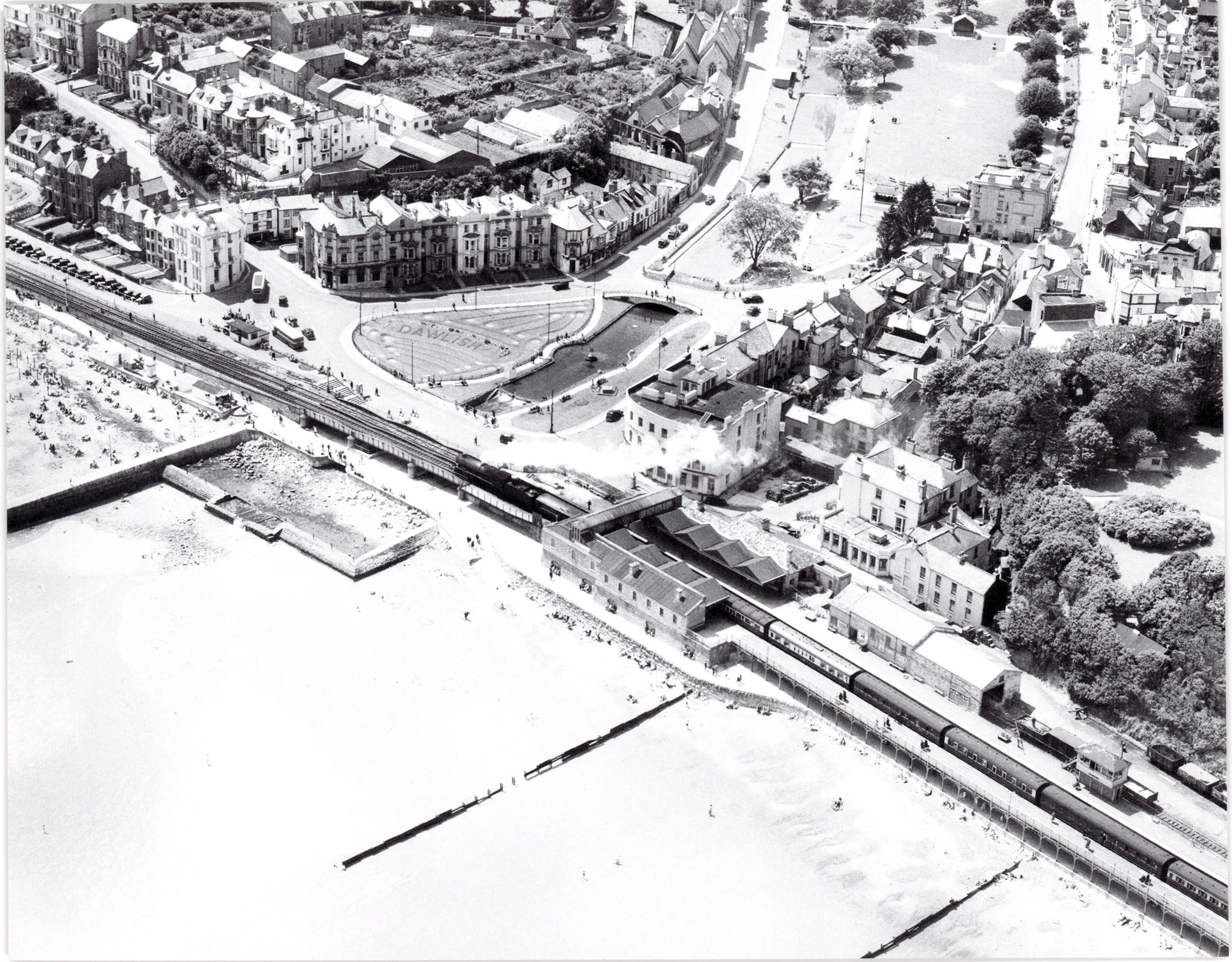
DAWLISH

Dawlish railway station and York Gardens, Dawlish, Devon
1947

Seaside resorts were one of the main beneficiaries of the emerging railway system. During the 1840s, many existing resorts began to be connected to the rapidly growing railway network. Brighton led the way followed by more than a dozen resorts including Weston-super-Mare, Great Yarmouth, Scarborough, Margate, Hastings, Teignmouth, Whitby and Torquay. Six rival schemes were proposed in 1834–5 for a route from Brighton to London, with the most direct line being chosen in 1836 and opening in 1841. In 1840, the Preston & Wyre Railway opened, running to the new port and resort of Fleetwood, and in 1846 a branch line was established into the heart of Blackpool. As the 19th century progressed, railways spread to smaller, more remote resorts and areas of the country. Perhaps the most surprising latecomer to the railway era was Bournemouth, which only acquired its first two stations during the 1870s.

The arrival of the railway transformed the character of seaside resorts; once the preserve of the leisured class, people with free time and disposable income, increasingly they came within the reach of ordinary working people. Dawlish was visited by Jane Austen in the early 19th century and she used it as the location for the honeymoon of Lucy and Robert Ferrars in *Sense and Sensibility*. An 1810 guidebook described the genteel settlement: 'The town is most delightfully set on the sea coast, and is much frequented during the summer season for sea bathing. Of late years many elegant buildings have been erected and it is now in a flourishing state'.

In May 1846, the railway station opened at Dawlish; the local geography required the line to pass along the seafront, cutting the town from the beach, except today by an underpass. The population of Dawlish in the 1841 census was actually less than 10 years earlier, but with the arrival of the railway it grew by between 10% and 15% each decade for the next 50 years. The original wooden station and train shed were burnt down in August 1873 and the new station shown here opened in April 1875. The photographer has been fortunate to catch a train standing at the station heading towards Cornwall to the west. This photograph also shows the central park with the stream running alongside it that flows down towards the sea.

Dawlish's railway line made the headlines as one of the victims of a series of more than a dozen major storms that struck Britain from the south-west between October 2013 and February 2014. The sea defences along the seafront were severely damaged, washing away the ground beneath the railway line. The tracks were left hanging in mid-air, leading to the closure of the main route into Cornwall for two months.

EAW007656

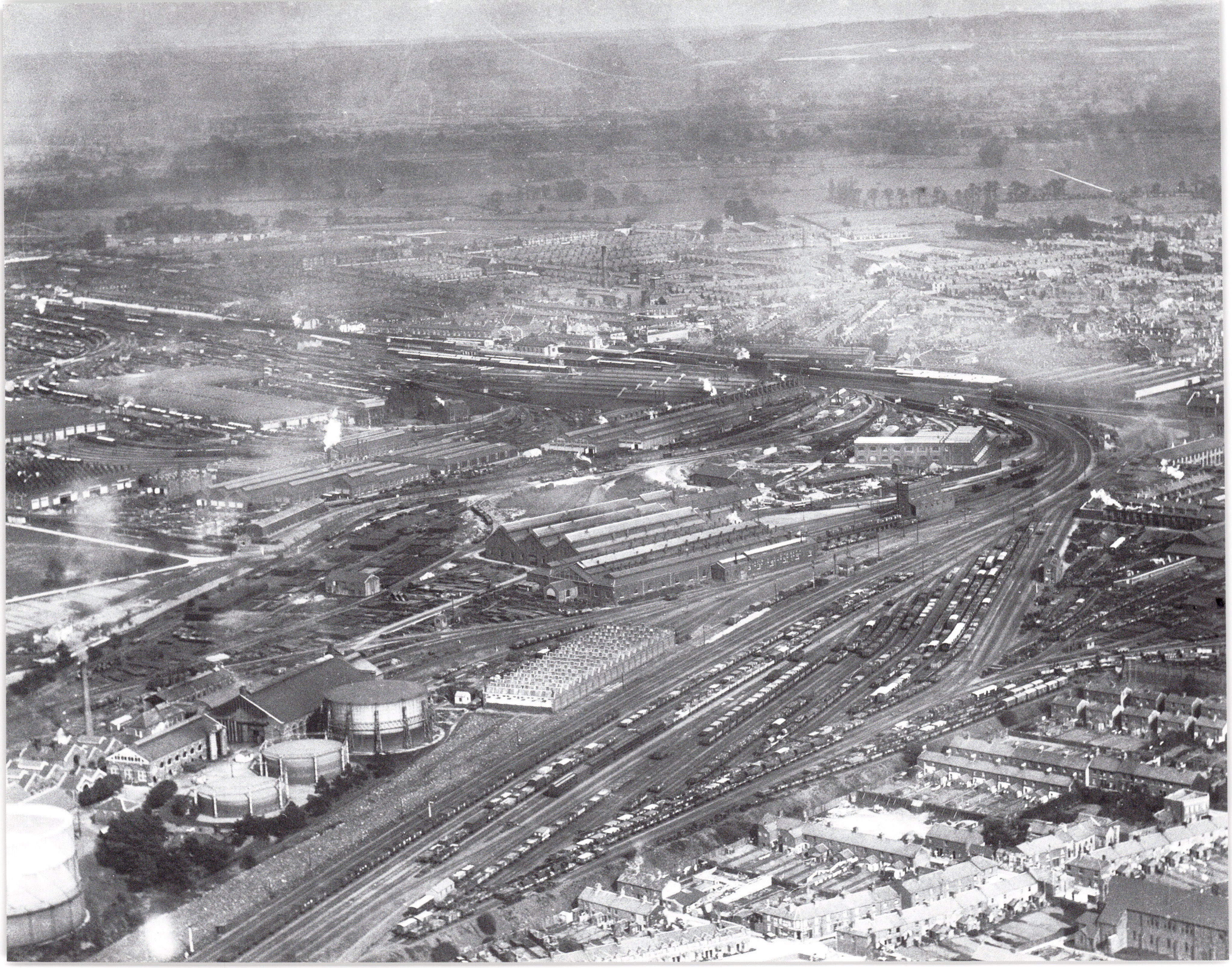

Great Western Railway Works, Swindon, Wiltshire
May 1920

Almost as far from the sea as it is possible to get in England, nevertheless Swindon, and specifically the works of the Great Western Railway Company, were at one time intimately linked to the seaside, and notably Weymouth. This highly evocative photograph, tainted with cloud, smoke and age, shows the scale of a major industrial concern in the early 20th century. It depicts the rows of good-quality housing that had been provided by the company, but it also vividly illustrates why these workers needed respite at the seaside.

As the 19th century progressed, the seaside became accessible to a wider section of society. In 1841, Thomas Cook arranged his first trip from Leicester to a temperance fete in Loughborough and was soon arranging visits to seaside towns. Apart from Cook, there were other private excursion organisers and a wide range of philanthropic trips. Mechanics institutes arranged trips that were both pleasurable and educational and organisations of working people, including the Oddfellows and the Foresters, also put on their own excursions. Enlightened employers were also important providers of trips. In 1848, Sir Titus Salt, the founder of Saltaire, took 2,000 employees to the country, and from 1865 Bass provided family day trips to the seaside. In 1903, office staff at Cadbury's Factory at Bournville had a hectic day trip to Weston-super-Mare. It included lunch, dinner, a boat trip and a ride on a charabanc, and all this had to be fitted in after they had completed their paperwork at the factory. However, not all workers were fortunate to have a philanthropic employer. Employees at Portsmouth dockyard had to form their own excursion committee in 1883 and they ran their first trip to the Fisheries Exhibition in London.

An annual holiday from the Great Western Railway Works in Swindon attracted thousands of visitors to Weymouth and other seaside resorts, and the 'Swindon Week', which latterly became the 'Swindon Fortnight', became a regular event at the beginning of July. The annual trip of GWR workshop employees from Swindon to Weymouth by the 1890s carried 21,000 people in 500 carriages, an operation matched in scale only by mobilisations of armies. Weymouth was the most popular seaside destination, attracting over 6,000 visitors in some years. While Weymouth had once been a magnet for Royalty and high society, by the late 19th century the arrival of the railway made it a playground for industrial workers.

EPW000940

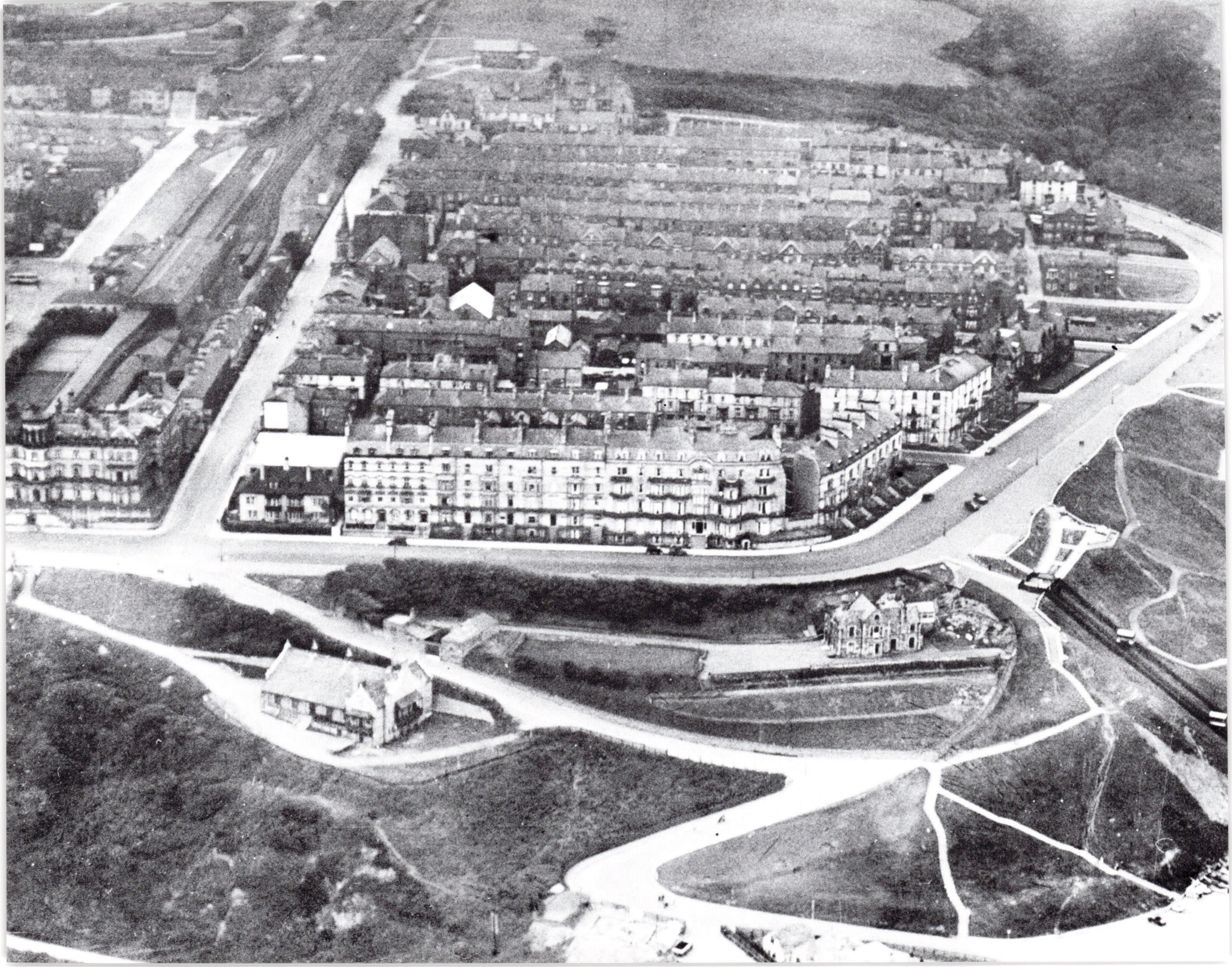

Marine Parade, Saltburn-by-the-Sea, North Yorkshire
September 1929

Most seaside resorts grew rapidly from the 1840s onwards because of railways, but Saltburn-by-the-Sea is more unusual as it was created by the arrival of the railway. There was a small hamlet here before the 19th century, approximately beneath the location of the aircraft, but everything in the photograph dates from the 1860s onwards. This image shows the funicular railway rising from the pier to the clifftop, and the new town and hotel on the clifftops. In 1869, a hoist is mentioned at Saltburn 'for raising and lowering people thus avoiding the toilsome ascent by road'. Tall cliffs were a significant reason for slow development at some resorts, but once technology in the form of the cliff lift and the cliff, or funicular, railway existed, it came to the aid of holidaymakers who had to trudge up cliffs back to their lodgings and hotels. Saltburn's hoist was superseded in 1884 by the cliff railway.

Large developments involving railway companies were usually partnerships with local landowners, though the precise arrangement varied in each case. The Stockton and Darlington Railway Company was authorised in 1858 to extend its line from Redcar to Saltburn. Henry Pease saw the development potential and negotiated with Lord Zetland in 1859 to buy land. Here the developers were a group led by the Pease family rather than the railway company, and an Improvement Company was set up to manage the development. The railway opened in 1861 and new streets were laid out by George Dickinson of Darlington on a regular plan flanking the station. The railway company erected some cottages for its men and a row of six speculative houses, the grandly named Britannia Mansions. In 1863, William Peachey, the architect of the station, completed the 50-bedroom Zetland Hotel with Alfred Waterhouse as a consultant. A unique feature in England, the railway ran into the hotel; the main platform reached up to the building's back windows.

EPW029133

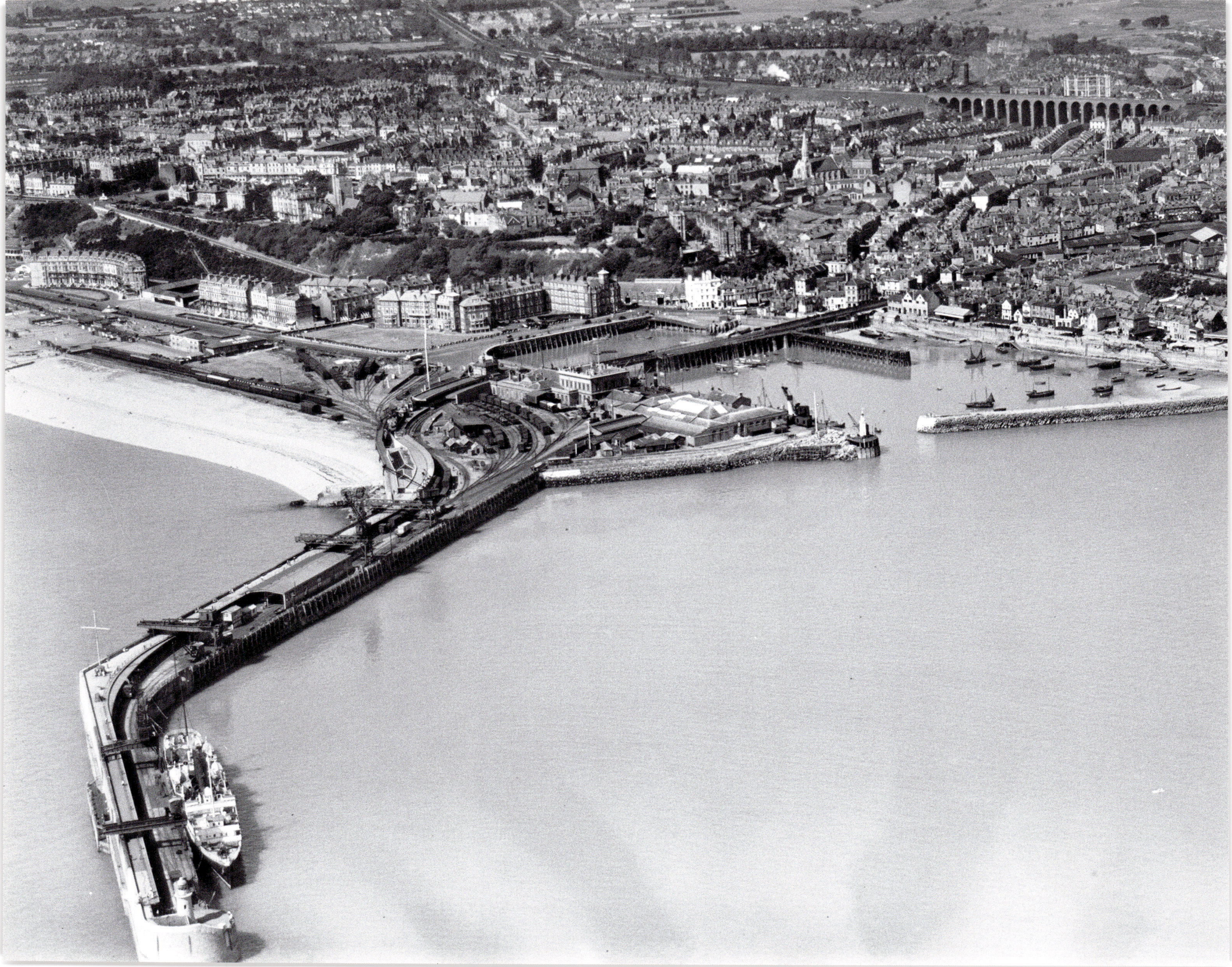

The Harbour Pier, inner and outer harbours and the town, Folkestone, Kent
August 1933

Between 1851 and 1901, the population of Britain grew by just over half from 27.5 million to 41.6 million, but many seaside resorts grew much faster. Blackpool, most spectacularly, increased by almost 1,400%, as much a result of its low population in 1851 as its huge popularity in 1901, and similar reasons explain Southport's growth by 588%. In Kent, a heartland of early resort development, the population of the parish of Hern with Herne Bay increased by 173% and Margate, after a mid-century dip, grew again ultimately by 165% over 50 years. However, the most impressive growth in Kent was at Folkestone, whose population increased by 310%.

This was a reflection of its new, central role in cross-channel communications as much as its growing resort function. The station at Folkestone opened in 1843 and the town soon became established as a fashionable watering place on the growing route from London to Paris. In the distance can be seen the substantial railway viaduct constructed by William Cubitt; it consists of 19 round-headed brick arches spanning the Foord Valley and is nearly 100ft (30.5m) high in its centre. A little further to the east, just to the right of this photograph, a railway line left the mainline and snaked its way down through the town to run along to the harbour to connect with cross-channel steamers. One of these ships can be seen at the end of the harbour.

Folkestone grew in size and enjoyed an elevated status due to its strategic location. It also became a prestigious resort, with high-status new developments along the seafront, and particularly on the clifftop Leas. Some of these new terraces and crescents can be seen on the left-hand side of the photograph. The large building immediately beside the harbour is the Royal Pavilion Hotel, a popular place to stay before or after a cross-channel voyage (*see* p 35).

EPW042865

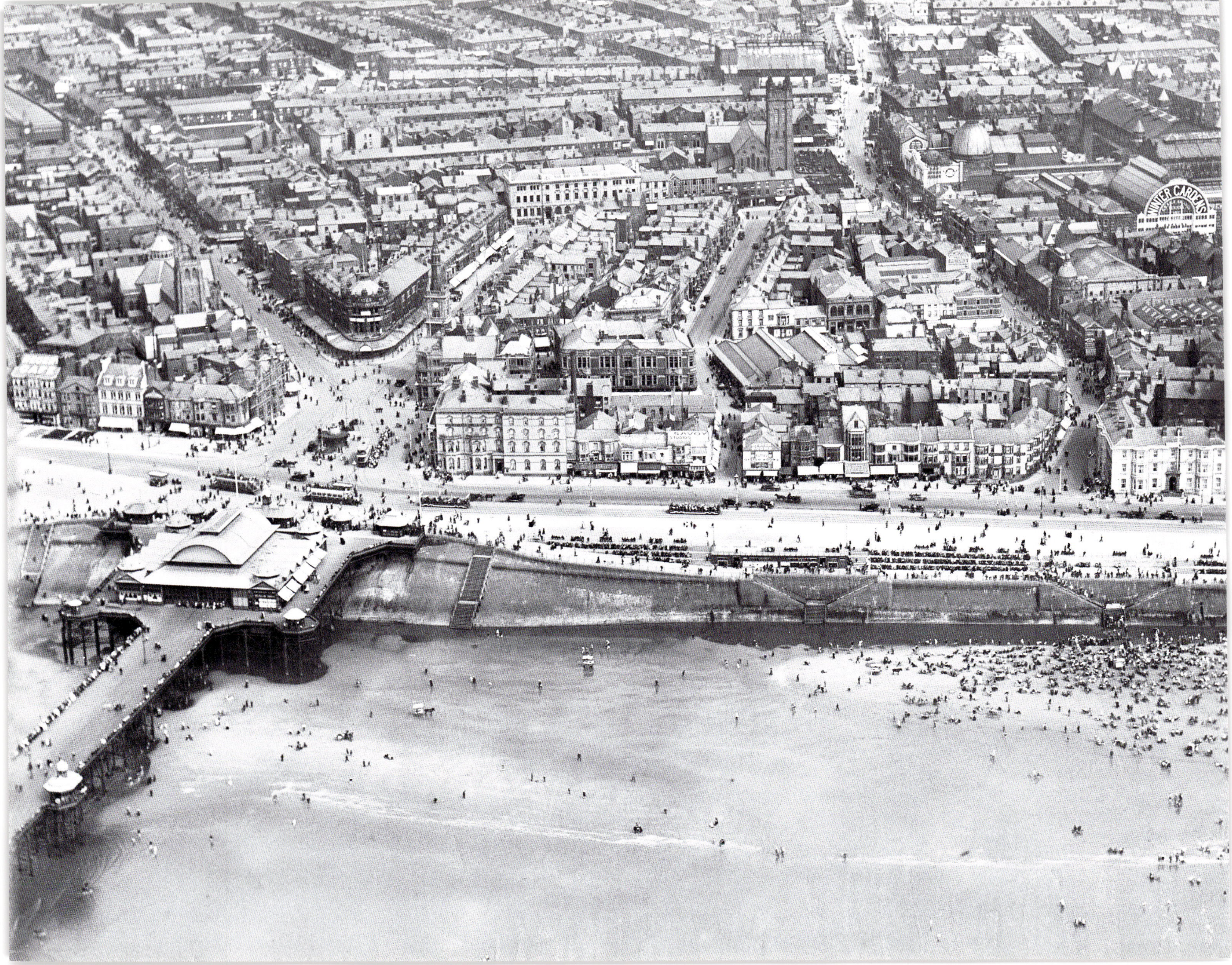
WINTER GARDENS

Birley Street and environs, Blackpool, Lancashire
July 1920

The arrival of the railway and the subsequent increased ease of access for mass tourism had an impact on seaside resorts, with Blackpool being particularly affected. It had been a site of sea bathing since the 1750s and by the early 19th century it was a small village with houses along its low cliffs and clustered around Church Street, where the parish church was completed in 1821. This is the wide street extending back from the seafront on the right-hand side of the photograph.

Blackpool's first railway station opened in April 1846; in 1841 its population numbered just under 2,000 and just over 2,500 in 1851, but by the 1860s Blackpool had shifted from being a village to a small town. In two decades its population doubled to almost 4,000, but this relatively slow initial growth was due to the limitations caused by there only being a single railway track into the resort. This route was doubled in 1865, but it was the provision of a second service into Blackpool that would be key to the town's late 19th-century expansion. The new Central Station, which lies a short distance beyond the right edge of the photograph, comprised little more than a cabin when it originally opened in April 1863, but it was the creation of this route that would eventually allow millions of visitors to reach the resort each year.

As a result of the improvements to the railway infrastructure, in the mid- to late 19th century the town's population was growing at around 30% to 50% per decade, but in the years immediately before the First World War, Blackpool's population grew even more rapidly, increasing by around 70–80% per decade. This photograph of 1920 shows how far the town was already extending inland, and vast areas of housing had been constructed to meet the needs of the growing population.

Blackpool's resident population was growing rapidly, though probably not as quickly as the number of its visitors. By 1879, nearly a million people arrived annually by train, rising to almost two million in 1893 and nearly 4 million on the eve of the First World War. Two features in this photograph relate to the growth in railway tourism: the central street of Blackpool was no longer Church Street, but was instead Talbot Road, which linked the railway station to the seafront. Where Talbot Road reached the sea was the logical location for Blackpool's first seaside pier, which opened in May 1863, the end of which is obscured in this photograph by the wing of the plane.

Four of Blackpool's trams catering for tourists can be seen; there are two open single-deck 'toast rack' cars and two of the open-top 'Dreadnought' type with four staircases, two at either end to cope with the significant numbers of passengers carried.

EPW002061

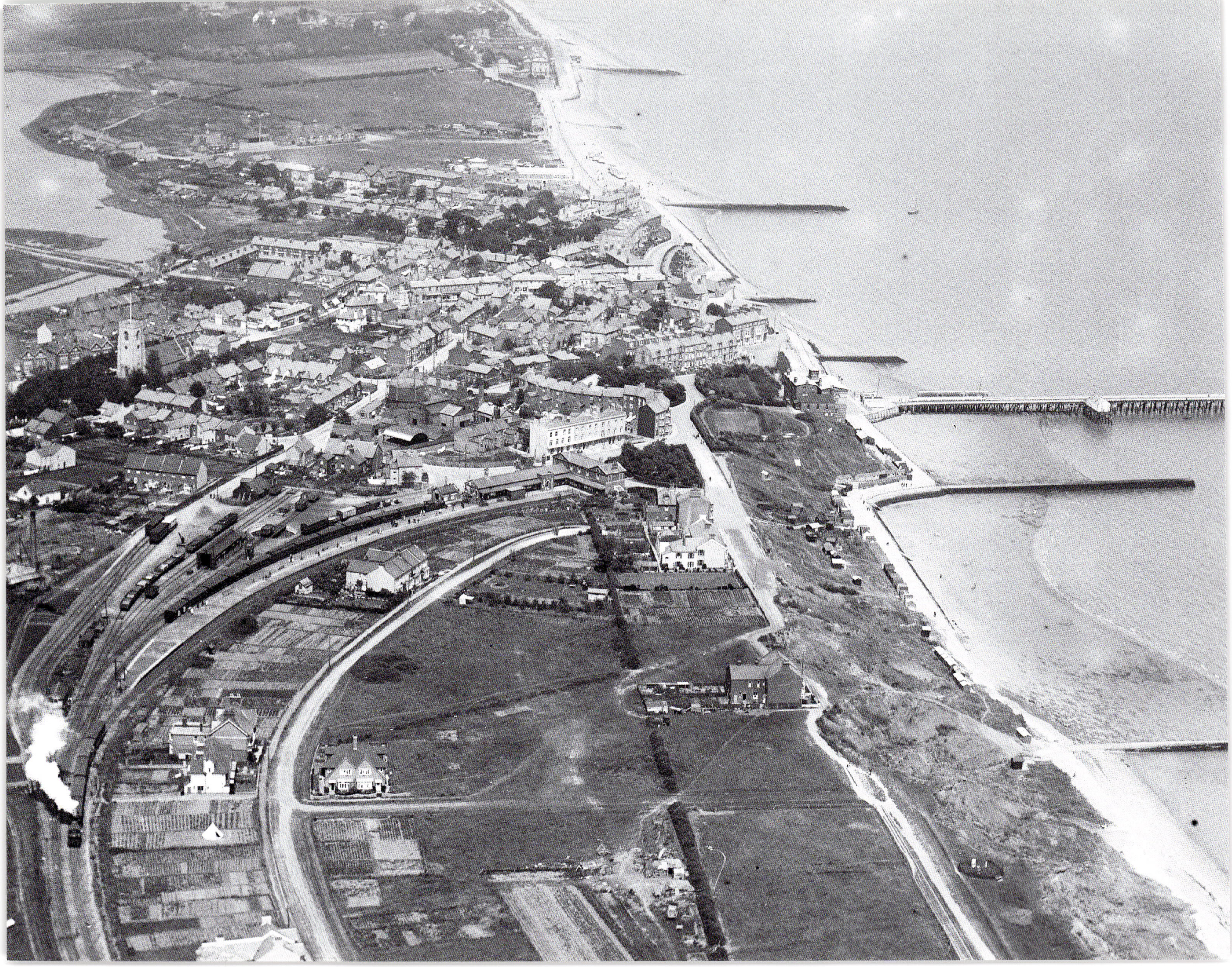

Walton-on-the-Naze and the Tendring Hundred Railway, Walton-on-the-Naze, Essex
June 1920

This photograph vividly shows one of the factors that have caused many seaside resorts to suffer economically in the late 20th century. They are literally at the end of the line, or at the end of the road, from major conurbations, making communications difficult and at Bank Holidays leading to legendary traffic jams. It also illustrates that by the mid-19th century there was such an appetite for the seaside that companies were willing, and financially able, to invest in lines to relatively small and isolated resorts around the coast.

Walton had a small timber pier as early as 1829 in an attempt to attract steamers travelling between London and Ipswich. It was gradually lengthened, but in 1871 another pier opened, built by a rival company led by the railway engineer Peter Bruff, who had opened the branch from Thorpe-le-Soken to Walton in 1867. The new pier was designed by Joseph Cochrane & Son; it was initially 530ft (162m) long, which was still short of what was required at low tide. The Coastal Development Company, which was establishing steamer services between Felixstowe, Harwich, Clacton and Southend, bought the pier in 1898 and increased its length to 2,600ft (792m). A single-track 3ft 6in-gauge (1.1m) electric railway was opened in 1899 on the pier and in the following year a 750-seat pavilion opened at the pier head, which lies to the right of the edge of this image. The landward end of the pier, as can be seen in this photograph, remained largely undeveloped until the construction of the Sea Spray Lounge in 1927.

In the 1870s, when Walton was mapped by the Ordnance Survey, the Old Pier was still intact to the north of the recently opened New Pier. There had been some development, but the town was still awaiting plots to be infilled and some of this had taken place by the time the aerial photograph was taken in 1920. Walton's population in 1871 was only 1,070, but had less than doubled to 2,007 by 1901, suggesting only slow growth in residents and visitors and a similarly slow return on investment for the railway and pier company. This may explain why the pier was lengthened and improved at the turn of the 20th century, in an effort to increase visitor numbers.

EPW001843

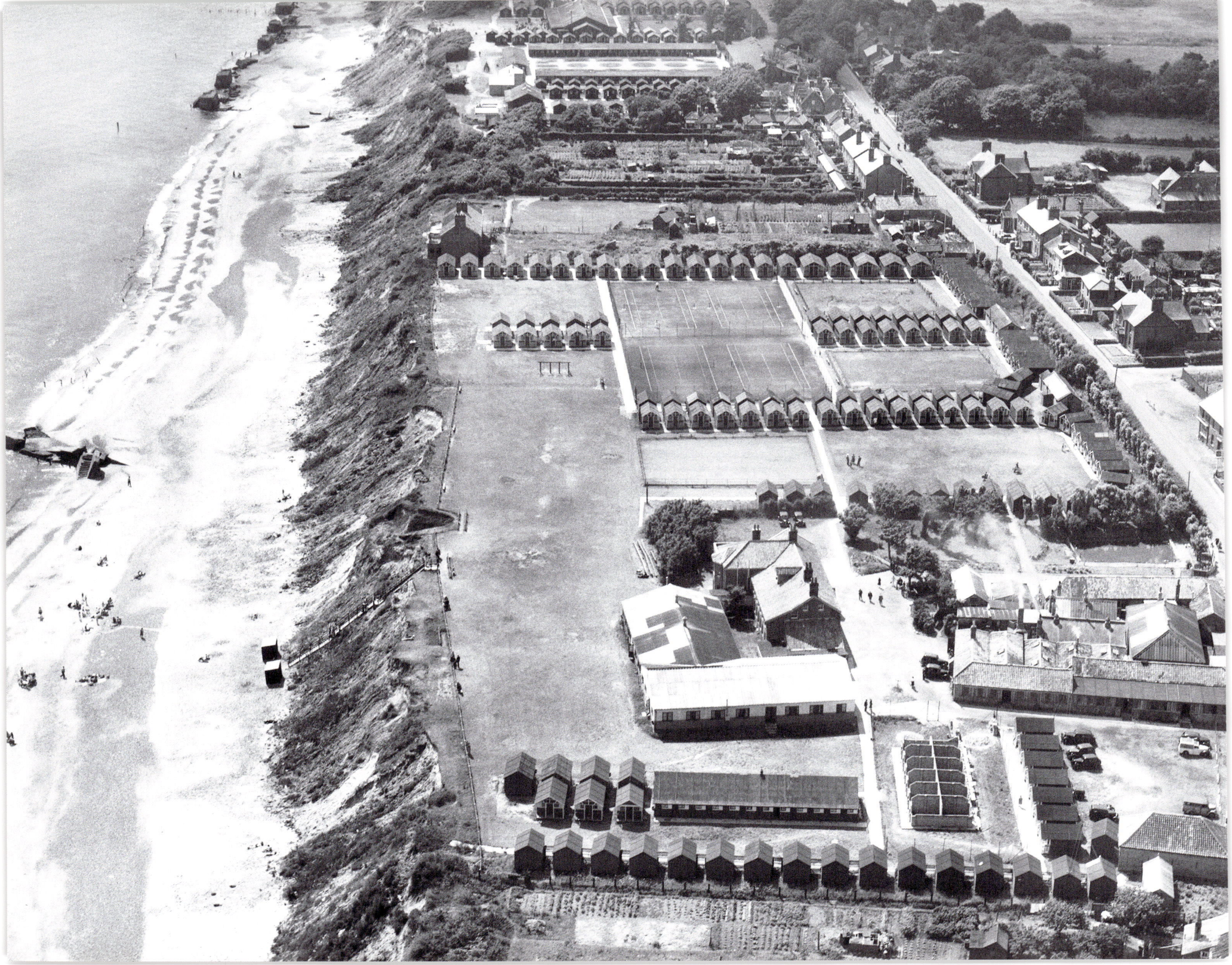

Corton Holiday Camp at Manor Farm, Corton, Suffolk

12 July 1947

Although railways were improving and extending access to the sea, to enjoy anything longer than a day trip might incur considerable expense, and this was one of the motivating forces behind the development of the holiday camp. In 1894 Joseph Cunningham established what is accepted as Britain's first holiday camp when he leased a piece of land on the Isle of Man and attracted campers from a number of Sunday schools, clubs and temperance leagues from the Liverpool area. In 1904 Cunningham bought another site and immediately built a 100ft-long (30.5m) dining and social room and erected 1,500 four-man tents set on wooden floors. Campers could enjoy activities such as billiards, mini golf, tennis, a bowling green, a 90ft-long (27.4m) covered swimming pool and a concert hall. To cater for visitors, there were shops, a bank, a post office, a bakehouse, photographic darkrooms and a chaplain. Gradually a series of increasingly grand and elaborate buildings were erected. In 1907, a miniature castle housing washrooms and latrines was built and other buildings were created with minarets, in a mock-Tudor style and, after the First World War, using neo-classical forms. When Billy Butlin visited the camp in the 1930s, he saw many features that he adapted and introduced into his own camps.

A range of other organisations, such as The Children's Country Holidays Fund, the Boys Brigade, the Catholic Church and most famously the Boy Scouts created rudimentary, temporary camps for children. However, some early permanent camps were created to allow children from industrial cities an opportunity to enjoy fresh sea air. The Wood Street Mission in Manchester established a holiday camp in 1897 at St Annes-on-Sea for children from the slums of central Manchester and Salford. In 1893, a boy's club in Leicester created a charity to pay for trips to the seaside, and by *c* 1900 longer holidays were being organised. A children's holiday camp was also opened by the City of Salford at Prestatyn on 28 September 1928.

As well as being founded by local authorities and philanthropic organisations, some early holiday camps emerged from a political or trade union background. A camp was established at Caister-on-Sea in 1906 by John Fletcher Dodd for the Independent Labour Party, but due to its lack of entertainment facilities it never prospered. However, by about 1911 many of the canvas tents were being replaced by huts and chalets and more permanent facilities.

W J Brown, General Secretary of the Civil Service Clerical Association (CSCA), inspired by a visit to Dodds' holiday camp at Caister and a grim, wet family holiday at a boarding house, described immodestly in his autobiography how we went on to found 'A New Industry'. He found a site at Corton near Lowestoft, and despite initial support from his Association, he had instead to seek patrons willing to buy £1 shares to raise the capital. Although technically perhaps a trade union camp, it was run on commercial lines and does seem to have offered a blueprint for many subsequent commercial holiday camp developments. In 1946 the camp was sold to Harry Warner and was extensively rebuilt in the late 1980s with new two-storey chalet accommodation. It is still owned and operated by Warners today.

EAW008179

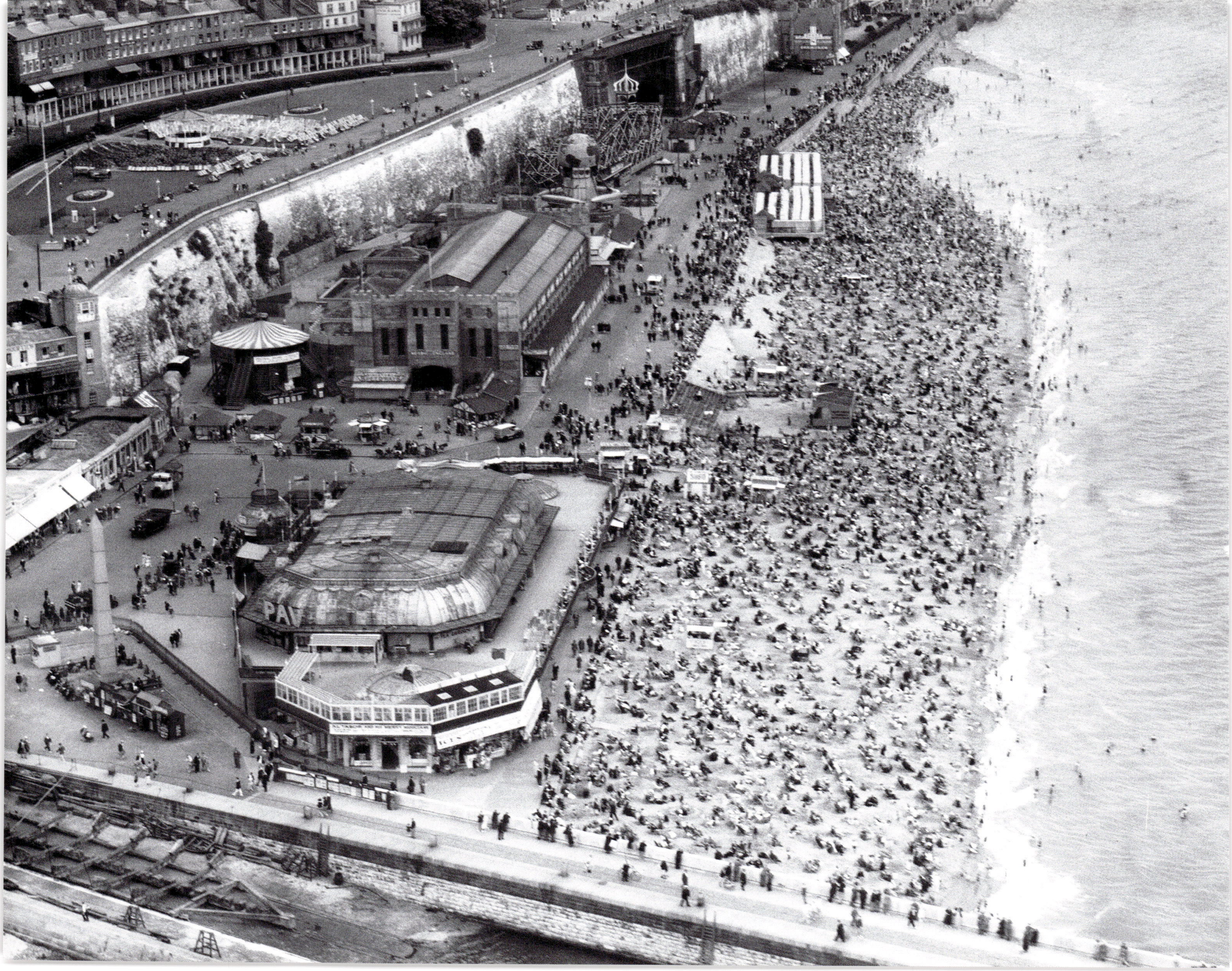

The Royal Victoria Pavilion and 'Pleasurama', Ramsgate, Kent
July 1932

A difficult subject to address is the simple question of how many people went to a seaside resort in any year. When rail travel dominated the way that people would get to the seaside, it is possible to make a reasonable estimate of the number of visitors to a resort, but once the motor car began to replace the train in the post-war years, such estimates become more like guesstimates.

At the beginning of the 19th century, around 20,000 visitors arrived annually at Margate by sea and in 1835–6 this peaked at 108,625, the figures being derived from the record books of the pier company. In 1837 stagecoaches are estimated to have brought 50,000 travellers to Brighton, but in a single week in 1850, 73,000 people arrived by train. On 3 August 1863, over 30,000 people travelled by train to the newly opened station at Cleethorpes, with a further 4,000 arriving on horse-drawn vehicles. Blackpool, still a modest-sized resort in 1861, dealt with 135,000 passengers, and by 1879 this had risen to almost 1 million. By 1914 around 4 million passengers were travelling to Blackpool each year. In the late 1930s, it was estimated that 7 million holidaymakers visited Blackpool, Southend had 5.5 million visitors, Hastings 3 million and Bournemouth and Southport 2 million. No figure was given for Ramsgate at this date, but something in the region of 2 to 3 million would fit in with other similar resorts. That type of number would equate with the appearance of this busy beach in July 1932.

Until 1926, Ramsgate had a railway station on the beach, where the large, castellated building can be seen in the centre of the photograph. As people were often reluctant to travel too far from where they arrived, and this beach was hemmed in on its south side by the large harbour, it must have been a very crowded spot in the height of summer.

Despite growing foreign competition, the peak of domestic holidays seems to have occurred in the early 1970s; one writer placed it in 1973 using evidence from holiday camps, while in 1974, 40.5 million people took a holiday in Britain of four days or longer, perhaps exacerbated by the 'Oil Crisis'.

The problem of assessing visitor numbers after the Second World War can be seen at Blackpool. At its pre-war height, Blackpool could boast around 7 million visitors per year and in the 1930s, its entertainment venues could seat more than 60,000 people each night. In 1972, 6 million people made 16 million visits. A similar survey 15 years later found that around 7 million people made 12.4 million visits to Blackpool, with both day trips and overnight stays showing a significant decline. In 1999, there were around 13 million visits, after which the numbers fell to nearer 10 million, though in 2011 it was reported to have returned to the level it had enjoyed 12 years earlier.

EPW039325

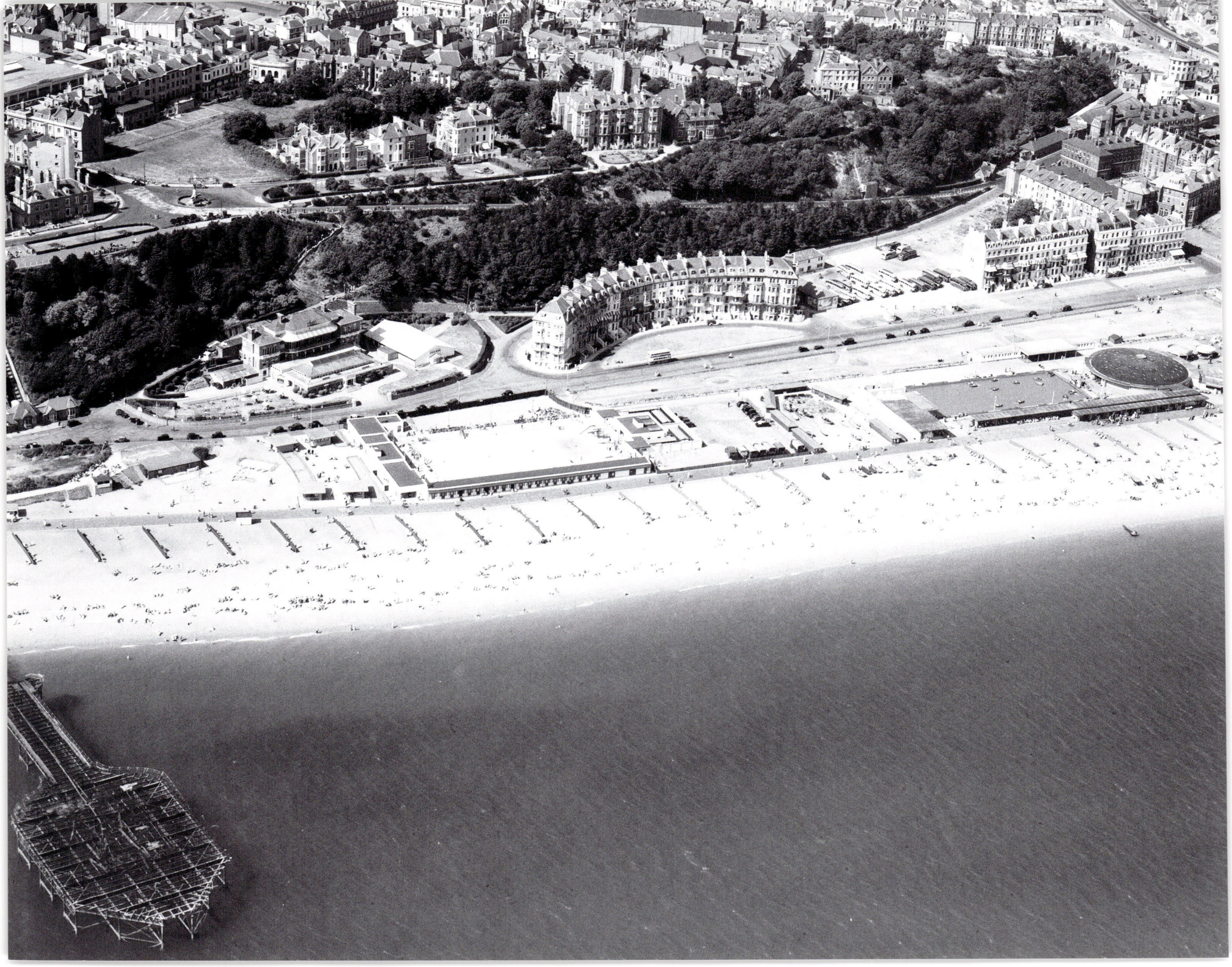

Marine Gardens and Marine Parade, Folkestone, Kent
12 July 1949

This image provides a useful reminder of the extent to which the seafronts of seaside resorts have changed during recent decades and the interesting seaside heritage that has been lost. On the left can be seen the last vestiges of Folkestone's pier, which opened in 1888 after more than a decade of debate and troubled fundraising. It was designed by Noel Ridley and was constructed by the Manchester engineers Heenan & Froude, who are perhaps more famous for their work on Blackpool Tower (*see* p 101 and p 105). At the end of the pier was a large pavilion that could seat 800 patrons. Despite the modest fee of 2d to walk along the pier, it never seems to have been sufficiently popular and economically successful and passed through a number of operators.

Due to Folkestone's proximity to the Continent, the pier had to close at the outbreak of the Second World War, although it was subsequently reopened for a short period. However, on 11 June 1940 the pier was closed again to allow the centre section of the structure to be blown up as a defensive measure (*see* p 283). The gap was closed by the addition of a small bridge in 1943, but on 20 May 1945, a fire destroyed the pavilion and severely damaged the seaward end of pier. The structure was beyond recovery and demolition began in 1952.

Behind the pier can be seen the cliff railway, which was constructed as part of the same scheme as the pier, and in recent years has at times been closed as it was too expensive to run and maintain (*see* p 73). To the right of the cliff railway can be seen the Bathing Establishment, a multifunctional bathhouse and entertainment complex that opened in July 1869 and was extended in the 1870s with the construction of a swimming pool.

The mid-19th-century crescent of houses and the nearby terraces survive today, but the hotel on the right-hand side of the image has been largely replaced by the Grand Burstin Hotel Folkestone; incorporated into the rear of the mid-1980s hotel are fragments of the original 1843 Royal Pavilion Hotel seen in this photograph, a once vital facility for passengers using ferries across the English Channel (*see* p 25).

At the top of the beach can be seen the substantial entertainment facilities for visitors, including a bathing pool on the left, a boating lake in the centre and the Rotunda Amusement Park. The amusement park closed in 2003 and declined slowly during the following years until the site had been entirely cleared.

EAW024832

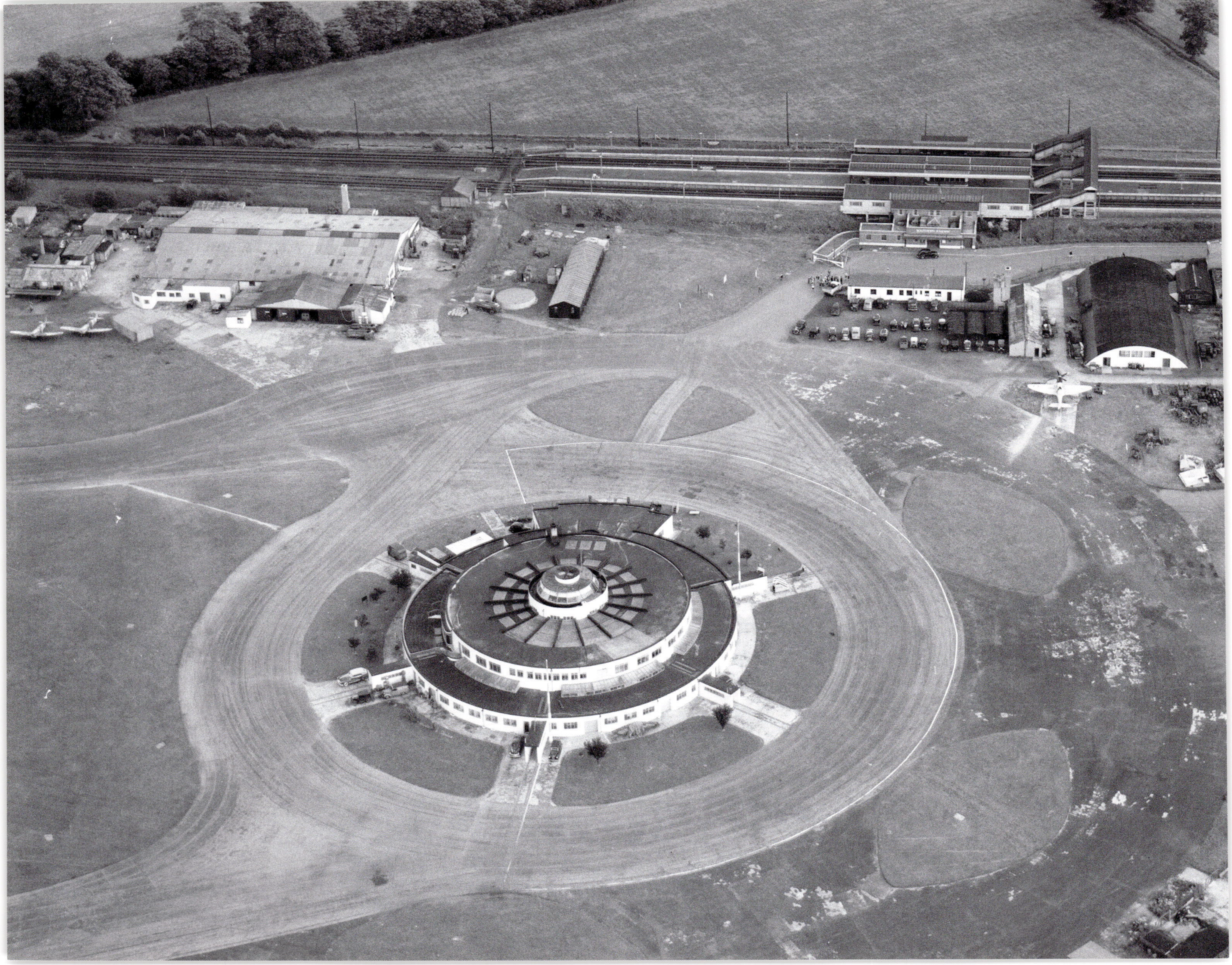

The railway station near The Beehive (Gatwick Airport South), Crawley, Surrey
15 July 1953

During the second half of the 19th century, the rapidly expanding rail network opened up seaside resorts to the masses; similarly, the aeroplane in the second half of the 20th century ushered in an era of foreign package holidays and cheap flights, first to the sunshine of the Mediterranean and subsequently to more distant parts of the world. The roots of this change lie in the interwar years when local authorities began to develop a network of regional airports. Shoreham Airport's terminal building opened in June 1936 using cubic and curvilinear forms in the fashionable streamlined Modern Movement style. Although some people undoubtedly flew to Shoreham to enjoy a holiday on the south coast, the net effect was to begin the process of improving access to the Continent for the upper end of the British market, as well as to other parts of Britain.

The growth in international air travel due to increased disposable income and cheaper airfares has had a significant impact on the popularity of the English seaside resort. Gatwick Airport, which opened officially in June 1936, had a circular terminal building, nicknamed The Beehive, designed by the architects Hoar, Marlow & Lovett. Extending from this were six 20ft-long (6.1m) covered corridors with telescopic canvas canopies radiating out from the central concourse, allowing six aircraft to be handled simultaneously; three corridors were for arrivals and three for departures. In the space where the seventh corridor could have been attached, a subway connected the terminal building to the nearby railway station. Its design anticipated the hubs found today at many airports around the world.

In 1951, the first terminal at Heathrow opened, and in the following year the Comet provided the first jet service on the route from London to Johannesburg. This aircraft would usher in the future of long-distance air travel, even though its lifespan proved short due to major technical problems. In 1970, the first Boeing 747 entered service and six years later Concorde made its inaugural commercial flight between the USA, France and Britain. In 1950 there were 195,000 landings and take-offs at British airports, but by 2002 this had risen to just over 2 million in much larger aircraft. Consequently, over the same period the numbers of passengers passing through airports rose from just over 2 million to almost 200 million.

The main impact of air travel was to bring cheap foreign travel within the reach of most holidaymakers. Nevertheless, a major part of the shift from domestic to foreign tourism can also be attributed to the motor car, which opened up the western part of Europe to holidaymakers and second-home owners. British Travel Association figures recorded that in 1951 1.5 million people took holidays abroad, a figure that rose to around 5 million during the 1960s and to 8.5 million in 1972. Despite growing foreign competition, the peak of domestic holidays seems to have occurred in the early 1970s, but from the mid-1970s onwards, tourism to foreign destinations increased rapidly. In 1978 9 million holidays of four nights or more were taken abroad, but nine years later this had risen to 20 million. The main victim of improved and more affordable transport, greater disposable income and more leisure time has inevitably been the English seaside resort.

EAW050736

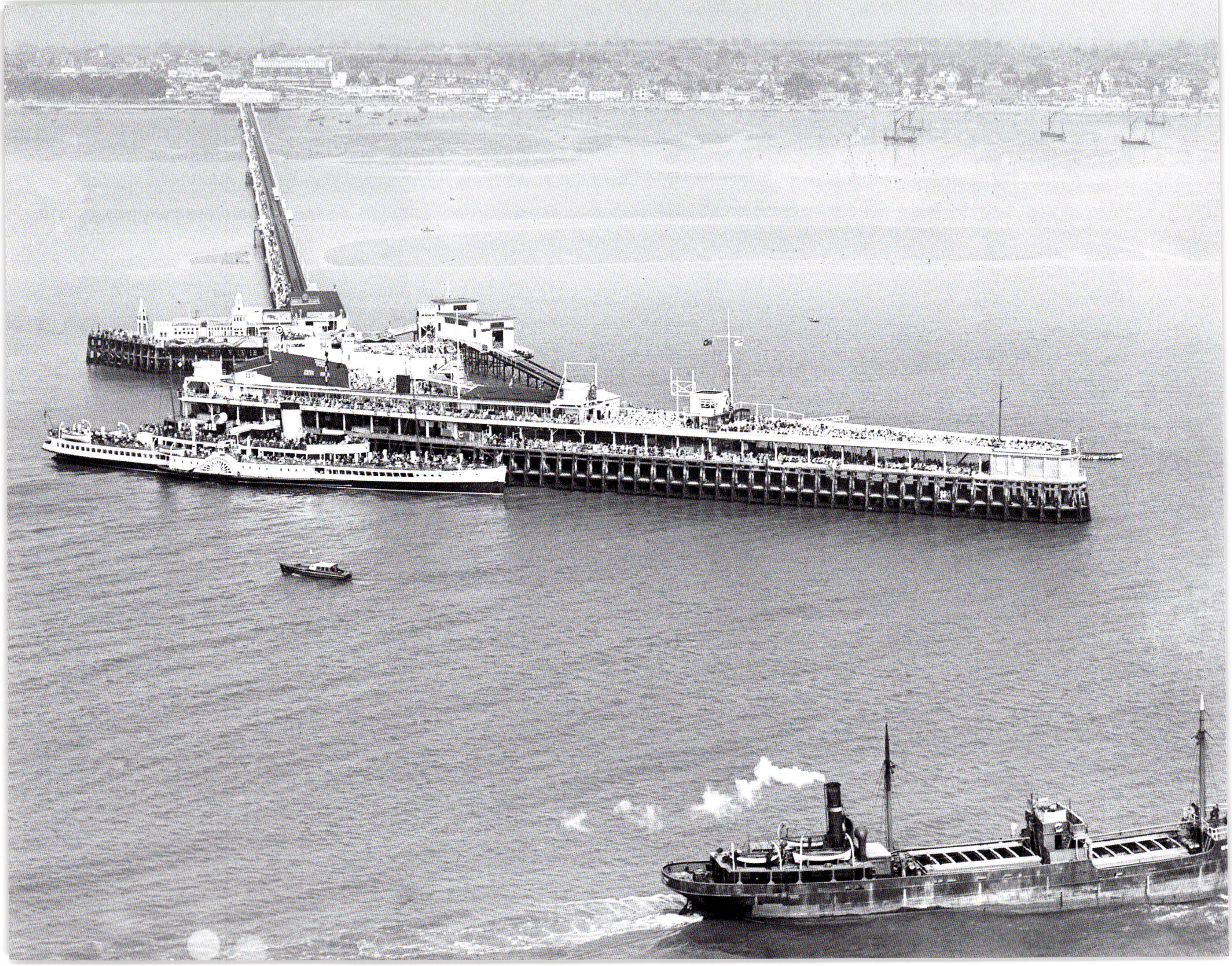

Southend Pier, Southend-on-Sea, Essex
21 August 1939

Taken only 10 days before the outbreak of the Second World War, the sight of the paddle steamer carrying holidaymakers and the crowded pier head suggests that it was business as usual at Southend. Soon after this photograph was taken, the pier would be taken over by the Royal Navy and renamed HMS *Leigh*. The pier in the photograph opened completely on 24 August 1890, but steamers were still struggling to land passengers and therefore, in January 1898, an extension was ready for use, bringing the total length to 2.2km (1.4 miles) (*see* p 125).

When people first went to the seaside during the 18th and early 19th centuries, the vast majority of holidaymakers travelled by road. An exception was resorts in Kent, particularly Gravesend, Margate and Herne Bay, where considerable numbers of visitors arrived on sailing boats, known as hoys, travelling along the Thames. From 1815 onwards, steamers began to replace sailing boats and therefore had a profound impact on tourism along the Thames. In 1763, hoys were able to carry 60–70 passengers, while a guidebook in 1797 estimated that over 100 could be transported. Steamers were considerably larger; in 1820, the *London Engineer* steam yacht transported 270 people along the Thames. By the end of the 19th century, the steamers that plied the route along the Thames were huge compared with their predecessors: for instance, the steamer *La Marguerite* measured 104m (341ft) long and weighed 2,204 tons. The size of boats and growing competition between rival companies contributed to driving down fares, resulting in growing passenger numbers. Another consequence of larger ships was that piers had to be longer, so that passengers could embark or disembark at low tide.

The ships seen in this photograph are the paddle steamer PS *Royal Eagle* moored alongside the pier and the 631-ton cargo ship *Moelfre Rose* passing by. Built in 1932 by Cammell Laird at Birkenhead, the PS *Royal Eagle* was 89m (292ft) long and weighed 1,539 tons. It entered service on the route along the Thames from London to Southend, Margate and Ramsgate and heroically made three trips to Dunkirk at the end of May 1940 to evacuate troops. It spent the remainder of the war as an anti-aircraft vessel and returned to civilian service in 1946, primarily on the route from London to Margate, though for a few weeks in 1950 it also served Southend and Clacton. Although steamers continued in use into the second half of the 20th century on the Thames, they became very much secondary to railways, and therefore the *Royal Eagle* was sold in November 1953 and scrapped.

EPW062734

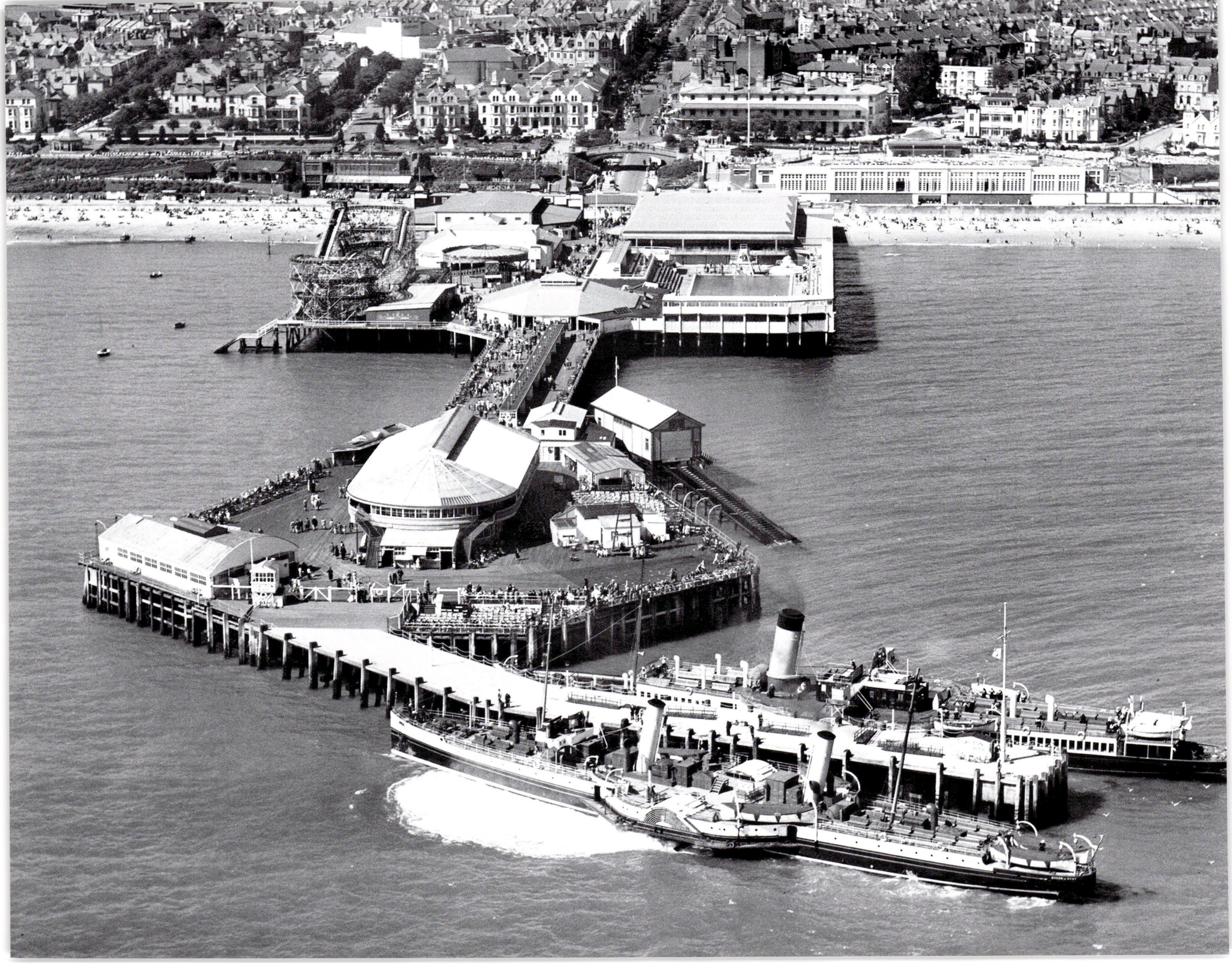

The pier, Clacton-on-Sea, Essex
23 August 1938

This photograph shows two steamers alongside the pierhead at Clacton-on-Sea, but what it also illustrates is the diversity of activities taking place at a seaside pier, which could combine this function with providing entertainments, a fun fair, a lifeboat station and a swimming pool.

The first Clacton pier opened on 27 July 1871 and was 146m (479ft) long. A lifeboat station was added in 1878 and a pavilion was built on the previously uncluttered deck in 1883. The pier was extended to 360m (1,181ft) during the 1890s, and included a new polygonal head and steamer landing stage. A one-inch gap covered by wrought iron plates was deliberately left between the pierhead and neck to help withstand the vibrations caused by visiting boats. Belle Steamers began operating from the pier at the turn of the century and continued there until the 1930s.

The ship moored at the front of the pier is the *Queen of Kent*. It was built as an Ascot-class paddle minesweeper HMS *Atherstone* by the Ailsa Shipbuilding Co in 1916. After the war, it was bought by The New Medway SP Co and rebuilt as the passenger steamer *Queen of Kent*. In 1949, the ship was sold to the Southampton, Isle of Wight & South of England Royal Mail Steam Packet Co Ltd, also known as Red Funnel Steamers, and it was renamed *Lorna Doone (2)*. It was sold for scrap in 1952.

EPW058702

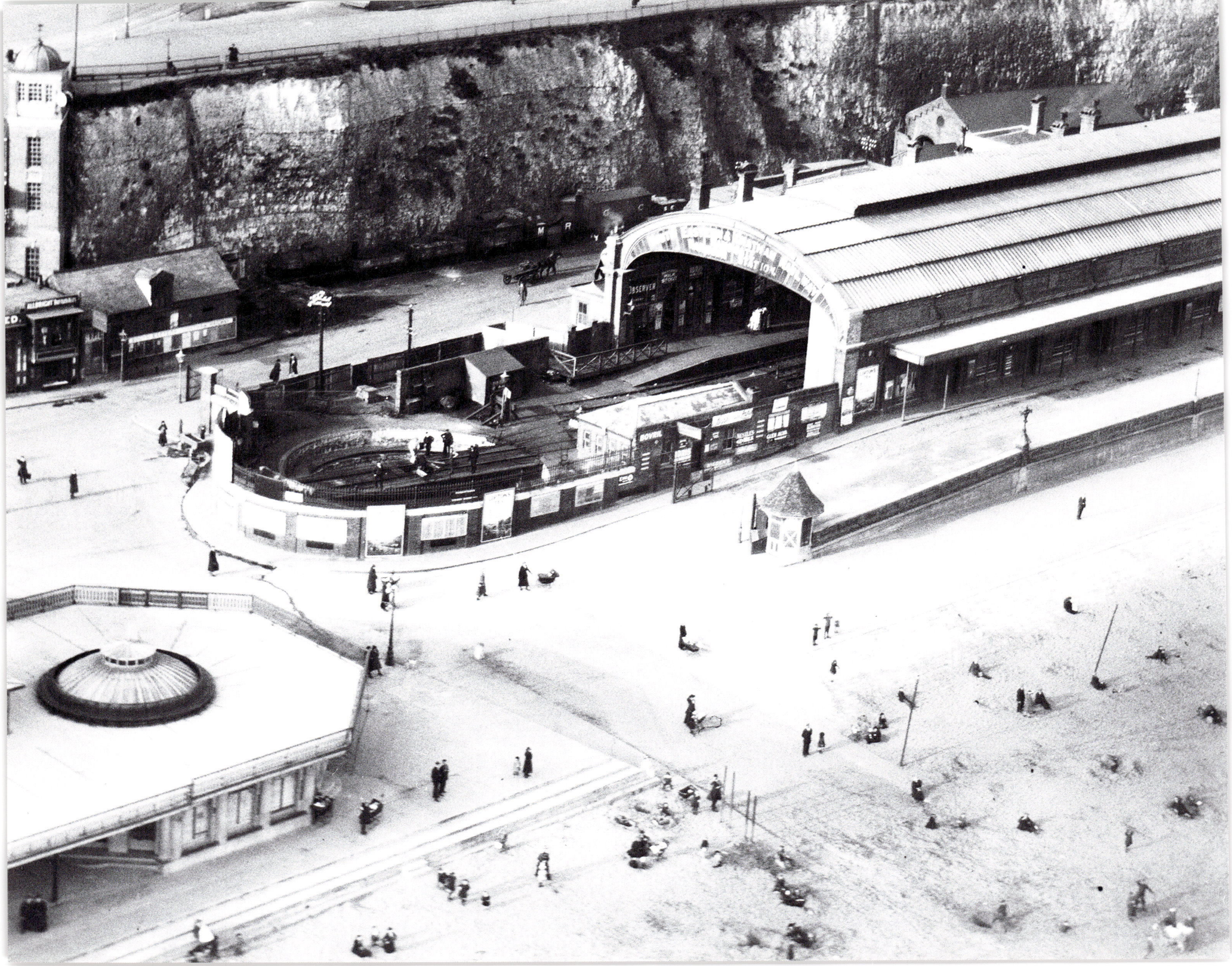

Ramsgate Harbour Station, Ramsgate, Kent
February 1920

On 13 April 1846, the Canterbury to Ramsgate branch of the South-Eastern Railway Company's line from London to Dover opened, but the railway station was a considerable distance inland. The Kent Coast Railway's line reached Ramsgate on 5 October 1863, arriving at this new terminus on the seafront. The presence of a railway station, and the consequent increased access to the beach of visitors and trippers, changed the character of Ramsgate's Sands, once a place enjoyed by sedate, genteel visitors.

By 1920, the station was called the Ramsgate Harbour Station, as can be seen on the sign on the arch above the railway lines. At the end of the station can be seen a turntable; as this was a terminus, the locomotives of trains would have to be turned through 180° for the return journey.

Ramsgate's third railway station was opened on 2 July 1926 by Southern Railway and replaced the original Town Station and this seafront Ramsgate Harbour Station. The old terminus at the Sands was converted in 1930 into an amusement park entitled Merrie England. The attraction was modernised in 1935, and in 1938 the 900-seat Coronation Hall opened. The building was destroyed by fire in May 1998 and the site has remained undeveloped since.

In early 1903, Ramsgate Corporation asked S D Adshead to draw up plans for an entertainment pavilion. The Royal Victoria Pavilion, part of which can be seen to the left of the photograph, was opened in June 1904 by Princess Louise, Duchess of Argyll. By the early 21st century, it was derelict, but in 2017 it reopened as Britain's largest branch of the J D Wetherspoon chain of pubs.

EPW000093

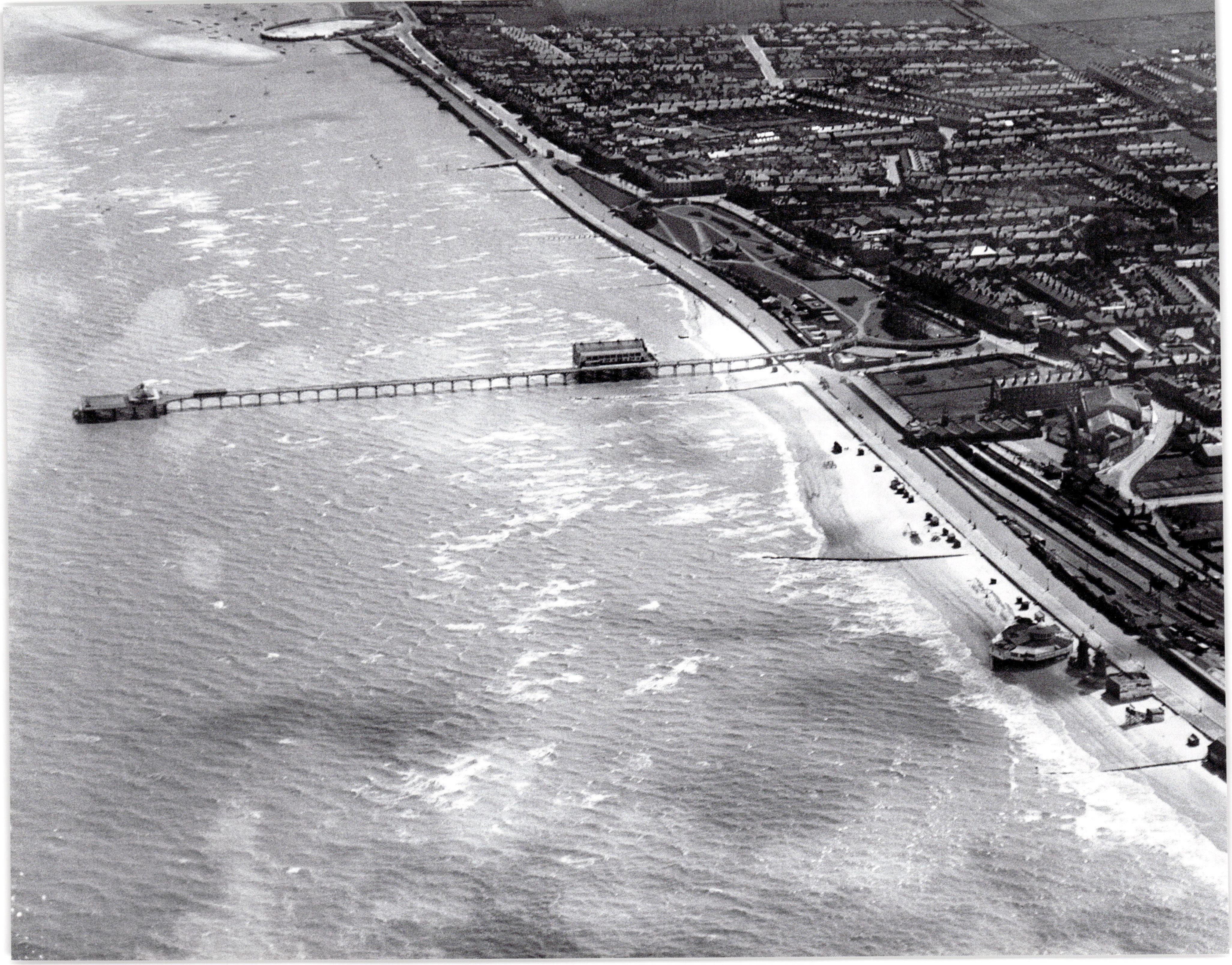

The railway station, pier and town, Cleethorpes

May 1930

This photograph shows the close relationship between the railway station, the pier and the seafront at Cleethorpes. In the 18th century, Cleethorpes was a fishing village with an inn established around 1760 that was used by people wishing to bathe in the sea. The first stirrings of Cleethorpes as a health holiday resort took place during the early 19th century, but major development began with the coming of the railway. More than 30,000 people travelled by train to the newly opened station parallel to the coast on 3 August 1863, with a further 4,000 arriving on horse-drawn vehicles.

The Manchester, Sheffield and Lincolnshire Railway also invested over £100,000 to build an exhibition hall, a museum, aquarium, amusement park and baths, as well as the promenade and gardens. Encouraged by this investment, the main landowners in the town, Sidney College Cambridge and the Earl of Yarborough, took advantage of this investment by laying out large numbers of building plots for speculative development.

The arrival of the railway prompted investment in a seaside pier, its natural location being close to the station, and therefore convenient to catch the eye of new arrivals. Similar arrangements can be found at a number of resorts, such as at Blackpool (*see* p 47) and Hunstanton. When the pier opened on 4 August 1873, it was 366m (1,200ft) long to allow steamers to land passengers at all but low tides. It was begun by John Dowson, but after his death in 1868, the work was completed by Head Wrightson of Stockton. In 1883, a concert hall was erected at the pierhead but it was destroyed by fire in 1903 and replaced by shops and a café. In 1905, a new pavilion was built on an extension attached to the side of the pier.

As the railway company had invested so much in its new station, the decision was taken to invest in new sea defences. The initial stretch of sea wall was built in 1884 and was continued in the early 20th century as a result of the Cleethorpes Improvement Act 1902. This led to the creation of a new 610m-long (2,000ft) sea wall, which was 5.5m (18ft) high, 2.1m (7ft) thick at the base and built with 15,000 tons of concrete.

EPW031924

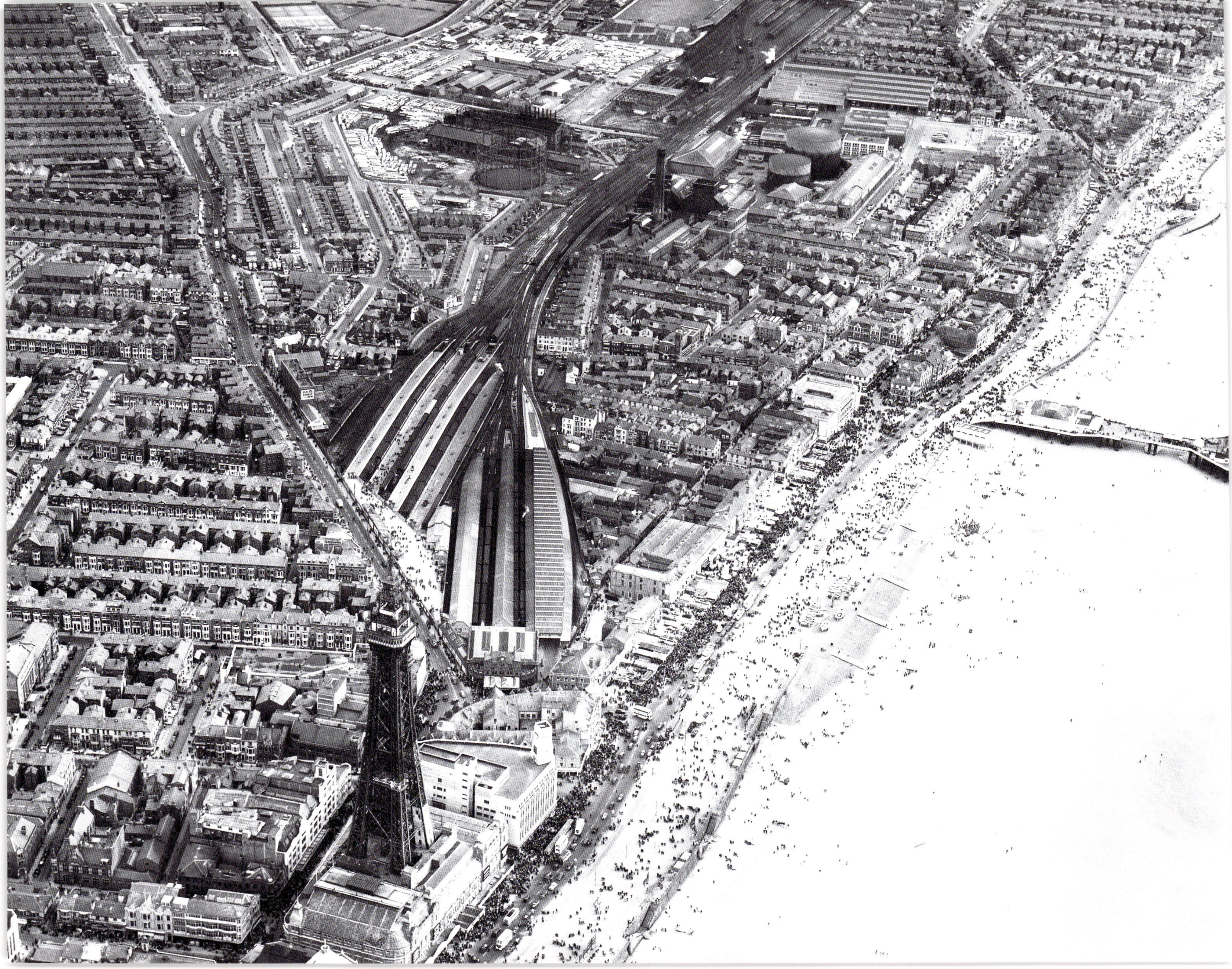

Blackpool Tower, Central Railway Station and the seafront, Blackpool, Lancashire
10 October 1952

From 1846, Blackpool had a single railway track arriving at Talbot Road and this route was doubled in 1865, though Preston remained a bottleneck that seems to have restricted the number of passengers. The provision of a second route to Blackpool would prove to be key to the town's late 19th-century expansion. Work began on the line in September 1861 and the new station, comprising little more than a cabin, opened in April 1863. The substantial Central Station seen in this photograph was the result of major reconstruction in 1899–1901.

The creation of this second route into Blackpool would eventually allow millions of visitors to reach the resort each year. However, the most immediate impact was to shape the development of the southern part of Blackpool, providing a major barrier between seafront development and more inland areas. The eventual size of the rail lines, and the presence of industrial facilities including the gas works, the electricity station and the tram depot, would also lead to the streets near the tracks being filled with some of the most modest housing and cheapest lodgings.

The creation of Central Station prompted investors to construct Central Pier, the second of Blackpool's piers, which opened in 1868. As it was located near the station, it proved popular with visitors and excursionists as a venue for dancing, an activity that would have been frowned upon at the earlier, more genteel North Pier.

The other impact of the new railway station would be to stimulate the creation of an area of large lodging and boarding houses to the east of Central Drive, the larger houses to the left of the diagonal road behind Blackpool Tower.

After the war, the Borough Surveyor's Department of Blackpool Corporation had begun to plan for a future that primarily involved the use of cars and coaches. Central Station closed in 1964, leading to all major rail services being rerouted into Blackpool North. The site of the closed station was the subject of various redevelopment plans until its eventual demolition in 1974, by which time the long-mooted creation of a new civic centre on the site was already underway. However, only the police station and magistrates' court were built and today the site of the railway station is a huge car park.

EAW047419

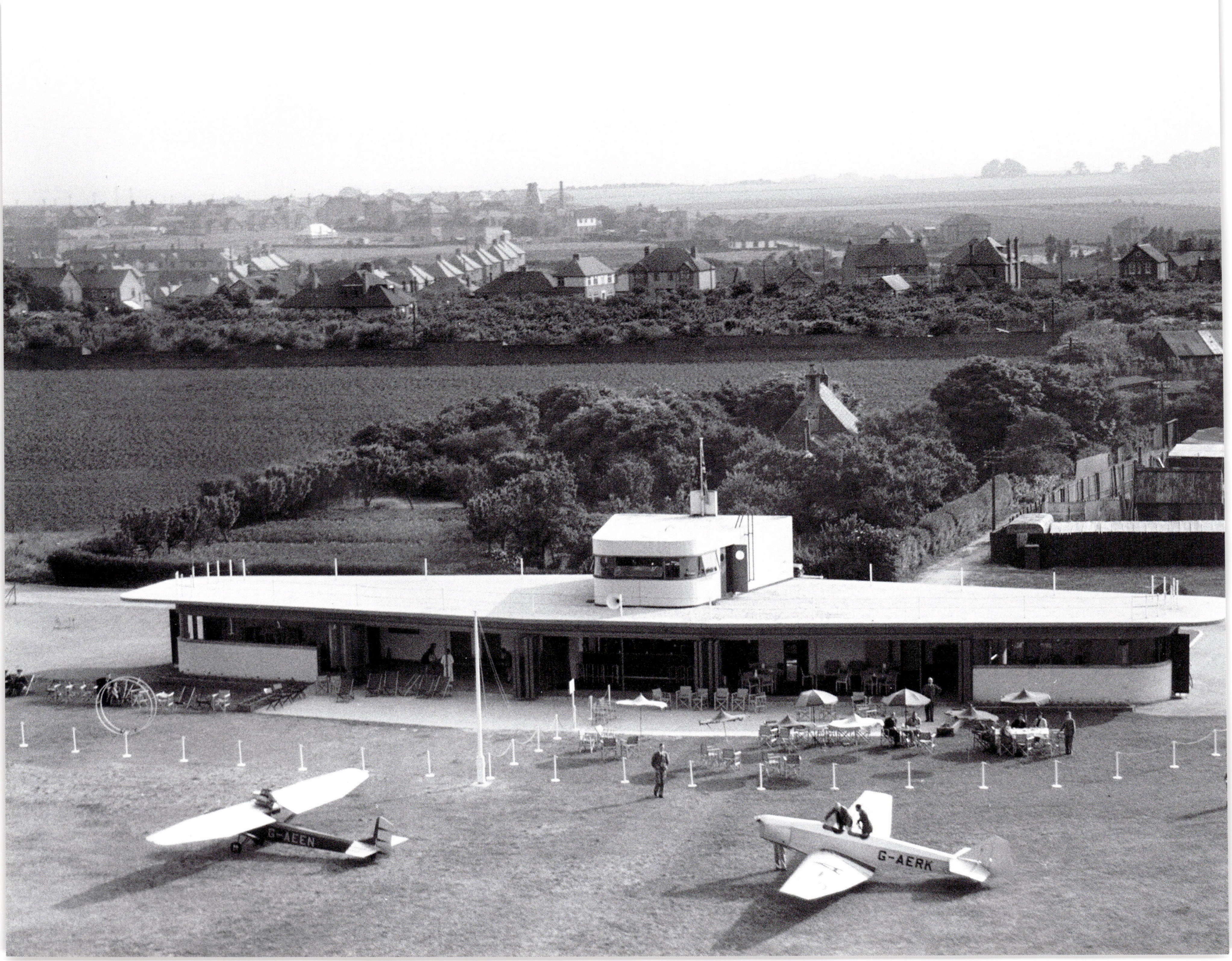
G-AEEN
G-AERK

Ramsgate Aerodrome Pavilion, Northwood, Kent
June 1937

The caption of the Aerofilms photograph helpfully identifies the two aircraft in front of the 'Ramsgate Aerodrome Pavilion' as a BA Swallow L25C Mk.2 (G-AERK) and a BAC Drone (G-AEEN). The information in the Aerofilms caption also reveals that 'airport terminal' was not yet the established term in everyday use.

Seaside resorts figured prominently in lists of airports during the interwar years. In August 1936, *Flight* magazine ran a feature about the new airport at Weston-super-Mare and as a result of an analysis of passenger numbers, the author concluded that 'holiday-makers will use the air while business people still view it with misgiving'. In fact, this was perhaps a slight exaggeration, though there were early airports at Blackpool, Shoreham, Weston-super-Mare and Ramsgate. It is perhaps ironic that a facility that might have originally brought holidaymakers to resorts would in the future take the customers abroad and contribute to the decline of England's seaside resorts (*see* p 37).

Ramsgate Municipal Airport was designed by David Pleydell-Bouverie and opened in 1937, the year that this photograph was taken. The terminal at Ramsgate resembles the elegant wings of a contemporary monoplane. The evocation of the theme of flight might seem an obvious idea for an airport architect to employ, but in Britain the only other clear example is the 1939 terminal at Birmingham Airport. It incorporates cantilevered canopies flanking the building resembling wings under which aircraft could embark and disembark passengers, a practice known as dry boarding.

At the centre of Ramsgate's terminal building is a small control tower projecting above the roofline of the wings. The rebuilding of Croydon Airport in 1927–8 introduced the idea in Britain of a combined control tower/airport terminal, a model for future airport design, the control tower serving like the bridge of a ship. Regional and municipal airports across the country during the 1930s predominantly followed this example, including the terminal here at Ramsgate. The building closed in 1968 and was demolished.

EPW053975

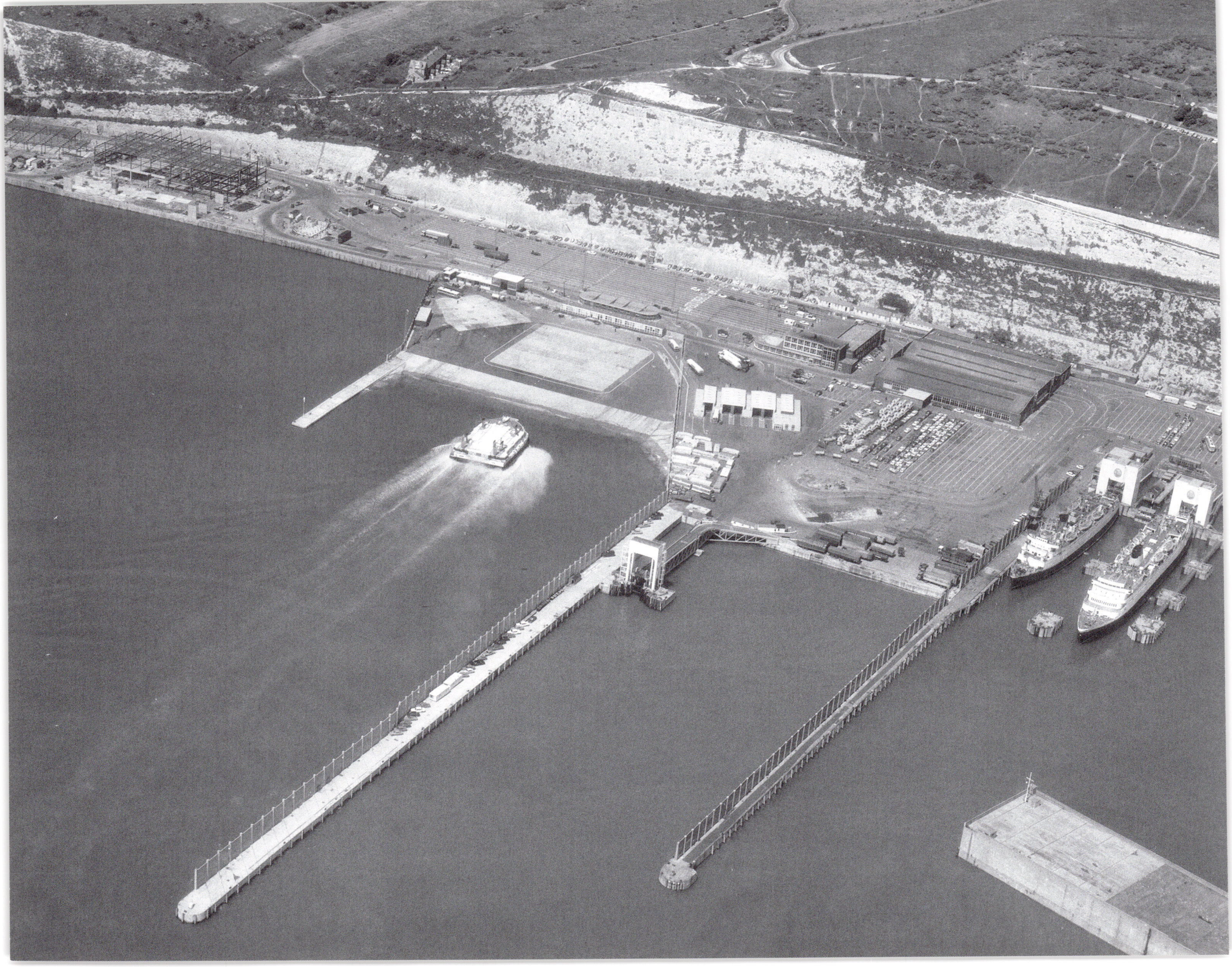

Hovercraft coming into port at Eastern Docks, Dover, Kent
1 June 1969

Since the Middle Ages, Dover has been the key port connecting Britain to mainland Europe. Today there is a huge port infrastructure handling large numbers of passengers and a substantial part of Britain's imports and exports. In this photograph of 1969, the edge of the ferry passenger facilities can be seen on the right-hand side. One thing that is absent today is the hovercraft.

The world's first hovercraft crossed the English Channel from Calais to Dover on 25 July 1959 with its inventor Sir Christopher Cockerel on board. Passenger services began between Pegwell Bay, near Ramsgate, and Calais in 1966 and by June 1968 the world's first hovercraft car ferry made its maiden trip from Dover to Boulogne in 25 minutes, reaching speeds of 50 knots. The craft shown in this photograph appears to be one of the SRN4 craft, either the *Princess Margaret* or *Princess Anne*.

This photograph shows one of the great advantages of the hovercraft; it needs very little in the way of facilities beyond a dedicated section of beach or harbourside, with some accompanying ticket office and waiting room facilities. In 1978 a new hoverport at the Western Docks at Dover was commissioned and at the peak of the service in 1982 hovercraft were carrying in one six-month period 2.5 million passengers and 400,000 cars. However, the opening of the Channel Tunnel in 1994 marked the beginning of the end for the hovercraft service, which ended on 1 October 2000.

The transport solution of the future is now something largely consigned to the past. However, there is still one hovercraft service operating in Britain in the Solent, between the mainland and the Isle of Wight, with terminals located on the seafronts of Southsea and Ryde. The route across the Solent began operating from Stokes Bay to Ryde on 24 July 1965, the first in the world, but soon the mainland departure point became centred on the seafront at Southsea.

EAW193516

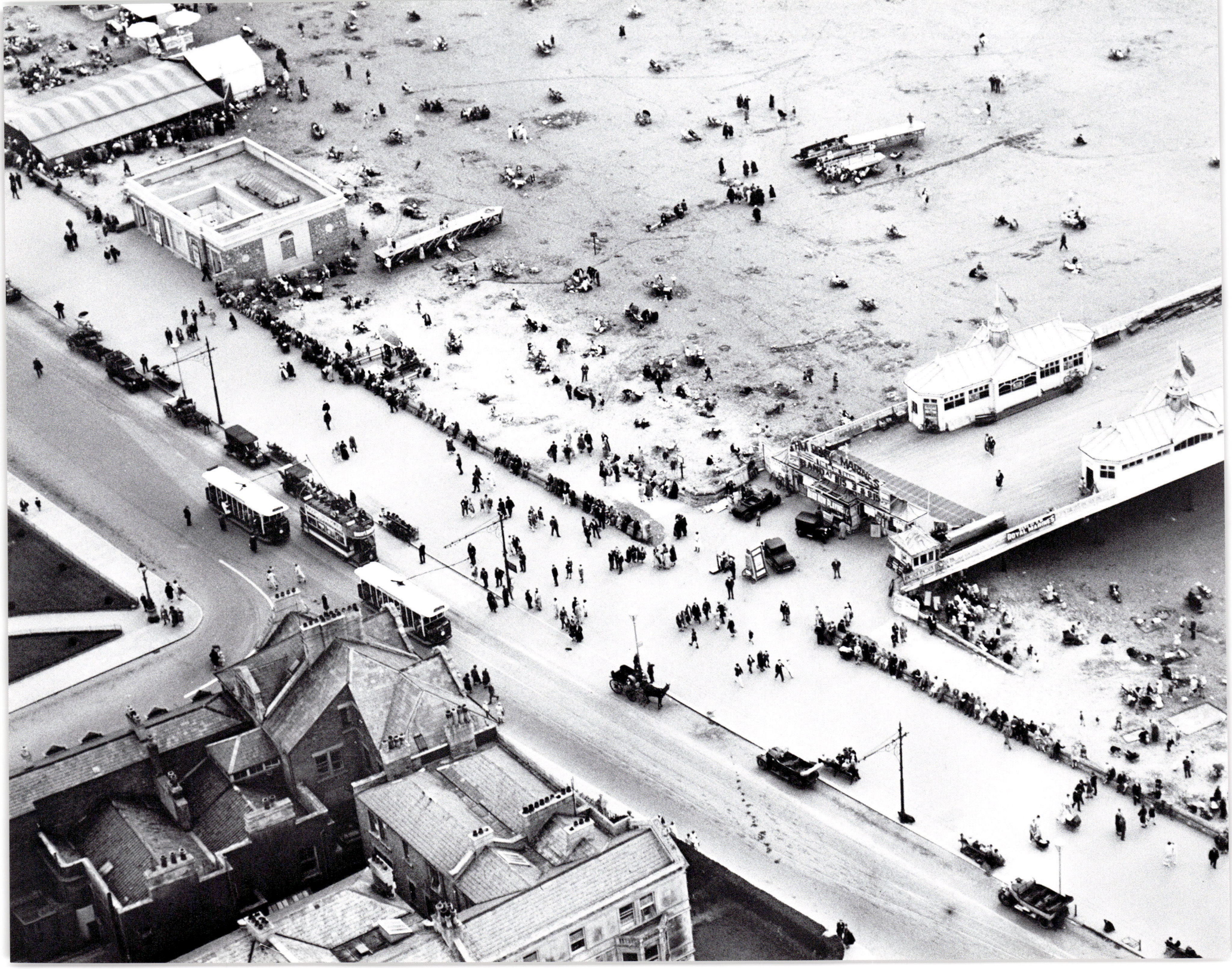

The entrance to the Grand Pier, Weston-super-Mare, Somerset
September 1928

This close-up photograph shows the variety of forms of transport being used by visitors to a seaside resort in the 1920s. In 1928, most visitors arrived at Weston-super-Mare either by train or by landing from steamers arriving at Birnbeck Pier. However, the motor car and the charabanc were becoming an increasingly common sight at seaside resorts. A few cars can be seen in this photograph, ranging from some smaller examples to larger, wider ones that are similar to small versions of charabancs. A number of the cars appear to be taxis, and alongside them can be seen some horse-drawn carriages, providing a practical form of transport as well as perhaps beginning to be seen as a novelty.

Electric-powered trams are also visible; electricity came to Weston-super-Mare in May 1901, surprisingly late for a major resort. The provision of electric lighting only came about when the Weston-super-Mare and District Electric Supply Company realised the possibility of running trams by day while lighting the streets by night, maximising their potential income. The company was established in 1899 and a Tram Order was obtained in 1900 to give it the necessary powers. Work began in January 1902 and by April the first trial runs of trams were taking place. The official opening of the service took place during the following month and in the first year of operation trams carried 778,965 passengers.

From the outset, trams faced competition from buses, and opposition from taxi drivers. In the 1930s, the Bristol Tramways Co began operating buses on the tram route during the summer and soon reached an agreement to close the tramway, purchasing it for £15,000, while paying the Urban District Council another £5,000 to lift the rails. The last tram ran in April 1937. During their lifetime, Weston's trams carried over 51 million passengers. Weston-super-Mare was the 102nd tramway system to close in Britain, and by 1962, Blackpool alone continued to operate a service. For 30 years it was the sole town with trams running in Britain until 1992 when Manchester's Metrolink opened.

EPW023970

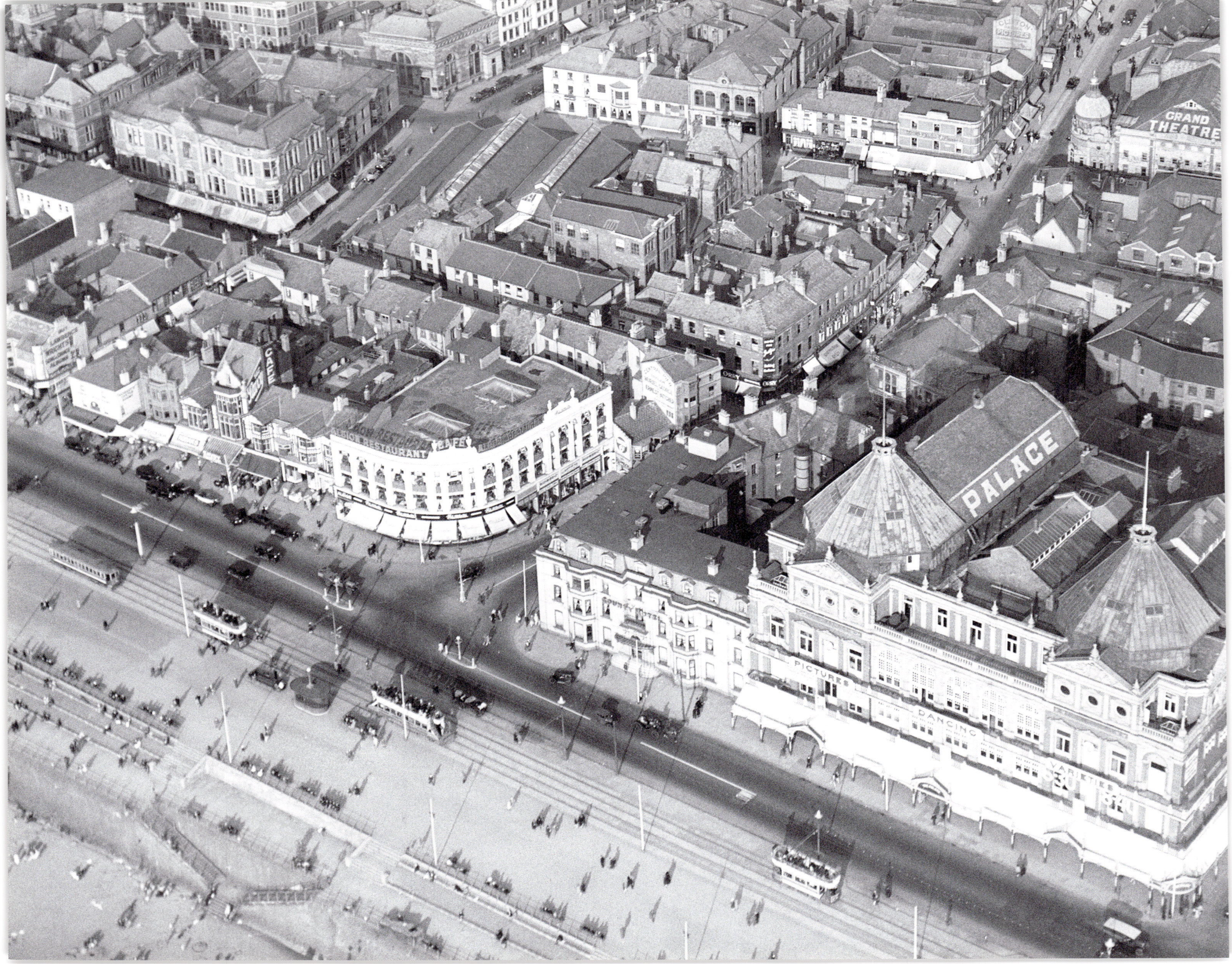
GRAND THEATRE
PALACE
PICTURES
DANCING
VARIETIES
RESTAURANT

The Palace and Promenade, Blackpool, Lancashire
12 September 1929

As well as travel to and from seaside resorts, provision was made for travelling within these towns. As people valued a view out to sea, there was a natural desire to build new homes on the seafront and consequently seaside resorts often have a very long diameter. Therefore, local authorities had to provide a good road along the seafront and many resorts also had trams following the same route.

Most early electric-powered services relied on the transmission of power via their rails and wheels, but Blackpool's initial system, installed by September 1885 by the Halifax engineer Michael Holroyd Smith, drew its power from a conductor rail in a conduit between the rails. Initially the two-mile-long service ran on a single track with a number of passing places. This arrangement can be seen in a number of early photographs, but by the end of the 1880s the limitations of the power system had been recognised. Water caused the electrical supply to be earthed and sand collected in the conduit. Therefore, Blackpool followed other towns in employing collectors to draw power from overhead trolley wires. The switchover of power transmission systems in the original line, which took place between 1899 and 1905, was accompanied by the doubling of the tracks. Therefore, the promenade was widened and new sea defences were created.

Think of the seafront at Blackpool today, or 100 years ago, and the first thing that comes to mind is Blackpool Tower. However, beside it was a major rival for the hard-earned savings of the millions of visitors. The Palace, originally called the Alhambra, had its foundation stone laid in December 1897 and the building was designed by Wylson and Long of London. Although the Palace could not boast the tower of its neighbour, it outshone its rival in terms of its lavishness. At the heart of the public spaces were marble halls, with floors laid with Italian marble and Venetian mosaic, while the stairs were built using solid Carrara marble.

The Alhambra opened in August 1899, but went bankrupt in November 1902. The building was acquired by the Blackpool Tower Company and reopened as the Palace in July 1904 following a redesign of its interiors by Frank Matcham. It was demolished in 1962 and was replaced by a large department store, which was in turn replaced 30 years later.

EPW029210

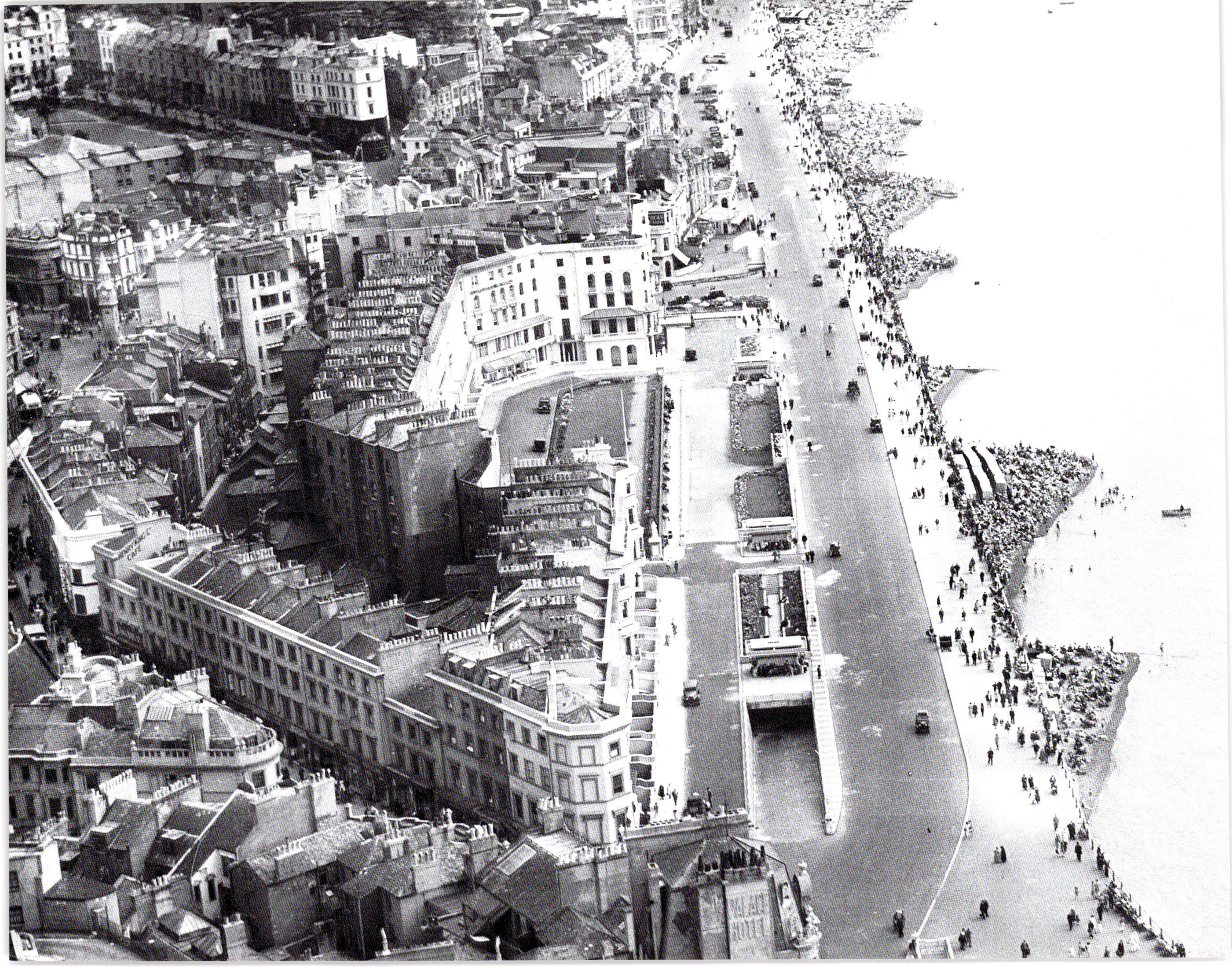
QUEEN'S HOTEL

The entrance to the Carlisle Parade underground car park and the seafront, Hastings, East Sussex

August 1932

Many seafront roads created during the 19th century proved, at least initially, capable of handling the new vehicles. Cars were parked on seafront roads parallel to the pavement and larger charabancs and buses were often catered for in empty spaces back from the seafront. At some resorts with wide seafront roads, it was possible to park large numbers of cars, but the rapid growth in car ownership soon meant that new purpose-built facilities would be required. In 1920 there were 591,000 licensed vehicles in Britain, but a decade later this figure had almost quadrupled to 2.25 million.

At Hastings, the seafront had developed in a piecemeal fashion during the 19th century and by the 1920s, there was no continuous single road from one end of the resort to the other. To rectify this, and to create new parking, Hastings undertook a major reconfiguration of its seafront. Between 1925 and 1939, a 2.2km-long (1.4 miles) two-tier promenade was created from Carlisle Parade to Marina Court under the supervision of the borough engineer Sidney Herbert Little (1885–1961). This was achieved by constructing a new set of seawalls closer to the sea and infilling the area between these and the original sea walls. At the upper level, the new seafront consisted of a long, wide road, while beneath there was a series of car parks, two swimming pools and long, sheltered walkways. When the Carlisle Parade car park opened in 1931, it was Britain's first underground car park. Its wide exit can be seen in the foreground, while the entrance was further back and to the left side of the seafront.

An alternative solution to providing parking was to create a multi-storey car park. In 1906, Caffyn Brothers opened a three-storey garage on Marine Parade at Eastbourne that could accommodate around 100 cars. At Bournemouth, a multi-storey car park was built in 1932, a year after the underground car park at Hastings opened, while at Blackpool the continuing shortage of car parking spaces and facilities for buses led to the creation in 1936–7 of a combined bus station and car park near Blackpool North railway station.

EPW039366

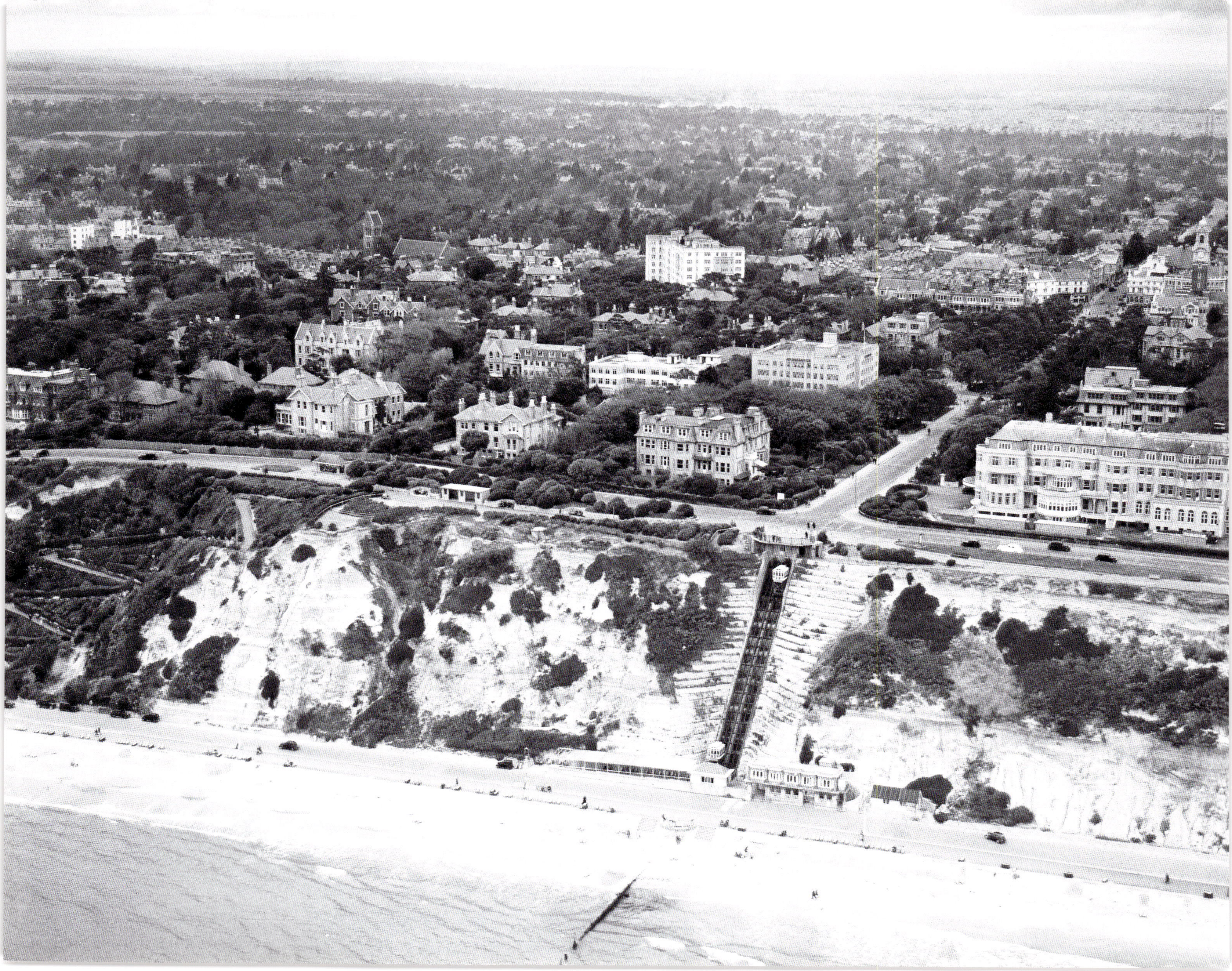

The East Cliff Railway and the town, Bournemouth, Dorset
3 October 1946

A number of the largest seaside resorts developed where there were tall cliffs and therefore there was a need to provide easy transport between the seashore and the cliff tops, where most of the housing was located. In 1869, a hoist is mentioned at Saltburn 'for raising and lowering people thus avoiding the toilsome ascent by road' and in the following decades a few resorts installed lifts or inclined railways. The first lift at Shanklin was built in 1892, but was demolished in 1957. The vertical lift may be more practical than the cliff railway, but it lacks its thrill and the aesthetic appeal.

By 1876, the first cliff railway, the South Cliff Railway, had opened at Scarborough as a result of an initiative by Mr Hunt of the Prince of Wales Hotel for his guests. When the weight of the top carriage of the pair of linked, counter-balanced carriages running on parallel tracks was increased by pumping water into a tank beneath the upper carriage, it descended, pulling up the lower carriage on the adjacent track, which had an empty tank.

This was the favoured method until the beginning of the 20th century, when the water system began to be superseded by the use of a counterweight and electric motors, eliminating the need for a second, counter-balancing carriage. A precursor of this technology was employed by the Central Cliff Railway at Scarborough. It opened on 1 August 1881 and used steam-powered winding gear to raise the cars.

The number of cliff lifts and cliff railways at a resort depended on the height of the cliffs and the length of the seafront; therefore Scarborough had five at one time and Bournemouth three. Bournemouth East Cliff Railway, the oldest of its three funicular railways, opened in April 1908 and is the oldest surviving cliff railway originally powered by electricity. Constructed for Bournemouth Corporation by Waygood and Company Limited, its two passenger cars, running on two parallel tracks, had a 25hp winding motor powered by mains electricity. The second cliff railway at West Cliff opened later in 1908 and originally used the same kind of motor, while the third cliff railway at Fisherman's Walk began operating in 1935.

EAW002995

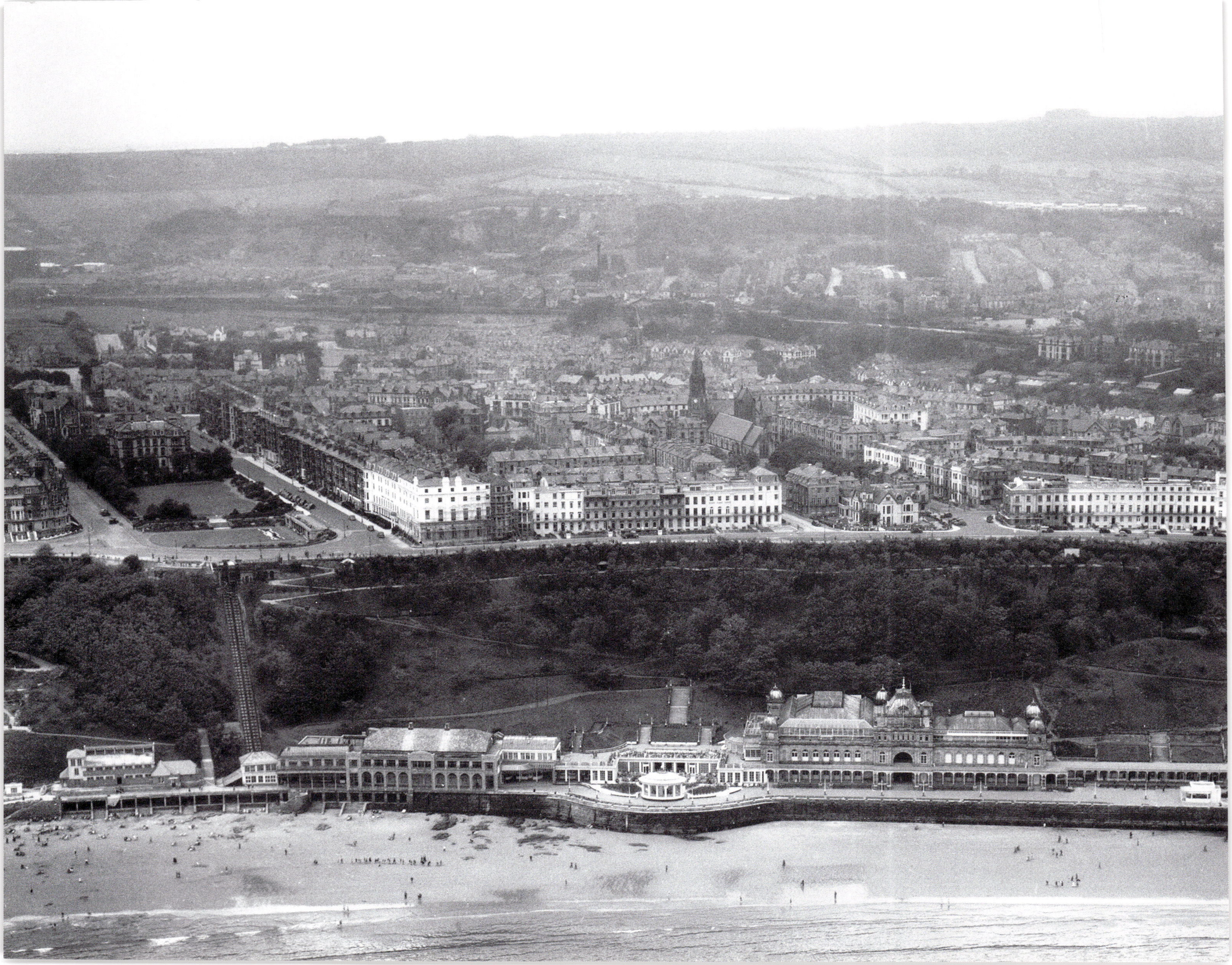

The Spa and South Cliff Gardens, Scarborough, North Yorkshire
23 June 1948

Seaside resorts originated at the beginning of the 18th century. Medical writers and doctors inspired people who had previously gone to spa towns to drink mineral waters to head to a number of coastal towns where they could enjoy seawater. Sir John Floyer (1649–1734) in 1702 explicitly made the connection between the medicinal effectiveness of spa waters and the sea when he said that 'Since we live in an Island, and have the Sea about us, we cannot want an excellent Cold Bath, which will both preserve our Healths, and cure many Diseases, as our Fountains do'.

In the 16th century, the most popular spa town in England was Bath; the Romans established *Aquae Sulis* to exploit its springs, the only naturally hot mineral waters in Britain. During the Middle Ages, Bath remained a popular destination for religious and commercial, but also for health, reasons. In the north of England, Buxton had been settled by the Romans who called it *Aquae Arnemetiae*, and during the Middle Ages, St Anne's Well seems to have been a popular local destination. Behind the popularity of Buxton in the 16th century was George Talbot, 6th Earl of Shrewsbury (*c* 1522–90), who was responsible for Mary, Queen of Scots' imprisonment from 1569 until 1584. During this period she was allowed to enjoy the baths, and although Elizabeth I never visited the spa, her Lord High Treasurer, Lord Burghley (1520/21–98), did visit it.

By the late 16th century, new sources of mineral water were beginning to be identified and popularised. Harrogate was close to Knaresborough, which was famous for its petrifying well associated with Mother Shipton, an alleged witch and prophetess who appears to have flourished around 1530. The first mineral spring was discovered at Harrogate in 1571 and during the early 17th century it became a popular destination. By this date, the number of spa sites began to increase rapidly, including new ones at Tunbridge Wells and Epsom, which were convenient for London.

In the long term, the most important of these new spas was at Scarborough on the east coast of Yorkshire. Its spa waters were discovered in *c* 1626. In 1660, a local doctor, Robert Wittie, while promoting the spa at Scarborough, warned that internal consumption of seawater could be detrimental to health, but in the 1667 edition of his book, he noted that seawater bathing had rid him of his gout. In the late 17th century, Scarborough seems to have been the most prestigious and most popular spa in the north of England, despite travel to such a remote town being difficult.

Scarborough may be where people first bathed in the sea around the English coast in a systematic, organised fashion. In this photograph can be seen the rebuilt Victorian spa, which had ceased to be a place for drinking mineral waters, but instead had become a popular entertainment complex. It lies to the south of the historic town and harbour and is the successor to the Georgian spa building, which existed by the early 18th century, and was rebuilt after a major landslide in 1737. The beach to the right of the spa in this photograph is the site of the earliest depiction of sea bathing, an engraving of 1735. During the 19th century, the previously undeveloped cliff tops behind the spa began to be filled with prestigious housing and to the left of the spa can be seen the cliff railway (*see* p 75).

EAW016691

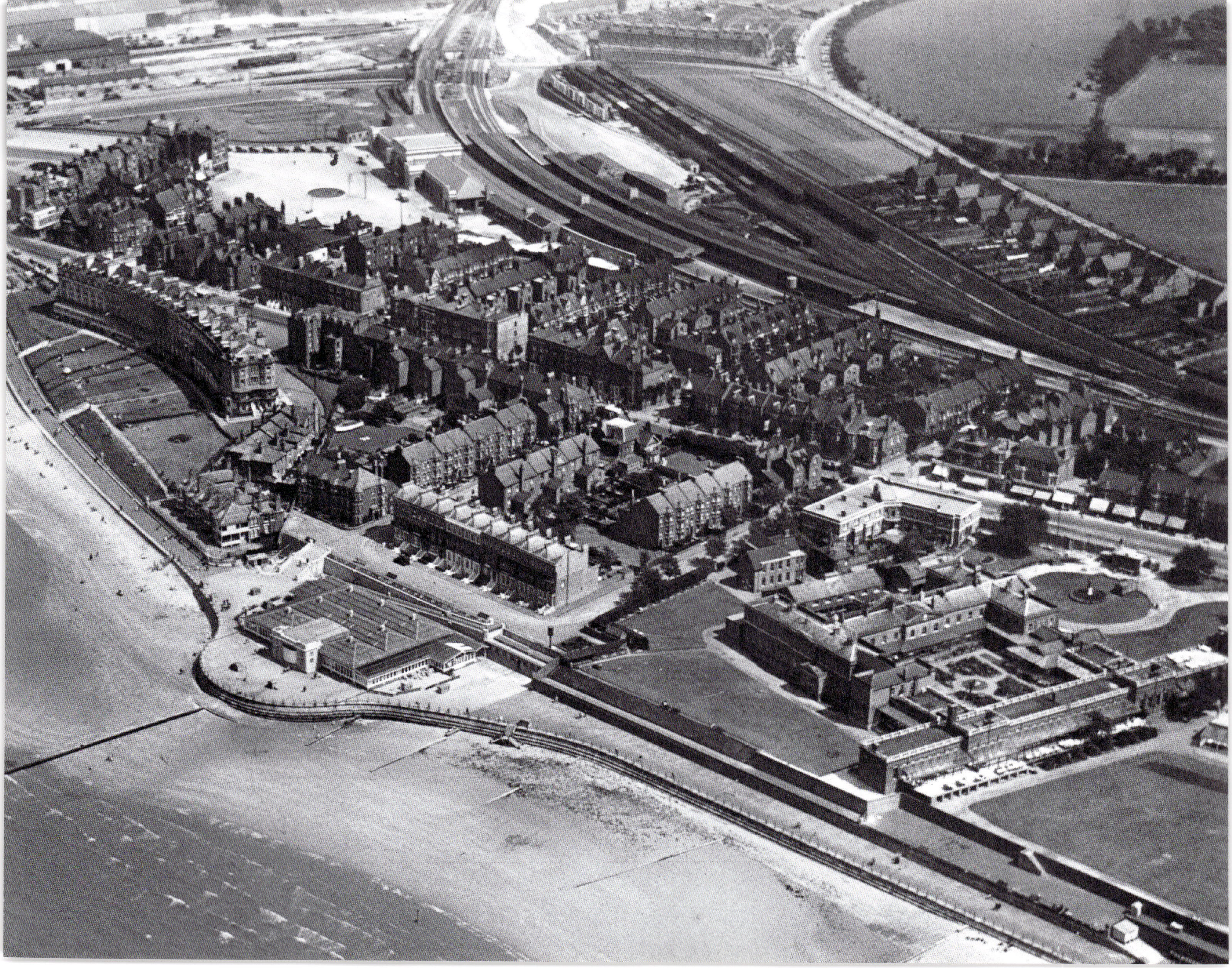

The Westbrook Pavilion and beach, Margate, Kent
22 June 1927

The first people to benefit from a visit to a seaside resort were the wealthy, with the time and money to spend a few weeks bathing in the sea and enjoying the health-giving sea air. However, by the end of the 18th century it was realised that it was the urban poor, and especially their children, who might benefit from time in or by the sea. John Coakley Lettsom was a Quaker physician who believed that seawater bathing and sea air were suitable treatments for the kind of scrofula he witnessed amidst the squalor of London. Scrofula was a disease with glandular swellings, probably a form of tuberculosis. At a meeting of like-minded gentlemen at the London Coffee House on 2 July 1791, 'The Margate Infirmary, for the Relief of the Poor whose Diseases require Sea-Bathing' was established. The Margate area was selected due to its long association with sea bathing and because it could be reached easily, and cheaply, by boat along the Thames.

The first hospital building, initially to care for 30 patients, was designed by an amateur architect, the Reverend John Pridden, and opened in 1796. Its design comprised open colonnades, where patients could sit in front of the wards flanking the central, two-storey staff and administration block. The early treatment at Margate relied not only on sea bathing, but also exposure to fresh air and sunshine. Patients were initially admitted during the bathing season, which ran from May to the end of October or early November. The sea-bathing treatment was conducted using the infirmary's own bathing machine, and by 1853 various baths had been installed in the hospital and seawater was pumped from the shore by a horse-powered pump. It was not until the installation of indoor seawater baths in 1858 that patients were treated during the winter. A large, heated seawater baths block, designed by James Knowles junior, was added to the site in 1883. However, in 1910 the swimming bath was converted into a ward, and although a heated hydrotherapy pool was opened in 1972, Lettsom's formal seawater bathing treatment at the hospital effectively ended before the outbreak of the First World War.

This photograph shows, on the right-hand side, the complex of buildings that existed by the 1920s. When first established, the hospital was distant from the centre of Margate, but with the arrival of the railway in the 1840s, and the opening of a link road along the seafront in the early 19th century, this part of the town became a popular destination for holidaymakers, as well as an attractive place to live.

EPW018606

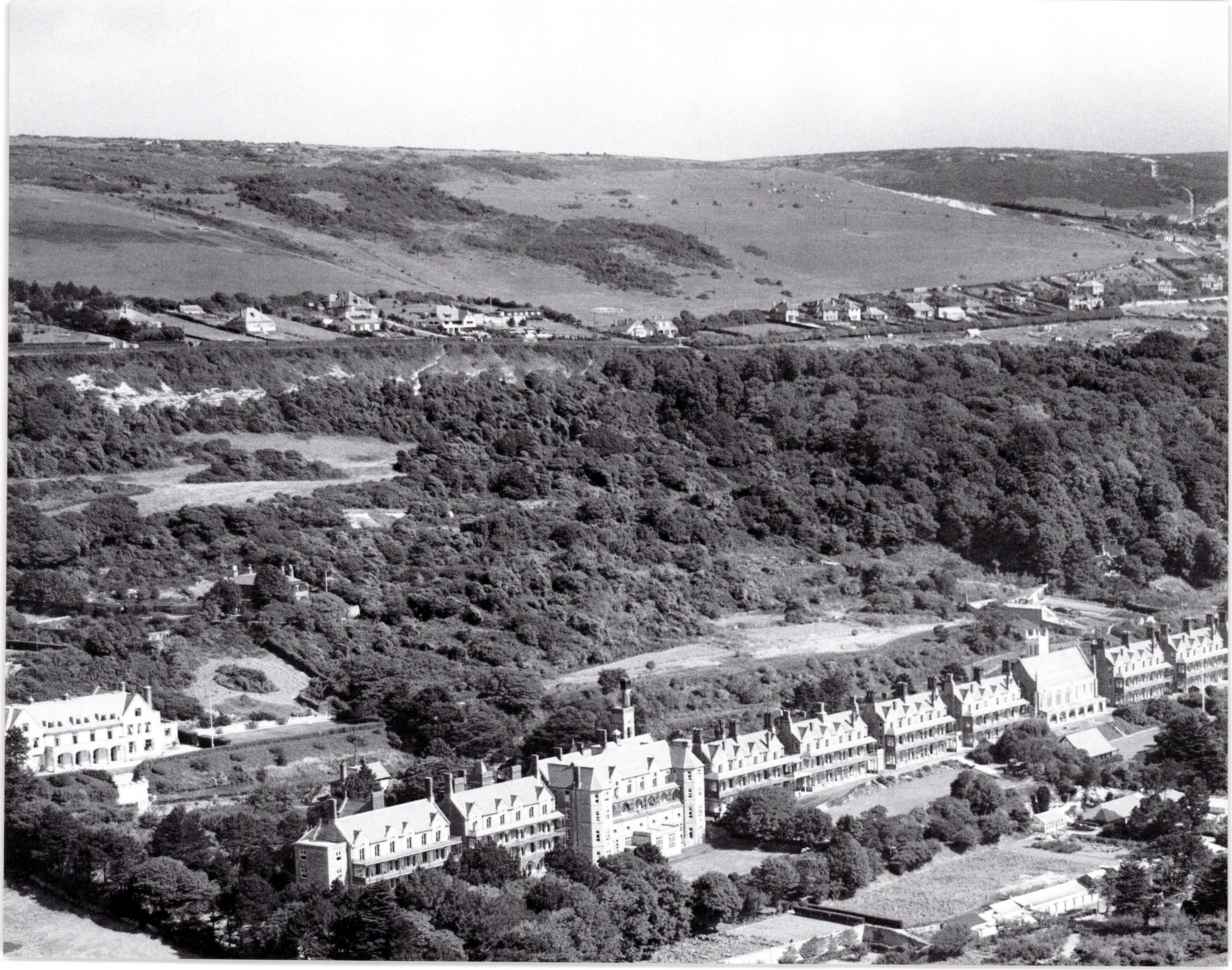

The Royal National Hospital, Ventnor, Isle of Wight
August 1933

The sea-bathing hospital at Margate was followed by a similar, but slightly later, facility at Scarborough. Following fundraising by a number of local gentry and the support of local MPs, including William Wilberforce, the Royal Northern Sea Bathing Infirmary was established there in 1812 to cure the 'sick poor who were proper objects for warm sea bathing'. The infirmary's building still survives on the seafront near the harbour and, unusually for a medical facility, it was located near the heart of the historic town. It is more common for medical institutions, such as at Margate, to be located at the margins of resorts, on less commercially desirable sites; for instance the Promenade Hospital at Southport was built at the north-eastern end of the seafront in 1852–3 to act as a convalescent hospital and sea-bathing infirmary.

In 1868–70, the Royal National Hospital for Consumption and Diseases of the Chest was constructed in large, landscaped grounds on a south-facing coastal site to the south-east of Ventnor on the Isle of Wight. It was arranged as ten separate three- or four-storey blocks, connected only by a corridor, and forming a line over a quarter of a mile long. Each 'semi-detached' block had 12 small bedrooms plus living rooms for groups of three patients, all opening onto multi-storey, cast iron balconies providing patients with a maximum of sunshine and sea air. Interspersed along the line were a four-storey administration and central dining-hall block, and a chapel (1871–2) in a neo-perpendicular style with a square, battlemented tower. The architect for the whole hospital was Thomas Hellyer of Ryde, whose other works included at least ten churches. The detached building behind and to the left of the hospital was the nurses' home.

The hospital closed in 1964 and was demolished five years later. The site is now the Ventnor Botanic Gardens.

EPW043012

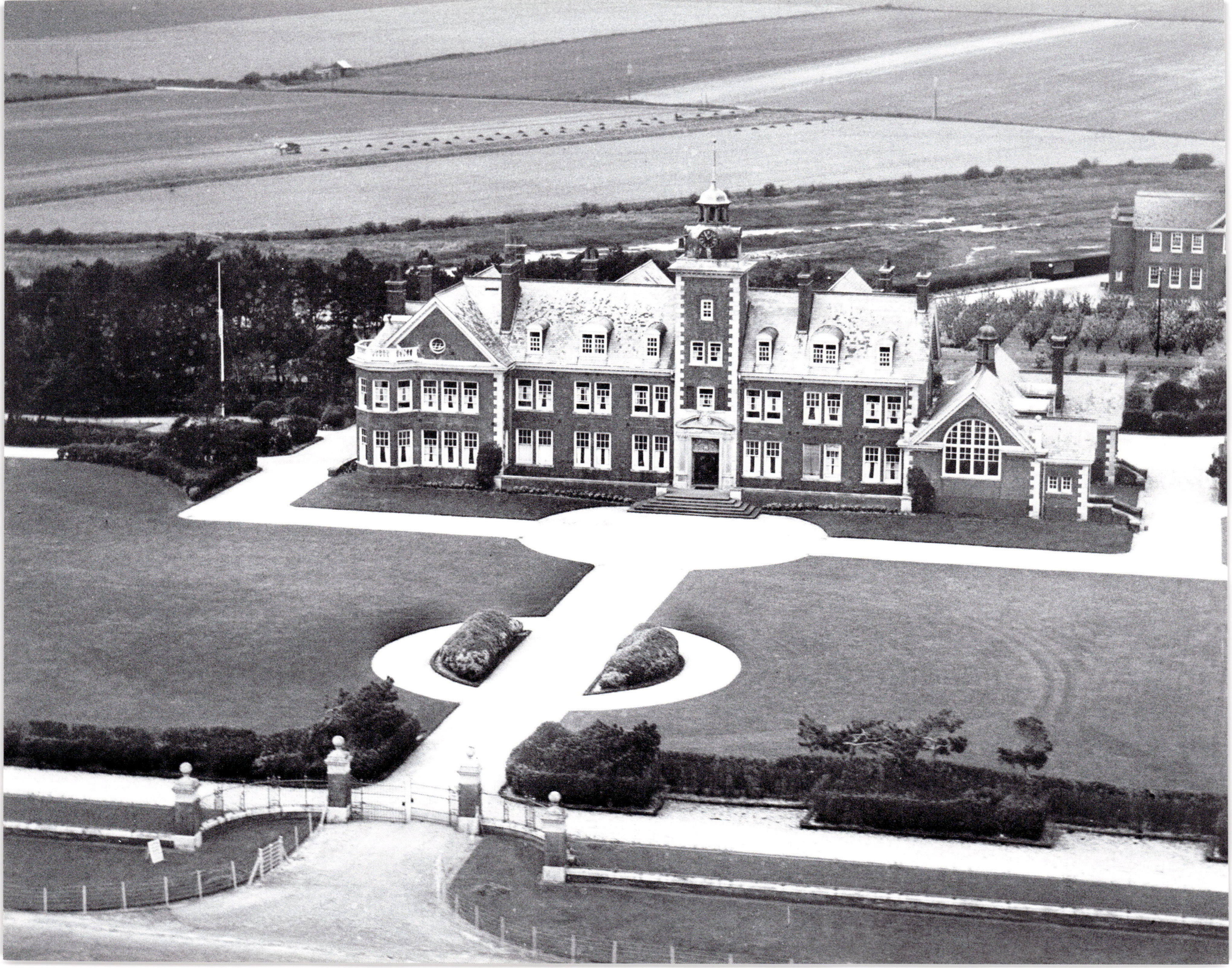

Rustington Convalescent Home, Rustington, West Sussex
April 1927

During the 19th century, seaside resorts became popular locations for convalescent homes for patients recuperating from operations or injuries sustained elsewhere. The sea-bathing hospitals established in the 18th and early 19th centuries gradually became more devoted to recovering patients, and dedicated convalescent homes began to be established in England from the mid-19th century, and especially after 1870. Prior to this, patients were generally sent home, a practice that was not always conducive to the restoration of good health. Like sanatoria, the favoured locations for convalescent homes were in the countryside and at the seaside, where the quality of the air was superior to that in towns and cities. Florence Nightingale was an advocate of seaside convalescent facilities and even went so far as to specify which part of the English coast would be suitable for different types of patient.

Some convalescent homes were established by organisations representing specific industries. For instance, the Lancashire and Cheshire Miners' Convalescent Home was built in Blackpool in 1925–7 to house 132 men on a 7.5-acre (3ha) site. A second purpose-built convalescent home for Derbyshire miners, built in 1928 on a 4-acre (1.6ha) site at Ingoldmells, near Skegness, could accommodate 124 male and 34 female patients. The ground floor contained communal recreation rooms at the front of the building with adjacent open-air rooms, sheltered from the coastal winds by larger billiard and recreation rooms on their east sides.

Rustington Convalescent Home, set in 7 acres (2.8ha) of gardens, was purpose-built in 1897 by Sir Henry Harben, President of the Prudential Assurance Company and Master of the Carpenter's Company, in 1893. This home, designed by Harben and the architect Frederick Wheeler, provided a place where working men could convalesce after an illness or accident and enable them to become fully active again. It was bequeathed to the Carpenters' Company when Sir Henry died in 1911. The brown-brick home is built in a 17th-century style and is still in use today as a convalescent home.

EPW017752

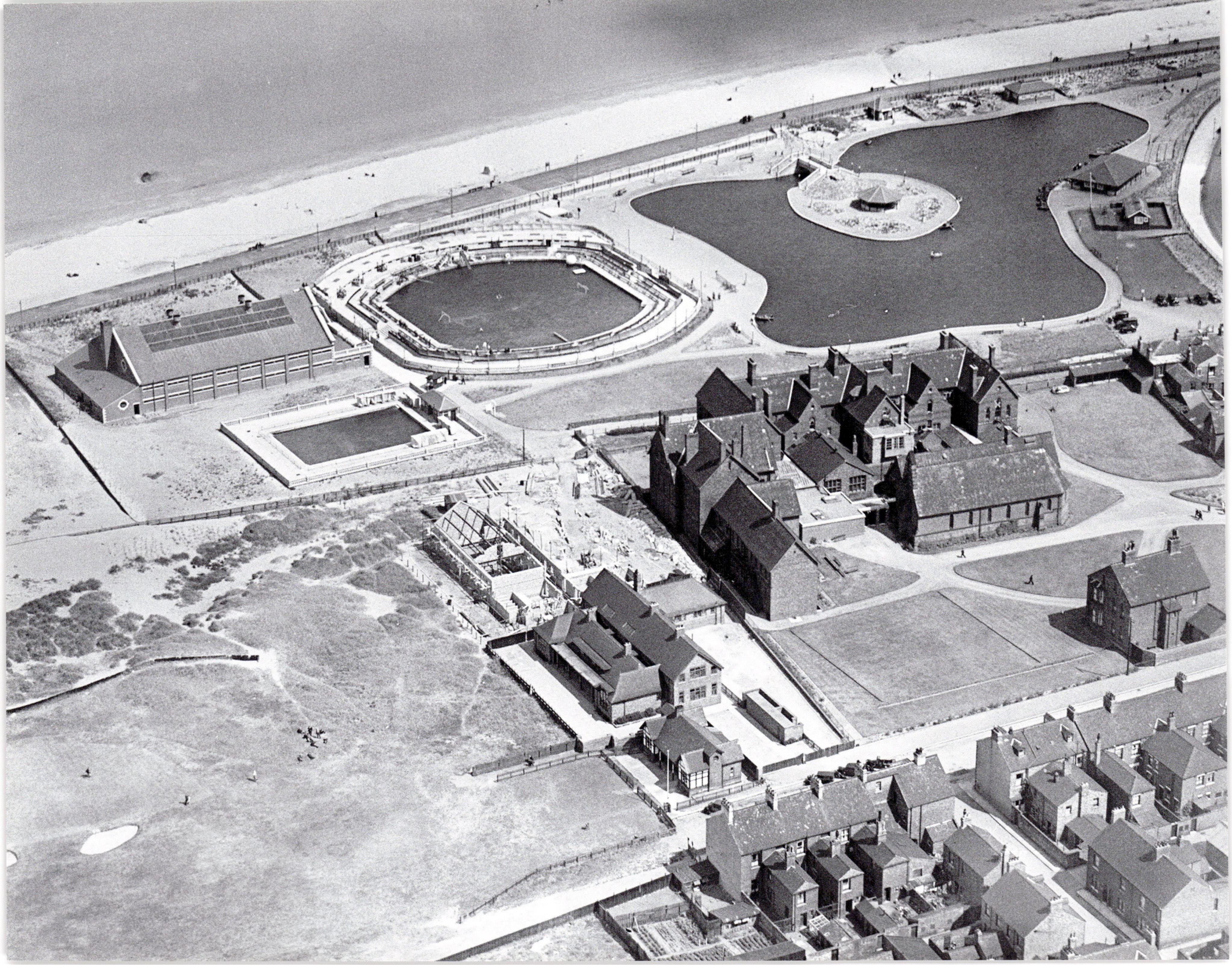

The Coatham Convalescent Home and Children's Hospital and the Redcar bathing pool and boating lake, Redcar, Cleveland

July 1932

As well as creating convalescent homes for people working in specific industries, some were established for specific types of patients. At Bognor Regis, the Convalescent Home for Women of Surrey was founded in 1897 in Surrey House on the Esplanade. This two-storey, red-brick building was opened by the Duchess of York in 1900. There were also convalescent homes for children: the Hornsea Children's Convalescent Home (Humberside) was built on the seafront to the north of the resort in 1907–8 for children recovering from bone diseases. The Children's Convalescent Home for Surrey was in Clarence Road on the seafront at Bognor Regis. It was donated by Sir Max Waechter in 1906 and rebuilt in 1930 by Sir Jeremiah Colman to accommodate 40 children and two mothers with babies in a separate flat.

A convalescent home for children was established at Coatham in 1861 and extended in 1869. A chapel was built in 1878, designed by G E Street. In July 1878, a local newspaper article described the opening of the new hospital beside the children's home. The building, designed by Norman Shaw, had been supervised by Robert Moore, a local architect, suggesting only an arms-length involvement of the main architect. The article was already foreseeing the extension of the hospital, which would take place in 1883, when a further 32 children could be treated. The patients in the hospital, like the convalescent home, of which it was a part, were cared for by women who volunteered their time. The building to the right of the main home, rather worryingly, included a mortuary, a reminder that not all of the young patients might recover from their treatment. The complex was demolished in 1951.

The institution was run on a Christian model, the presence of the chapel at the rear of the building providing evidence of this original ethos. However, between the publication of the Ordnance Survey map in 1929 and this aerial photograph in 1932, the boating lake, outdoor swimming pool and other leisure facilities were constructed in front of the hospital and hopefully its recovering patients would have had the opportunity to enjoy them.

EPW038941

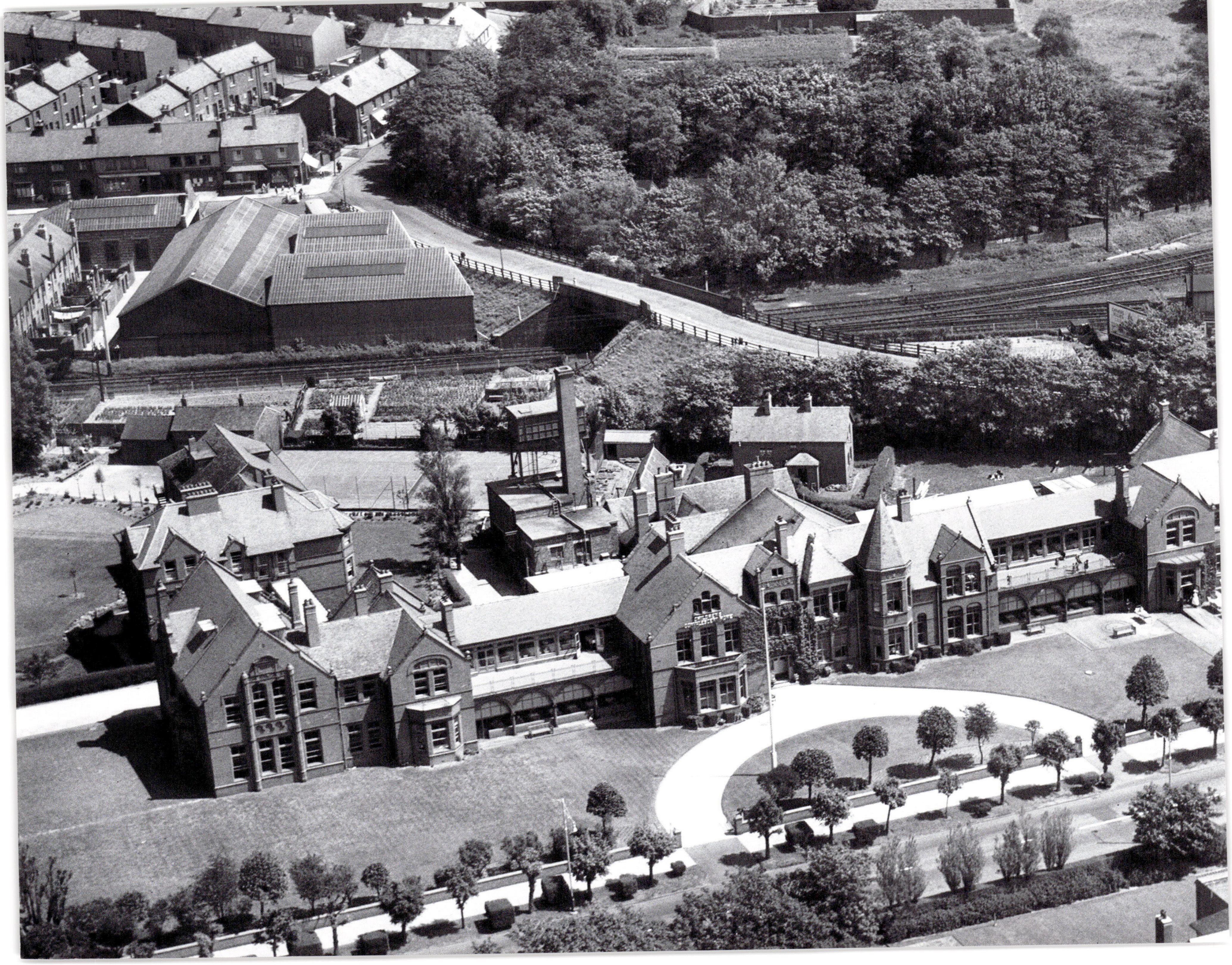

The Children's Convalescent Home, West Kirby, Merseyside
16 June 1938

The number of children suffering from the effects of life in industrial England and diseases associated with dense urban living and poverty prompted the founders of the Children's Convalescent Home to provide the first accommodation in Filey Terrace. Facilities were established for six convalescing children to benefit from fresh air, good food and good-quality care. The present site beside the railway line, and close to the railway station, was acquired and the hospital block was built in 1899. In this photograph, at the right-hand side, can be seen the main entrance to the complex. A nurse is standing there beside a group of unoccupied beds, which were probably awaiting occupants to enjoy some summer sun.

The presence of children staying at the Convalescent Home for a lengthy period led to the introduction of a programme of teaching, including the appointment of a certificated teacher as headteacher, and a day school attached to the home was opened in 1901. This is the block that can be seen at the left-hand side of the hospital. This was the first school in the country to be recognised for the education of children with physical disabilities and in 1905 it became a boarding school. The improvement in medical treatment, including the discovery of antibiotics, led to less demand for places, and therefore a greater emphasis on education. West Kirby School and College today provides educational and residential provision for children and young people with a range of complex social communication difficulties and associated learning needs.

EPW057575

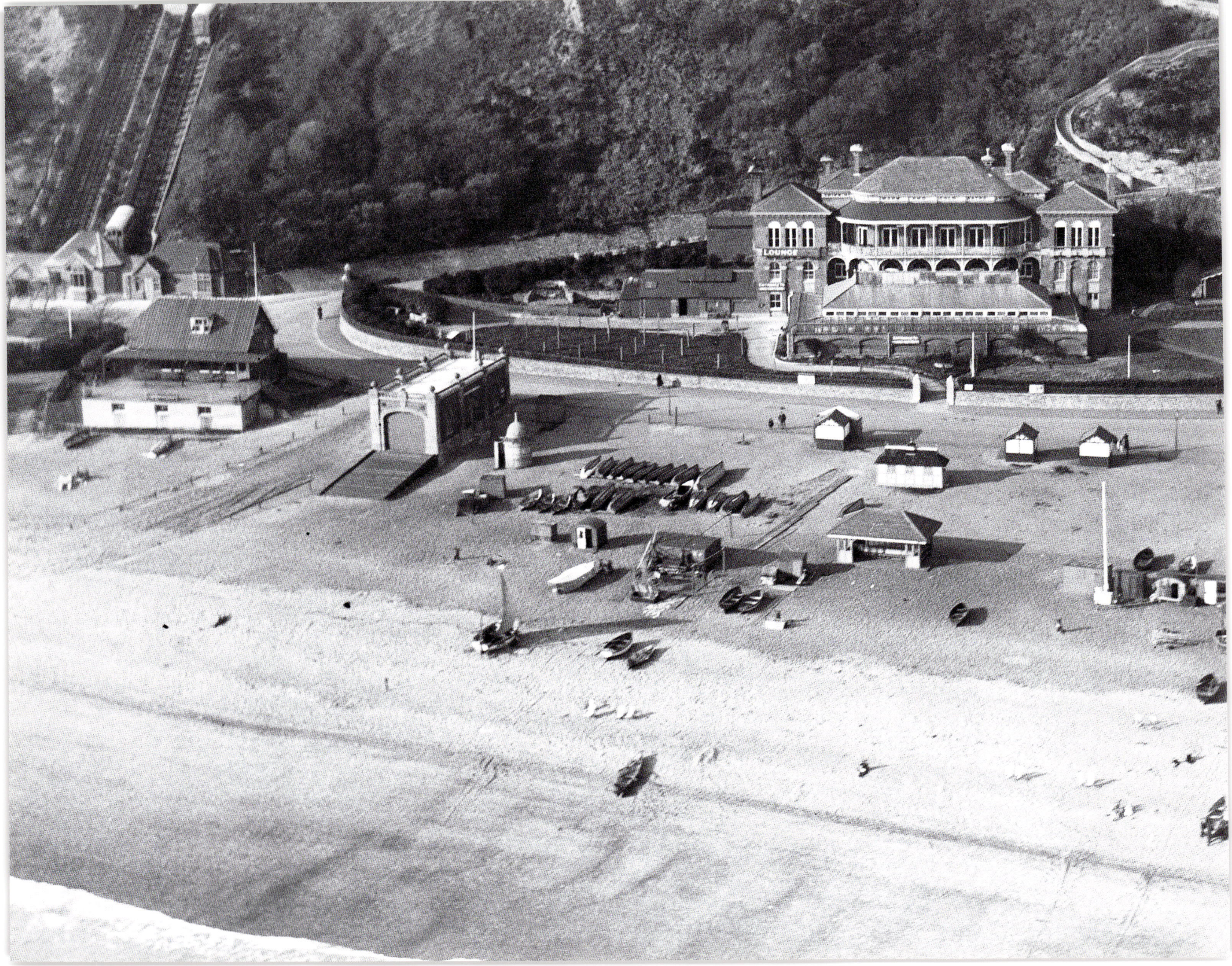
LOUNGE

Folkestone lido, Folkestone, Kent
February 1920

The initial reason for visiting the seaside during the 18th century was to improve your health, predominantly by bathing in the sea, but also by spending time in a healthy environment, the air at the seaside apparently having health-giving properties. From the 1730s onwards, a number of seaside resorts also had bathhouses, and during the course of the 18th century these became larger and more sophisticated. However, as bathing was only supposed to take place during the morning, this left these buildings largely unused for the remainder of the day; to make them more economically viable, a number of other functions were often included alongside the baths, such as providing a circulating library or offering accommodation for visitors.

The ultimate expression of the multi-functional nature of 19th-century bathhouses was the Bathing Establishment at Folkestone, which opened in July 1869. The building was designed by Joseph Gardner with a swimming pool and plunge bath and a variety of medicated baths and invalid baths at beach level. On the first floor, there were warm and cold baths, and on the top floor separate Subscription and Assembly Rooms.

In the Georgian period, bathhouses provided their 'patients' with individual baths or larger baths that might accommodate a few people bathing rather than swimming. During the 1870s, swimming came to the forefront of the public imagination and featured explicitly in legislation for the first time. In August 1875, Captain Matthew Webb successfully swam the English Channel and duly became a national hero. The Public Health Act of 1875 included clauses allowing funding for swimming pools, while the 1878 Baths & Washhouses Act empowered local authorities to provide covered swimming baths.

As early as 1878, the lack of a large swimming pool was recognised by the Directors of the Folkestone Bathing Establishment Company at their Annual General Meeting. Therefore, an extension was added to the front to provide a larger swimming pool, recognition of a changing attitude to the sea and an acknowledgement of a new activity that would be at the heart of people's relationship with the sea in the late 19th and 20th centuries.

The Bathing Establishment was constructed on the seafront at Folkestone, a short distance from the cliff lift shown to the left. The Leas Lift opened on 21 September 1885 and from 1890 consisted of two parallel 1.5m-gauge (5ft) tracks extending to a length of almost 50m (164ft). It employs the water balance principle; the cars were linked via a cable so that when water was supplied to a tank beneath the upper car it would descend, and therefore pull up the lighter car on the other track, which had emptied its tank when its downward journey had been completed. The cliff lift survives today but alas the Bathing Establishment has been demolished.

EPW000080

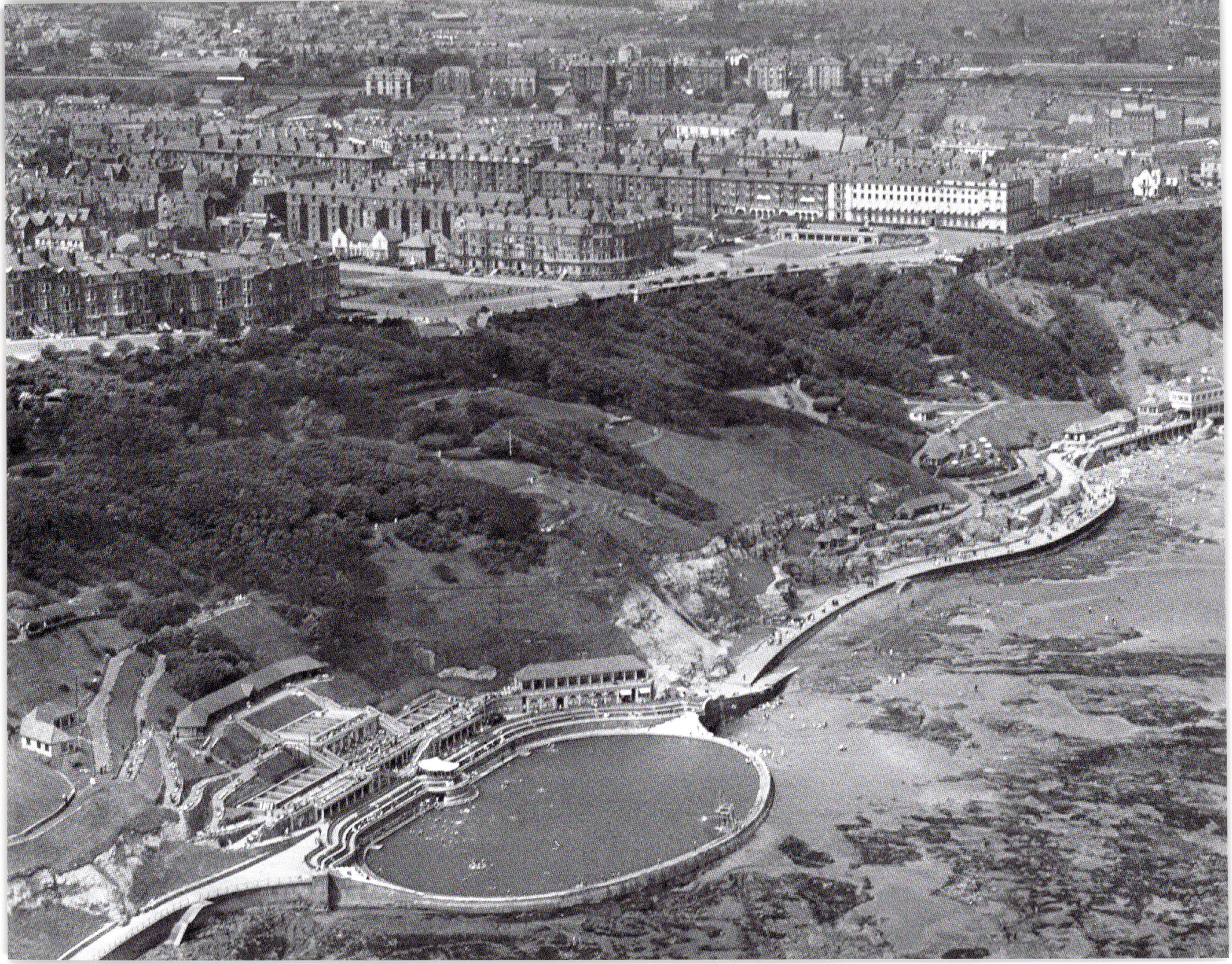

The bathing pool and South Cliff, Scarborough, North Yorkshire

July 1932

Scarborough may be where people first bathed in the sea around the English coast in a systematic, organised fashion. At the top of the picture can be seen the Victorian spa building, a new entertainment complex constructed on the site where a mineral water spring was discovered during the 1620s (*see* p 61). This had become a popular spa by the late 17th century, and soon people were visiting Scarborough to drink seawater and to bathe in the sea. This took place using bathing machines on the beach near the spa. During the 19th century, the previously undeveloped cliff tops behind the spa began to be filled with prestigious housing, and by the early 20th century there was a need for sea defences to protect the cliffs from coastal erosion; included within this scheme was a large, oval bathing pool.

During the late 19th and early 20th centuries, indoor pools were erected in great numbers in large urban conurbations and, while some seaside resorts such as Blackpool and Brighton might be in that category, the availability of the sea, and the existence of early baths, seems to have been sufficient to limit later expenditure on covered pools. Some seaside resorts also began to invest in outdoor pools, especially between the wars, as they could provide facilities for hundreds, or even thousands, of people. They also fitted in with an emerging interest in sun worship and the body beautiful, and they allowed people to play in the water, as much as formally swimming.

One of the earliest outdoor pools was the Table Rock Bathing Pool at Whitley Bay; it was first developed in 1894 and enlarged in 1896 and *c* 1908. This pool was presumably created by exploiting a natural hollow in the rocky foreshore and enlarging and regularising it into a rectangle. It was scarcely more than a hole in the rocks, but by the outbreak of the First World War, a much more ambitious outdoor pool was being created at Scarborough. The South Bay Pool was the brainchild of Harry W Smith, the town's borough engineer from 1897 to 1933. He believed that the provision of outdoor swimming pools might improve Scarborough's image and therefore attract more visitors. Construction began on the South Bay Pool in April 1914 and it opened on 21 July 1915. This pool, and some of the subsequent interwar open-air pools, were huge compared to the standard Olympic swimming pool, which is 50m long by 25m wide. Work continued despite the First World War as the pool's monumental concrete wall also served as a seawall to protect the cliffs behind. Initially the pool was provided with 137 dressing cubicles, hot and cold showers, first-aid rooms and a separate block housing the pumping plant and laundry. Between the wars Scarborough Corporation added a café, restaurant and more seating for spectators on a terrace hewn out of the cliff face, while further up the cliff blocks of holiday bungalows for rent were created. South Bay Pool closed in 1989, and after being left to decay, it was infilled.

EPW038934

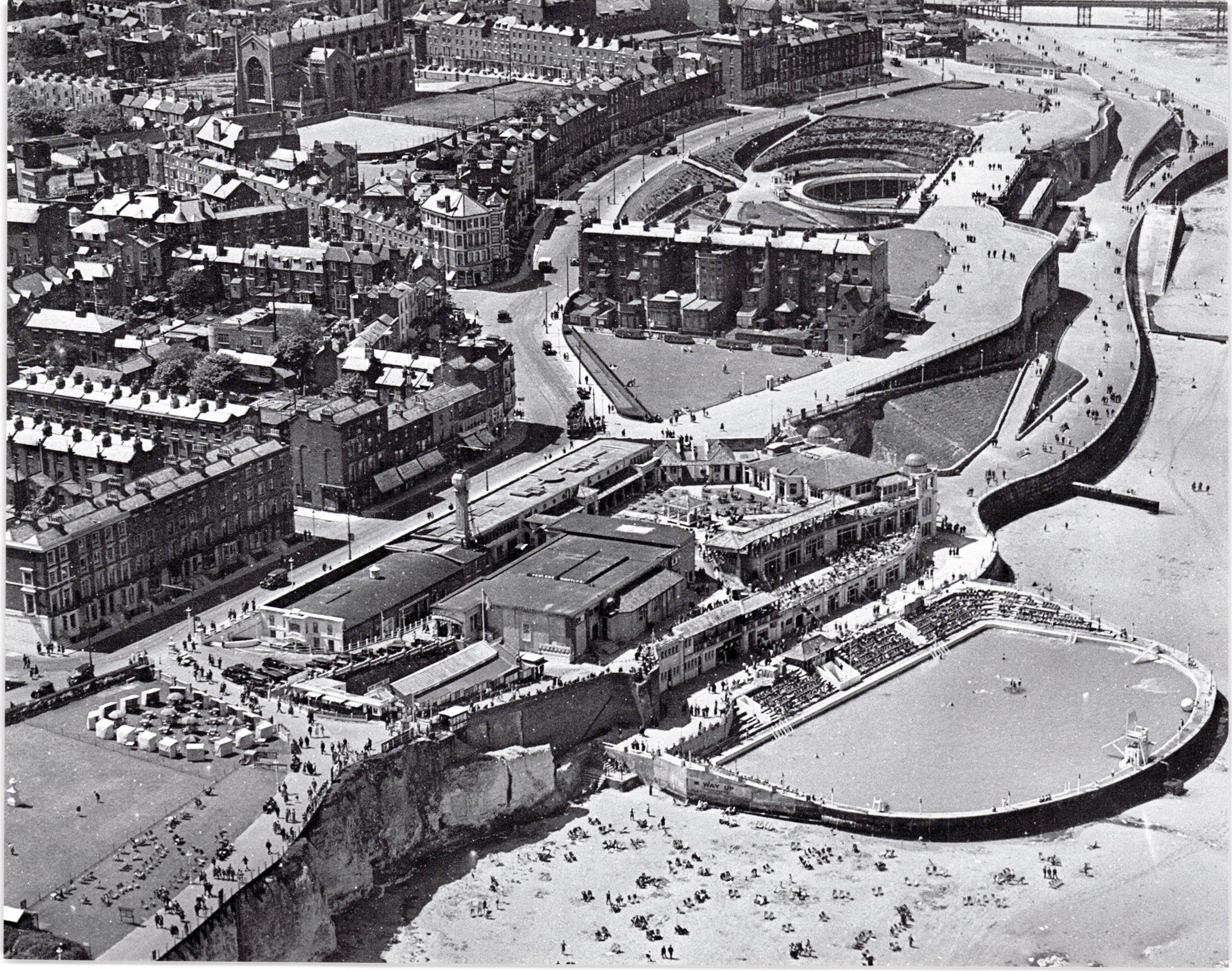
WAY UP

The Clifton Swimming Baths, the Winter Gardens and environs, Margate, Kent

May 1931

This photograph shows the first of Margate's outdoor tidal pools, the bathing pool at Cliftonville, which opened on the seafront in 1927. It was created by John Henry Iles, a leading figure in the amusement park industry between the wars, who also owned the Dreamland Amusement Park in Margate (*see* p 87 and p 147).

This was the site of the Clifton Baths created a century earlier; it was constructed in 1824–8 by John Boys at a cost of £15,000 by excavating into the cliffs at Fort Green. The complex originally consisted of a dwelling house, warm and cold baths, dressing rooms and a reading room. There was also a large entrance to the complex at beach level allowing the storage of bathing machines at the base of the original vertical complex.

Iles turned the old site into a large modern seaside complex of bars, cafés and restaurants on several levels, with the large open-air swimming pool projecting into the sea. From 1938, the name was changed from the Clifton Baths to the Cliftonville Lido and it continued to provide an important bathing facility until it closed in 1977 and was infilled. The illuminated sign for the Margate Lido, dating from near the end of the site's life, cunningly utilised the surviving chimney from the original 19th-century Clifton Baths. The complex of rooms and passages within the cliffs survives today, but has not yet been reused.

Towards the top of the photograph can be seen the Winter Gardens. It was built by excavating into Fort Green and it opened in August 1911, providing the kind of year-round concert facilities that had not been available since the demise of the town's Assembly Rooms. The complex was designed to host indoor and outdoor concerts, and was home to the resort's Municipal Orchestra. During the Second World War, the Winter Gardens acted as a receiving station for troops evacuated from Dunkirk and was damaged during a bombing raid in 1941.

On the clifftop can be seen the prestigious houses that had been built in Cliftonville, a more exclusive part of the town due to its distance from Margate's railway stations and the consequent frequent influxes of day trippers. At the top of the photograph can be seen Holy Trinity Church, which was destroyed during the Second World War (*see* p 281).

EPW035474

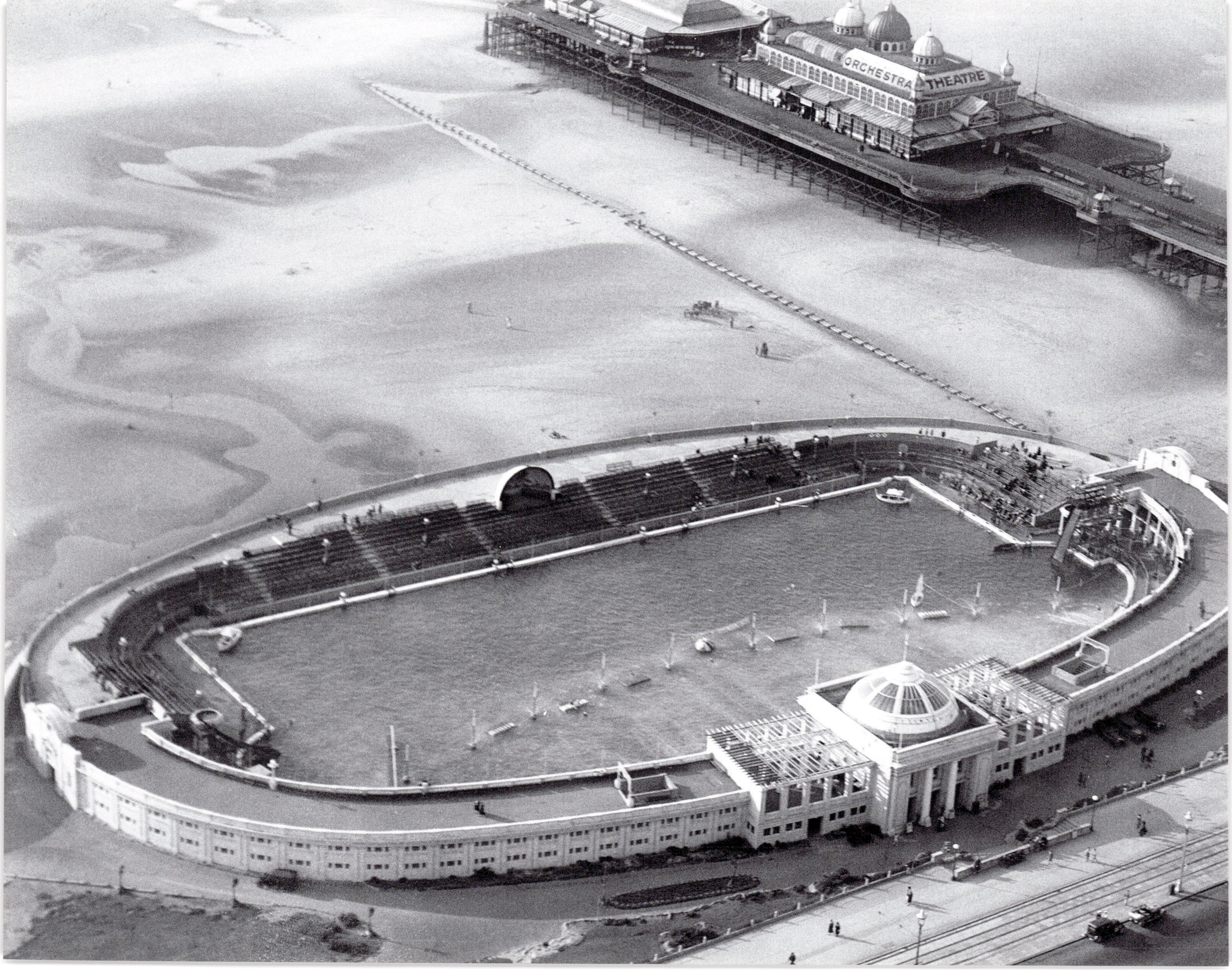
ORCHESTRA
THEATRE

The Open Air Swimming Baths and Victoria Pier, Blackpool, Lancashire
12 September 1929

During the early 20th century, Blackpool was undergoing a programme of southward expansion and a key element in this was the construction of the Open Air Swimming Baths, which opened on 9 June 1923 between the South Pier and the Pleasure Beach. Blackpool Corporation embraced wholeheartedly the growing taste for open-air swimming by providing probably the largest such facility in the world. The baths were designed to promote the outdoors and good health, and their architecture was designed to convey this wholesome message.

The open-air baths, designed by J C Robinson, cost £80,000 and had a pool measuring 115m by 52.4m (377 by 172ft), much larger than a modern Olympic-size pool. Around the outside, there was a colonnade of Doric columns flanking a central Beaux Arts domed entrance and a café with a pergola-style roof terrace, open to the elements. This was as much a civic celebration as a leisure facility. There were 574 dressing rooms for bathers accessed from a third-of-a-mile-long concourse around the pool and tiers of seating could accommodate around 3,000 spectators on three sides. Interestingly, spectating during the interwar years was as popular as bathing in the pool.

By the 1960s, the popularity of the open-air pool at Blackpool, and outdoor pools in general, was in decline and so it closed in 1981 and was demolished in 1983. Since 1986 its site has been occupied by the Sandcastle Waterworld indoor leisure centre.

EPW029209

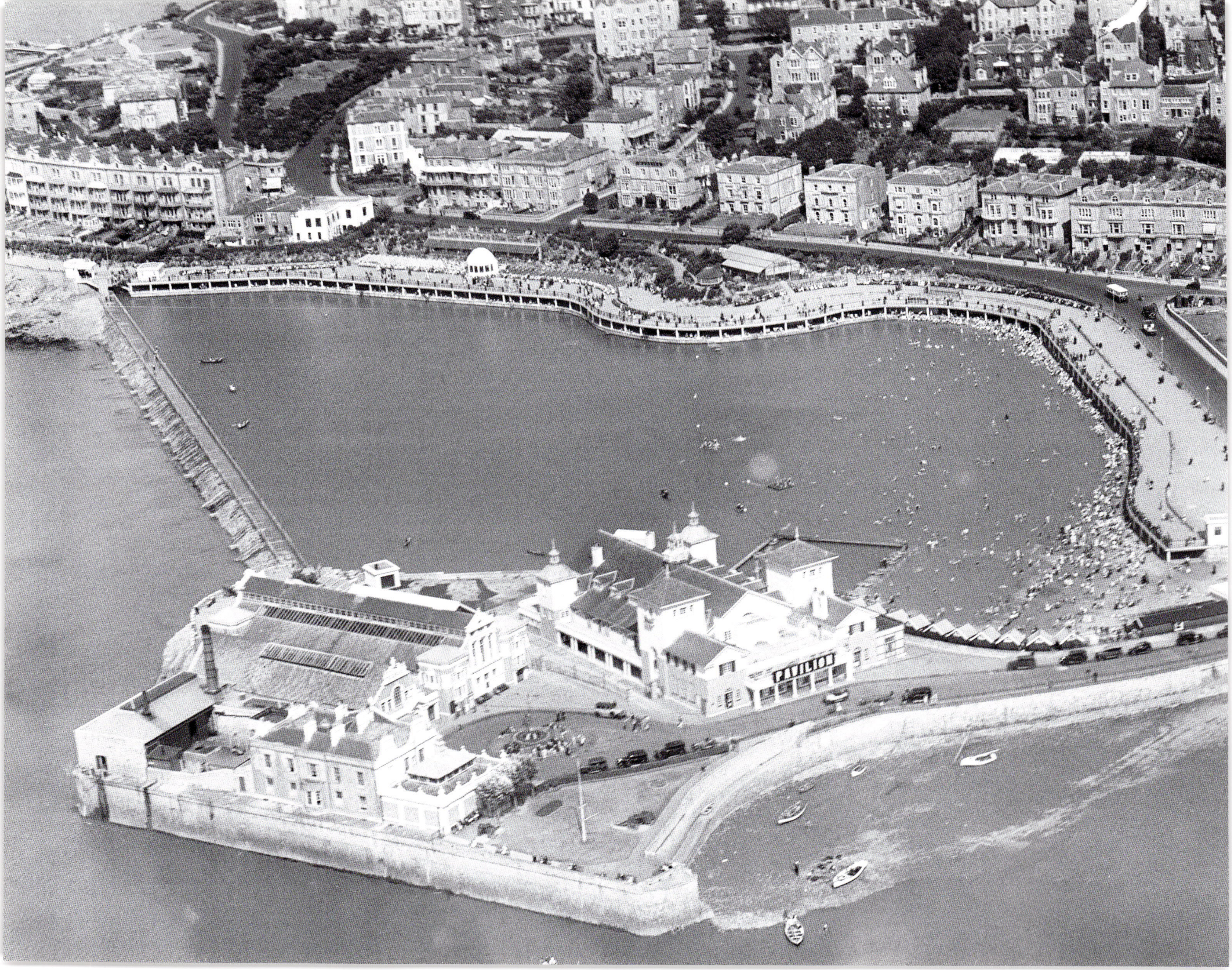
PAVILION

Glentworth Bay Marine Lake and Knightstone Island, Weston-super-Mare, Somerset

August 1932

Weston-super-Mare began to be visited by sea bathers at the end of the 18th century, but it has always been bedevilled by its geography. It has a very wide tidal range, so that the difference in height between low tide and high tide, the second highest in the world, means that because of its shallow, sandy beach, the sea can appear very distant at low tide.

Knightstone Island was critical to the early provision of bathing facilities for Weston's visitors. The first bathhouse and pool were constructed in 1820; at this date Knightstone was still an island, only connected to the mainland by a ridge of pebbles, but when the Revd Thomas Pruen took it over later in the 1820s, one of his main projects was the construction of a causeway. On 5 August 1828, the island was put up for auction and was acquired by Dr Edward Long Fox (1761–1835), a Quaker physician from Brislington House lunatic asylum in Bristol, who advocated sea bathing for the treatment of mental illness as well as for physical complaints. The present bathhouse on Knightstone Island (the white buildings seen at the bottom of the island) was built in 1832 and, despite damage in a fire in 1844, is now in use as offices and a salon. There was also a series of houses originally, but these were demolished at the end of the 19th century to make way for the new swimming pool (on the left of the island) and pavilion/opera house (to the right of the island) that both opened on 13 May 1902.

One of the main concerns of the local authority at Weston during the interwar years was to cater for the growing number of visitors who wished to swim and play in the sea, something that was problematic at low tide. A scheme had been mooted as early as 1871 to enclose Glentworth Bay to allow bathers easy access to a body of seawater regardless of the tide. The idea was revived in 1888 when an impractically vast marine lake measuring over 457m (1,500ft) long by almost 50m (164ft) wide was proposed. In 1895, the newly created Urban District Council decided to support a proposal that envisaged creating a barrage from Knightstone Island to Black Rock at Uphill, an eye-watering distance of 3km (1.86 miles).

By the 1920s, a more realistic scheme had taken shape, and by 1929 the barrage seen in this photograph had been constructed between Knightstone Island and the shoreline near the southern end of Claremont Crescent, a more manageable distance of 270m (886ft). This new Marine Lake was equipped with a diving stage, rafts, rubber boats, water chutes, children's paddle boats and hundreds of bathing tents and dressing enclosures. It proved to be an instant success, being used by more than a quarter of a million people during 1929.

EPW039937

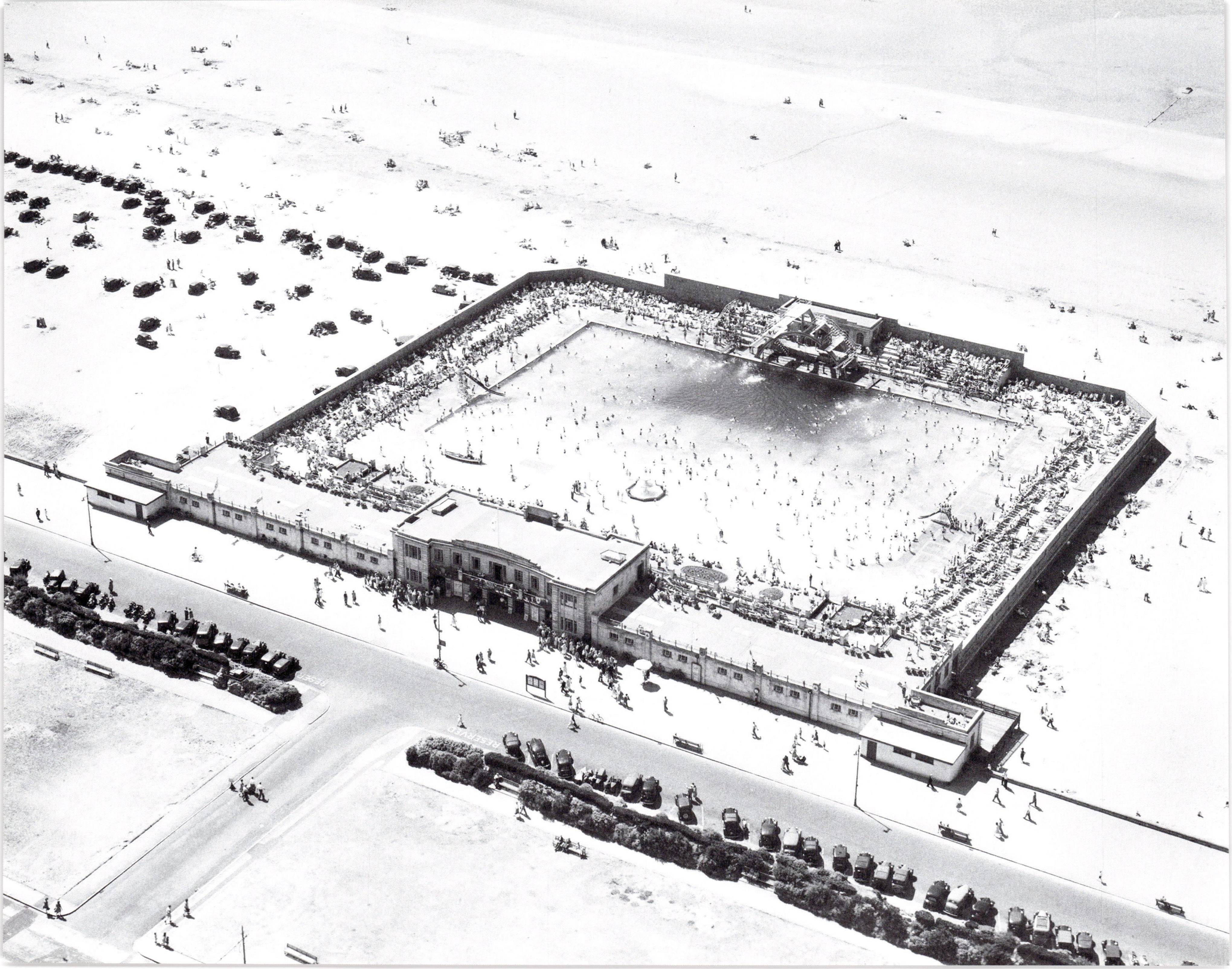

The Swimming Pool (Tropicana), Weston-super-Mare, Somerset
25 July 1949

The local authority at Weston during the interwar years looked for ways to cater for the growing number of visitors who wished to swim and play in the sea, something that was impractical at low tide. After having improved access to the sea by creating the Marine Lake, Weston Urban District Council decided to construct an open-air bathing pool further south. Its opening ceremony took place in July 1937, at which a message from the government was read out: 'Any money which may have been expended upon [the pool] will come back a hundredfold … not necessarily in cash, but in health, which is better than wealth'. After the usual round of speeches, the assembled crowd of 4,000 spectators were entertained by a display by members of the local diving club, including a sequence of synchronised diving from the top stage. This was followed by a 'mannequin parade of bathing fashions for 1937' and a demonstration of 'physical culture' by the Women's League of Health and Beauty, all against a backdrop of music played by the Municipal Orchestra. In the evening, a repeat performance of the afternoon programme ended with a water polo match.

The entrance to the bathing pool on the seafront is a two-storey pavilion flanked by single-storey wings containing changing rooms and roof terraces. Designed by the office of the borough engineer, Harold Brown, the architecture is an essay in stripped-down civic classicism and is in striking contrast to the elegant modernism of the diving platform at the seaward end of the pool. It was described from the outset as 'the finest diving platform in Europe' and immediately became used as a symbol of the town, frequently featuring in posters produced by railway companies. It was built by Messrs George Pollard of Taunton, with reinforced concrete steelwork provided by Messrs Coignet of London. The structure consisted of two parallel reinforced concrete arches, 26ft (8m) high, faced with a band of coloured tiles from which seven boards at 3m, 5m, 7m and 10m (10ft, 16ft, 23ft and 33ft) were cantilevered. These were reached by steps from the rear.

In its opening year, the bathing pool attracted 109,000 bathers and 156,000 spectators. However, by the 1960s, with the number of tourists declining and a greater interest in promoting swimming as a sport, the bathing pool was becoming less popular, and in 1976 the diving stage was cordoned off on safety grounds. The diving stage was demolished in February 1982, and during the following year the bathing pool was transformed into a £1 million water theme park, featuring slides, a fibreglass elephant and a giant pineapple. This may explain why the relaunched Tropicana Pleasure Beach was advertised as 'fun, fruity, wet and wild'. Today, the pool is closed and the site is used for occasional public events, such as ice skating in the winter and a fun fair during the summer. From August to September 2015, it was the location of Banksy's Dismaland, which he described as a 'family theme park unsuitable for children'.

Compare the seafront road in this photograph with the image on p 53 taken 20 years earlier and the marked increase in the number of cars is obvious. Weston was fortunate to have a wide road on which cars can still be parked, and at all but high tide, part of the long beach is often used for additional parking, as was the case here in 1949.

EAW025157

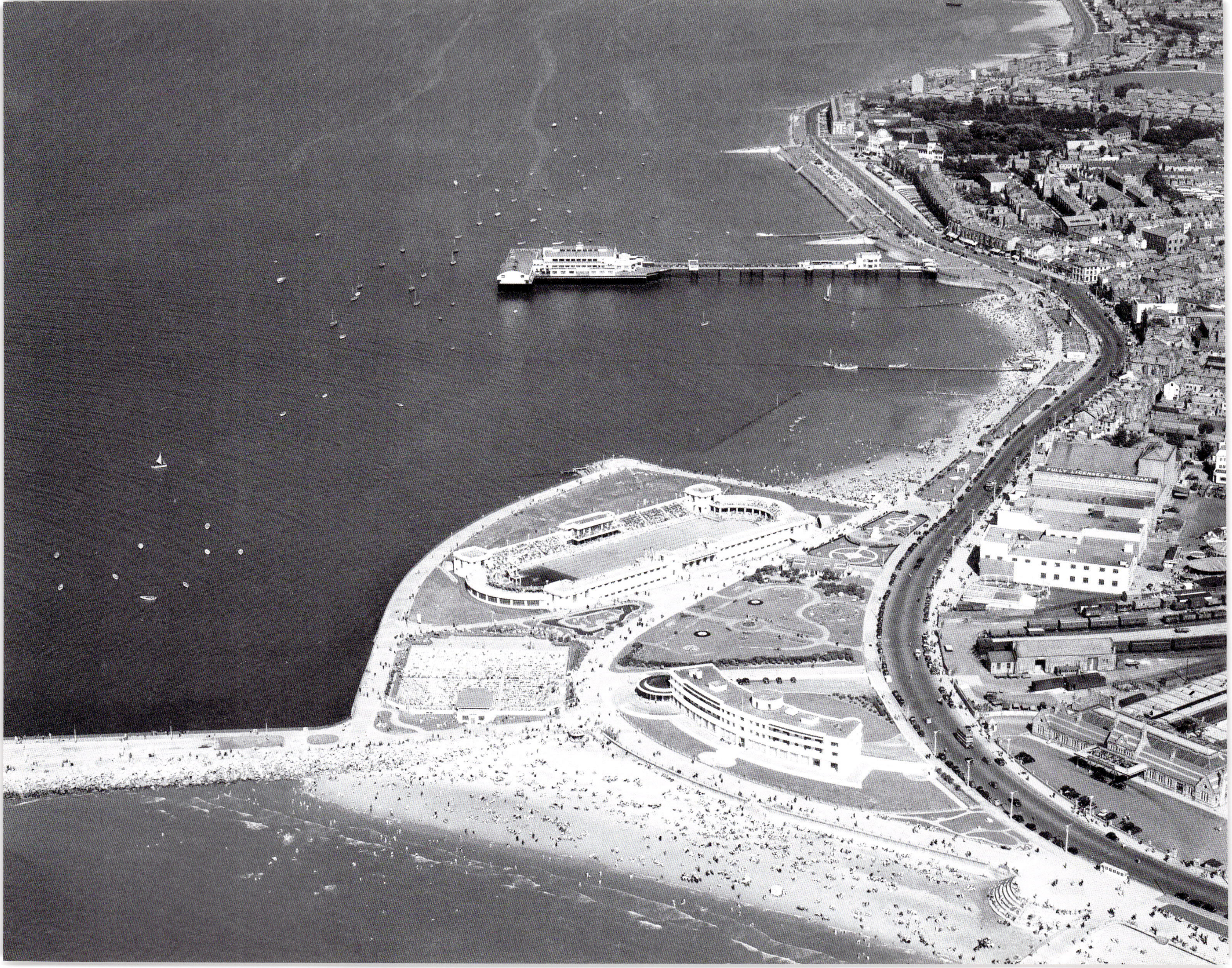
FULLY LICENSED RESTAURANT

The Midland Hotel, Swimming Stadium and Central Pier, Morecambe, Lancashire
15 August 1949

This photograph of Morecambe at the height of the summer holidays shows the major facilities available for holidaymakers on the seafront. Just above the busy beach at the bottom of the photograph can be seen the Midland Hotel (*see* p 205). It was built in 1932–3 by Oliver Hill in a striking, modernist form with elegant interiors filled with contemporary art.

Above the hotel can be seen the enormous Super Swimming Stadium. During the 1920s, around 50 outdoor pools were built, while in the following decade another 180 were opened, predominantly in large towns, with only a few being on the seafront of seaside resorts. In 1928, the Sea Bathing Lake at Southport opened at a cost of almost £70,000, its form, scale and style being inspired by Blackpool. During the 1930s, Blackpool's and Southport's monumental classical style was replaced increasingly by more or less radical versions of Art Deco. In 1936, the Modern Movement style was adopted for Morecambe's Super Swimming Stadium, which was similar in scale to Blackpool's baths of a decade earlier.

Seafront bathing pools and pavilions were a popular location for beauty pageants; the oldest competition in Britain was established in 1945 at Morecambe and in 1956 it became the Miss Great Britain contest, which was held, at least in part, at the seafront Super Swimming Stadium until the mid-1970s. To cater for television, the format of the Grand Final was changed in 1971 and therefore was recorded in three parts, with the Swimwear Parade staged at the Super Swimming Stadium, the Daywear Parade taking place at the Promenade Gardens and the Evening Wear Parade on the stage of a local theatre. The pool closed in 1975 due to structural problems and was demolished a year later.

At the top of the photograph can be seen Morecambe's pier, which opened on 25 March 1869 and was enlarged in the early 1870s. In 1897–8, a pavilion was added, but it was destroyed by fire on 31 July 1933 and the 2,000-seat pavilion/ballroom seen in this photograph was built in 1935–6. The pier closed at Easter 1986 after some of the decking collapsed, and a fire on 4 February 1987 damaged the amusement arcade at the shoreward end. Despite a change of ownership, and some repairs taking place, the demolition of the pier began in March 1992.

EAW026226

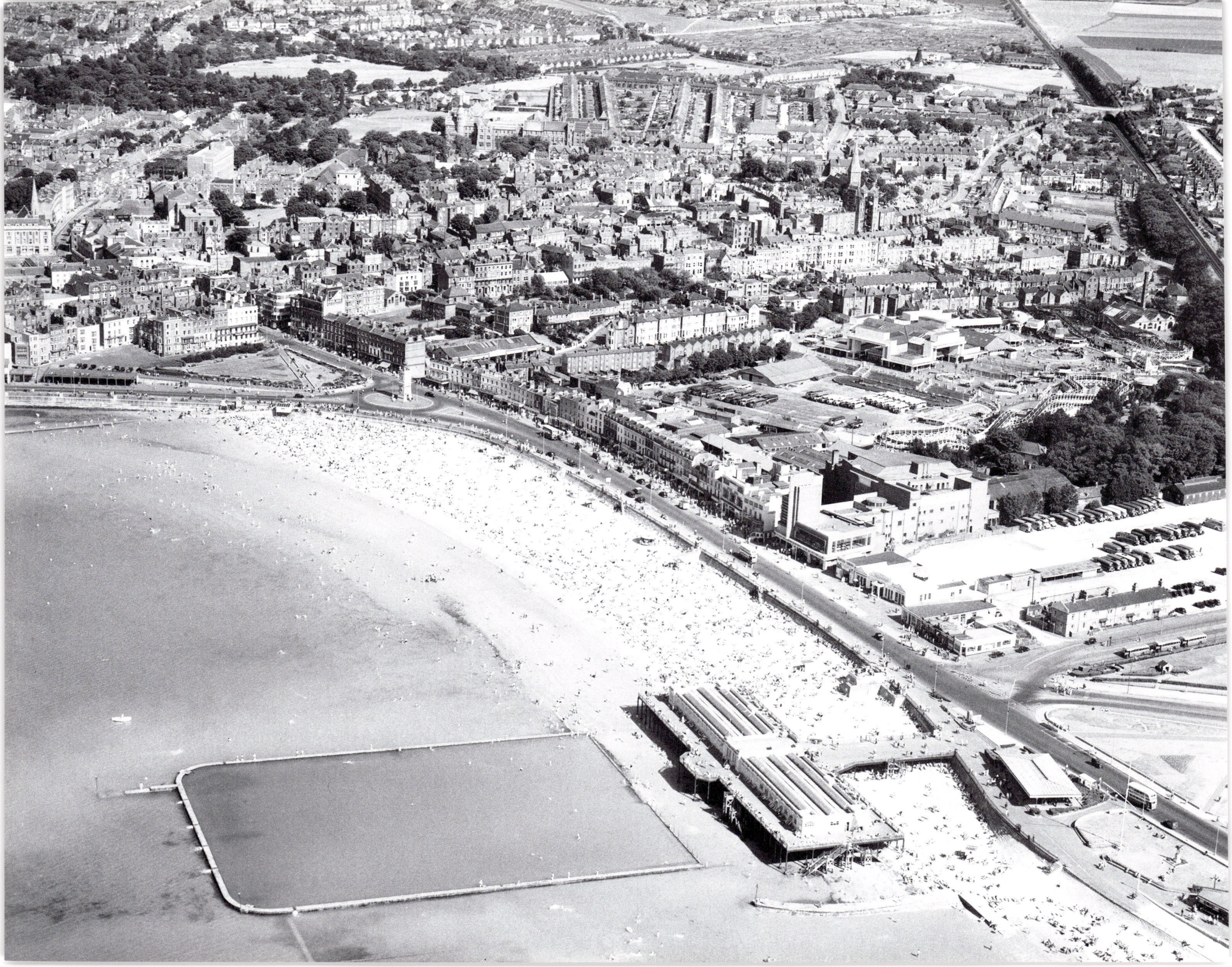

The Marine Terrace Bathing Pavilion, Dreamland and the town centre, Margate, Kent

12 July 1949

At the height of summer, Margate's famous sands are busy with holidaymakers, many of whom have come from the railway station beside the seafront. The large structure standing on the beach is a bathing station. In 1926 this structure was built near the Lifeboatman memorial, providing bathing cabins and facilities; it was demolished in 1990 (*see* p 99).

On 18 June 1937, a pair of tidal bathing pools opened in front of the Marine Terrace Bathing Pavilion, and further east at Walpole Bay. There was also a smaller tidal bathing pool off Marine Drive, directly opposite the site of the former High Street Bathing Rooms. These pools were submerged at high tide, but as the tide receded the water was retained within the concrete walls, allowing people to swim in seawater regardless of the state of the tide.

The other major feature in this photograph is the Dreamland Amusement Park, which lies just behind the seafront road behind the beach (*see* p 147). It opened as an amusement park in April 1920 and its largest ride, the Scenic Railway, which can be seen just above the trees, opened in July of the same year. A rebuilt version of this ride is still in operation today.

EAW024852

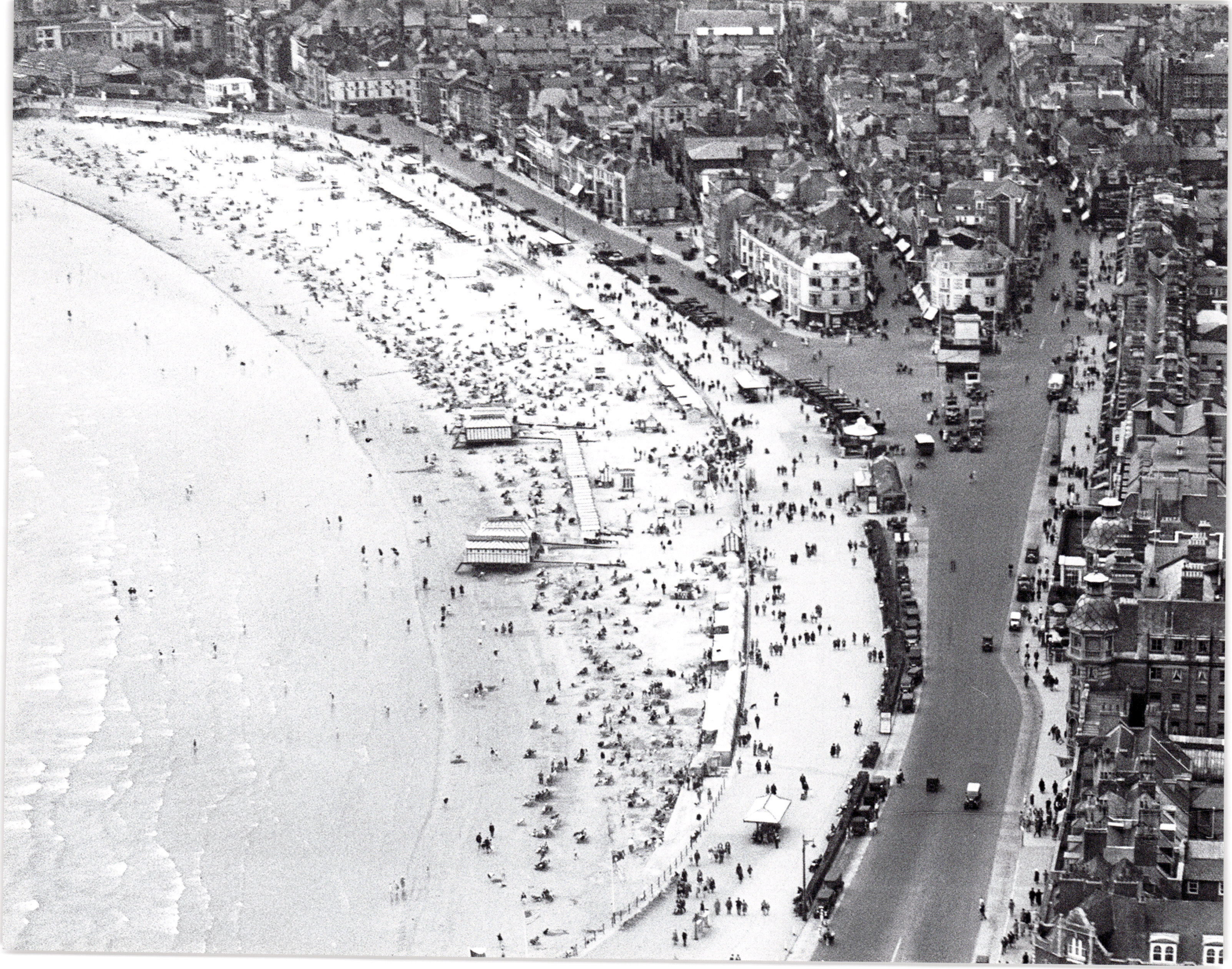

The Esplanade, the beach and the town, Weymouth, Dorset
August 1932

From the origins of the seaside holiday in the 18th century, the bathing machine was at the forefront of how people ventured into the sea. At a time when people were not confident in the sea – indeed, many could not swim at all – a bathing machine allowed them to be taken to the water, where they briefly dipped in it before returning to the shore. These contraptions were changing rooms on wheels, smaller but superficially similar to the beach huts that line the seafronts of many resorts. Typical 18th-century bathing machines were designed for one, or perhaps two bathers, though by the late 19th century larger, multiple-occupancy saloons were employed at a number of resorts, including Weymouth. The bathing machine became an increasingly rare sight during the interwar years, and disappeared finally as a result of the clearance of beaches to make way for anti-invasion defences at the outbreak of the Second World War.

There was a more or less strict observance of segregating male and female sea bathers during the 18th and 19th centuries. On some smaller beaches, the ringing of a bell might indicate when one gender's time in the sea was over, while on larger beaches, there might be separate areas. In this aerial photograph some of the last remaining bathing machines were used to enforce the separation between the male and female saloons. These new facilities had been blamed for a new relaxed attitude to bathing, and therefore in 1897 the local council required that the male and female saloons should be 75 yards (69m) apart, hence the separating line of bathing machines still in evidence 30 years later. By this date, these bathing saloons provided bathers with changing rooms prior to bathing in the sea. During the 1920s, bathing tents, manufactured locally by Messrs Marsh and Wright, would be spotted on the beach, and these could be hired from the Royal Arcade. Lining the seafront, there seems to be a series of these bathing tents with awnings in front.

On the beach, midway between the two saloons can be seen two small booths. These are probably predecessors of the Punch and Judy booth that can still be found on the beach at Weymouth today. This type of entertainment appears to have been in existence by the 1660s, and by the early 18th century there are references to puppet shows taking place in at least one seaside town. During the 19th century, the Punch and Judy show added features that make the modern show so distinctive; the glove puppet superseded the marionette, the dog Toby appeared around 1830, the Crocodile replaced the devil during the 1860s, and by the mid-19th century, the swizzle stick was being used to create Mr Punch's voice.

EPW039703

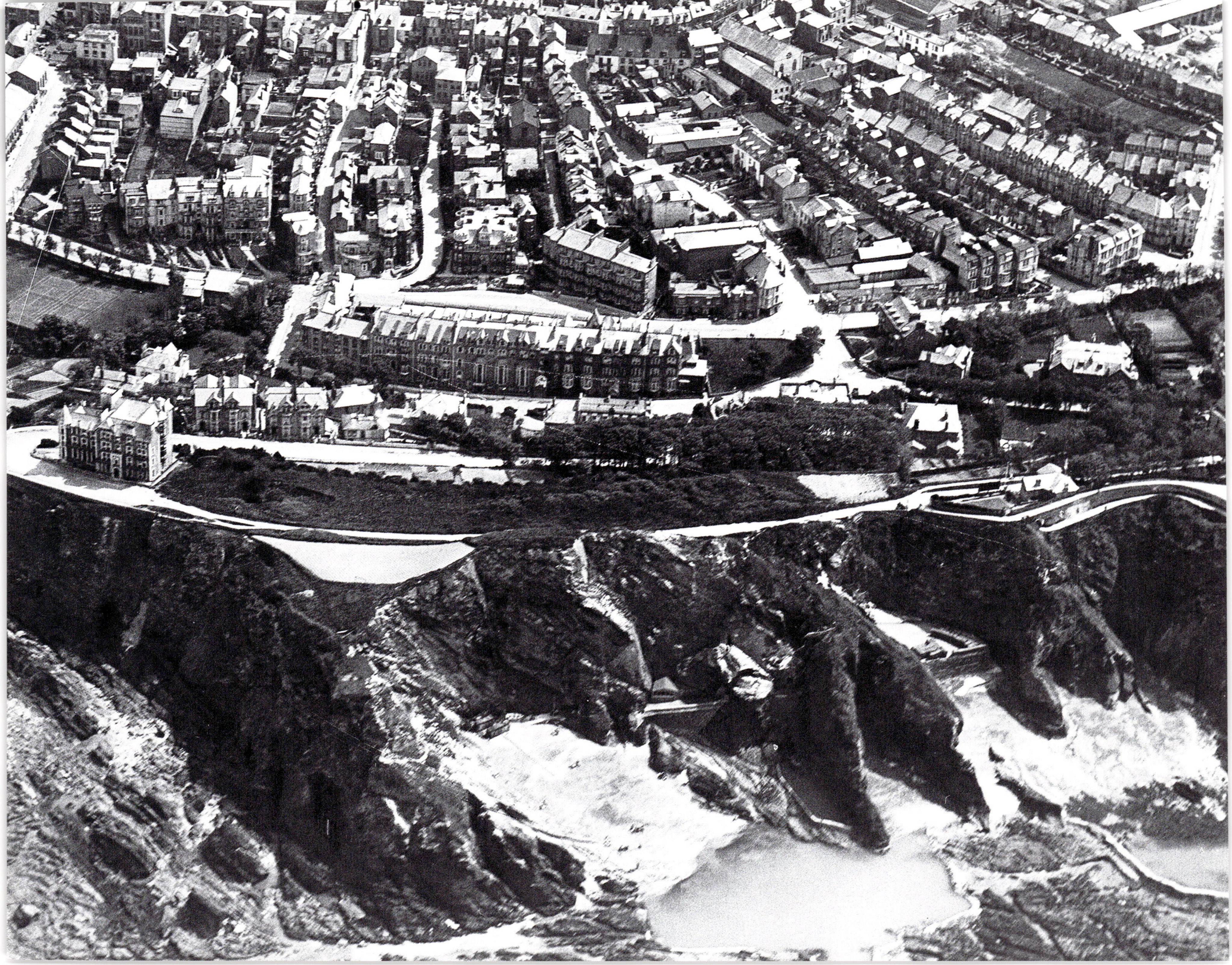

Granville Road and Wilder Road area, Ilfracombe, Devon

May 1920

For a seaside resort to be successful, access to the sea is a vital prerequisite. On the north coast of Devon, Ilfracombe is an ancient settlement with an important harbour. It is therefore not a surprise that people would wish to bathe in the sea, but due to the cliffs along the shore there was no easy access to the sea. Access was gained by climbing the cliffs, rounding the point by boat, swimming or, at the lowest tides, clambering around the rocks of the point.

Ilfracombe's beaches, now known as the Tunnel Beaches, were only made practically accessible after Welsh miners cut a tunnel through the cliff in 1823. The creation of the tunnel also allowed the project's investors to control a valuable revenue stream. The two beaches were made more practical for bathers by the creation of separate tidal pools for male and female bathers. Women had to wear clothing while bathing, but, as was the case at other resorts around the coast, men generally swam naked. The male pool can be seen at the right-hand side of the photo, while the whole of the women's pool is closer to the centre of the image.

At the landward mouth of the tunnel through the cliff, a bathhouse was built; the single-storey building's main entrance was through a pedimented Greek Doric portico, leading to an interior containing hot and cold baths. In the town, the variety of accommodation that developed during the 19th century can be seen, ranging from terraced houses and villas to large hotels to cater for the town's growing number of visitors.

EPW000956

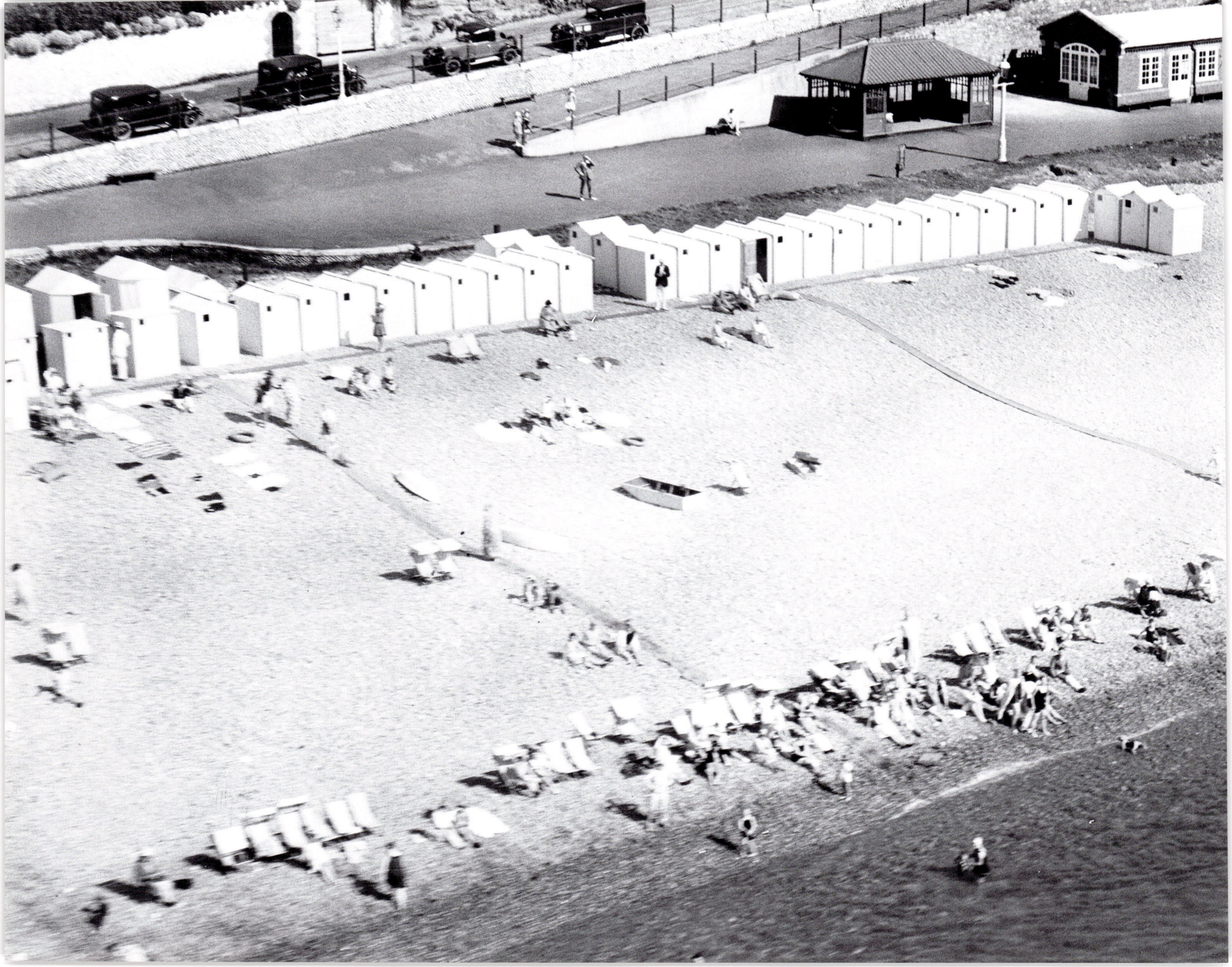

Beach huts at the bottom of Coastguard Hill, Budleigh Salterton, Devon
September 1928

This photograph shows holidaymakers enjoying sitting in deckchairs along the water's edge and a seafront lined by beach huts. The type of chairs shown in Victorian photographs is usually a lightweight type of chair, something like a campaign chair used by military officers on their travels. Some of these chairs may have come from the lodgings in which people were staying, but chairs were available to hire on the sands of Ramsgate as early as 1829. Photographs of that beach during the last quarter of the 19th century suggest that the chairs and some small benches were still being provided on the beach by enterprising local businessmen. These were fixed rather than folding, although folding wooden chairs, known as 'steamer chairs', began to be used on the decks of oceangoing liners from the 1860s. Although these were sometimes known as 'deck chairs', the portable, folding chair with canvas seating was only patented during the 1880s and was becoming common by the end of the 19th century.

Today the deckchair can be found on almost every beach and a similarly ubiquitous feature is the beach hut. These range in form and size from single timber sheds to multi-storey complexes of chalets, the exact configuration at any resort depending on the shape of the seafront and the likely number of customers. A line of timber beach huts along the seafront is the most common arrangement, echoing the lines of bathing machines from which they originate. The examples seen here at Budleigh Salterton are among the simplest, little more than a basic box, but at some resorts these small chalets have pitched roofs that might project in front of the cabin to create a sort of veranda, as at Southwold. At Scarborough, some of the chalets added beside the South Bay Pool between the wars shared a common roof, with the veranda area in front of them being defined by a light timber-framed arch, uprights and side panel.

Interestingly, there appears to be a narrow path, presumably a boardwalk, running along in front of the beach huts in this photograph, with two similar narrow paths leading down to the sea for bathers with delicate feet.

EPW023996

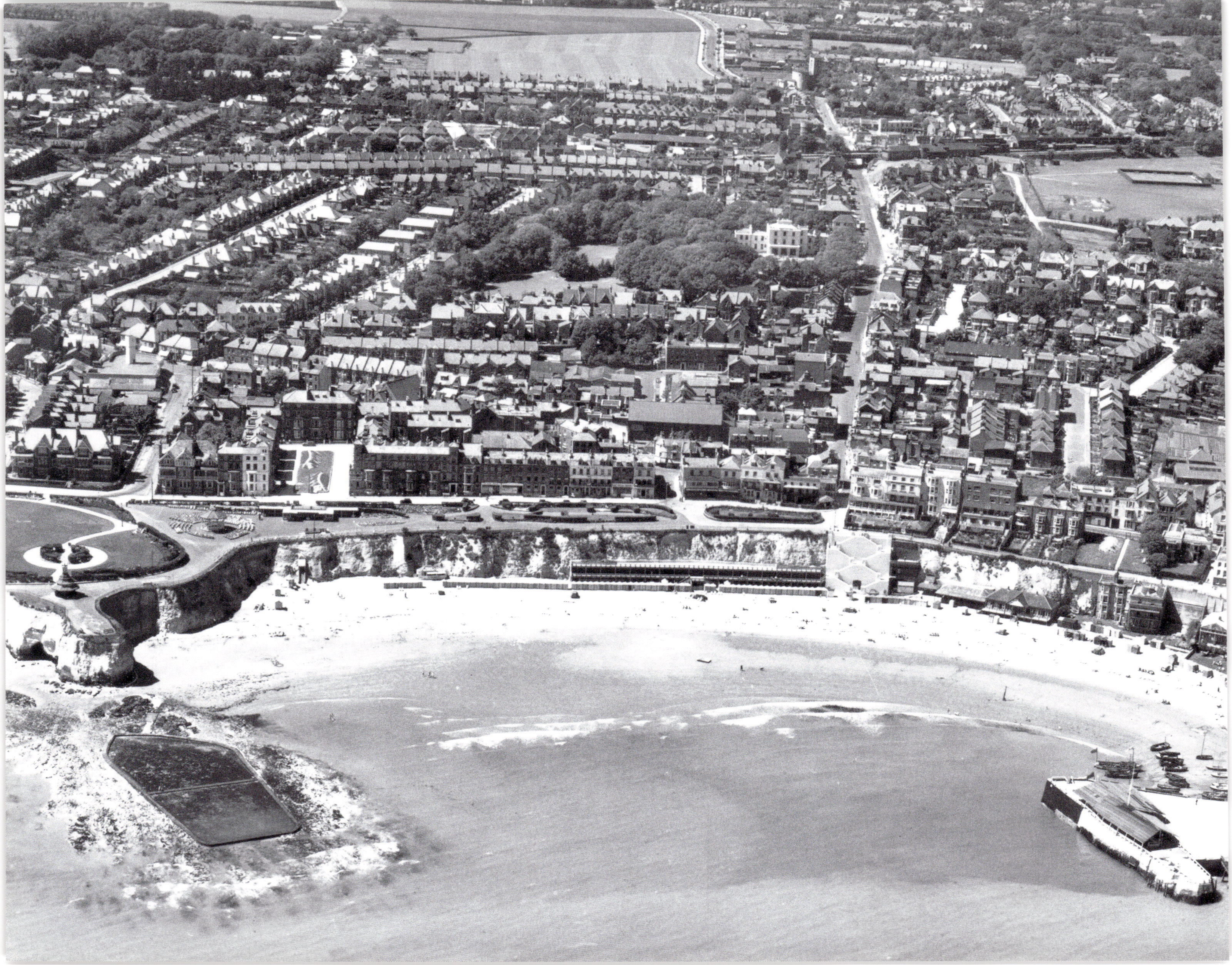

Viking Bay and environs, Broadstairs, Kent
19 May 1948

The classic image of a beach hut is the small, stand-alone, shed-like structure constructed of timber, often arranged in lines along the seafront. However, by the 20th century, facilities for changing, storing personal items and making a cup of tea were being provided in more substantial complexes of beach huts or chalets constructed of brick or concrete.

At Weymouth, two lines of 1920s chalets built at Greenhill Gardens have part of the tennis courts and bowling greens above them. A post-war line of chalets at Lowestoft has verandas partly enclosed by a brick wall and their more substantial construction has allowed the creation of a sun deck above. The desire to have individual beach huts in a more focused arrangement led to terraces of chalets. At Saltburn during the 1920s, two tiers of ten chalets were created on terraces cut into the cliff and a similar arrangement can be found at Porthmeor Beach at St Ives and at Folkestone, where tiers of white concrete beach huts resemble lookout towers.

Some resorts invested in more substantial complexes. In 1935 at Broadstairs, the Urban District Council erected a two-tier bathing station at the base of the cliff. It was constructed of reinforced concrete and provided 66 bathing cubicles and 32 larger chalets, while the flat roof acted as a promenade and sun deck. It was extended to the left after the date of this photograph.

To the left of the photograph can be seen a small paddling pool, which would be filled with seawater at high tide, but is shown here at a low tide, full of water.

EAW015846

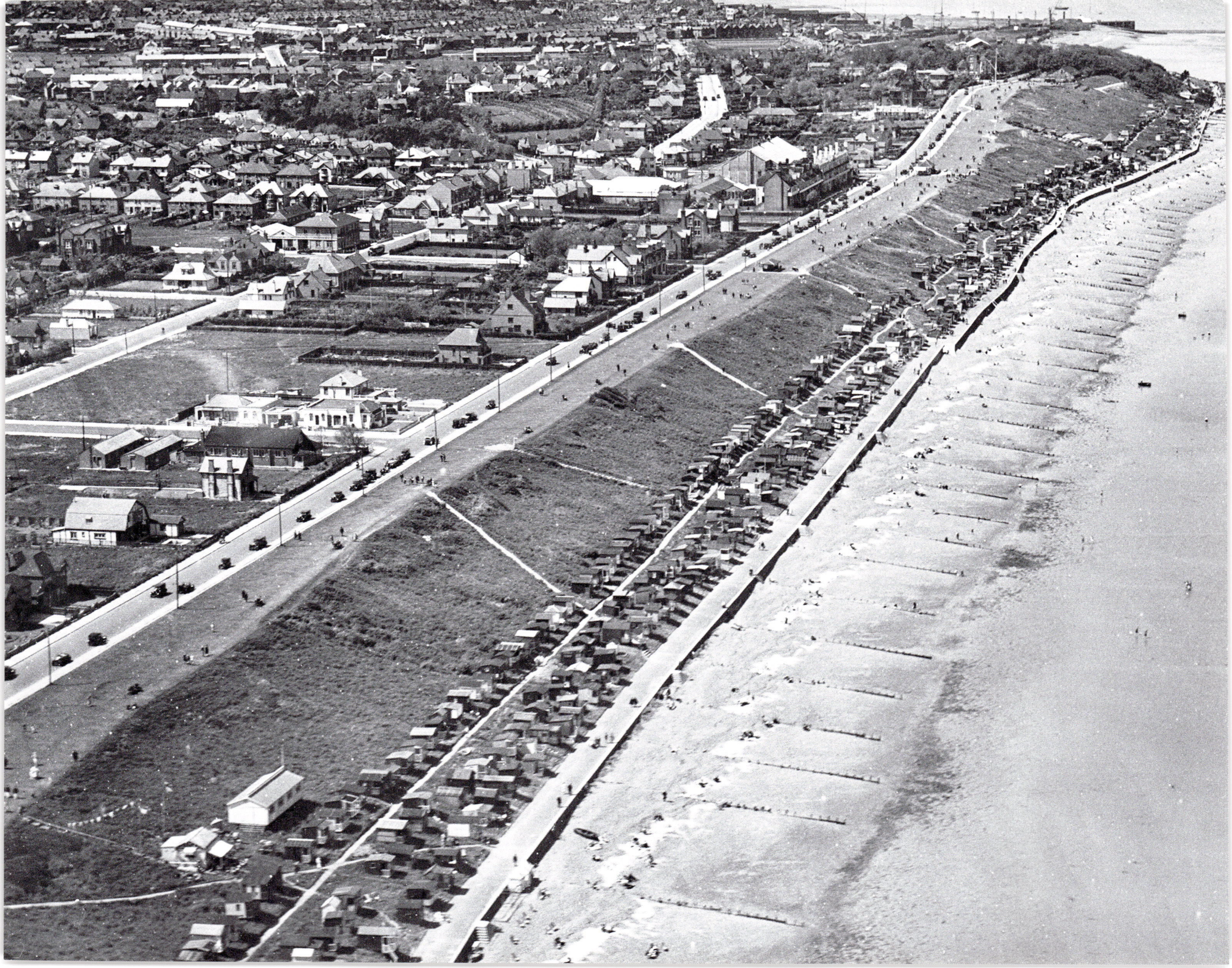

Tankerton Slopes and the town, Whitstable, Kent

May 1931

This aerial photograph shows the seafront at Tankerton, to the east of Whitstable. It is lined with a huge variety of bathing huts and cabins, and today there are still many examples on this stretch of the coastline.

The other, perhaps less obvious, feature is the form of the beach. Beaches have to be managed to ensure that they are sufficiently wide and high to prevent overtopping during high sea levels. Over time, beach material becomes finer due to the action of the sea grinding it and therefore it becomes easier to wash away. Groynes are a form of hard engineering designed to work as part of a soft engineering strategy to maintain and enhance a beach. They extend from the beach into the sea to slow the loss of beach materials through longshore drift as well as to encourage the deposition of new sediments.

Groynes can be constructed out of wood, stone, metal or concrete depending on the size of the native beach material, and, if required, a larger headland might also be employed to alter the littoral transport of sediment. The effectiveness of both groynes and artificial headlands can be easily measured by witnessing how much material builds up against them. Photographs taken of the beach at Tankerton in *c* 1900 show recently constructed groynes protruding up from the beach, but in this photograph, taken around 30 years later, they are far less prominent. Today, the sand of the beach almost overtops the groynes, indicating how successful they have been at stabilising the beach.

EPW035500

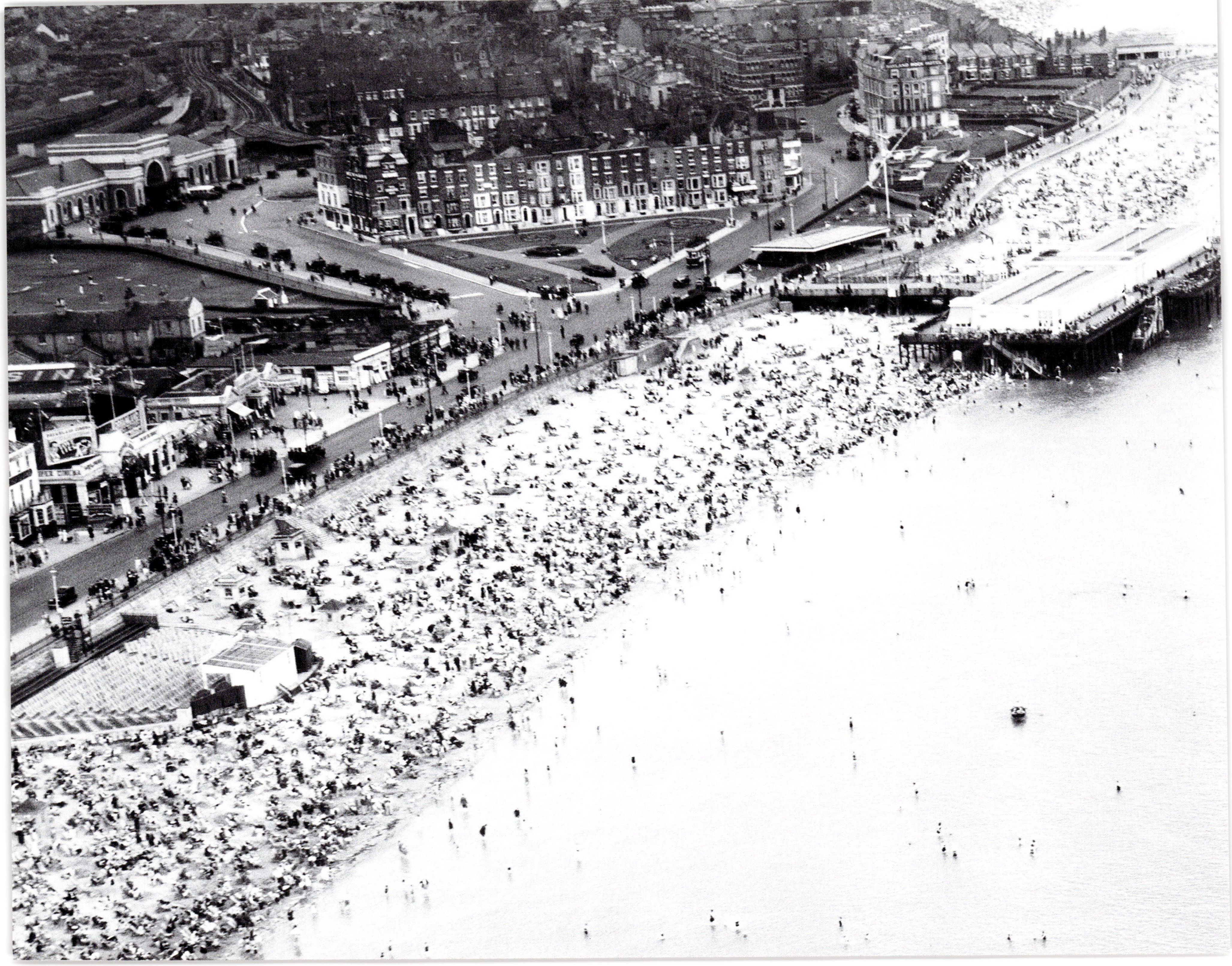

Marine Terrace Bathing Pavilion and environs, Margate, Kent
July 1932

This photograph shows Margate Sands at the height of a busy summer's day, with its crowded beach. The large structure standing on the beach is a bathing station, constructed in 1926, to provide bathing cabins and facilities. It was demolished in 1990. A few years after this photograph was taken, a tidal bathing pool would be constructed in front of the bathing station (*see* p 87).

As well as bathing in the sea and enjoying sitting on the beach, an enclosure with seats and a stage has been set up on the sands for entertainers. There is a long tradition of performers on the sand, relying on donations from happy customers to make a living, but this arrangement allowed them to levy an entrance fee, ostensibly for the use of the deckchairs. Behind the seafront road is the tip of the Dreamland fairground complex, including the casino building with the painted roof sign. Within a few years, this would be rebuilt as the Dreamland Cinema. Behind the bathing station is a large seafront shelter dating from *c* 1900; it is reputed to be where T S Eliot (1888–1965) wrote some lines of *The Wasteland* in 1921.

In the distance can be seen a haphazard row of houses; Buenos Ayres, a terrace of 13 houses, was begun in 1803 and was the first significant development to the west of the historic town. Although all the houses are four storeys and have bay windows, each builder has interpreted the detailing differently. To the left of the terrace can be seen the 1926 railway station, a replacement for the 1863 station Margate West.

EPW039326

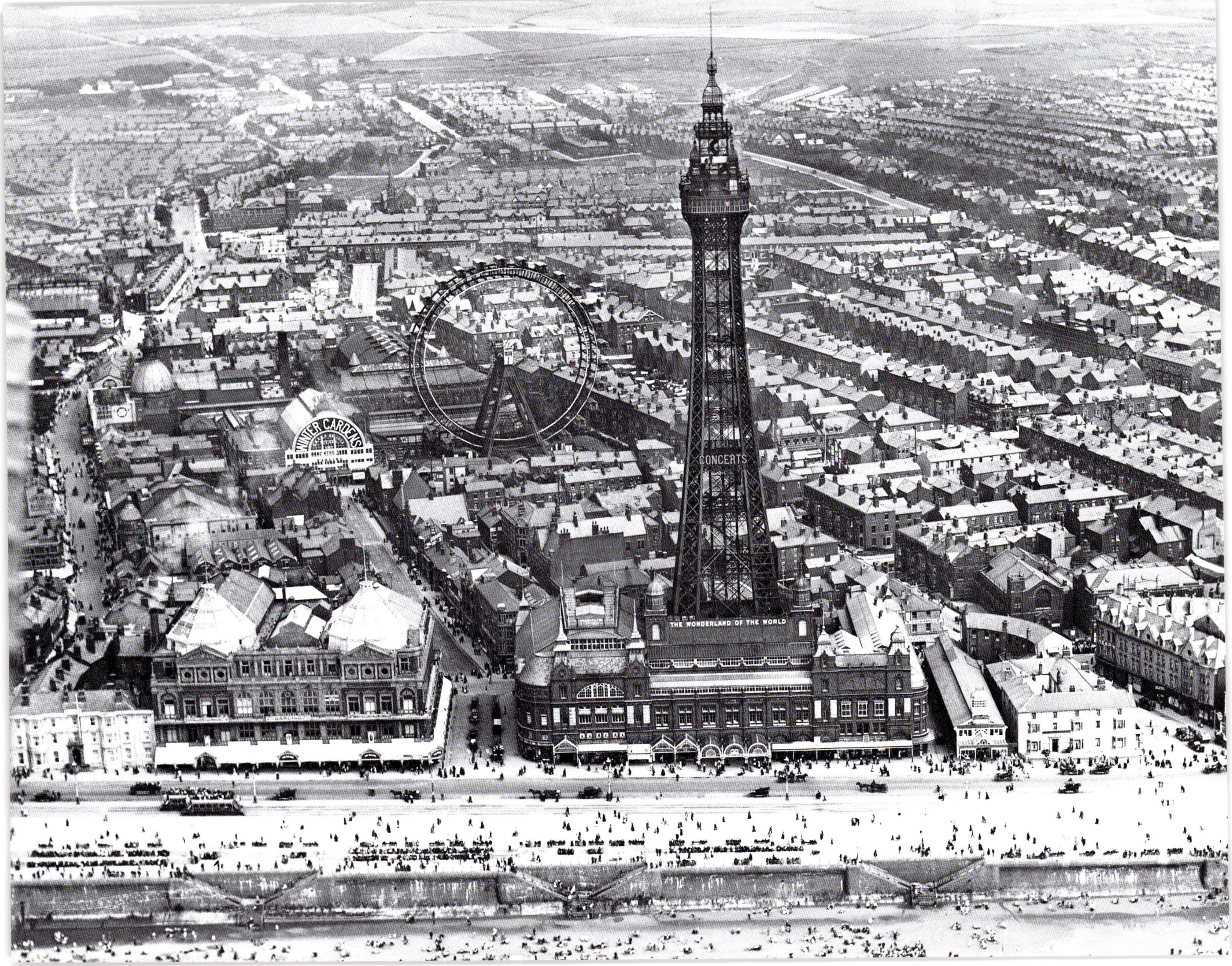
WINTER GARDENS
CONCERTS
THE WONDERLAND OF THE WORLD

Blackpool Tower and the Winter Gardens, Blackpool, Lancashire
July 1920

By the end of the 19th century, Blackpool was attracting millions of holidaymakers each year, and to entertain them huge new complexes were being created. Blackpool Tower was the ultimate expression of the scale that its holidaymaking infrastructure had reached. It exemplified the mass production of fun, providing customers with lavish interiors at an affordable price, relying on millions of visitors to make a profit.

The foundation stone of Blackpool Tower was laid on 25 September 1891, and by early 1893, the structure of the Tower had begun to rise above the roofline of the building being constructed around its base. It opened to the public on 14 May 1894. In this photograph of 1920, the owners of Blackpool Tower have modestly labelled it as 'THE WONDERLAND OF THE WORLD'.

Blackpool Tower was a technical triumph and an act of financial courage, particularly by John Bickerstaffe, mayor of Blackpool and chairman of the Tower Company. Designed by the Manchester-based practice of Maxwell and Tuke, the Tower, which was Britain's tallest building when it was built, measured 518ft 9in (158m) to the top of the flagstaff and was constructed in less than three years at a cost of £300,000. Blackpool Tower offered visitors a range of entertainments for 6d. For this fee they could visit an aquarium decorated with columns of rough rock supporting a cavern-like ceiling, a menagerie holding big cats and other creatures, a Monkey House and Aviary, the Seal Pond and Bear Cage, and roof gardens. The Tower's elevator hall was treated as a picturesque English village; there was also a Grand Saloon, refreshment bar, billiard saloon and the Grand Pavilion that would soon be reinvented as the celebrated Tower Ballroom. If visitors paid extra, they could ascend the Tower or enjoy a show in the 3,000-seat Circus. Its floor could be lowered to reveal a 6ft 6in-deep (2m) water tank to stage aquatic performances. This type of arrangement had been pioneered in 1871 at the 'Cirque' in Argyll Street in London, which closed in 1909.

To the left of the photograph can be seen the Alhambra and behind is the Winter Gardens with the large Ferris wheel (*see* p 105).

EPW002080

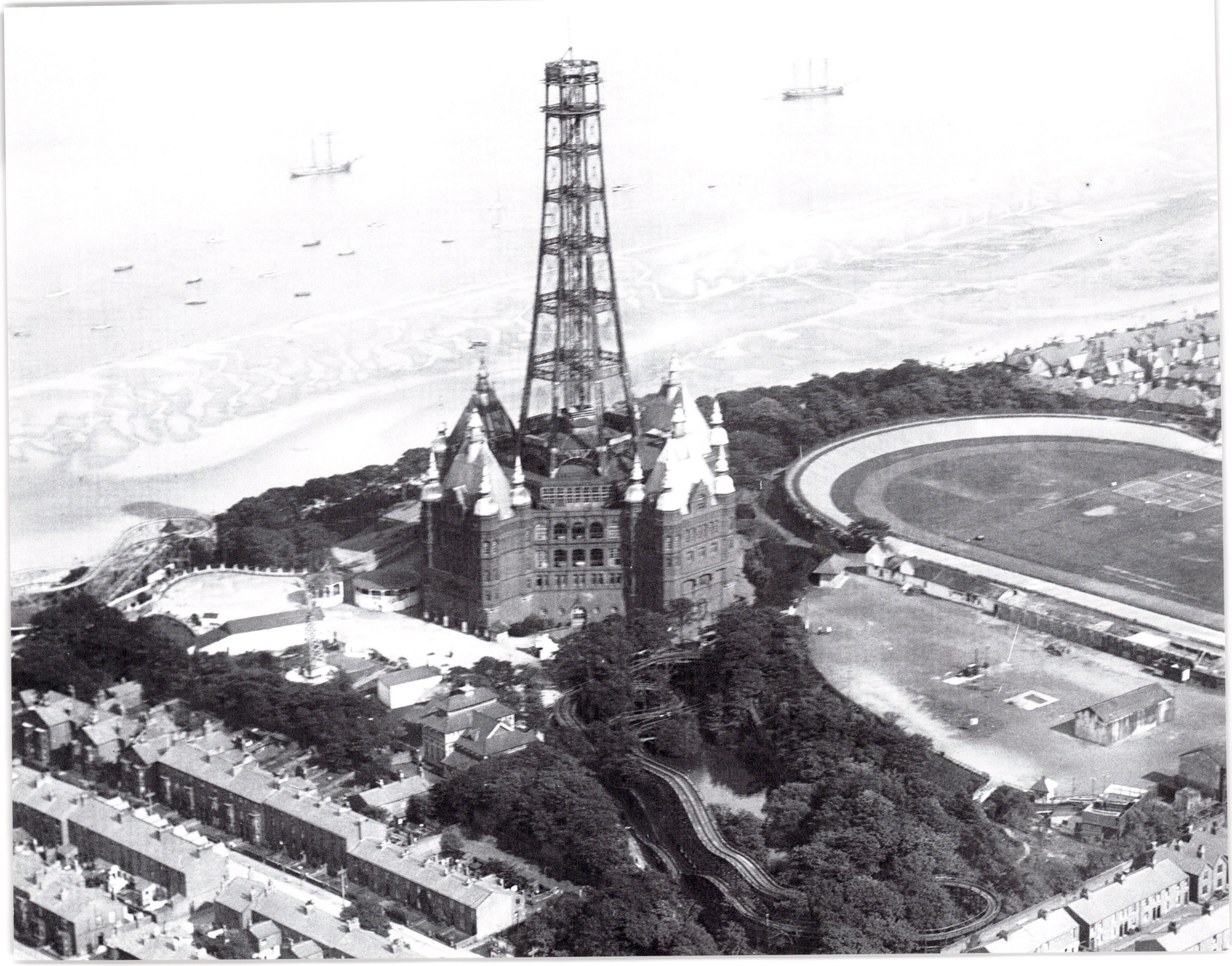

The Tower and Tower Grounds Amusement Park, New Brighton, Merseyside
August 1920

New Brighton Tower stood 567ft (173m) high and was the tallest building in Great Britain when it opened between 1898 and 1900. It was designed by the company Maxwell and Tuke, who had designed Blackpool Tower buildings and Southport Winter Gardens. Work began on the site on 22 June 1896, and the erection of the tower commenced in July 1897. The building at the base of the tower, which was to contain the ballroom, was constructed by Peters and Sons of Rochdale. It was a four-storey brick building with hexagonal, domed turrets. During the First World War, the building was neglected and as the structure required renovation that was beyond the means of the owners, the dismantling of the tower began in 1919, and the metal was sold for scrap. This photograph, taken in 1920, shows the dismantling process in progress. The building at its base, housing the ballroom, continued in use until it was damaged by fire in 1969.

In addition to New Brighton Tower and Blackpool Tower of 1894, there was also a tower constructed at Morecambe in 1898 and there was a plan to erect a 530ft-high (162m) tower at Southend's Kursaal, but this was never built. At Great Yarmouth, there was the Warwick Revolving Tower, which was built first in 1897, followed by similar examples at Morecambe, Douglas, Scarborough and probably Margate. The modern successor to this type of tower is Brighton's i360 in which customers ascend in a capsule up the shaft of the tower.

EPW004047

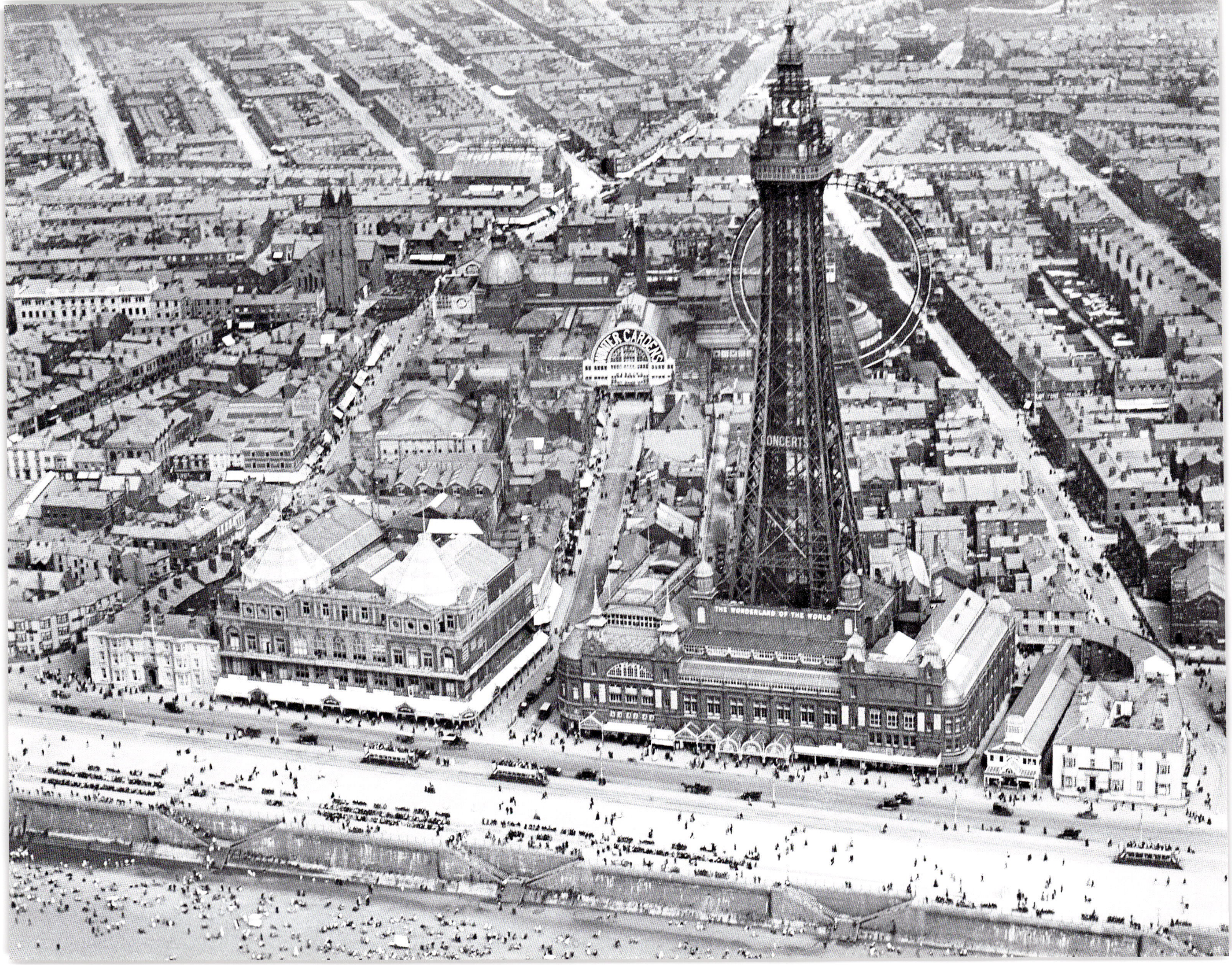
WINTER GARDENS
CONCERTS
THE WONDERLAND OF THE WORLD

Blackpool Tower and the Winter Gardens, Blackpool, Lancashire
July 1920

This photograph shows the three great entertainment complexes that were built at the end of the 19th century in central Blackpool. The most famous is of course Blackpool Tower, which opened to the public in 1894 (*see* p 101) but immediately to its left was the Palace, originally called the Alhambra. Its foundation stone was laid in December 1897 and the huge and opulent building was designed by Wylson and Long of London and opened in August 1899. Its theatre could hold an audience of 3,000 (though the local newspaper claimed 5,000 with 3,500 being seated), the circus could cater for an audience of 2,000, and the ballroom was designed for 3,000 people or 500 couples dancing. There was also a range of restaurants, lounges, roof promenades and balconies that catered for several thousand more customers. The venues were similar in size to those in the adjacent Tower, but what distinguished the Alhambra was its lavish marble and mosaic interiors. The company went bankrupt in November 1902 and the building was acquired by the Blackpool Tower Company. It was demolished in 1962 and was replaced by a large department store.

The third major complex can be seen behind the Tower. The Winter Gardens were Blackpool's first, almost industrial-scale entertainment facilities. The Blackpool Winter Gardens Company employed the Oldham architect Thomas Mitchell to build the Winter Gardens and by July 1878 it was open to the public, providing indoor attractions to enjoy during inclement weather. The Winter Gardens is an unrivalled complex of entertainment venues, including some of the largest and grandest in Britain. The earliest surviving part is the foyer behind the Church Street façade, topped with its tall rotunda and dome, which can be seen to the left of the large sign proclaiming the winter gardens. This leads through the Floral Hall to the horseshoe-shaped Grand Pavilion and Fernery, which had an iron and glass roof providing a perfect environment for exotic plants and enjoying a sedate promenade. This can be seen at the right-hand side of the complex, behind Blackpool Tower and the large Ferris Wheel. In 1889, the first Opera House, capable of holding 2,500 people, was added, and to compete with the newly opened Blackpool Tower a series of new attractions was built in 1896. The huge Empress Ballroom was designed by Mangnall and Littlewood, while the adjacent Indian Lounge, an elegant refreshment room, was created by J M Bookbinder. The Great Wheel, inspired by the Ferris Wheel first exhibited at the Chicago World's Fair in 1893, was created in 1896 on the site of the bowling green as a direct rival to the Tower. It remained in use until the late 1920s. In 1911, the second Opera House was built at the left-hand side of the complex in this photograph, and while it has been replaced, its magnificent foyer has survived on the first floor.

The takeover of Blackpool Winter Gardens Company by the Tower Company in 1928 led to the removal of the wheel and the construction of the Olympia indoor amusement park and exhibition hall, which opened in 1930. In 1931, a more extensive refurbishment of the Winter Gardens took place, with a series of themed rooms being created opening off the Floral Hall. Charles MacKeith's 3,000-seat Opera House opened in 1939 in an elegant Streamline Moderne style. It was constructed behind where the original foyer with its tall dome can be seen in the photograph.

EPW002059

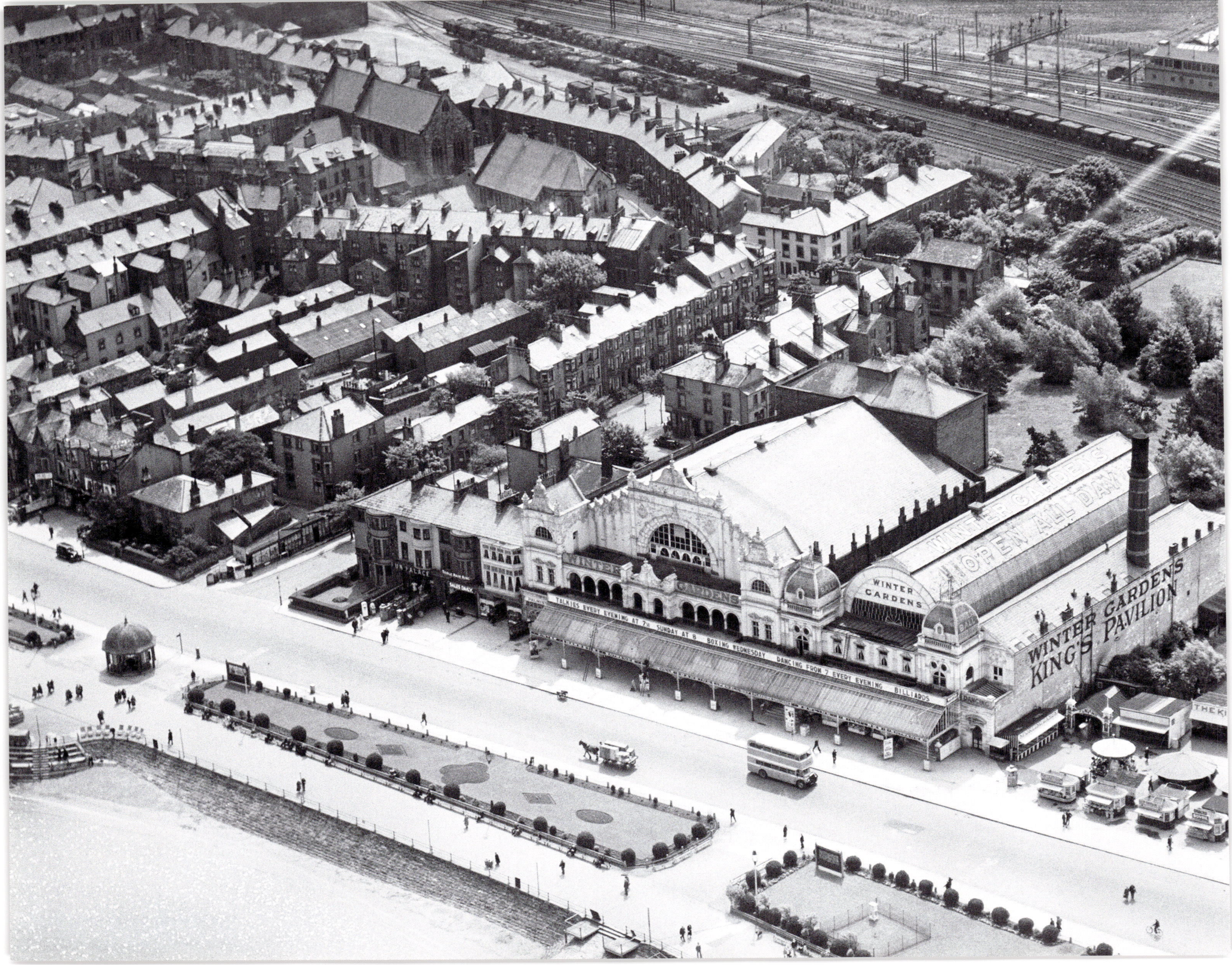
WINTER GARDENS
TALKIES EVERY EVENING AT 7½ SUNDAY AT 8 BOXING WEDNESDAY DANCING FROM 7 EVERY EVENING BILLIARDS
WINTER GARDENS
OPEN ALL DAY
WINTER GARDENS KING'S PAVILION

The Winter Gardens, Morecambe, Lancashire
June 1933

At a number of seaside resorts, winter gardens were created as indoor attractions for use during inclement weather, where visitors could promenade and admire exotic plants. The roots of this type of structure can be traced back to Henry Phillips' Athenaeum, a large glass conservatory designed to house palm trees as well as a literary institute. This project was abandoned due to a lack of funds, but the idea was revived in 1833 when the Antheum was built on the seafront at the west end of Hove. Unfortunately, this glazed, domed structure had serious design flaws and collapsed. However, the success of the Crystal Palace in 1851 demonstrated that the technology could be mastered, and during the 1870s a number of large examples were created in resorts in north-west England, as well as at Bournemouth, Torquay and Tynemouth. Due to the nature of the technology, using prefabricated iron and steel members, these structures could be dismantled and re-erected; Torquay's Winter Gardens were erected in 1878–81 on an inland site, but it was dismantled and reconstructed on the seafront at Great Yarmouth in 1903.

The Winter Gardens at Morecambe began life in 1878 as a complex of buildings that included seawater baths, a ballroom and bars. In 1897, the Victoria Pavilion Theatre was added, the large structure with the elaborate façade in the centre of the block of buildings. It was designed by the architects Mangnall and Littlewood, with the renowned theatre designer Frank Matcham serving as a consulting architect. The Winter Gardens closed in 1977 and the original building adjacent to the theatre was demolished in 1982.

EPW042133

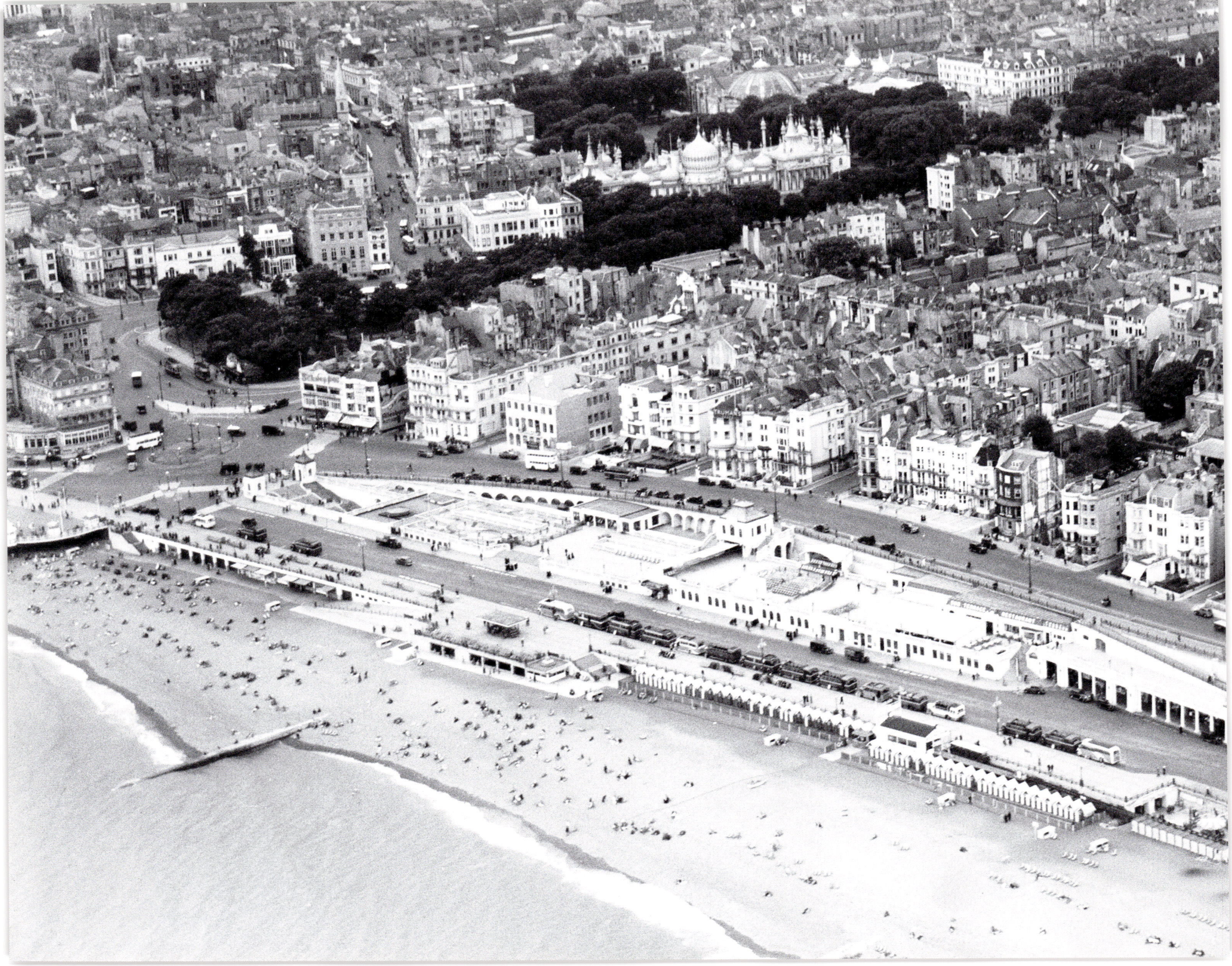

Brighton Aquarium and the town behind, Brighton, East Sussex
June 1937

In 1853, the world's first public, self-contained, self-sustaining marine aquarium opened in Regent's Park, and by the 1870s, the first aquaria had opened at seaside resorts, with Brighton leading the way. Brighton Aquarium was designed by Eugenius Birch, the pier engineer and designer of Brighton's West Pier (opened 1866), who conceived the idea following a visit to the aquarium at Boulogne. It was built close to the Chain Pier and its construction required the creation of a new sea wall and an extension of the promenade to create Madeira Drive. The Brighton Marine Aquarium Company was formed on 2 January 1868 and in the following year an Act of Parliament was obtained to allow work to take place. The whole project was completed in 1872 at a cost of £130,000.

A description of the building appears in a book designed to celebrate the opening of the building and to promote interest in the emerging science of home aquaria. This work and early photographs show that it was a large, complicated structure finished with highly decorative, architectural detailing. Its lavish Victorian interior featured polychromed brick, terracotta, vaults and fine stonework.

Aquaria were built in Southport in 1874 in the Winter Gardens complex, followed by others at Blackpool and Tynemouth in 1875, and Great Yarmouth in 1876 (now a cinema). A large, but short-lived, aquarium was also built at Scarborough in 1877, in an Indian style with caves and grottos complementing the fish tanks. Like the building at Brighton, it was designed by Eugenius Birch. The aquarium that can be seen in this photograph was the result of the almost complete reconstruction in 1927–9 by borough engineer David Edwards.

Running along the seafront is Volk's Railway, a pioneering electric railway, now the oldest surviving one in the world; it has been restored in recent years. In the distance behind the aquarium can be seen the Royal Pavilion, the lavish, oriental-style confection created for the Prince Regent (*see* p 167).

EPW054040

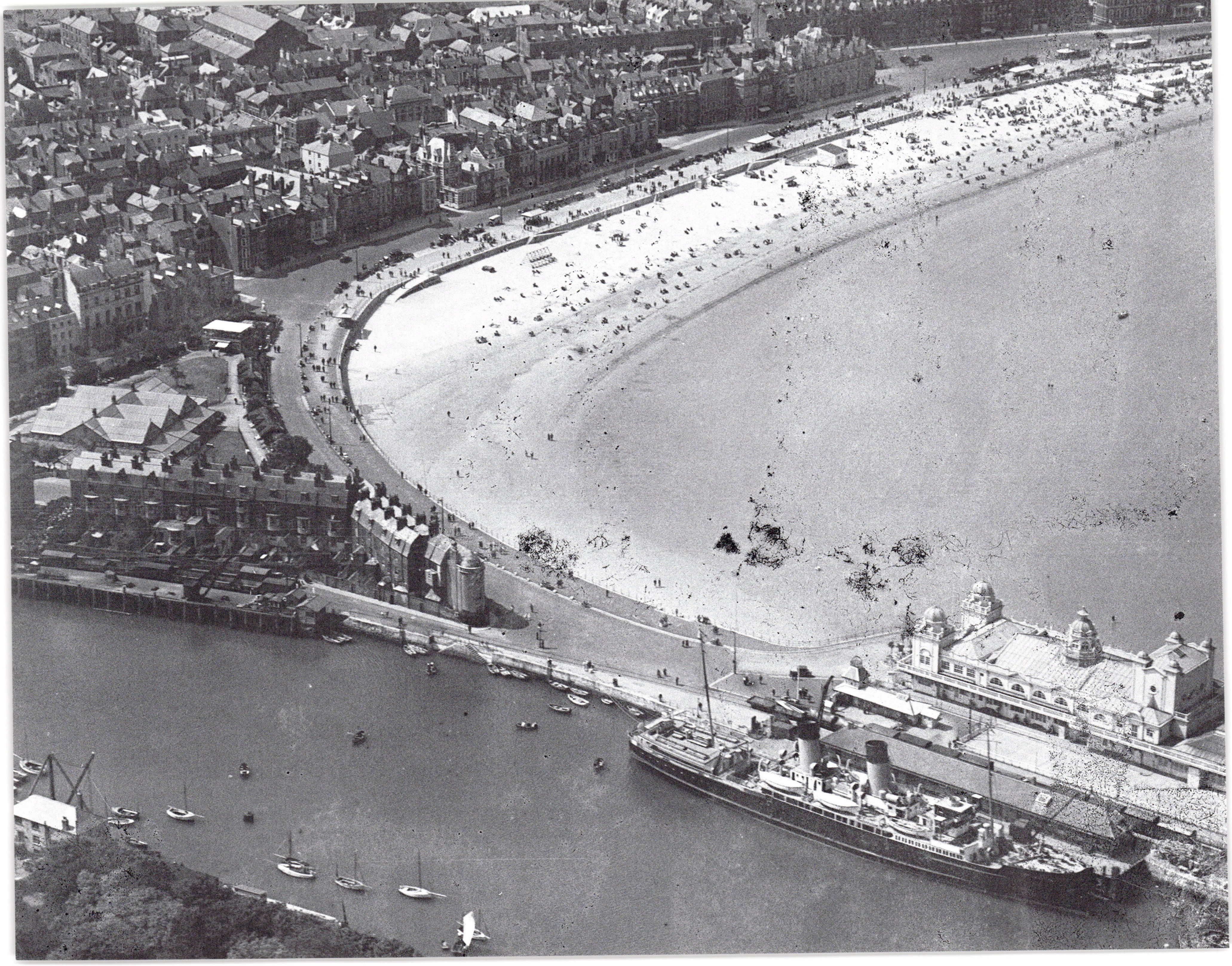

The Harbour, Pavilion Theatre and sea front, Weymouth, Dorset
June 1925

This print from a damaged negative shows the access to Weymouth's harbour with the Pavilion Theatre alongside the quay and the seafront in the distance. At this date, there was only a very narrow distance between the harbour access and the seafront; originally this was the location of the Pile Pier, which before its expansion during the later 19th century was a fashionable promenade, reminiscent of the Cobb at nearby Lyme Regis (*see* p 255).

One feature of the harbourside at the end of the 18th century was a floating bath for use by the royal family, which was moored beside the pier. Inside the hull there were three small pools, the largest one reserved for the king, and around the baths were dressing rooms.

As well as being a working harbour, the quay alongside the pier was also the departure point for ferry services to the Channel Islands and France and a moored ferry can be seen in the photograph (*see* p 253).

Although one side of the Pile Pier was obviously commercial, on the other side was the beach and the seafront. The Pavilion Theatre, originally known as the New Pavilion, was situated at the southern end of the Esplanade on reclaimed land beside the Pile Pier. Built in 1908, it had an auditorium that could seat 1,200. It was destroyed by fire in 1954 and the present Pavilion Theatre, designed by the Verity & Beverley partnership, opened in 1960.

EPW013595

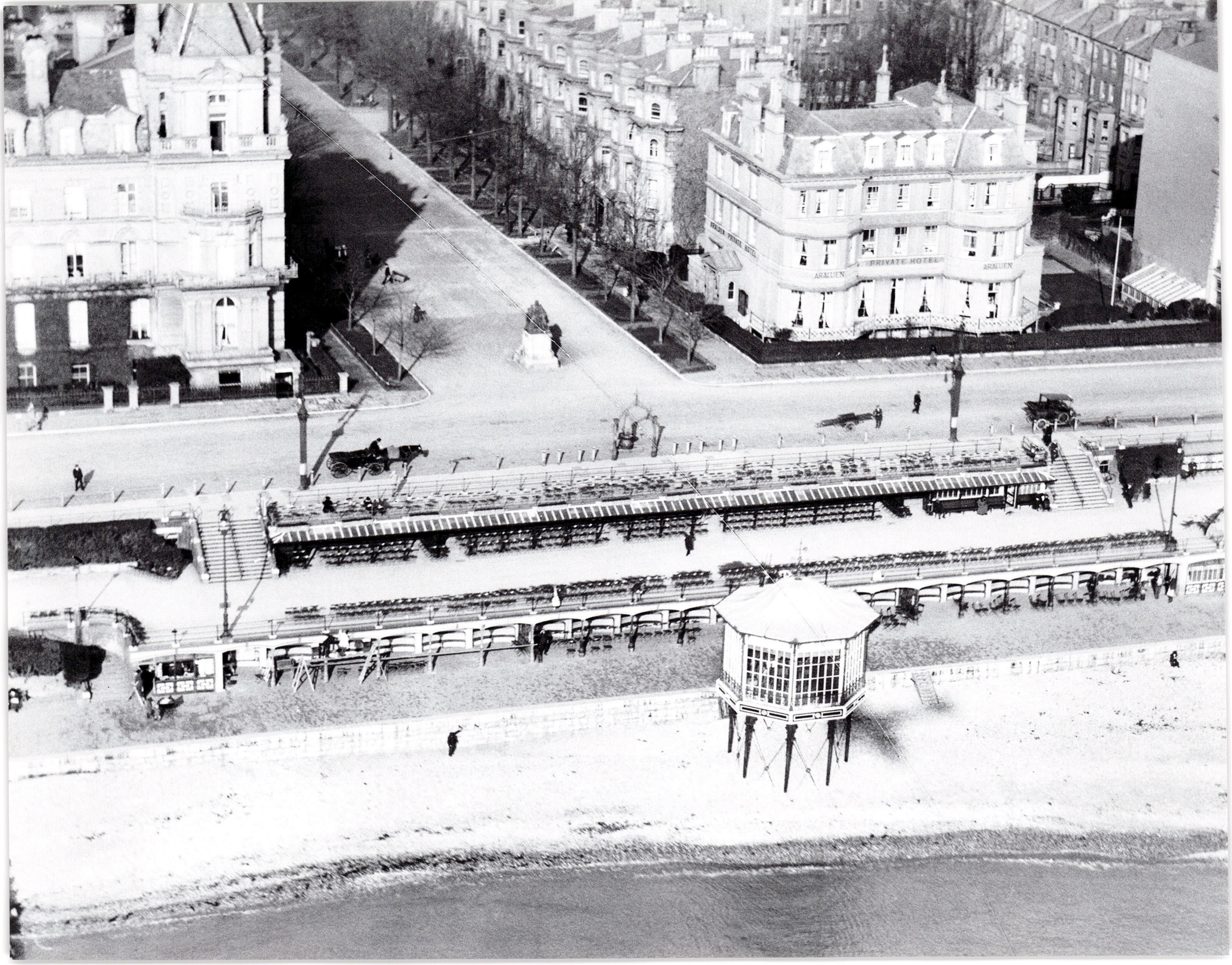
ARALUEN PRIVATE HOTEL
ARALUEN
PRIVATE HOTEL
ARALUEN

Seated statue of the Seventh Duke of Devonshire and bandstand, Eastbourne, East Sussex

February 1920

The bandstand has been a central feature in many seaside resorts for over a century. Their origins can be traced back to the structures erected in London's pleasure gardens for music performances during the 18th century, and facilities were also provided for music in spa towns, the best surviving example being the Georgian music gallery on the Pantiles at Tunbridge Wells. The seafront bandstand, or the band house as it was often known, also owed its origins to the need to provide a music venue in the growing number of municipal parks being established from the 1830s onwards. The first bandstands appear to have been erected in the Royal Horticultural Society Gardens in South Kensington in 1861. These were designed by Captain Francis Fowke of the Royal Engineers, who was also the architect of the main quadrangle of the Victoria and Albert Museum and was one of the designers of the Royal Albert Hall. These first bandstands were circular, domed pavilions supported on slender cast iron columns, resembling *chatri* from Indian and Islamic architecture. When the gardens closed in 1882, the bandstands were bought by the London County Council and re-erected in Southwark Park and Peckham Rye.

One of the earliest bandstands to be erected on a seafront was the elaborate 'Birdcage' bandstand at Brighton. Designed in 1883 by Philip Causton Lockwood and manufactured by Walter MacFarlane and Company of the Saracen Foundry in Glasgow, it is the sole survivor of 11 constructed in the town during the Victorian period. Its exotic detailing was a clear nod to the nearby West Pier and to the Royal Pavilion, which was ultimately responsible for the infusion of exoticism into the mainstream of seafront architecture. Other seaside resorts soon followed Brighton's example, including a bandstand on the Leas at Folkestone, which was manufactured by the Elmbank foundry and erected in 1886, and Clevedon's of 1887. There were also formerly examples at Worthing in 1897 and a Walter MacFarlane bandstand that opened at Clacton-on-Sea in 1899.

The Marine Parade Bandstand at Eastbourne had glazing around it to protect the musicians from the elements. It stood on slender iron columns at the top of the beach and this meant that the musicians were above their audience on the beach, but level with people in the seafront gardens. In this photograph taken in February 1920, the seats that would be occupied by an attentive audience during the summer are unoccupied. This structure was replaced in 1935 by a Neo-Grec-style bandstand, designed by the borough council engineer, Leslie Rosevere, and adorned with cream faience with some decorative blue, green and black faience.

The seafronts of seaside resorts were popular places to erect statues commemorating monarchs, local aristocrats and other national and local celebrities. Two of the Dukes of Devonshire are commemorated on the seafront of Eastbourne, the town they created. In this photograph can be seen the statue of the seventh Duke of Devonshire, William Cavendish (1808–91) situated at the foot of Devonshire Place. This 1.5m-high (5ft) bronze figure on a stone pedestal was unveiled on 17 August 1901 and was funded by voluntary subscriptions from the inhabitants of Eastbourne.

EPW000100

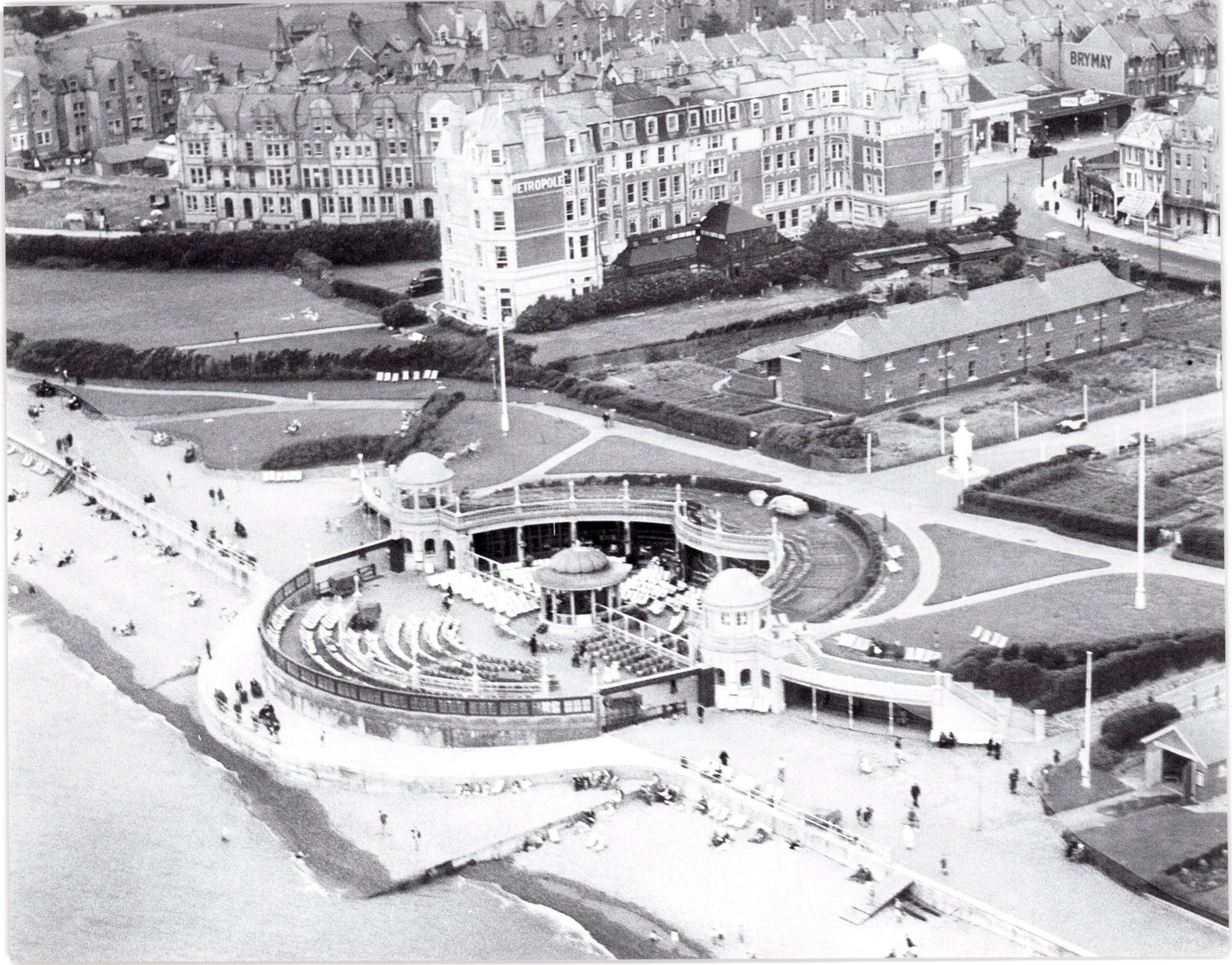
BRYMAY
METROPOLE
METROPOLE

The Colonnade and Metropole Hotel, Bexhill-on-Sea, East Sussex
July 1932

In 1914, a new band pavilion was opened at Clacton-on-Sea as a part of the town's General Beautifying Programme. The polygonal bandstand was set within a sunken pavilion with a glass front protecting the band and audience from sea breezes. A number of other seaside resorts employed this formula of setting a bandstand within an enclosure. During the mid-1930s, a new bandstand was built at Eastbourne in the vicinity of the seafront Redoubt, replacing a Victorian one. It consisted of a central, circular bandstand finished with classical detailing, along with a two-storey, curved structure to the east providing shelter and seating on the lower deck. Another new bandstand at Eastbourne, which dates from 1935 and survives, was erected in the centre of the main beach. It was designed by the borough council engineer, Leslie Rosevere, and is an example of a bandstand combined with an enclosed seating area. Its predecessor can be seen on p 113.

Perhaps the earliest example of this formula of combining an enclosed seating area with a bandstand was at Bexhill-on-Sea. An Edwardian bandstand with classical detailing was constructed as part of the development of the Central Parade in 1910–11. The rear part of this structure survives today, but is often unnoticed because of the building that was built behind it. Where one of a pair of parallel blocks of coastguard houses is shown in this photograph, the striking Art Deco De la Warr Pavilion was constructed in 1935.

EPW039349

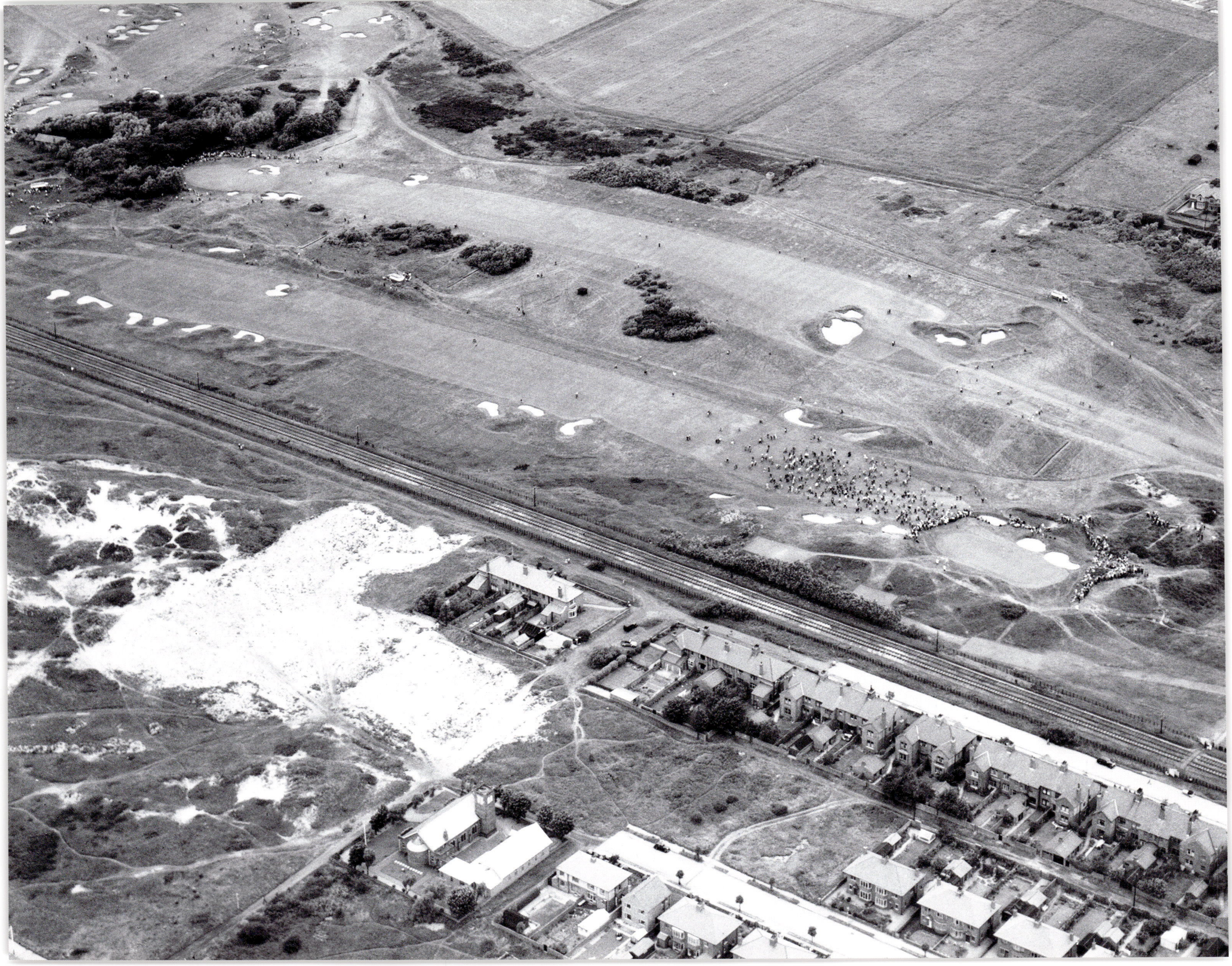

The 1952 Open Golf Championship (9–11 July) in progress at Royal Lytham St Annes Golf Course, Lytham St Annes, Lancashire

July 1952

The wilder dunes and heathland on the peripheries of resorts have sometimes become homes for links golf courses. This was the kind of land on which golf originated on the east coast of Scotland during the late Middle Ages and prospered in the following centuries before arriving in England with the Scottish court at the beginning of the 17th century. Scotland led the way in codifying the rules of the sport in 1744 and in the creation of golf clubs. By the late 19th century, golf was an essential part of many people's seaside holiday by the Scottish coast. In 1850, England boasted only one golf club, Blackheath (founded in 1766), but the situation changed dramatically during the late 19th century. By 1880 there were around a dozen golf clubs, rising to 50 by 1887 and to over 1,000 courses by the outbreak of the First World War.

The Open Golf Championship, first staged in 1860, has four English golf links on its schedule of active venues. Royal St George's at Sandwich was first used in 1894 for the competition and there are three courses in the north-west of England, at Hoylake on the Wirral (established in 1869), and two on the Lancashire coast, at Birkdale and Lytham St Annes. The Royal Lytham & St Annes Golf Club was founded in 1886 and the present course was constructed in 1897. The winner of the 1952 Open was Bobby Locke, who won a mere £300 for his victory. This is in marked contrast to the most recent Open Championship at the same course in 2012, when the winner Ernie Els collected £900,000.

EAW044946

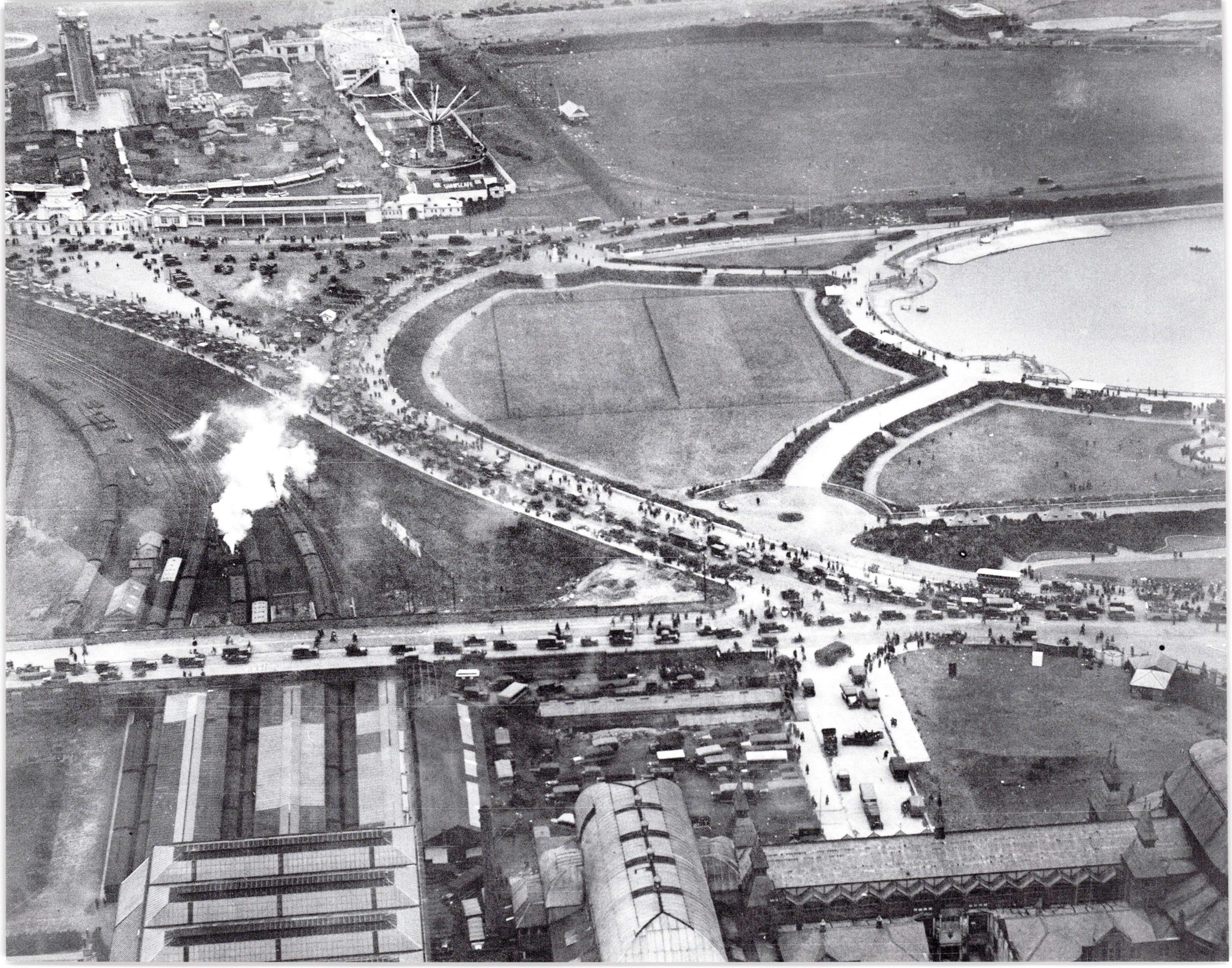

Crowds gathered for the total solar eclipse, Southport, Lancashire
29 June 1927

Aerofilms Ltd actively tried to capture events taking place around the country and on a number of occasions they tried to record the crowds at sporting events such as the FA Cup final or the Open Golf Championship (*see* p 117). This photograph, one of a series taken on that day at Southport, shows the crowds that had gathered to observe a total eclipse of the sun on 29 June 1927.

A solar eclipse occurs when the moon passes between the earth and the sun, thereby totally or partly obscuring the sun; a total solar eclipse occurs when the moon blocks briefly all direct sunlight, turning daytime into almost total darkness. With day becoming night, stars can be seen and as totality begins and ends, a series of visual phenomena can be witnessed, including Baily's Beads, where the sliver of the sun visible is like the diamonds of a ring. The occurrence of a total solar eclipse relies on the astonishing coincidence that the distance between the earth, moon and sun, and the relative size of the latter bodies, means that the moon can precisely obscure the sun from view from earth. The path of totality in June 1927, where a total eclipse would be experienced, crossed northern Europe and Asia, including the United Kingdom, and was the first total eclipse visible from British mainland soil for 203 years.

The site where people had gathered in this photograph was beside the railway station seen on the left of the image and in front of Southport's large Winter Gardens, which had been built in 1874. It was one of the first glass and iron structures to emulate the engineering of the Crystal Palace. In the distance can be seen Pleasureland, which opened on the seafront in 1913 and to the right is the large Marine Lake.

EPW018659

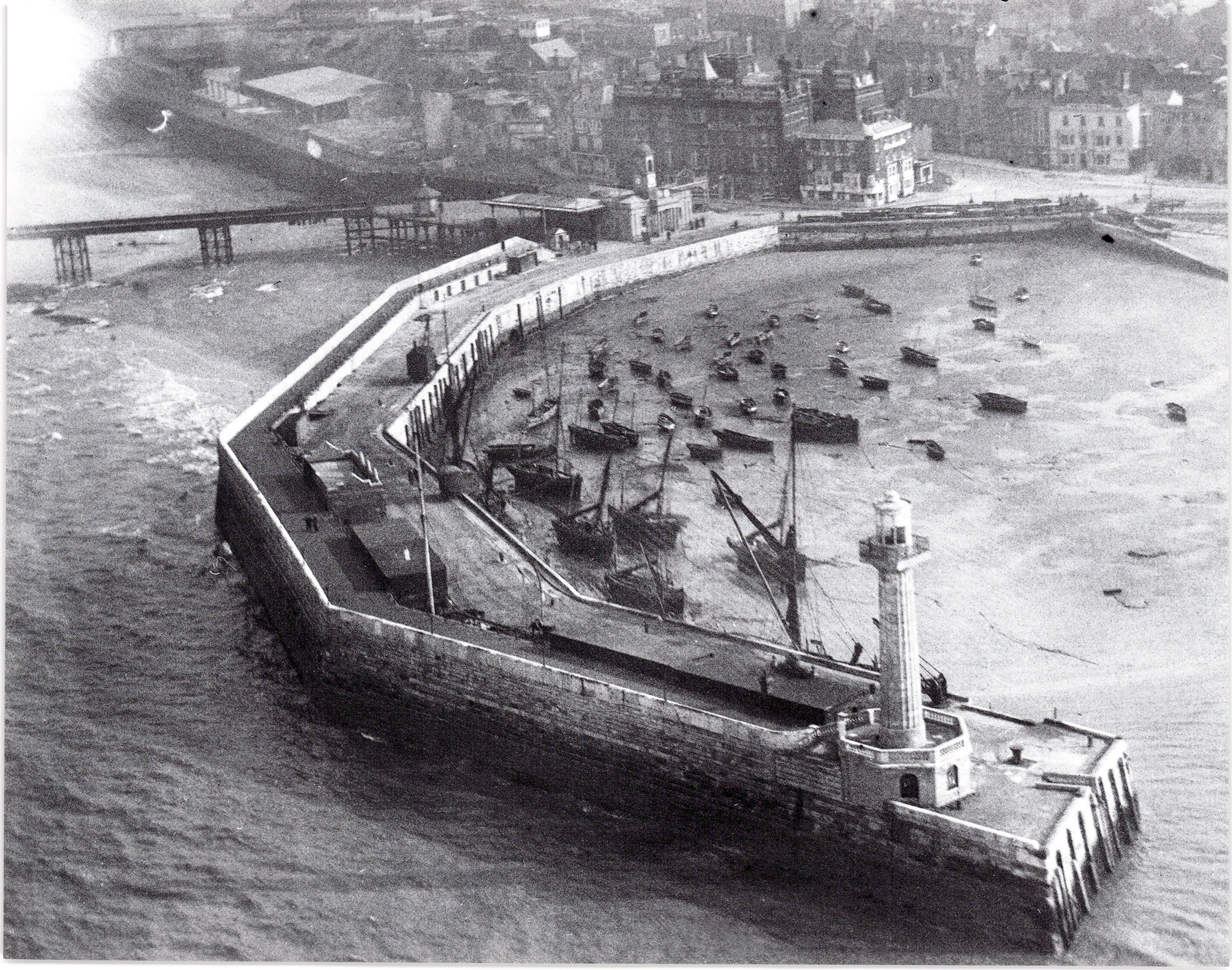

The Harbour Pier, Margate, Kent
February 1920

On 26 July 1814, the pier at Ryde on the Isle of Wight opened to boats landing passengers, initially with difficulty at low tide until it was lengthened, but it also catered for promenading holidaymakers. It consisted of a simple wooden deck carried on brick arches at the shore end and driven wooden piles further out to sea. Although Ryde may have been the first structure erected specifically for people to walk out to sea, it was a recognition of a practice that had perhaps been taking place probably since the first visitors came to the seaside during the first half of the 18th century. At some early resorts the harbour became a destination and a place to walk. At Scarborough, the harbour was improved and enlarged in the 1730s, the decade in which the first documented influx of people for sea bathing was taking place. In the late 18th century, a stone pier at Weymouth separated the mouth of the harbour from the beach; it is shown in a 1774 map as a short, narrow structure, but a 1789 drawing suggests that it had been extended and was a place for well-dressed visitors to promenade. The Cobb at Lyme Regis, which was rebuilt during the late 18th and early 19th centuries, offered shelter for working boats, but it also served as a walk for visitors, including Jane Austen, who spent a holiday there in 1804 (*see* p 255). As well as substantial stone structures, some resorts had timber jetties that were used for promenading. At Great Yarmouth, the harbour was on the River Yare, while on the beach there was a wooden jetty that small boats could moor alongside and visitors could walk along. A successor to this jetty can be seen on p 127.

These varied structures were commercial in origin and were adopted by fashionable holidaymakers as a promenade, but at Margate the new harbour pier was constructed between 1810 and 1815 with visitors in mind. The harbour arm is always known as the pier, and therefore subsequent timber and iron 'piers' are always referred to as jetties. This new stone pier, constructed by the engineers John Rennie (1761–1821) and Josias Jessop (1781–1826), was completed in time for steamers to begin to ply the route along the Thames in 1815. It is roughly half octagonal in plan and visitors could walk along this if they paid a 1d toll, though the introduction of the toll in 1812 sparked a near riot.

The new stone pier is approximately 900ft (270m) long, but it still could not cope with steamers at low tide. Therefore a timber jetty, similar in form to the pier at Ryde, was erected. Jarvis's Jetty, named after Daniel Jarvis in recognition of his services to the Margate Pier and Harbour Company, survived until the 1850s, when a cast iron pier, the first designed by Eugenius Birch was constructed. The landward end of the structure can be seen beside this stone pier.

The stone pier still survives today, but the lighthouse at its seaward end and the Droit House for the collection of tolls at its landward end were both reconstructed after the Second World War.

EPW000162

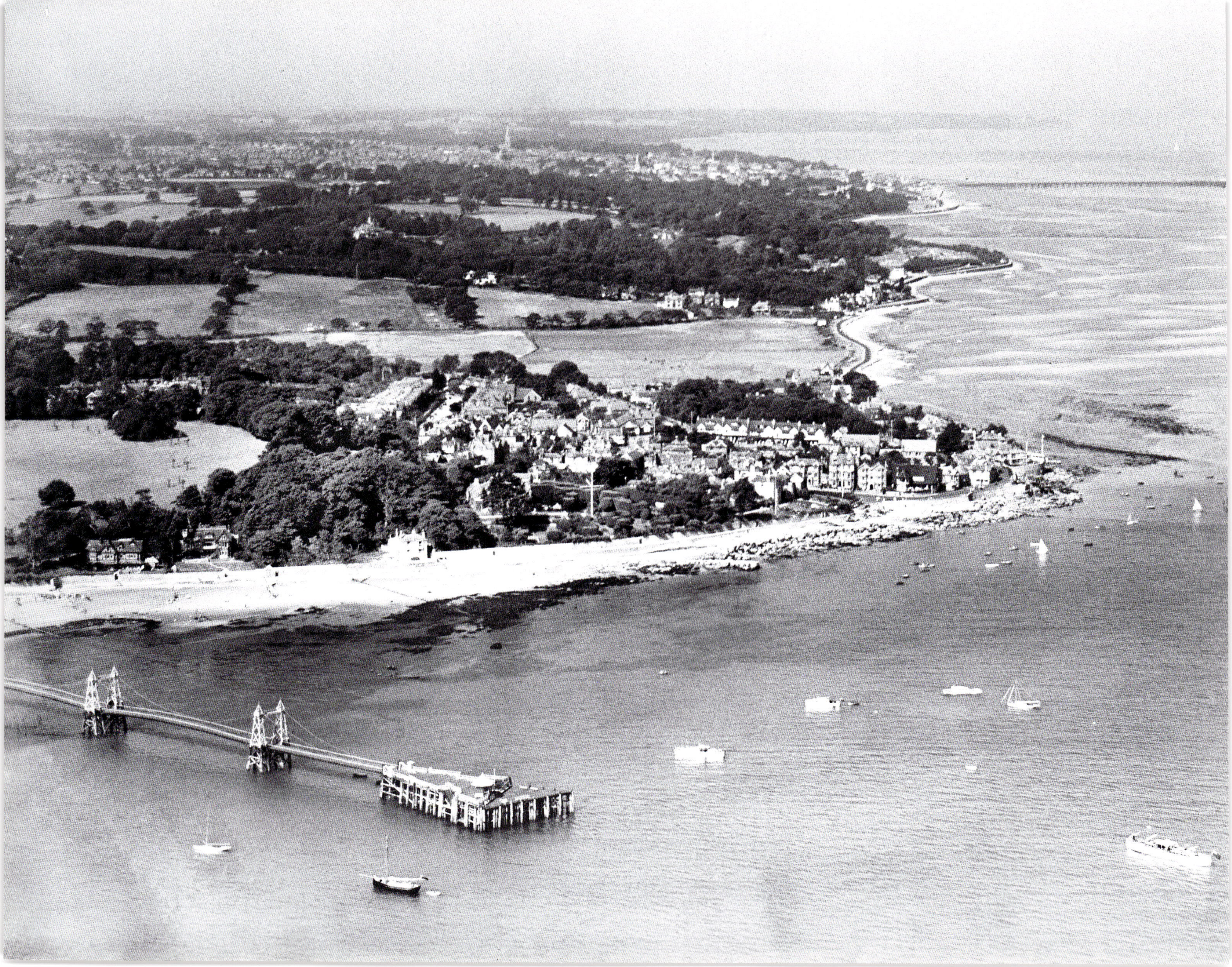

Nettlestone Point and the coast towards Ryde, Seaview, Isle of Wight

August 1933

At the north-east corner of the Isle of Wight is the small seaside resort of Seaview, and a short distance to the south of it can be seen its pier, a structure built using the same form of engineering as a suspension bridge. This was one of four such seaside piers constructed during the 19th century and was the last to survive.

Like the pier at Ryde, Jarvis's Jetty at Margate was a simple structure consisting of a wooden deck with wooden piles that had been driven into the seabed. However, an alternative, more ambitious approach to pier design was pioneered by the civil engineer and naval officer Captain Samuel Brown (1776–1852). In 1816 he had installed the first machine in his workshops for testing chain cables and those destined for the steamship *Great Eastern* were manufactured at his works in Pontypridd. As a result of his expertise, he became involved with the construction of suspension bridges, including the Union Bridge across the Tweed near Berwick, completed in 1820. In the following year, he erected the Chain Pier at Leith near Edinburgh and in 1823 he constructed another pier with a suspension structure at Brighton and this remained a central feature of the resort until its destruction in 1896. Although the chains and the upright elements of the superstructure of Brighton's Chain Pier were made of iron, the pier was still constructed on wooden piles. The chain piers at Leith and Brighton were destroyed by storms in 1898 and 1896 respectively.

Although this design was closely associated with Samuel Brown, two other examples were erected at Greenhithe on the Thames in the 1840s (demolished in 1875) and at Seaview on the Isle of Wight in 1881. The Seaview Pier Company was formed on 20 December 1877 and work began in September 1879 to the design of Frank Caws. The unfinished pier officially opened on 7 June 1881. In 1889, a 50ft (15.2m) extension and a new pierhead increased the length to 320m (1,050ft), while a still-larger pierhead was erected in 1901. The Royal Navy took over the pier during the Second World War. By 1945, it was in poor condition and despite being sold off it seemed to have had no clear future. A series of storms between October 1950 and December 1951 severely damaged the structure and its last remnants were demolished in 1952.

EPW043021

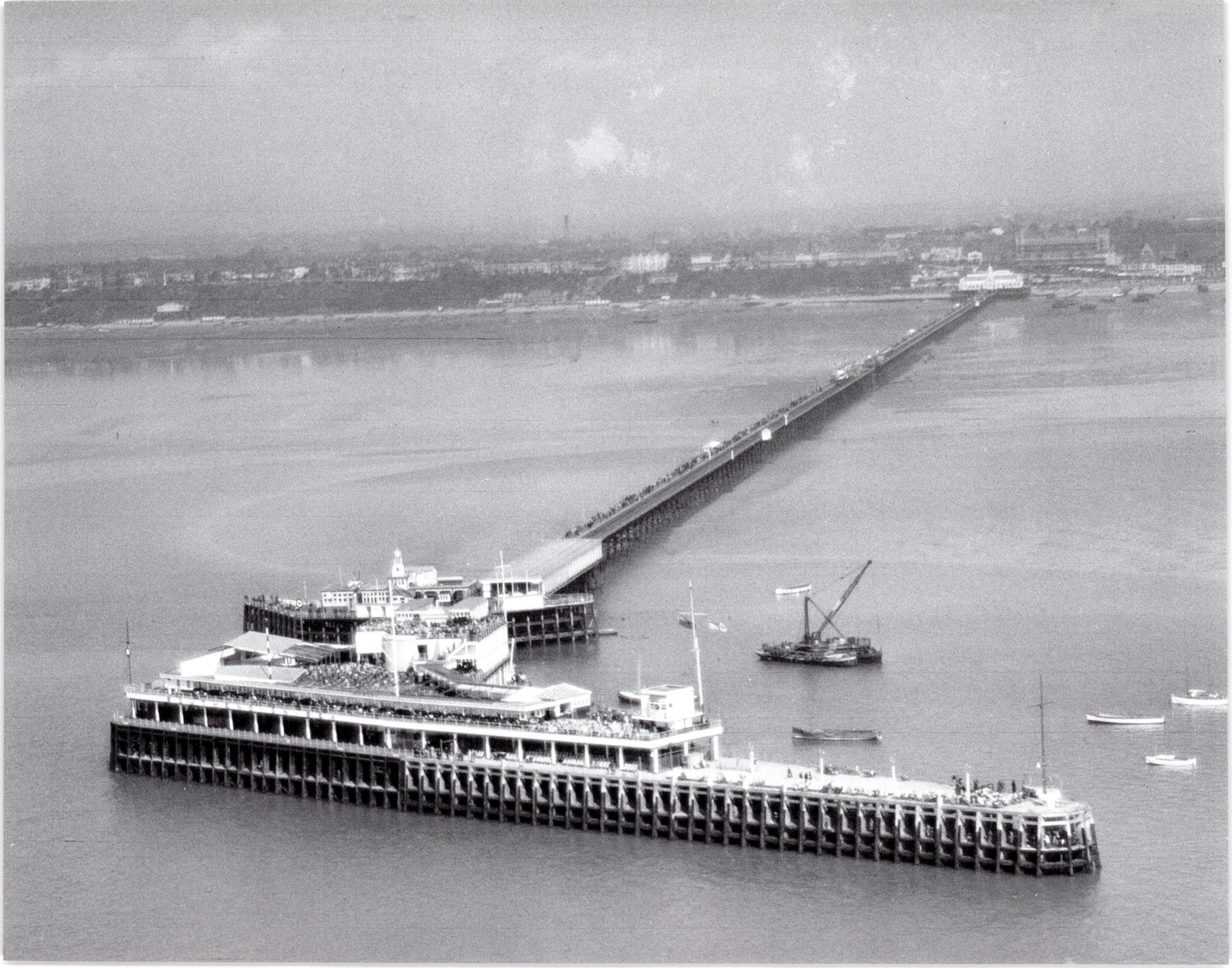

Southend Pier, Southend-on-Sea, Essex
April 1933

This aerial photograph shows Southend Pier, which is clearly the longest pier in the world, its length being necessary for steamers to be able to disembark passengers at low tide. Witnessing the popularity enjoyed by Margate because steamer passengers could be landed there at the harbour, the decision was made to build a pier at Southend to try to capture some of the lucrative Thames holiday market.

In 1802, a landing jetty had been erected by Sir Thomas Wilson for boats to land passengers at Southend, and in 1821, people wishing to disembark from steamers at low tide had to use two gravelled causeways. Therefore, in 1829 construction began on a wooden pier and the 183m-long (600ft) structure opened in June 1830. This soon proved to be too short for steamers and was first lengthened to 457m (1,500ft) in 1833 and then to 2km (1.24 miles) long in 1846. The early pier was constructed using driven wooden piles, but due to decay and damage by small, wood-boring marine creatures, the pier required significant repairs within a few years of its construction.

On 18 January 1880, the timber pier was severed by a ship striking it, and in combination with growing numbers of visitors arriving from London, the decision was taken to build a new iron and steel pier. James Brunlees, the designer of the pier at Southport, was employed, and the first part of the structure opened in July 1889. The pier opened completely on 24 August 1890, but steamers were still struggling to land passengers and therefore in January 1898 an extension was ready for use, bringing the total length to 2.2km (1.37 miles). Long piers could be problematic for passengers. For their convenience, Herne Bay's pier in the 1830s led the way with a sail-powered car for transferring luggage, which had to be pushed when the wind was light. In August 1890, the new, lengthened pier at Southend began operating a passenger train service and soon longer trains were introduced to cope with the growing numbers of trippers; for instance in 1895, a quarter of a million trippers embarked or disembarked (*see* p 39).

This 1933 photograph shows the enlarged pierhead in the foreground; on 8 July 1929, the Prince George Extension, constructed of reinforced concrete, was opened. At the outbreak of the Second World War, the pier was taken over by the Royal Navy and renamed HMS *Leigh*. It reopened to the public on 27 March 1945.

EPW040976

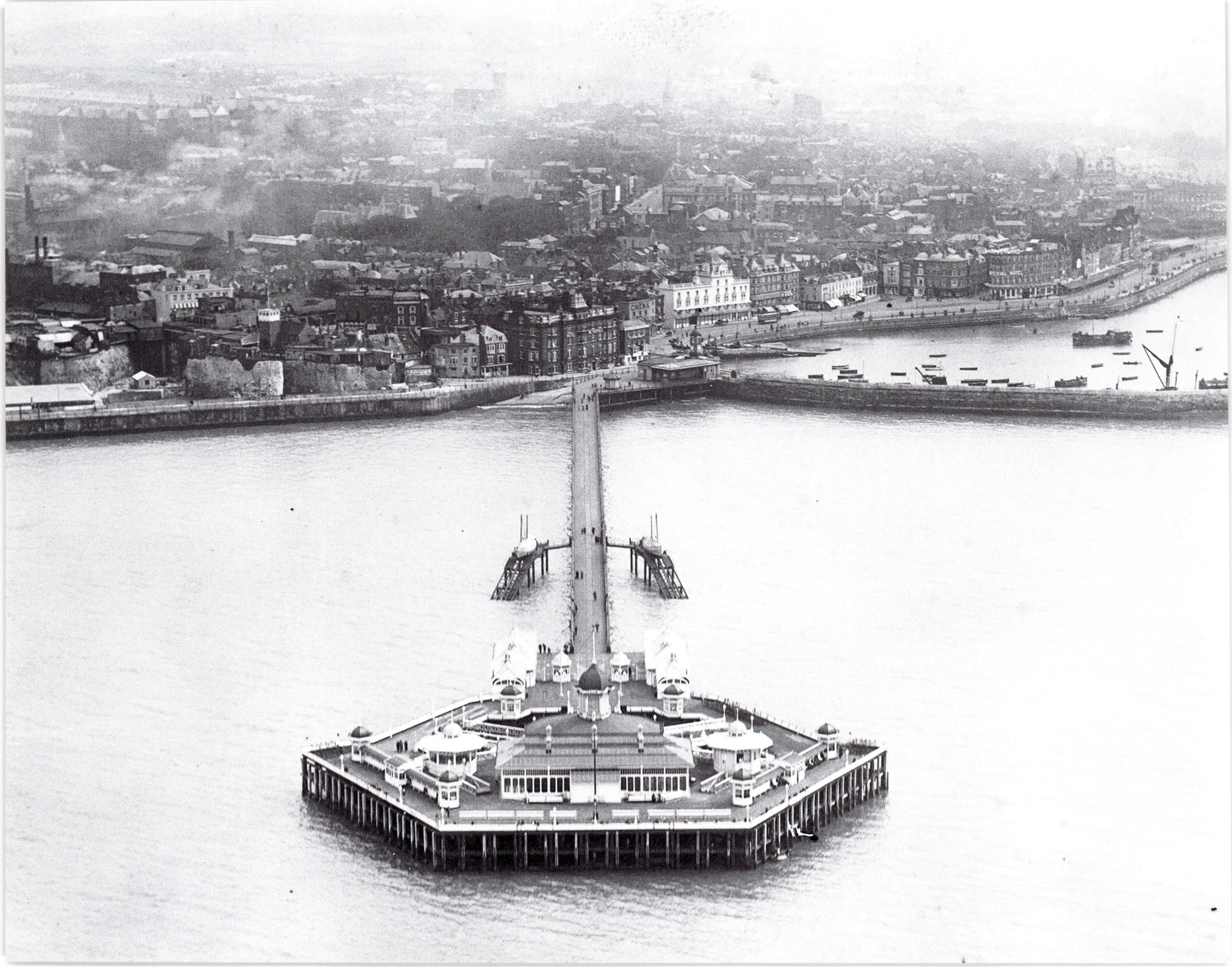

The jetty, Margate, Kent
April 1920

The main form of pier construction until the 1850s was to employ wooden piles driven into the seabed. However, wood was prone to decay and to damage by small, wood-boring marine creatures; the new piers at Southend and Herne Bay both required significant repairs within a few years of their construction in the 1830s. The obvious alternative was to use iron and the earliest surviving example in the world was the Town Pier at Gravesend, designed by the engineer William Tierney Clark (1783–1852). Another iron pier opened at Sheerness in 1835, and in 1842 the timber Royal Terrace Pier at Gravesend was replaced in iron.

The definitive shift to using iron piles only took place in the 1850s, with the construction of the new jetty at Margate by the distinguished civil engineer Eugenius Birch (1818–84). This was his first pier and he would be responsible for 14, a career that helped to define the essential characteristics of the seaside pier. His first contribution to pier design was to employ the screw pile, which was patented by Alexander Mitchell (1780–1868) in 1833. This was a technique using a screw on the end of an iron rod to fix the pile into the seabed. Mitchell employed this technique in a number of lighthouses before constructing his first jetty at Courtown Harbour in County Wexford in 1847.

Margate's new iron jetty was constructed to replace the timber Jarvis's Jetty, which was located in the same location beside the stone pier of the harbour. The first pile of the new structure was driven in May 1853 and it opened in April 1855, although the 1,240ft-long (378m) pier was not finally completed until July 1856.

In 1875–8 the pierhead was enlarged to allow the creation of a pavilion and to increase the number of steamers that could land at the pier, as well as to cope with larger vessels. Further additions were made in 1893 and 1900. During the Second World War, the jetty was used for troop and supply movements, including many soldiers rescued from Dunkirk. Steamer services resumed after the war, but ended in 1966. The jetty was forced to close in 1976 on safety grounds, and was largely destroyed by a storm on 11 January 1978.

EPW000619

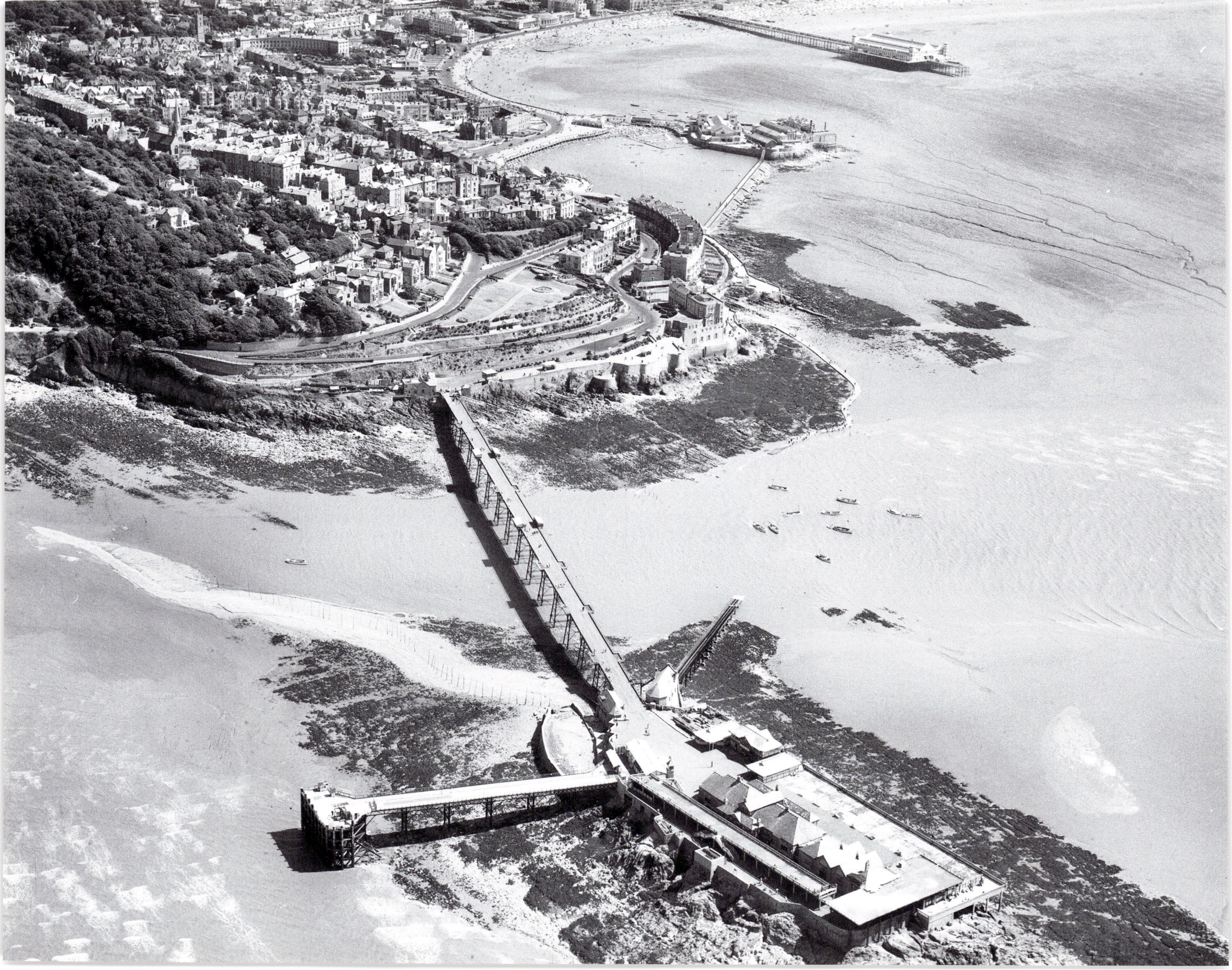

Birnbeck Island looking towards Weston Bay and the town, Weston-super-Mare, Somerset

25 July 1949

This 1949 photograph shows clearly why Birnbeck Pier is unique in Britain; it is the only pier that extends out to an island, meaning that its pierhead could accommodate larger, heavier structures than conventional wooden or iron examples. However, it also meant that a series of elaborate landing stages were required for the steamers that were bringing holidaymakers to Weston-super-Mare from Bristol and South Wales.

Prior to the construction of the pier, Birnbeck Island was used to catch fish in nets hanging between stakes set into the foreshore; stepping-stones provided a causeway out to the island at lower states of the tide. In the 1840s it was the site of Weston-super-Mare's first short-lived and never-completed pier; work began on the vertical supports of the pier in 1847. It was to be a 1,100ft-long (335m) suspension-bridge design with a central span of 545ft (166m) carried on substantial stone piers that stood a short distance into the sea on either side of the channel. However, a major storm later in the year swept away the first stonework of the uprights, leaving only foundations. There were no funds to continue work, the engineer William Dredge was declared bankrupt, and the pier company was wound up.

The idea of a pier in this location was revived by the Weston-super-Mare Pier Company, which was registered in January 1860. The foundation stone of the pier was laid on 28 October 1864, the components of the pier being prefabricated by Messrs Toogood at their Isca Foundry across the Severn in Newport (Monmouthshire). Birnbeck Pier was officially opened on 6 June 1867, and during the first three months of operation, 120,000 people passed through the turnstiles; receipts during this period totalled £5,000. The designer was the renowned Victorian pier engineer Eugenius Birch (1818–84).

Birnbeck Pier consisted of a 317m-long (1,040ft) main structure between the mainland and Birnbeck Island, with originally a 12m-long (39ft) timber jetty resting on iron piles extending westwards. The jetty was dismantled in 1872 and replaced by another one, 76m (249ft) long, facing north. In 1882, a lifeboat was first stationed on the island, though a boathouse was not constructed for another eight years. The stone pavilion was built in 1884 and it contained a concert hall and refreshment rooms. It was destroyed by fire on 26 December 1897, but was replaced by a new building that opened for business in July 1898. A low-water landing stage was added in 1898, but in September 1903 both jetties were badly damaged. The north jetty (seen on the left of the island) was rebuilt in steel and extended to 91m (299ft) in length, but the low-water landing stage remained closed until 1910.

The large area and the stable footings provided by the presence of an island allowed substantial fairground rides to be erected by the early 20th century. Among the attractions were a water chute, a switchback railway, a shooting gallery, a helter-skelter, a merry-go-round, and a flying machine, its design being derived from the Sir Hiram Maxim's Captive Flying Machine of 1904 at Blackpool Pleasure Beach (*see* p 139). A large concrete platform was constructed to increase the area of the south side of the island, allowing the erection of the theatre, a bio-scope (cinema) and a roller-skating rink.

These entertainments and amusements helped the pier to achieve a profit of over £3,000 during the summer of 1913. It also benefitted from having a monopoly of steamer services landing passengers from around the Severn Estuary and especially from South Wales. The construction of the Grand Pier nearby at the beginning of the 20th century had threatened this monopoly, but difficulties with navigation and currents prevented steamers from mooring alongside this pier despite the building of a low-water jetty extension (*see* p 131).

During the Second World War, Birnbeck Pier became HMS *Birnbeck* and was used by the Admiralty's Department of Miscellaneous Weapon Development. By the 1960s, steamers and their successors along and across the Severn were in decline due to the opening of the Severn Bridge in 1966 and the relaxation of licensing laws in South Wales. The last steamer service arrived in 1979, fatally undermining the economic viability of the pier. The pier then went into a long period of decline and had to close to the public in 1994.

EAW025154

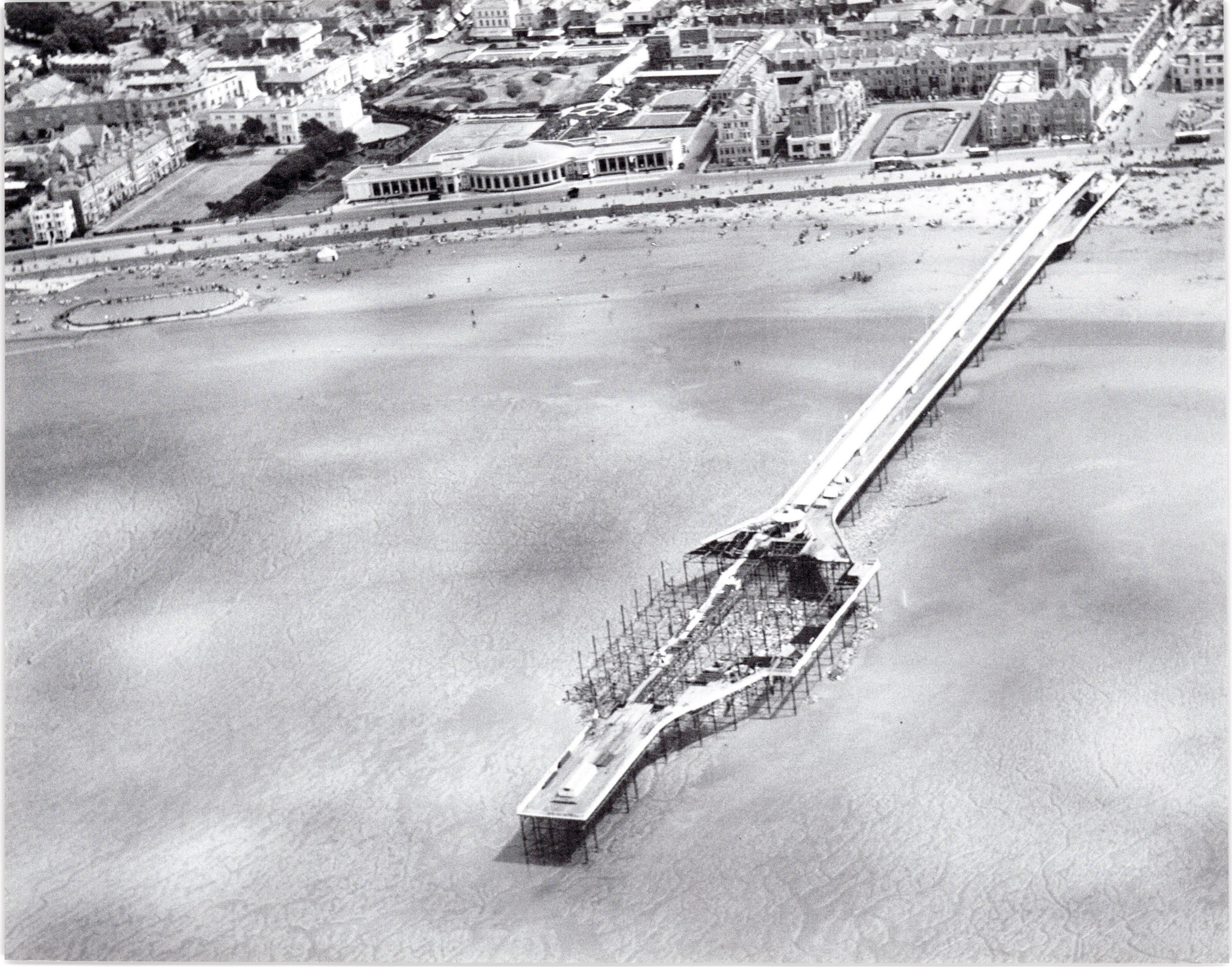

The Grand Pier, Weston-super-Mare, Somerset
July 1930

This topical photograph shows the Grand Pier at Weston a few months after a major fire had destroyed the pavilion at the end of the pier. As early as 1861, a proposal had been put forward to construct a pier at this site, effectively the closest point on the seafront to the railway station. This idea was revived in 1883, when the Weston-super-Mare Board of Health approved plans for a new promenade pier, over a mile in length, which would cost £70,000. This was to be part of the revamping of the whole seafront, including the provision of new sea defences.

In July 1884, an Act of Parliament received its royal assent, allowing the construction of the new pier, but despite enthusiastic local meetings, no work took place. During the 1890s, this idea was revived and another Act of Parliament received its royal assent in 1893, though again no work took place in its immediate aftermath. Work finally began on 7 November 1903 to designs produced by Peter Munroe, and by summer 1904 the contractors, Mayoh and Haley of London, had completed the pavilion and the first stage of the pier; these opened on 11 June 1904. The initial structure was 329m (1,079ft) long, but a narrow, low-water landing stage was added, taking the pier to a total length of 786m (2,579ft), less than half the anticipated length of the original design. Such length was necessary because of the wide tidal range at Weston-super-Mare, meaning that at low tide the sea is hundreds of metres from the beach. As a result, only three steamers ever attempted to use the pier, and once the approach channel had rapidly silted up, other pleasure steamer captains refused to call there.

Without income from steamers, the pier had to focus on raising revenue by entertaining visitors. A 1910 guidebook described how it was famous for its high-class instrumental music and entertainments. At the end of the pier there was a pavilion in which musical entertainments and vaudeville parties were staged for audiences of 2,000. A 1913 guidebook described how the pavilion's interior was tastefully decorated in white and gold, and had a blue-tinted panelled ceiling. There was also a bandstand in front of the pavilion and the pier also offered roller skating, confetti carnivals and many other seasonal attractions.

In January 1930, a fire destroyed the Grand Pier's pavilion, and construction of a new building began in the autumn of 1932. The pierhead was enlarged and strengthened to support the larger structure. The new pavilion opened during 1933 and a café and ballroom were added in 1935.

The relative remoteness from mainland Europe meant that the Grand Pier, like its neighbour Birnbeck Pier, was not breached during the Second World War, but it was guarded round the clock. While Birnbeck Pier's fortunes declined during the late 20th century, the Grand Pier proved to be more successful as it was more centrally located. On 28 July 2008, the 1930s pavilion caught fire and was destroyed, but a new pavilion was rapidly constructed, housing a range of attractions, rides and facilities; this opened on 23 October 2010.

EPW033286

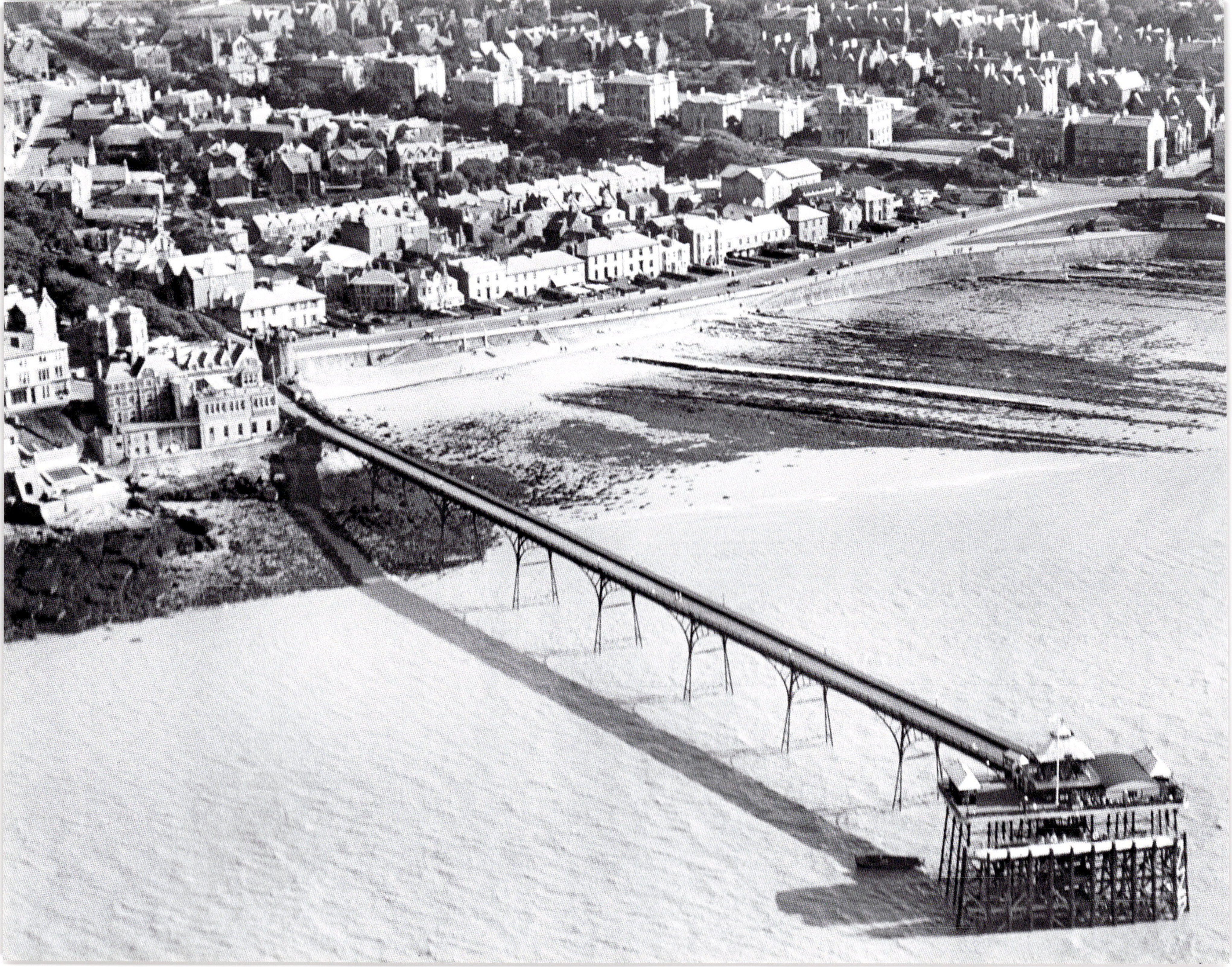

The pier, Clevedon, Somerset
September 1928

Today, most seaside piers are covered with kiosks, pavilions and entertainments, but in the mid-19th century their decks were still predominantly uncluttered, to maximise the number of passengers landing from steamers and to cater for people promenading on the pier. Two seaside piers still have largely clear decks, at Saltburn-by-the-Sea in North Yorkshire and at Clevedon, both piers, coincidently, opening in 1869.

The Clevedon Pier Company was established in 1867 and employed Richard Ward (1817–81) and John Grover (1836–92) as engineers. To cope with the wide tidal range in the Severn Estuary, the pier was built as an openwork wrought iron structure to offer as little resistance as possible to wind and water. The elegant, arched structure that they designed reputedly made use of discarded rails originally employed in the construction of the Great Western Railway. The pier, with its eight graceful spans of around 30m (98ft) in length, is in marked contrast to the standard piled-pier construction, and due to Clevedon Pier's elegant structure, it is a grade I listed building; the only other grade I listed pier is the West Pier at Brighton, now only a skeletal ruin.

The pier opened on 29 March 1869 and it remained largely unaltered until 1894, when a pavilion and shelters were built in a Japanese style. The pier suffered storm damage in 1899 and 1910, and a new cast iron landing stage was opened in 1913. In 1970 two of the spans collapsed into the sea, leading to the pier's closure and the threat of demolition. However, the local community acted energetically and the pier reopened. It still welcomes passengers using the last seagoing paddle steamer in the world, *Waverley*, while it travels down the Severn; in 2020 the ship was undergoing a major refit.

EPW024065

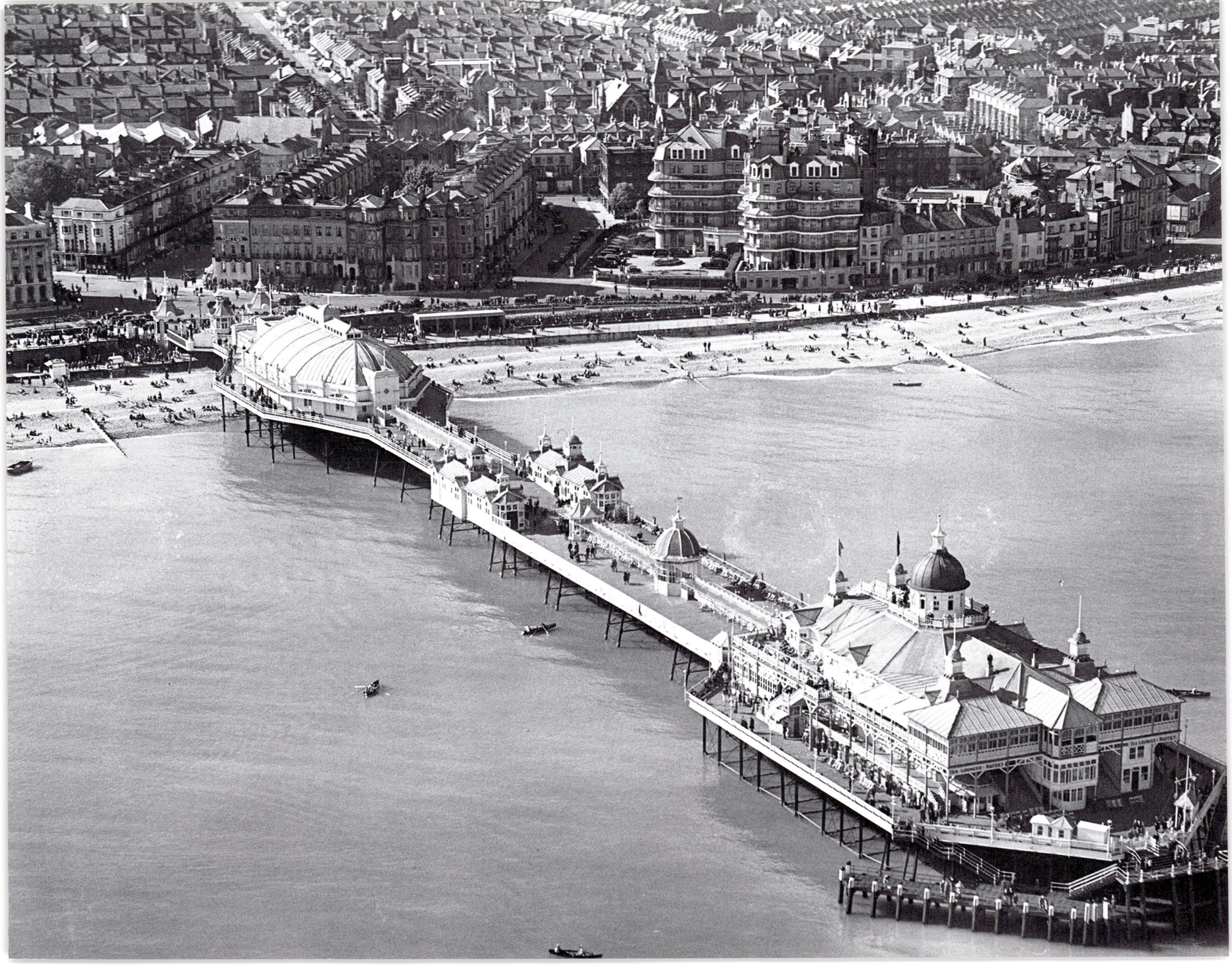

The pier, Eastbourne, East Sussex
25 May 1931

Margate's jetty, like other piers being built during the 1850 and 1860s, had a plain, uncluttered superstructure that maximised the area for promenaders and passengers disembarking from steamships. However, changes were already underway in the detailing of the seaside pier; at Blackpool, Eugenius Birch erected the town's first pier, which opened in 1863, and he included a series of kiosks on its deck. Three years later he completed Brighton's West Pier using a similar formula, but included the first hint of exotic forms inspired by the nearby Royal Pavilion. This oriental vocabulary would come to dominate the detailing of piers for several decades and culminate in the extravagance of Brighton's Palace Pier (1899) and the Grand Pier at Weston-super-Mare (1903–4). Birch had introduced, albeit tentatively, the kiosk and a hint of the exotic, and in 1872 at Hastings he constructed the first pier to be designed with an integral and large pierhead entertainment building.

All these innovations were incorporated into the pier at Eastbourne. The Eastbourne Pier Company Ltd was formed in 1865 and the first pile of the structure was driven on 18 April 1866. The pier, designed by Eugenius Birch, opened on 13 June 1870, though work was not finally completed until 1872. The first 400-seat theatre was constructed on the pierhead in 1888, but was replaced by a 1,000-seat theatre, bar, camera obscura and pier office complex in 1899–1901. A new landing stage was constructed in 1893 and two saloons were constructed halfway along the pier in 1901. In 1912, new entrance buildings were added and in 1925, a 900-seat music pavilion was constructed at the landward end. The theatre was destroyed by fire in January 1970; the large domed structure at the landward end of the pier was destroyed by fire in 2014.

This aerial photograph shows Eastbourne pier at the height of its interwar popularity. Visitors could enjoy a wealth of entertainments in buildings embellished with oriental-influenced detailing, particularly in the rooflines. The timber landing stages at the end of the pier have a handful of people on them, not waiting for a passing boat, but instead fishing.

EPW035324

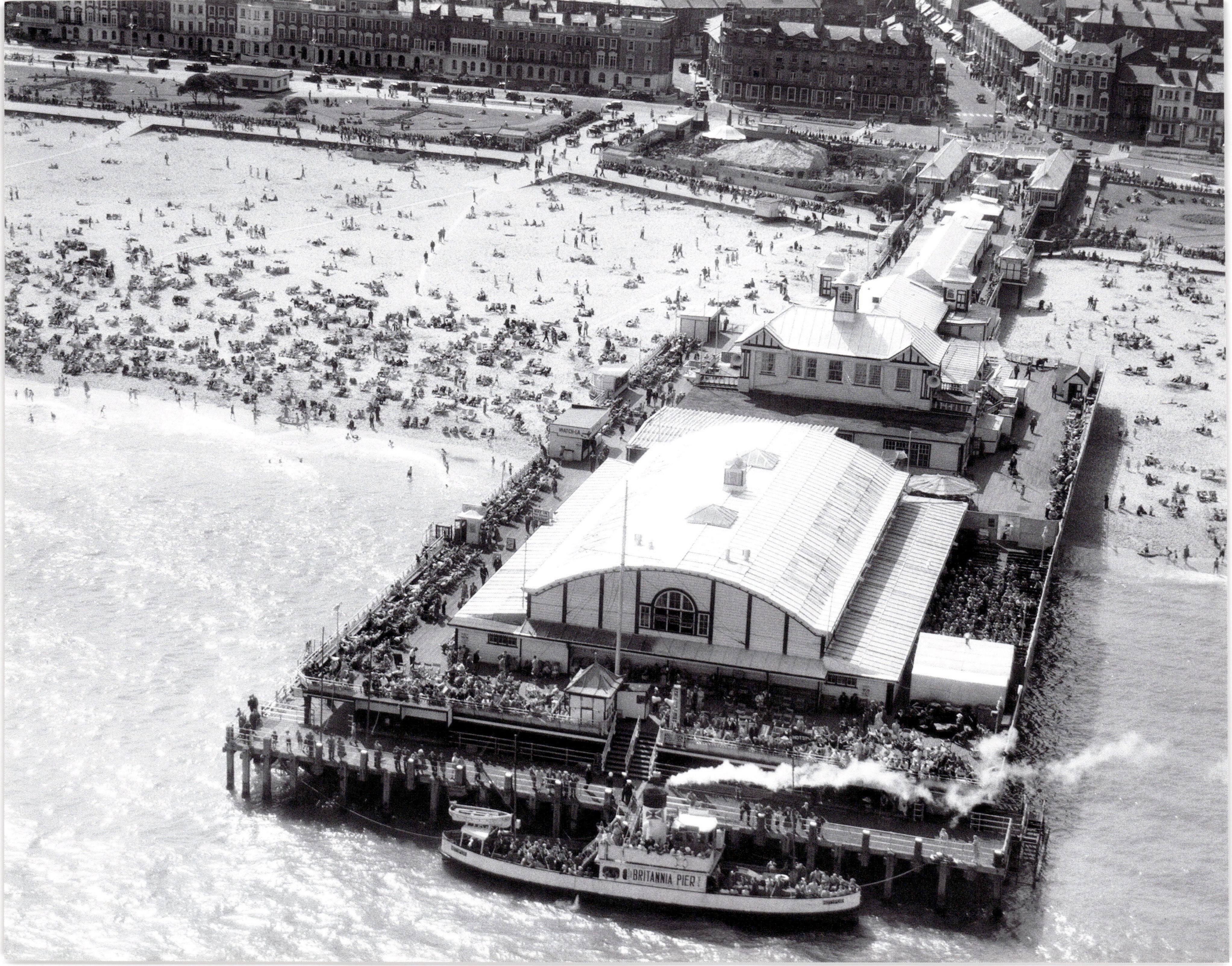
BRITANNIA PIER

Britannia Pier and the town, Great Yarmouth, Norfolk
31 July 1952

Britannia Pier was constructed on the site of a previous wooden pier; it had been designed by A W Morant and opened on 13 July 1858. That pier was demolished and its replacement, shown in this photograph, was officially opened in June 1902. It was designed by James and Arthur Mayoh and built by Boulton & Paul of Norwich, who employed 104 steel screw piles to support the deck. The original domed and turreted Grand Pavilion, costing £1,500, opened on 21 June 1902 and burned down on 22 December 1909; its replacement, which opened during the following July, met a similar fate in April 1914. This was allegedly the result of an action by the suffragettes who had been refused permission to hold a meeting in it. A Floral Hall, which opened in 1928, succumbed to a blaze in 1932. The structure shown in this photograph of 1952 was a combined ballroom and theatre; on Easter Monday 1954 it too caught fire and the present theatre opened on 27 June 1958.

At the end of the pier can be seen a small pleasure boat, to provide a trip out to sea rather than for bringing tourists to the resort. As this photograph was taken at the end of July in 1952, it is no surprise that the deck of the boat, the pier and the beach are all crowded with holidaymakers.

EAW045607

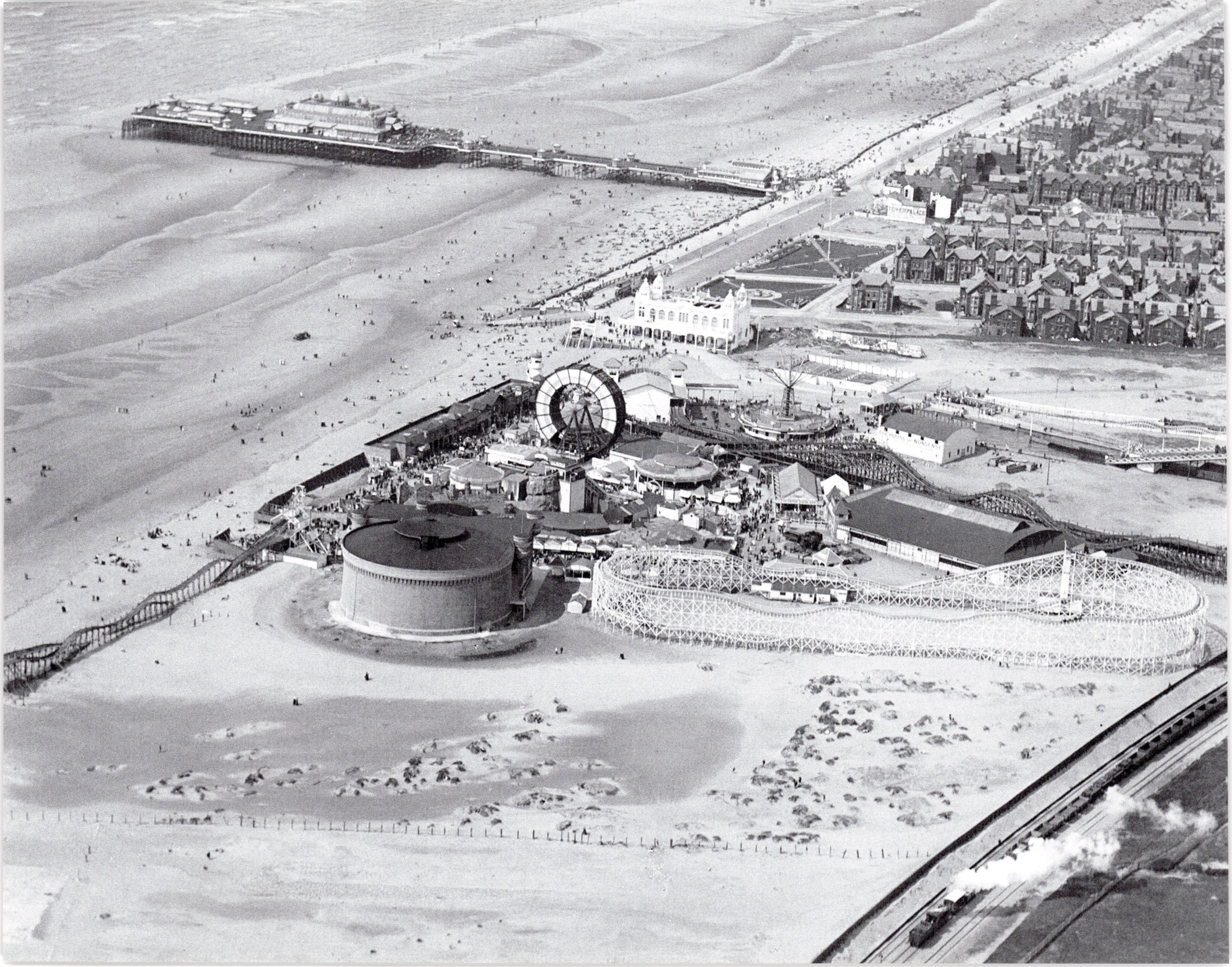

The Pleasure Beach and Victoria Pier, Blackpool, Lancashire
July 1920

New technology developed for manufacturing would in due course give seaside resorts roller coasters and other fairground rides. Britain's first enclosed seaside amusement park evolved from the mid-1890s on a stretch of Blackpool's shoreline south of the Victoria Pier. The men behind the creation of Blackpool's Pleasure Beach were William George Bean (1868–1929), a Londoner who had become involved with the emerging American amusement business in Philadelphia, and John William Outhwaite (*c* 1855–1911) from Shipley (Yorkshire) who had family connections to the American amusement industry. However, the original partnership that sub-leased 20 acres of the Watson's Estate in 1897 was between Outhwaite and Albert Ellis, a phrenologist, fortune teller and occultist who was already well established on the Golden Mile. They leased out plots of land on which rides and stalls were created as concessions. By 1898, Bean had become involved with Outhwaite and they were renting out sites and operating their own rides. In 1903 they bought 30 acres of the Watson's Estate, and the title of 'The Pleasure Beach' first appeared on advertisements in 1905, indicating that the process of consolidating their ownership of the plots and rides was under way.

In 1906, over 3 million people visited the Pleasure Beach. Here they could enjoy Sir Hiram Maxim's Captive Flying Machine, the River Caves, the Hotchkiss Bicycle Railway and a switchback, as well as a range of other attractions, sideshows, a restaurant and a tea house. In this photograph, Sir Hiram Maxim's Captive Flying Machine can be seen in the centre to the right of the white Casino building. Today it is the oldest ride in continuous use in Europe; it first operated on 1 August 1904 at Blackpool and actually predates the foundation of the Pleasure Beach. Sir Hiram Stevens Maxim (1840–1916) was an engineer and the inventor of the Maxim machine gun. He was also experimenting with primitive flying machines, and in 1902 he devised this ride, which was first shown at the Earls Court exhibition in 1903 and was rebuilt at Blackpool. It consists of ten steel arms, from which gondolas hung from cables, spinning outwards as the central shaft of the ride rotated. The River Caves, a ride using ten-seater boats travelling around a cave past a series of tableaux, opened in 1905 and is also still operating today.

The prominent white building in the photograph is the 1913 Casino, designed by the local architect R B Mather. It contained a billiard hall, the park's first cinema, a grill room, restaurant and shop behind a white ferro-concrete façade decorated with white electric lights. It was demolished in the late 1930s to allow the construction of a new casino.

The most monumental structure on the Pleasure Beach was the cylindrical 'spectatorium' for the Monitor and Merrimac battle show, which recreated a naval engagement that occurred during the American Civil War. In 1914 it was adapted to present a review of the British fleet. To the right can be seen the wooden Velvet Coaster, built by William H Strickler; this ride was named after its velvet seating. It remained in use until 1932 when it was dismantled, though elements of it were incorporated into the Roller Coaster of 1933.

At the top of the image can be seen the Victoria Pier, now known as South Pier. It opened on 31 March 1893 and was designed by T P Worthington of Leeds. It featured a large theatre/music hall, and a pavilion housing 900 people adorned the entrance to the pier from 1911 and featured cinematograph performances. It was demolished in 1937 and replaced by the 1,300-seat Regal Theatre.

EPW002058

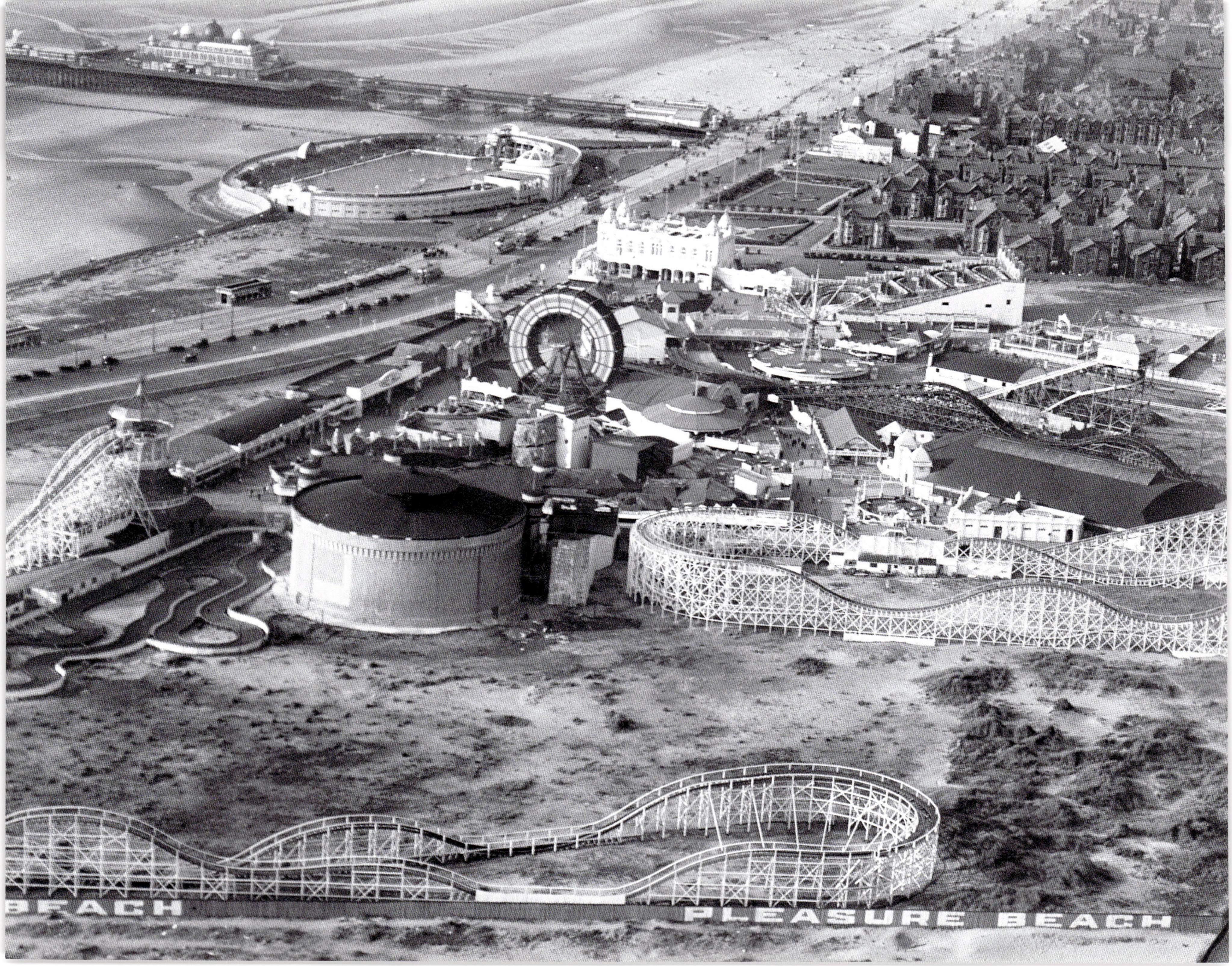

BEACH
PLEASURE BEACH

Blackpool Pleasure Beach, Blackpool, Lancashire
12 September 1929

This photograph, taken nine years after the one on p 139, shows a number of rides had been added to the Pleasure Beach. The Virginia Reel, behind the rotating arms of Sir Hiram Maxim's Captive Flying Machine, was added in 1922. It spun its passengers around as it twisted down a winding track through colourful scenery.

The largest new ride was the wooden Big Dipper, seen here at the bottom of the photograph. This type of new roller coaster, which first appeared in New Jersey in 1920, was designed by the leading roller coaster engineer of the day, John A Miller, and it was added to the Pleasure Beach in 1923 by William H Strickler. It was the first ride in Britain to use Miller's under-friction system in which wheels beneath the track held the car onto the ride. The rights to this technology had wisely been bought by William Bean, one of the founders of the Pleasure Beach. Despite all the new rides that were being added, there was still plenty of space for further attractions within the site, and the process of adding new rides continued during the 1930s and after the Second World War. This photograph of 1929 was taken just before the Pleasure Beach began the process of theming its rides and buildings in a modern, Art Deco style.

Between the Pleasure Beach and Blackpool's South Pier can be seen the Open Air Swimming Baths that opened on 9 June 1923, reputedly the largest such facility in the world (*see* p 79).

EPW029208

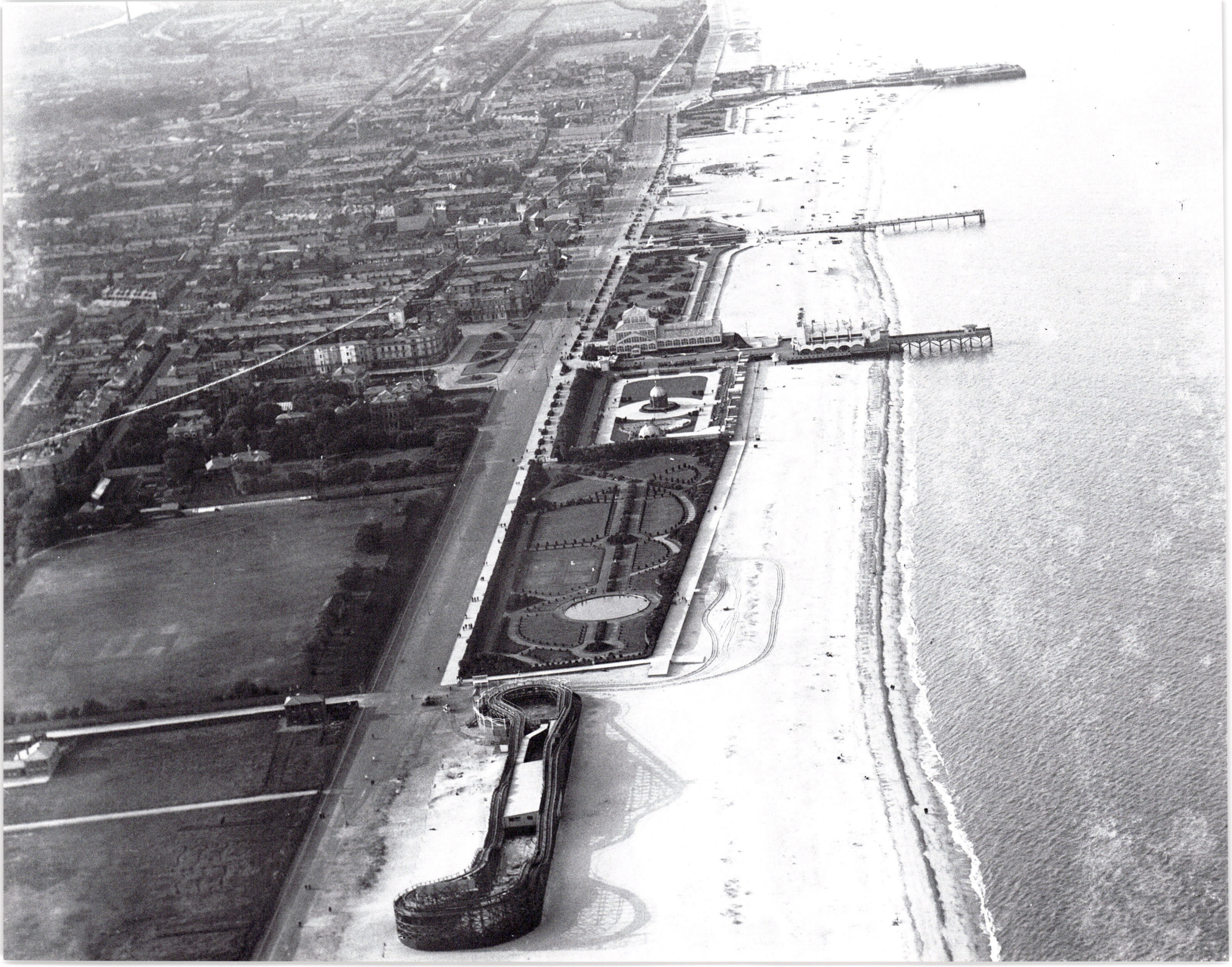

Britannia and Wellington Piers and Nelson Gardens, Great Yarmouth, Norfolk
June 1920

This photograph of the seafront at Great Yarmouth shows the resort's two piers with the jetty in between, and at the south end of the beach can be seen the Scenic Railway, which was in the process of being constructed.

The first amusement ride at Great Yarmouth was an L A Thompson Switchback Railway, erected at the northern end of the seafront in 1887. It remained there until the early 20th century, when it was relocated to Honley Pleasure Beach in Huddersfield. Instead, in 1909, the Pleasure Beach was established at the south end of the seafront and it included a wooden Scenic Railway set within a plaster mountainous terrain. It was destroyed by fire in 1919, but rebuilt quickly. This Aerofilms photograph of 1920 shows the scenic railway devoid of any scenery and standing alone on the sand, presumably awaiting other rides to be constructed around it. In 1928, the lease of the Scenic Railway ended and the ride was transferred to Aberdeen. A new wooden Scenic Railway was purchased from Paris and opened in 1932. Like its predecessor, an alpine landscape entertained the riders, who also enjoyed castles on the circuit. It is now a grade II listed building.

At the top of the image is the second Britannia Pier (*see* p 137). The southernmost of the piers is the Wellington Pier. The earlier of Great Yarmouth's two piers, it was designed by Peter Ashcroft and opened on 21 October 1853. Although the pier was named after the Iron Duke, its structure was actually timber. By the early 20th century, facing stiff competition from the Britannia Pier to the north, the Wellington Pier went bankrupt and was taken over by the local authority. Following a major investment, it reopened on 13 July 1903, with a pavilion for use by music hall artists. At the same time as the pier was being reconstructed, a substantial glazed Winter Gardens was erected beside the pier, having been transported from Torquay to become the home of the Wellington Pier Orchestra.

In addition to the two piers, in between was the jetty, which was in existence by the 18th century. It was used by fishermen, but was also a popular place for early holidaymakers to promenade.

EPW001875

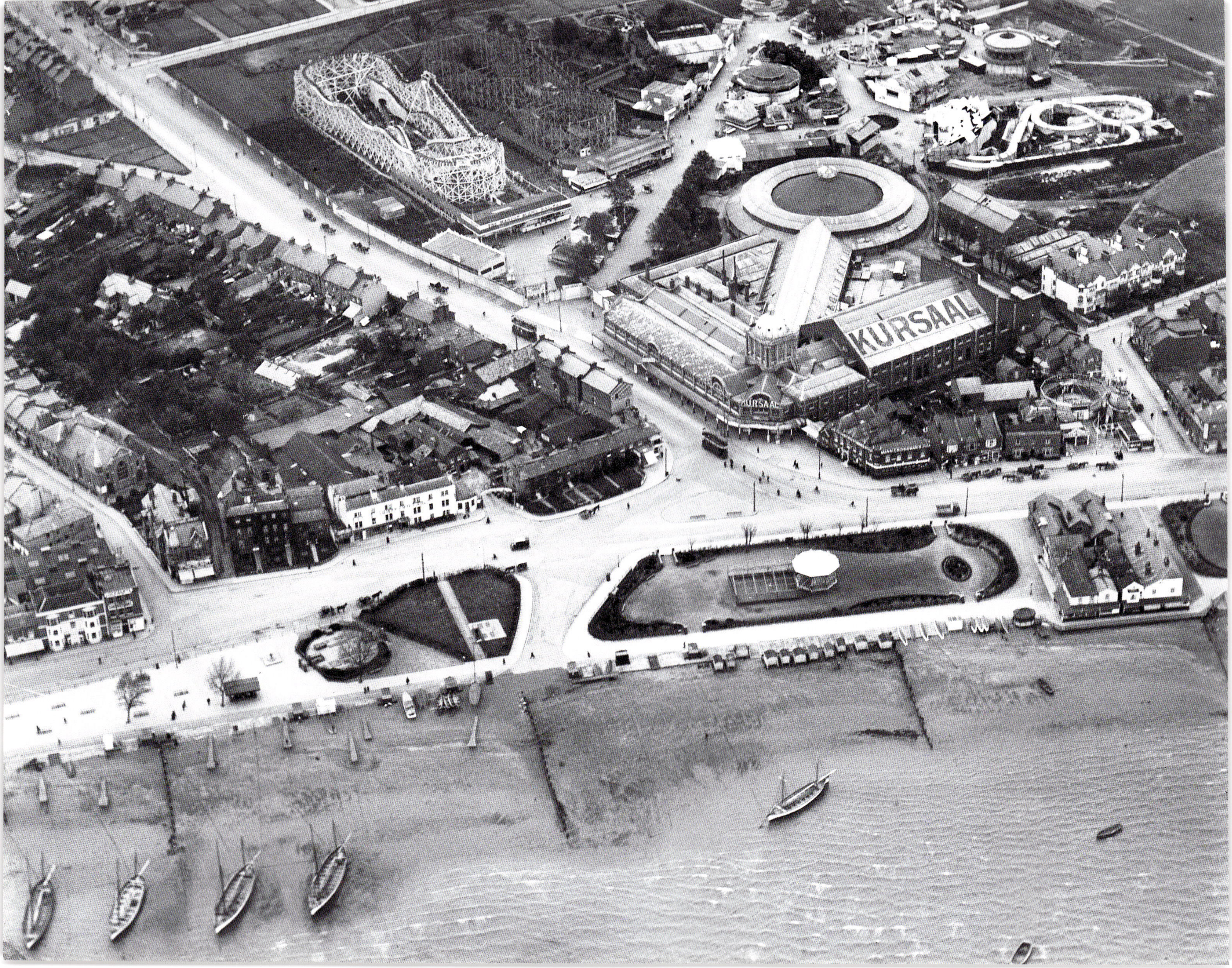
KURSAAL
KURSAAL

The Kursaal, Southend-on-Sea, Essex
April 1920

Blackpool Pleasure Beach served as an inspiration and a model for other seaside amusement parks. The Kursaal at Southend evolved from the pleasure grounds at Marine Park that had opened in 1894. After some financial difficulties, including a change of ownership, the Kursaal opened in July 1901, with enlarged gardens, amusements, a cycle track, a café, a menagerie and circus. The public face of the Kursaal was a large, red-brick structure with ashlar detailing and it was dominated by the tall, Wrennaissance-style dome, which can be seen in the centre of the photograph. There was a plan to erect a 530ft-high (162m) tower, which would have been taller than Blackpool Tower, but this was never built.

Faced with continuing financial difficulties, the site changed ownership in 1910 and became Luna Park, a dedicated amusement park with the Harton Scenic Railway and a Figure of Eight roller coaster, a miniature railway, Astley's Circus and a cinema. Despite new attractions, the financial problems continued, and a fire destroyed two profitable rides in 1911. In 1912, the site again exchanged hands and returned to its original name. Its new owner, Clifton Jay Morehouse, visited American amusement parks and by 1914 he had imported a number of large rides and shows. He died suddenly in 1920, and while his son David de Forest Morehouse kept the Kursaal afloat, he failed to push forward its development as others did for Blackpool's Pleasure Beach and Margate's Dreamland. Realising that the Kursaal was losing ground, de Forest Morehouse began in the 1930s to acquire more rides, including seven in 1933 alone. He died in 1934 and the trustees who managed the site arranged to extend the grounds and acquired three new, major rides. In 1936, Charles Paige's Cyclone arrived from the Brussels Exhibition of the previous year, though as it was owned and operated by Blackpool Pleasure Beach, little of the profits went to the Kursaal.

This photograph shows the site in 1920, when there were two wooden Scenic Railway roller coasters on the site, a Sir Hiram Maxim's Captive Flying Machine as seen at Blackpool Pleasure Beach (just above the top of the photograph), and a variety of smaller rides. At the east end of the park, to the right of the photograph, the full-size football pitch was still part of the site, though this disappeared during the 1930s to allow the construction of another roller coaster.

EPW000443

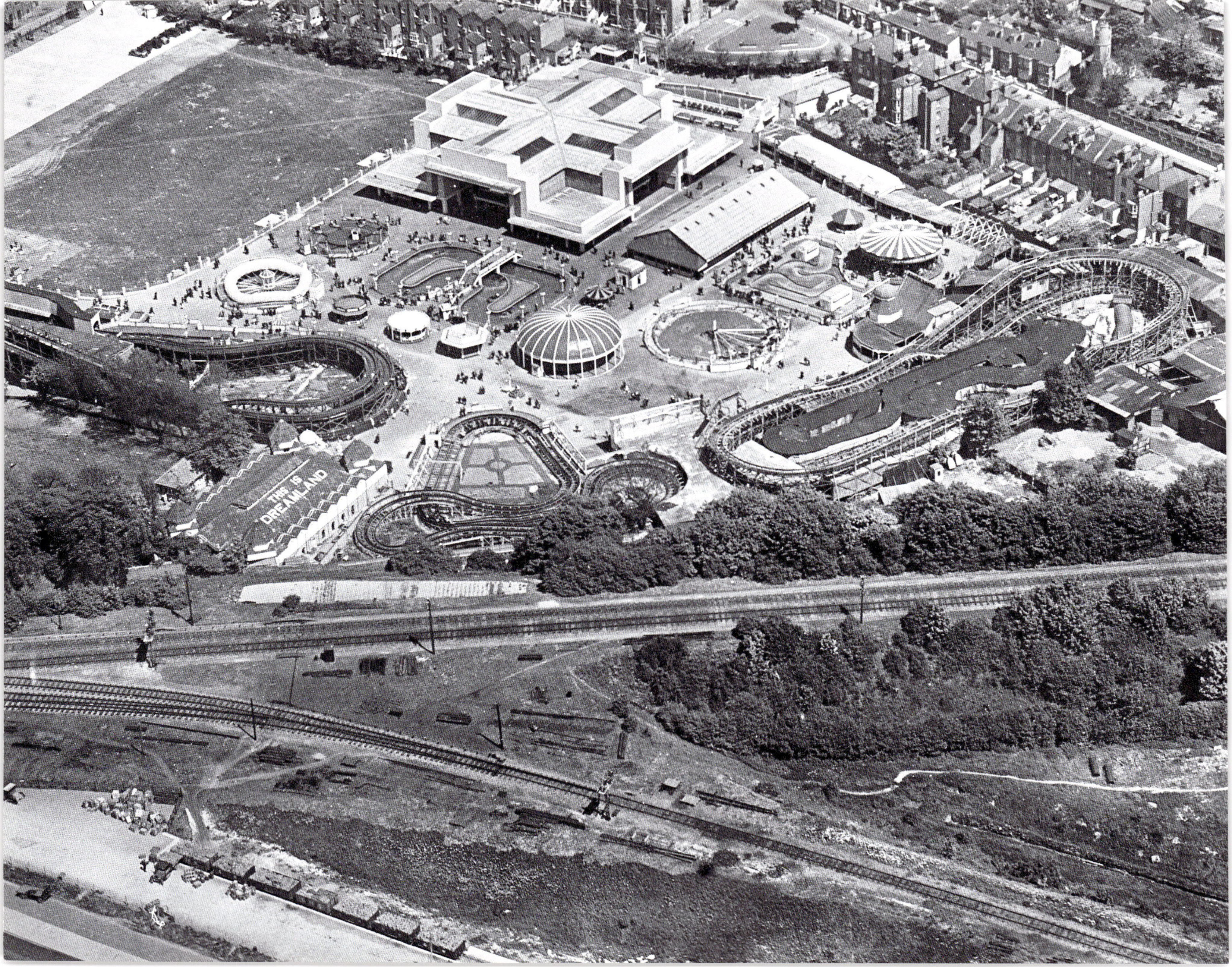
THIS IS
DREAMLAND

Dreamland Amusement Park, Margate, Kent
May 1931

Dreamland Amusement Park, which opened in 1920, was established on a large site behind a line of seafront buildings, Marine Terrace, which was built in the 1820s and 1830s. This land was left undeveloped until the mid-19th century as it was still too marshy for substantial development, but by 1867 the railway caterers Spiers and Pond opened an unused railway station booking hall as the Hall-by-the-Sea entertainment complex. It was then sold to Thomas Dalby Reeve, mayor of Margate, who also acquired land to the rear. Reeve's son Arthur married the daughter of the self-appointed 'Lord' George Sanger, a renowned showman, and in February 1874 he took over the Hall-by-the-Sea and converted it into a restaurant and ballroom. During the following years, he developed the land to include ornamental pleasure gardens, a small lake, a 'ruined abbey' folly, and a roller-skating rink. Sanger was the owner of the largest circus of English origin and he also used the site between the seafront and the railway line as his headquarters and as a place to lodge his animals when he was not travelling.

At the end of November 1919 the site was sold, and on Boxing Day 1919 the Hall-by-the-Sea reopened as the Palais de Danse, though it closed after two months. The site was soon renamed Dreamland and opened again in April 1920 with an amusement park and cinema. The name was chosen to reflect the glamour of Coney Island, the home of the world's leading amusement parks and fairground rides, including from 1904 to 1911 a park known as Dreamland.

Among the rides in the original park was reputedly 'THE LARGEST SCENIC RAILWAY IN EUROPE', which opened on 3 July 1920. This can be seen on the left-hand side of the photograph, and a rebuilt version survives today as part of the modern amusement park on the same site. During the course of the 1920s, various other rides were added, so that by 1931 the site was full of attractions (*see* p 87).

EPW035464

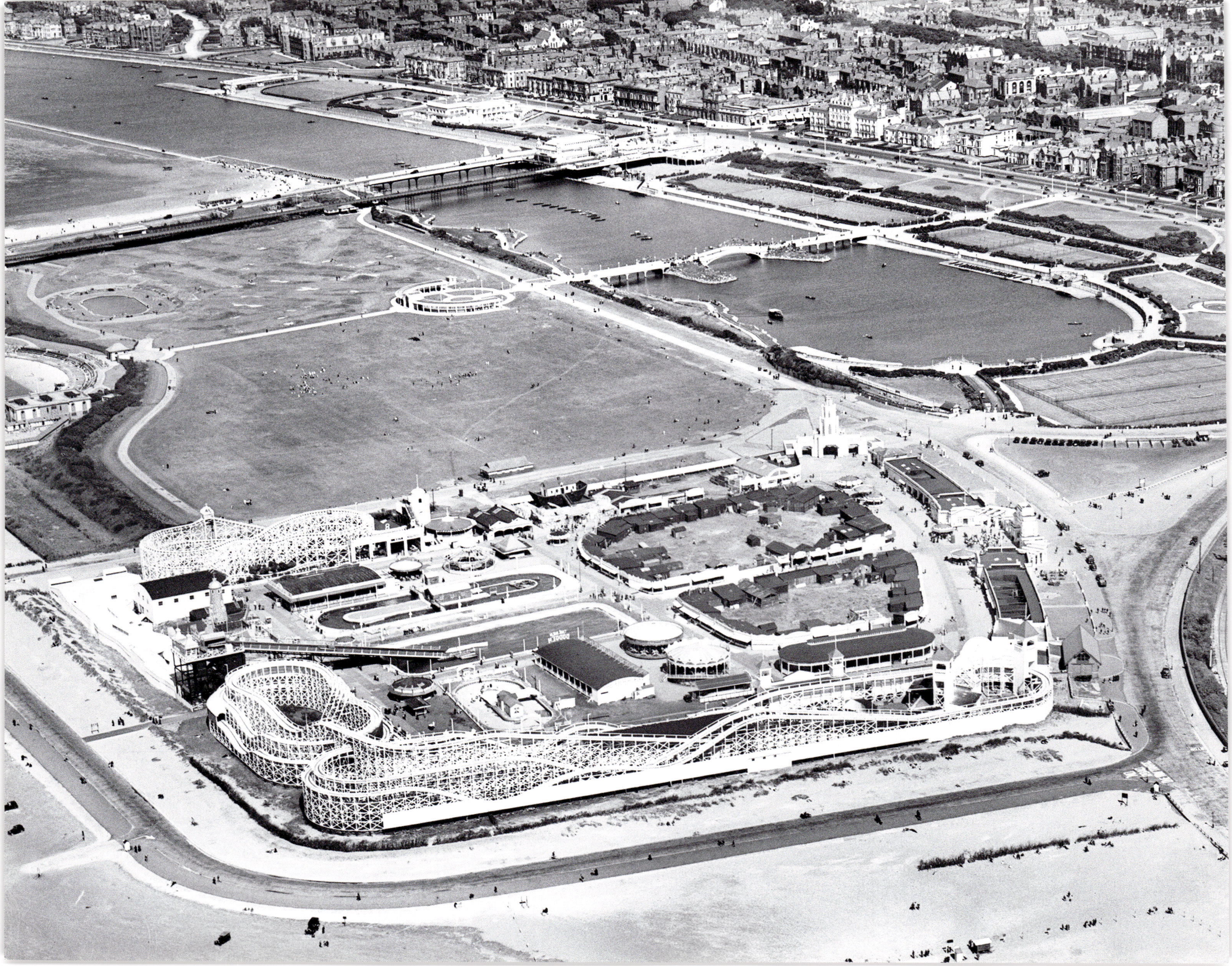

Pleasureland and Princes Park, Southport, Merseyside
July 1934

This photograph shows Pleasureland, located on the seafront at Southport. It was one of the first generation of amusement parks, all of which were influenced by Blackpool Pleasure Beach. The first Pleasureland operated from 1913 and had many rides in common with the nearby Pleasure Beach at Blackpool. As at Blackpool, some of the rides predated the foundation of the park, but in this instance, they were moved to the location in the photograph from a nearby site.

A water chute shown in the middle-left of the photograph beside the seafront was first constructed in 1903, followed a year later by a Sir Hiram Maxim's Captive Flying Machine. This can be seen in another Aerofilms photograph of 1928, but had been removed by 1934. The Southport site also had a River Caves, located between the water chute and the helter-skelter; the ride consisted of a number of boats passing through a series of caverns with tableaux lit by electric lights. The Southport ride had been at the White City at Southport since 1908 and was relocated to the new park in 1922. This type of fairly sedate ride has remained popular in some parks, as Disney's 'It's a Small World' demonstrates. A Noah's Ark can also be seen along the top edge of the site. The same type of attraction was constructed at Blackpool Pleasure Beach by William H Strickler in 1922, allowing visitors to take a trip in a boat to Mount Ararat, walking past animals on moving platforms with a rocking motion to simulate the sea voyage. Strickler also oversaw the construction of Noah's Arks at Morecambe and here at Southport in 1930.

The photograph also shows the wooden Scenic Railway erected in the mid-1920s at the bottom of the site, which survived until the 1940s, and the wooden Figure of Eight roller coaster at the top-left of the park. It was first built in 1908 on the nearby short-lived fairground site and was replaced in 1937 by the much larger Cyclone. At the top of the photograph can be seen the landward end of Southport's pier, the second longest in Britain.

EPW045243

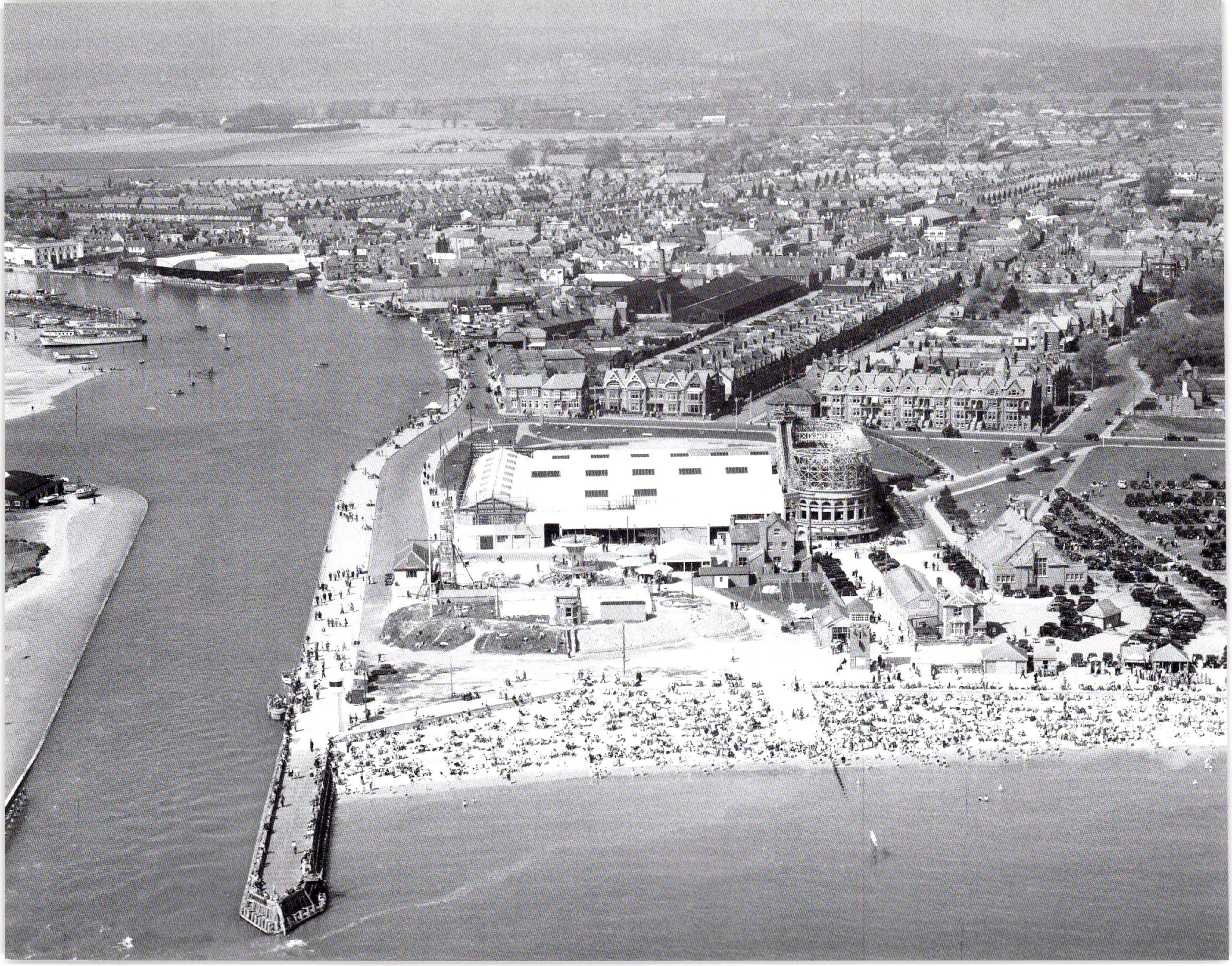

East Pier, Butlin's Park (Harbour Park) and the seafront, Littlehampton, West Sussex

17 April 1949

Billy Butlin is most famous for his holiday camps, the first of which opened near Skegness in 1936. However, before this he had a career in providing entertainment and amusements, an activity that he continued alongside his new business. William 'Billy' Heygate Edmund Colborne Butlin was born in Cape Town on 29 September 1899. His grandfather was a showman travelling around the fairs in Gloucestershire and Somerset, and his four sons all became showmen. As a young man, Billy travelled with his mother around West Country fairs before emigrating to Canada just before the First World War. He served in the Canadian Army during the war, including being stationed near Folkestone before returning to Canada in 1919.

He returned to England to join his relations working in fairgrounds and he became a travelling showman. In 1922 he employed his first assistant and they dressed in white coats with 'B' on the breast pocket and painted their stalls in red and white, marking the start of the Butlin image. He established a number of stalls and amusements at various fairs, winter fairs and seaside resorts, and in 1927 he opened a permanent amusement site in Skegness, which proved to be highly profitable. In May 1928, he obtained the first Dodgem Cars in Britain and subsequently bought the rights to sell them in Europe. He established other seaside amusement parks in England at Mablethorpe (opened 1928), Bognor Regis (1930), Hayling Island (1931), Felixstowe (1931), Southsea (1931) and at Littlehampton (1932). By 1935 most of his sites had an attached zoo and he also continued to operate fairs during the winter at Olympia, Glasgow and Edinburgh.

The Butlin's Park at Littlehampton, also known as Harbour Park, is located at the mouth of the River Arun, and was originally located behind a row of houses that were themselves set just behind the seafront. An earlier Aerofilms photograph of 1933 shows the smaller park behind the row of houses and in front of the circular pond. By 1947, these houses had been demolished and the area in front of the original park had been landscaped to accommodate other rides. The large building occupying the centre of the site, which seems to be in the process of construction, represents a consolidation of a number of smaller buildings and rides that previously existed in this part of the park. The large roller coaster to the right is the Big Dipper, which was constructed when the park opened. Harbour Park is still open today and is joined on the seafront at Littlehampton by reputedly one of the longest benches in the world and an iconic café designed by Thomas Heatherwick.

EAW022239

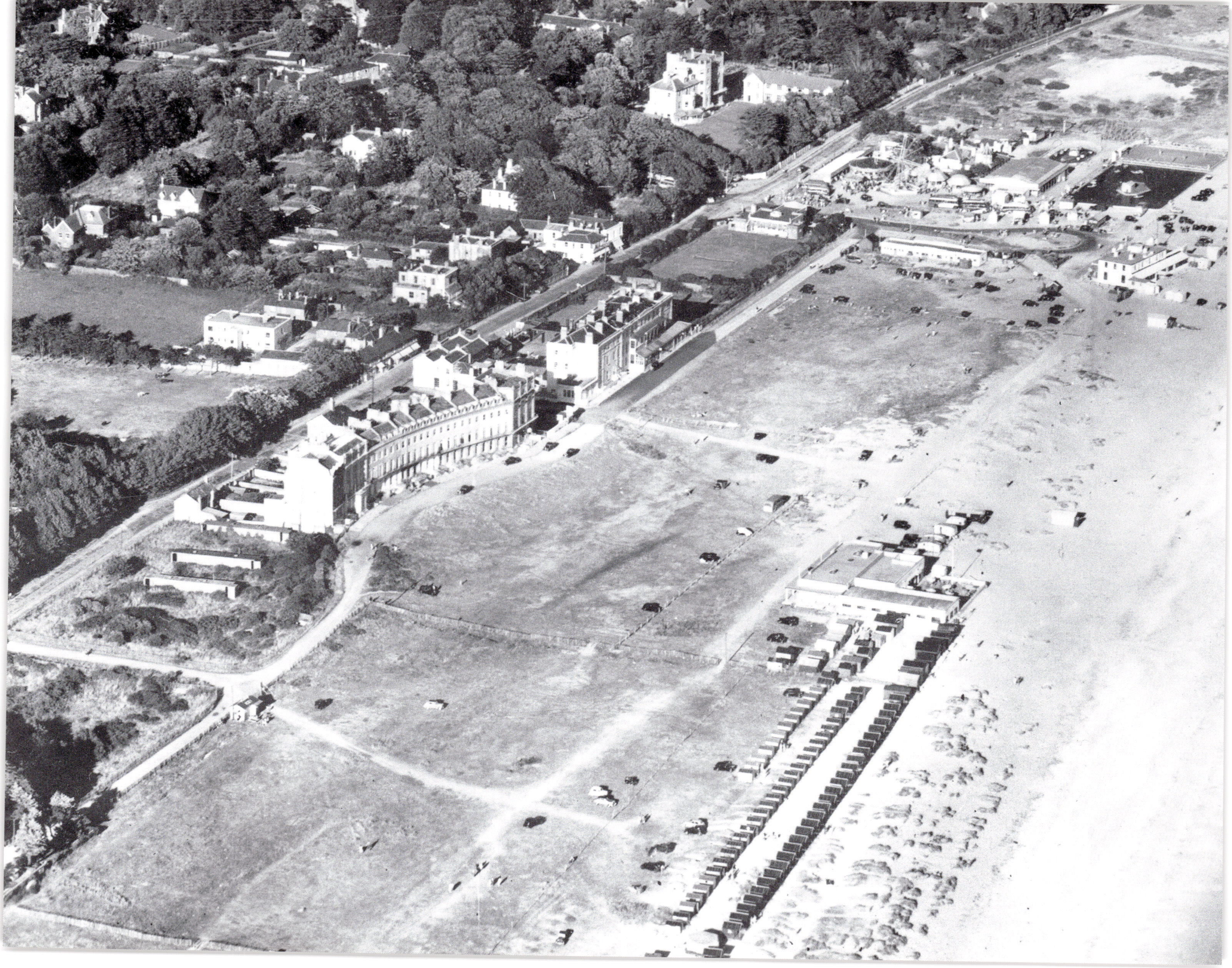

The beach by Norfolk Crescent, Hayling Island, Hampshire
10 August 1951

Until the early 19th century, Hayling island was effectively inaccessible for holidaymakers. However, the construction of a bridge in 1822–4 to link the island to the mainland appears to have been the immediate reason for the development of the previously remote island. Inspired by the emerging Kemp Town and Brunswick Town at Brighton and St Leonards beside Hastings, a plan was hatched to create a grandiose housing development, similar to these schemes, in what had hitherto been a natural wilderness.

The Duke of Norfolk, Sir George Thomas Staunton and William Padwick the younger were the three largest shareholders in the company that built the bridge, but once the bridge opened, the duke washed his hands of the island, apparently fearing that it would blossom into a watering place like Brighton. Padwick was the main force behind the immediate development as he had bought the land from the duke in 1825. Plans for villas were prepared by Robert Abraham of Torrington Street, Russell Square, London, and the foundation stone of the crescent was laid on 3 September 1825. A new hotel was also built beside the crescent, its foundation stone having been laid on 16 December 1825. In addition to accommodation, the fledgling resort offered visitors a library, a bathhouse and gardens. The library was a small temple-like building with a Grecian Doric portico located at the centre of what an 1843 guidebook described as 'a well-made esplanade three hundred yards in length, and which at one end is terminated by the Bath-house'. The Royal Hotel contained a billiard room, another essential for an early resort, but there is no evidence of a theatre.

Despite these grand plans, only a small part of the Crescent was built initially and as this photograph of 1951 shows, just over half of the Crescent had been built by this date. The remainder was constructed in the following years, but as a series of modern flats. The esplanade, including the baths and library, has gone, but the furze that once separated the hotel and crescent from the sea now dominates the shoreline. Today, apart from some car parking, a fun fair and a nearby golf course, the shoreline has recaptured something of its natural form.

EAW038551

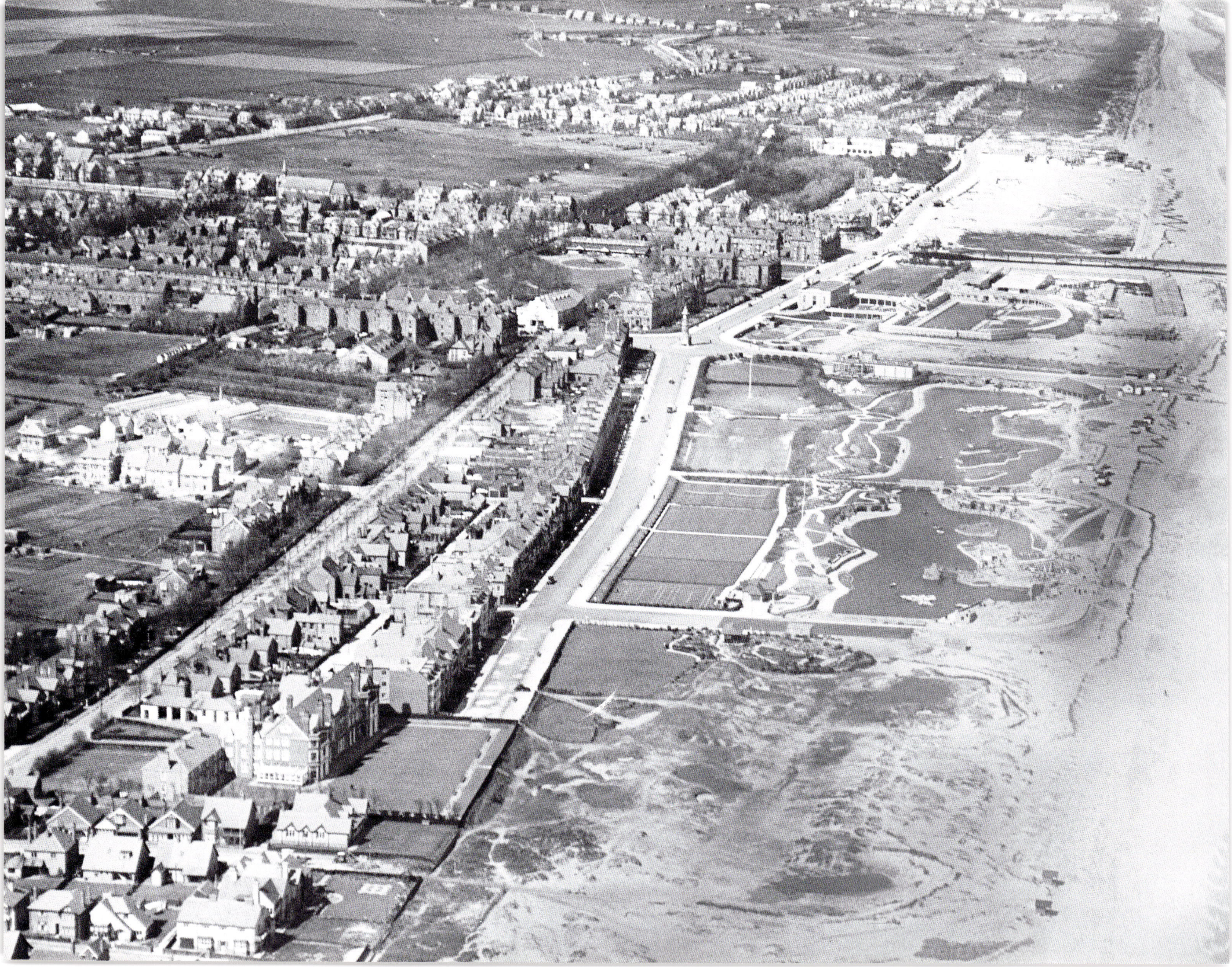

South Parade and environs, Skegness, Lincolnshire
7 May 1930

Although there is pressure to develop the seafront of seaside resorts as it is the most desirable location for lucrative accommodation and entertainment, some English resorts still retain something of their natural form at their peripheries. This may be because the numbers of holidaymakers being entertained means that these parts of the resort have not had to be exploited and because this land is less suitable for building development.

Although sand dunes may be seen by some developers as missed opportunities, or a potential future site for development, they can play an important part in preventing the sea from engulfing the towns behind. If properly looked after, sand dunes can absorb up to 90% of wave energy. Examples of dunes at resorts include an area to the south of the pier at St Annes and on St Mary's in the Isles of Scilly, where the dunes at Porthloo have recently been heightened to protect homes, businesses and the island's boatyard.

At the southern end of Skegness, seen here at the bottom of this photograph, the natural sand dunes can be seen, but further to the north, on either side of the pier, are the seafront Esplanade Gardens. These were designed by Skegness Urban District Council engineer, surveyor and architect Rowland Jenkins (in office 1912–1952) and date from 1922 onwards. Constructed within the former sand dunes, they incorporate waterways crossed by bridges, sunken formal gardens, pavilions, bowling greens and mock castles. Jenkins was sometimes apparently inspired by things that he had seen on his walking holidays on the Continent. An example of this is the walk alongside the south boating lake, formerly known as the Axenstrasse, which featured ferro-concrete simulated rocks, fences, arches, pathways, shelters, bridges and a castle ruin designed to evoke the St Gothard area of the Swiss Alps. By 1930, only the southern half of the gardens had been developed, with the northern half beyond the pier to follow soon after this photograph was taken. These two sections would be linked by a canal running beneath the pier.

Forming something of a contrast with the elegant gardens would have been Billy Butlin's first amusement park, which was located on the seafront beside the pier. In 1927 he opened an amusement arcade at Skegness and two years later followed this up with the large amusement park on the south side of the pier at Skegness.

EPW031866

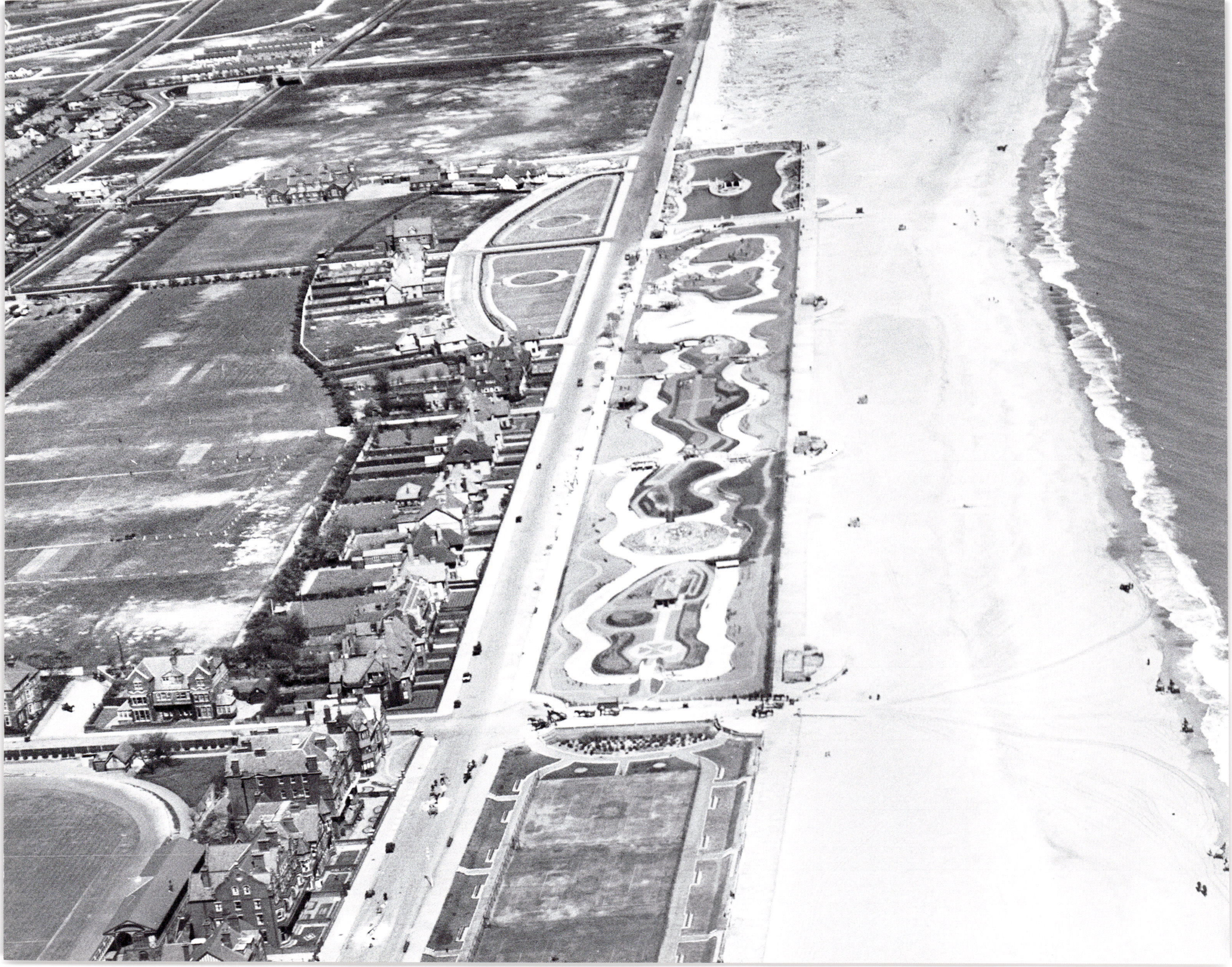

North Beach, Great Yarmouth, Norfolk
May 1928

During the 1920s, Great Yarmouth Borough Council began work to construct a major new sea wall running along the length of the seafront. In due course the resulting reclaimed land was developed as public pleasure gardens, including features such as a bowling green, yachting ponds and tennis courts. In 1926, a scheme for a boating lake, designed by the borough engineer S P Thompson, was constructed and opened on the northern end of the promenade, within part of the North Denes dune area. This roughly 1ha (2.5-acre) lake can be seen at the top of the photograph.

Following this work, Councillor Docwra's proposal for the addition of Venetian-style water gardens was adopted by the council. The gardens were again designed by S P Thompson and the Venetian Waterways were constructed between January and June 1928 as part of a programme of relief work for the unemployed. It is thought that the channels were all dug out by hand, using shovels and wheelbarrows, and 6,639 tons of soil were brought in from nearby Caister to replace the sand. The scheme contained winding rivers for gondolas, paths through rock gardens leading to picturesque bridges over the water, and several thatched shelters.

The Venetian Waterways were opened to the public on 2 August 1928 and cover around 3.3ha (8.2 acres). This Aerofilms photograph was taken during the construction work, hence the rather pale colour of the grounds around the waterways and the incomplete appearance of the gardens.

The Venetian Waterways became a great attraction and were developed to include illuminations, amplified music and a model of HMS *Nelson* in the central pool. The replacement of salt water with fresh water facilitated the creation of a skating rink during the winter. In recent years, the waterways began to look increasingly shabby and uninviting. However, in August 2019, they reopened after a major campaign of repair and restoration.

To the south of the gardens can be seen some of the tennis courts, and inland is the local stadium, which is still in this location. What is absent from this photograph is the scenic railway, which once dominated this part of the seafront. It was erected there in 1887, but the council required it to be removed in 1910. Instead, another scenic railway was erected to the south of the town and this became the location for Great Yarmouth's Pleasure Beach (*see* p 143).

EPW021190

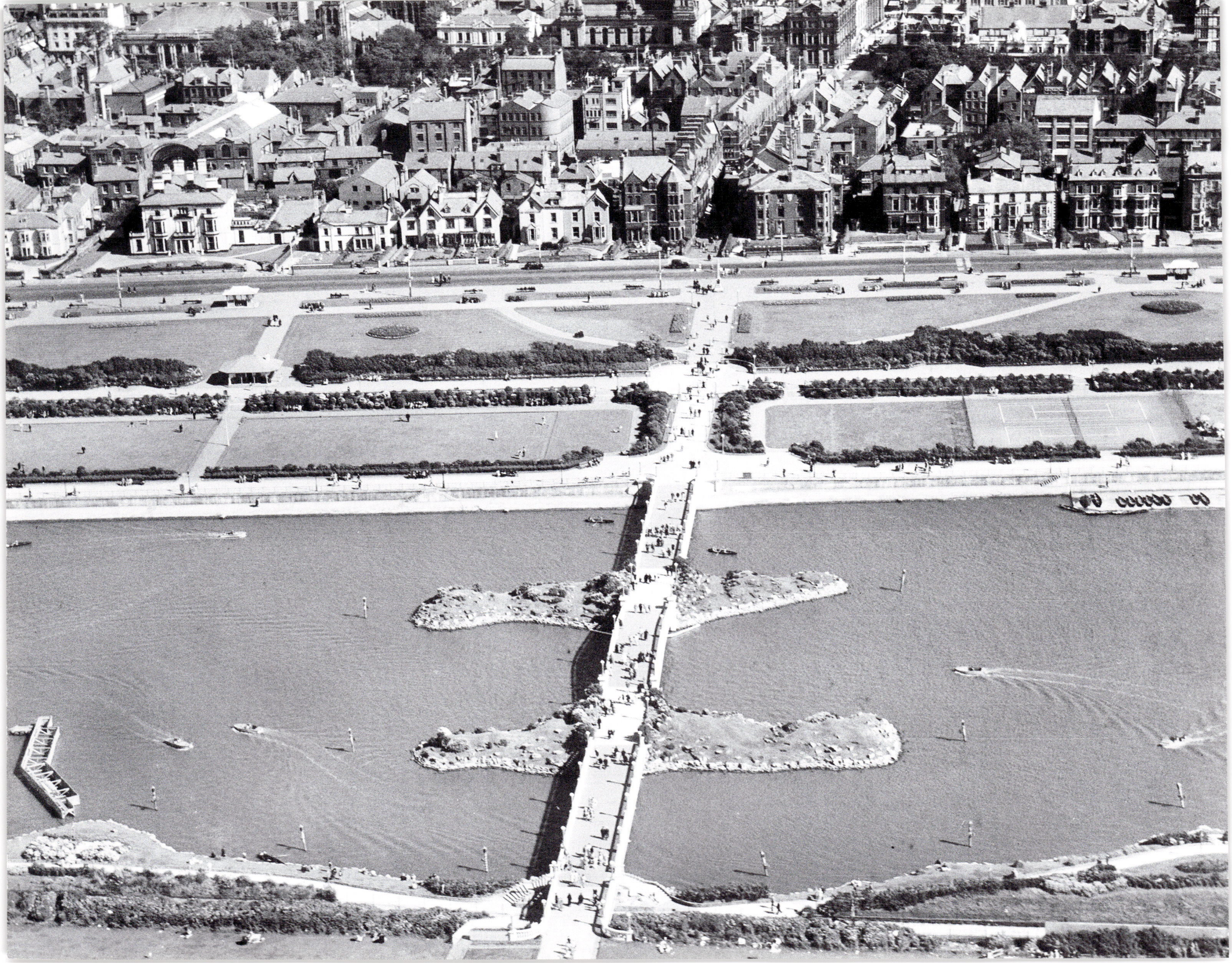

The Marine Lake, King's Gardens and South Marine Gardens, Southport, Merseyside

26 July 1938

On the seafront of resorts such as at Skegness, Great Yarmouth and Weston-super-Mare, a wide strip of land exists between the sea and the first line of buildings, allowing the creation of gardens and sometimes substantial water features. At Southport over the past 200 years, the rate of sand build-up and reclamation means that the beach is now around half a mile from the front of the town, creating an area for gardens and, today, also some less aesthetically pleasing industrial units and large entertainment facilities.

This aerial photograph provides a cross-section through the central part of the town's seafront. Just beneath the bottom edge of the image would be the beach and the seafront road, then the gardens with the large marine lake running through its centre. This was the site for pleasure craft and an aerial ride across the water. On the other side of the water, the gardens contain sports facilities, including bowling greens and tennis courts and then, after further gardens, a large road running along the rear edge of the built-up area of the town.

Southport had grown up on a previously undeveloped stretch of coastline; a bathing house was built in 1792 by William Sutton, followed by his hotel in 1798, and a range of other facilities were added during the early 19th century. The heart of the initial development was Lord Street, parallel to the sea; beyond the first blocks of buildings can be seen the tree-lined avenue. Although the form of the resort seems to have the regularity of a planned development, this was largely due to the practice of the two principal landowners, Miss Bold and Mr Hesketh. They carefully leased out to developers parcels of former 'waste land' along the seashore and saw the rise of a high-status resort, which was in marked contrast to nearby Blackpool with its working-class clientele and haphazard appearance.

EPW058480

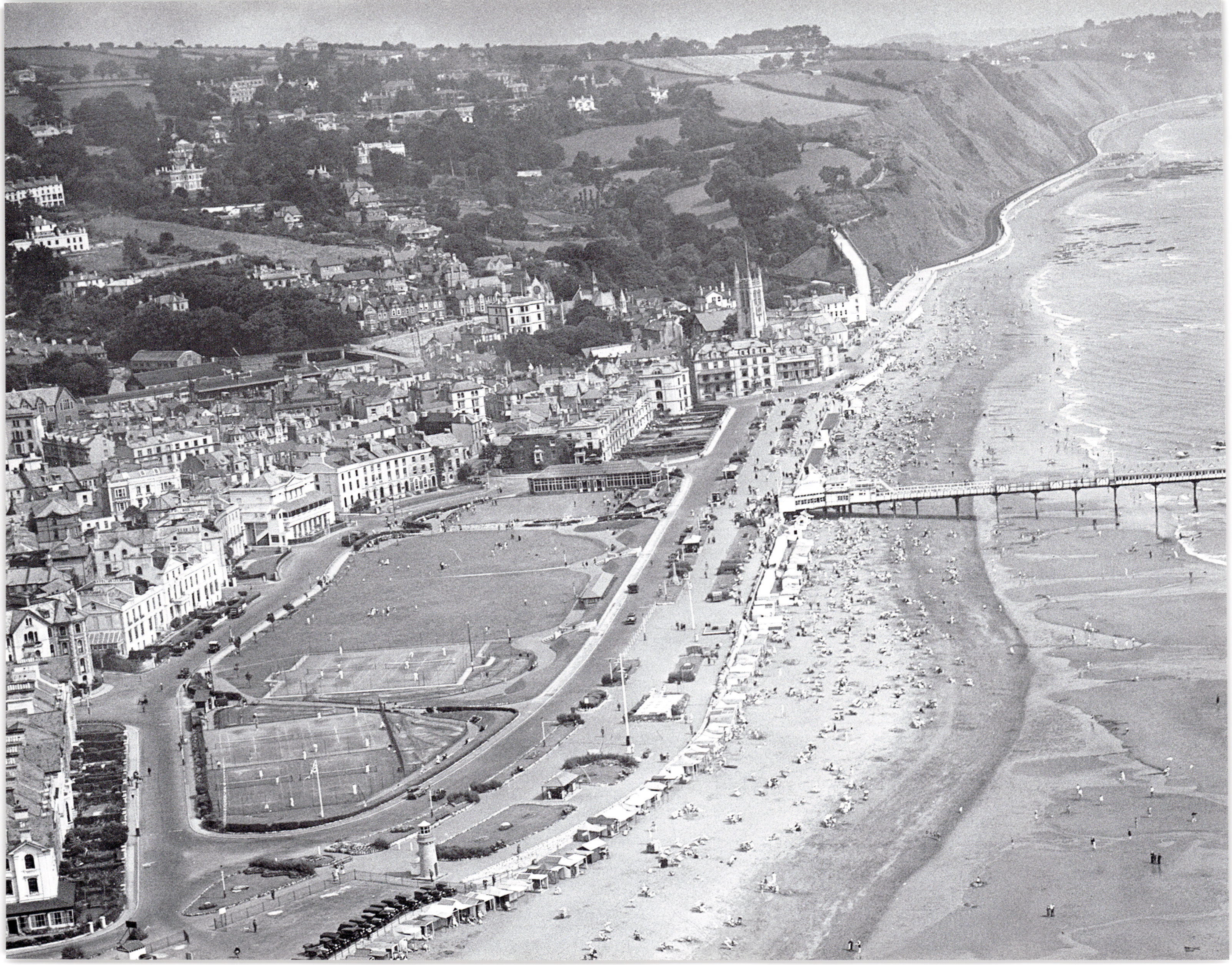

The Den, Teignmouth Pier and the beach, Teignmouth, Devon
August 1932

Sand dunes are a key part of the story of defending seaside resorts from the sea, though today they are usually only evident on the fringes of resorts, where development has not transformed them. At a number of seaside towns, a place name may reflect the former existence of dunes where the resort now stands. The Denes at Great Yarmouth or the Den here at Teignmouth are now topographically flat, but the names suggest the former existence of dunes.

Although responsibility for sea defences is now clearly vested with local and national government, at Teignmouth in 1823–4 there were 'excellent cold, hot and vapour baths', kept by Mrs Hubbard, who was responsible for the construction of the first sea wall, probably in this area. In 1869, the Board of Local Government acquired the Den from Lord Devon and created a pleasure ground, necessitating an extension of the sea wall to protect it. It was in this area that in 1825–6 the two sections of Den Crescent, with the Assembly Rooms between them, were built to designs by Andrew Patey from Exeter. Patey also built Cockram's Hotel for John Cockram in 1825, later known as the Royal Hotel, on the Den. It closed in 1988, and after years of dereliction it was demolished and replaced by a block of flats, Royal Court, the shape of which echoes its predecessor's form. The crescent, assembly room and hotel can be seen on the left-hand side of the photograph overlooking the Den.

The Grand Pier at Teignmouth was designed by Joseph Wilson, who had also been responsible for Bognor pier two years earlier and would go on to build piers at Hunstanton (1870–1978) and Westward Ho! (1871–80). It opened in 1867, cost £8,000 and was 600ft (183m) long. It could have had a short life because there was a proposal to dismantle it and transport it to neighbouring Paignton, but this did not materialise. It was originally a simple structure with four pagodas and a turnstile at its entrance, but improvements were carried out and the pier reopened on 24 July 1876. In 1887, a large pavilion was added at the entrance and included various shops and an amusement grotto. A permanent 300-seat pavilion was added to the pierhead in 1890, where a dance orchestra played twice daily except on Sundays. A perilous-looking footbridge led to a new landing stage at the end of the pier for the steamers that had been displaced by the new pavilion. In January 1908 huge waves breached the sea wall along the promenade and half of the entrance pavilion collapsed, but was rebuilt.

EPW039711

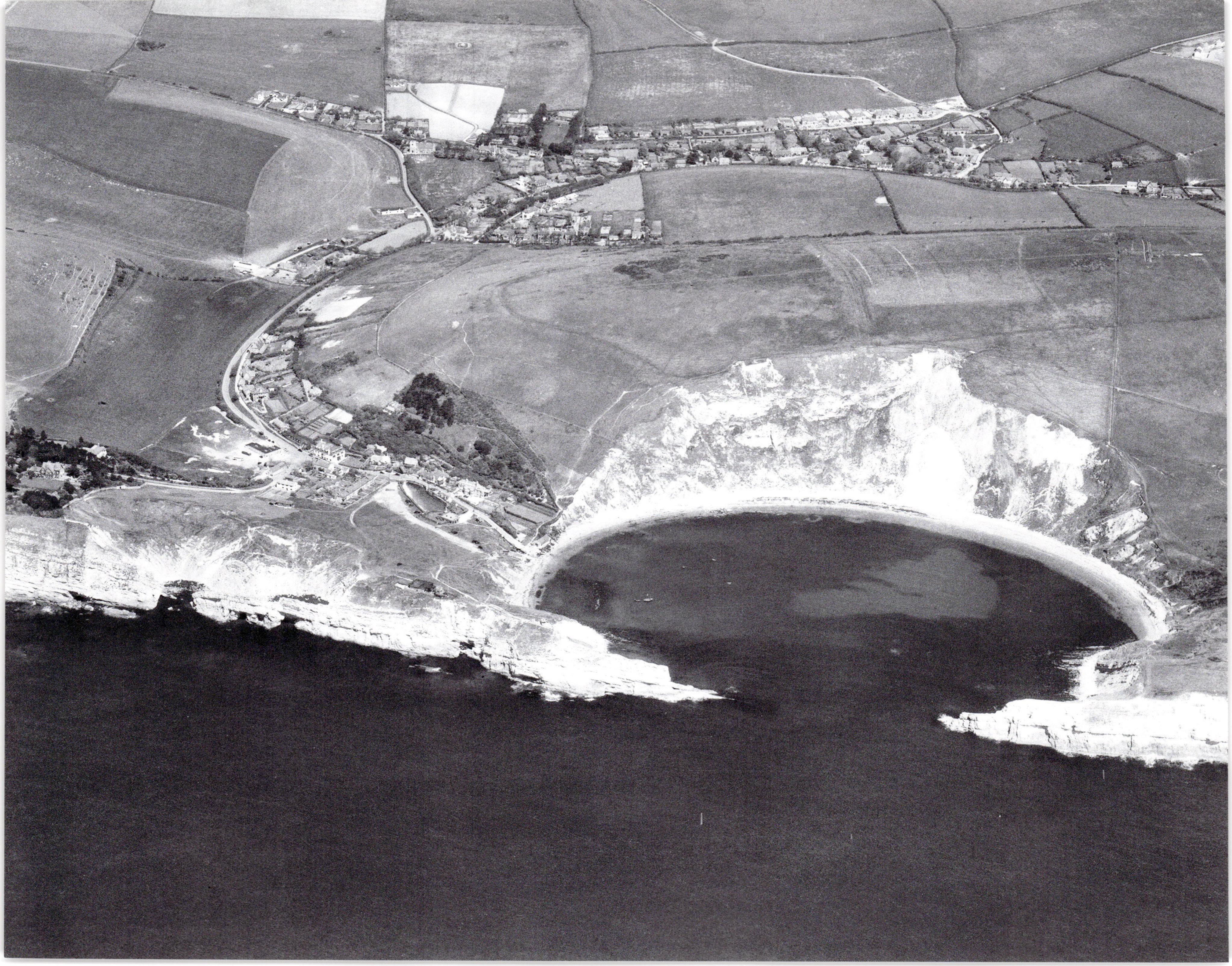

Lulworth Cove and the village, West Lulworth, Dorset
4 May 1953

Guidebooks to 19th-century seaside resorts often include suggestions about excursions and places of interest nearby. In the case of Weymouth, holidaymakers were often directed to ride over to the Isle of Portland (*see* p 235), visit country seats and admire picturesque villages. One of the most common destinations was Lulworth Cove, an important part of this coastline that was granted World Heritage Site status by UNESCO in 2001.

Lulworth Cove is a famed beauty spot because of its beautiful white pebble beach, blue waters and rock pools teeming with sea creatures. However, it is of more interest because of its complex geology and almost perfect semi-circular form. Sedimentary rocks were laid down over a period of 150 million years and many fossils are found in them. Among the rocks are Portland limestone, Purbeck limestone, greensands, Wealden clays and a band of chalk. Interestingly, due to folding, the sedimentary rocks no longer lie in horizontal bands; instead, they have been twisted so that the oldest rock is nearest to the sea and the youngest inland. Something of the complex striation can be seen on the cliffs of the coastline.

Each year Lulworth Cove is visited by around half a million visitors and around half of these walk to see the nearby arch of Durdle Door, around 2km (1.24 miles) to the west of the cove.

EAW049042

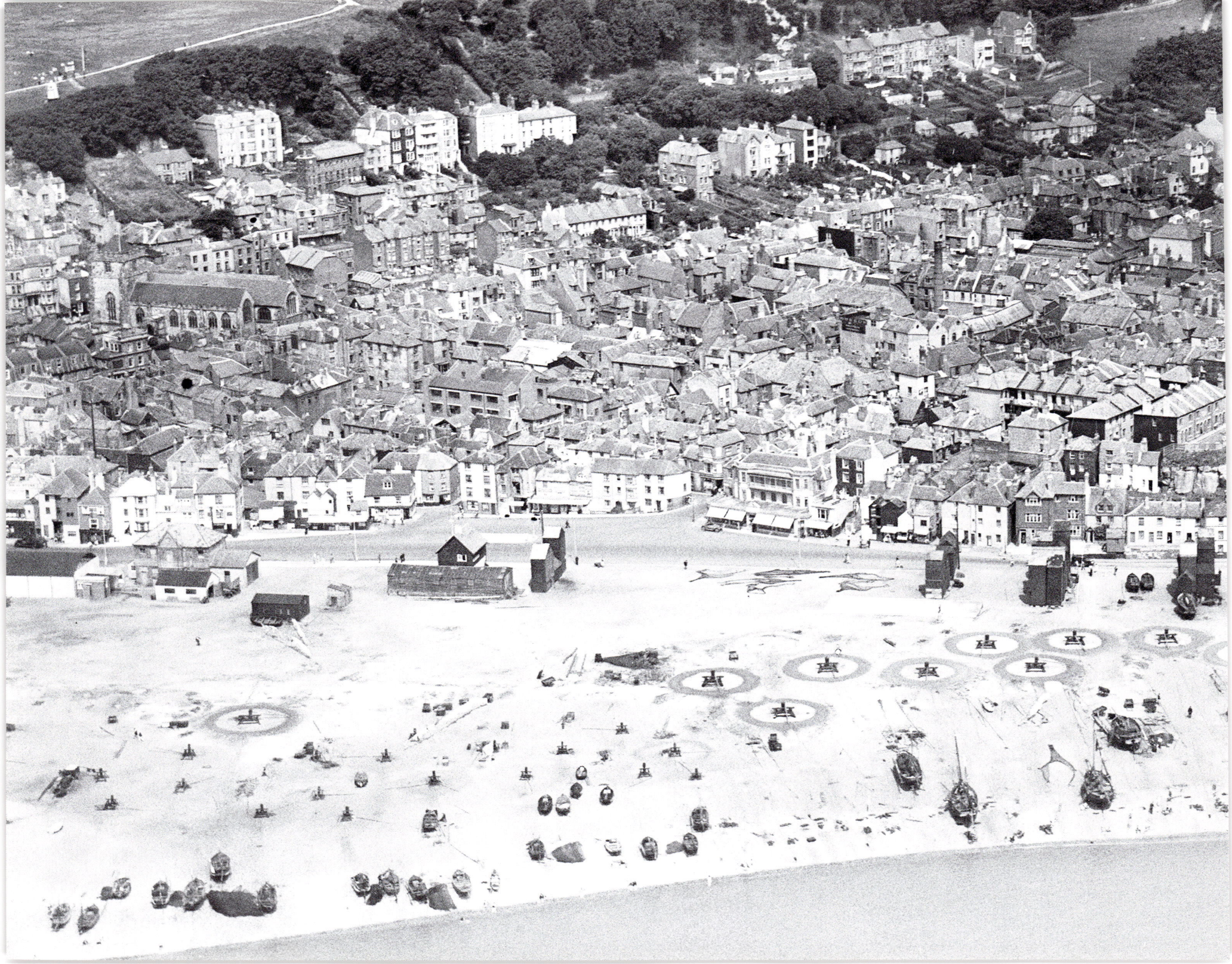

The Stade and the Old Town, Hastings
August 1932

This photograph shows the historic town of Hastings and the beach in front of it with an array of boats, the capstans for pulling the boats out of the water and the tall timber net lofts. The historic parish church can be seen to the left.

Hastings was one of the series of small ports around the English coast that began to welcome visitors seeking to bathe in the sea in the middle decades of the 18th century. Visitors came to these ports because they had access to the sea, but perhaps more importantly because they also had a range of housing to provide lodgings, and at least rudimentary entertainment facilities in the form of inns.

Historic Hastings consisted of a pair of streets running inland from the seafront with a stream in between. By the time that this photograph was taken, the stream had become a road, but the dense historic character of the town is still obvious. As was the case in other early ports that became resorts, such as Margate and Brighton, the pre-resort town covered a small area, with small plots, narrow streets and a dense pattern of relatively small-scale buildings. The town's development, which had taken place over several centuries, was piecemeal, with buildings varying in size, height and date. This variety is an expression of the lack of single ownership, but also reflects a time when regularity and uniformity was not a required objective of patrons or builders. What is clear in this photograph is that while the pattern of historic housing plots has been retained, most buildings along the seafront have been rebuilt during the 18th and 19th century in response to visitors wanting better and larger accommodation with a sea view.

Where there is no natural harbour, fishing fleets may be launched from beaches and this was the case once at Brighton and continues today at Hastings, where the area of the seafront and beach in front of the historic town is still dominated by the fishing industry, despite encroachment from the west by entertainment facilities. The most distinctive element of Hastings' seafront are the tall timber net lofts, covered in weather boarding and painted with tar. These were used to dry nets and originated from perhaps the Middle Ages, but as a result of regular storm and fire damage over the centuries, most have been rebuilt. The new Jerwood Art Gallery, which opened in 2012 on a site in the centre of this photograph, was given a black tiled external finish to match the net lofts.

EPW039362

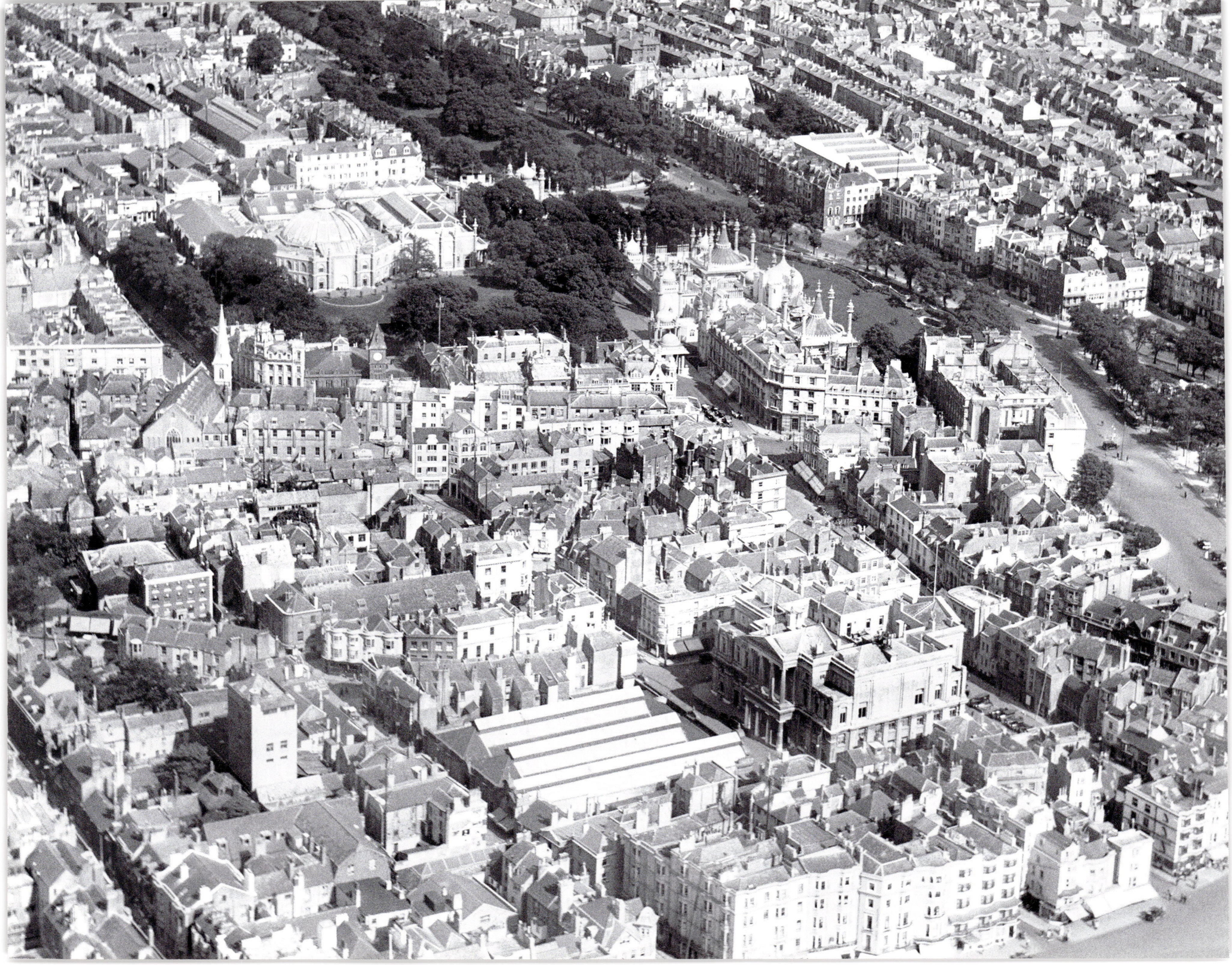

The Royal Pavilion and surrounding streets, Brighton
August 1926

In the heart of this photograph of central Brighton can be seen the Steine, the Royal Pavilion and the adjacent stable block set among densely packed streets of housing. The Steine is the open area in the centre of Brighton once used by fishermen to dry their nets, and latterly by wealthy visitors for promenading and socialising. Therefore, this was the logical place to construct the Royal Pavilion, the opulent and exotic seaside home created for the Prince Regent, who became George IV in 1820. His brother, and successor, William IV continued to use the Brighton Pavilion, and while Queen Victoria initially stayed in it, she felt uncomfortable being associated with the extravagance that it personified. As her family grew, she wanted more space and privacy and therefore sold the building to the town of Brighton in 1850 after its fittings and furnishings had been removed in anticipation of its expected eventual demolition. By this time, she and her husband, Prince Albert, had already decided to spend their summers at Osborne House on the Isle of Wight (*see* p 179).

The story of the Royal Pavilion began in 1786 when George, Prince of Wales and later Prince Regent, leased a farmhouse overlooking the Steine. During the following year, Henry Holland was employed to enlarge the house. He created a large, shiny, white-tiled but rather dour, neo-classical design incorporating the original farmhouse as one of a pair of buildings with a central domed structure between them.

In 1803, William Porden designed a large domed riding school behind the pavilion, seen to the left in this photograph. Decorated externally with Indian detailing, it was a building that the Prince reputedly believed was better than his accommodation. Therefore, he employed John Nash to extend and transform the neo-classical house into the current building that combines Indian, Islamic and even Gothic detailing on the exterior, with lavish, predominantly Chinese- and oriental-influenced interiors.

In 1822 William Cobbett described it as resembling the Kremlin, and a century later the renowned architectural historian Sir John Summerson likened its exotic charms unfavourably with the Granada Cinema at Tooting. However, although the building did not inspire many followers in the years immediately after its construction, it was highly influential in the development of oriental-influenced projects during the late 19th century, particularly in the design of buildings on seaside piers.

EPW016879

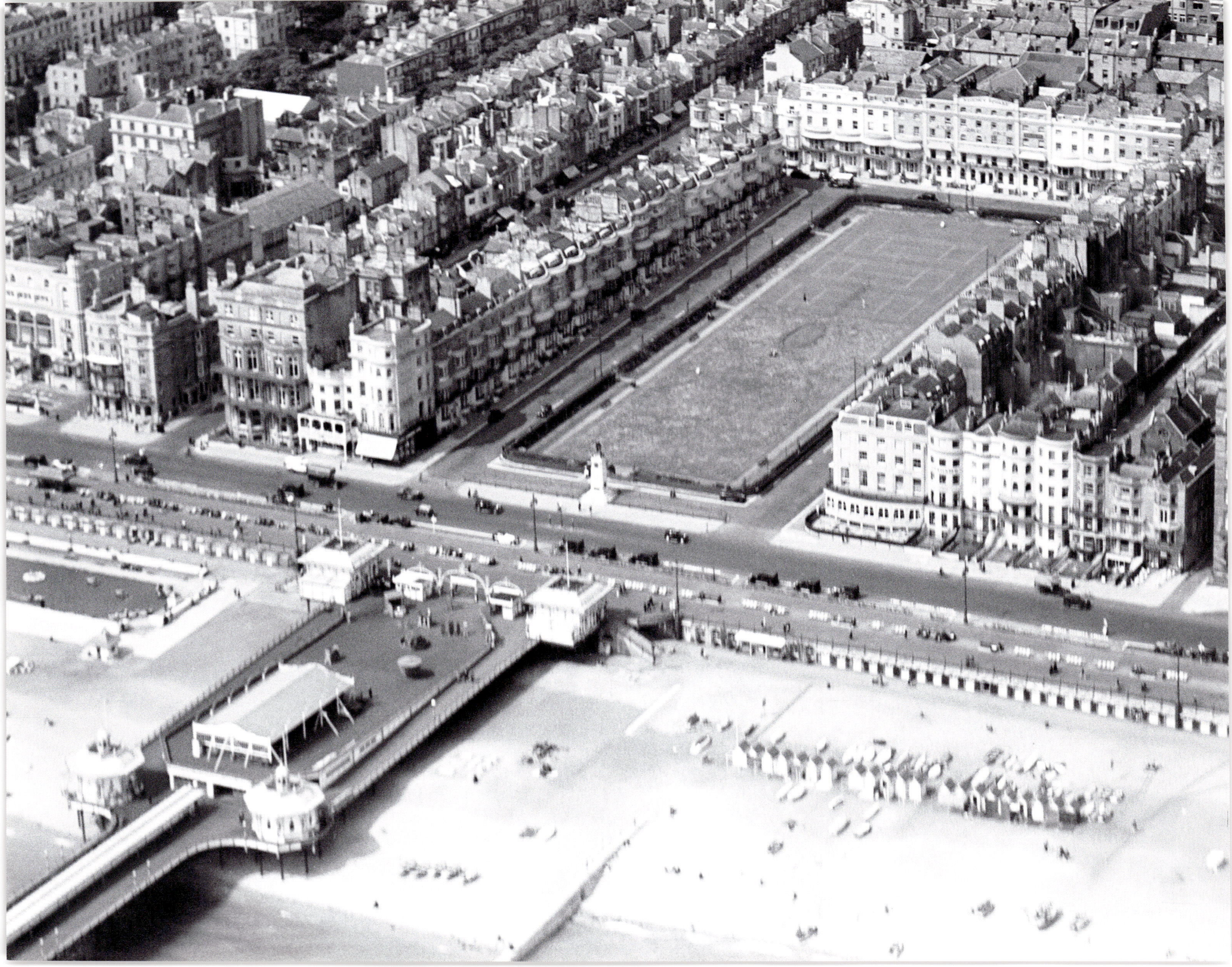

Regency Square, Brighton, East Sussex
May 1933

By the early 19th century, most new developments at seaside resorts consisted of terraces, often along the seafront or on a cliff top, but some of the larger schemes in the 18th century employed squares, some of which were set further inland at the social heart of the resort. At Margate, Cecil Square, built in 1769, contained the Assembly Rooms, a tavern, a row of shops and large houses built for fashionable families, including the Duke of Cumberland. The square remained a key feature of resort expansion in the 19th century. For instance, the failed new town of St Augustine's at Herne Bay, which was laid out in the early 1830s, consisted of a regular grid with the northernmost part of the design containing a chain of three squares linked by short roads.

A small number of resort towns, initially those on the south coast, employed a layout specifically designed to exploit their location by the sea. The three-sided square, with the fourth side left undeveloped to provide sea views, first appears during the early 19th century. This arrangement was inspired by the Steine at Brighton, the open area at the east side of the early town around which much of the earliest, fashionable construction was arranged, including the Royal Pavilion. Proof of this origin is provided by the fact that two of the early examples also adopt the name, the New Steine at Brighton and the Steyne at Worthing. Further afield, this form of three-sided square was adopted at Weston-super-Mare where Ellenborough Park has villas on two sides, with Ellenborough Crescent at the landward end of the development. Scarborough also has small examples, though they are too far inland to benefit from a prominent sea view.

Regency Square was one of the earliest examples of the three-sided square, being laid out in the years immediately after the defeat of Napoleon at Waterloo in 1815. The huge terraced houses were probably designed by the father and son combination of Amon Wilds (builder and carpenter) and Amon Henry Wilds (architect).

The prominent, central location of the square led to Brighton's West Pier being constructed on the seafront opposite and the landward end of the structure can be seen in this photograph. It was also chosen as the site for the South African War Memorial commemorating the men of the Royal Sussex Regiment who fell in that war. Erected in *c* 1905, it consists of a depiction of a regimental trumpeter on top of a tall pedestal.

EPW041375

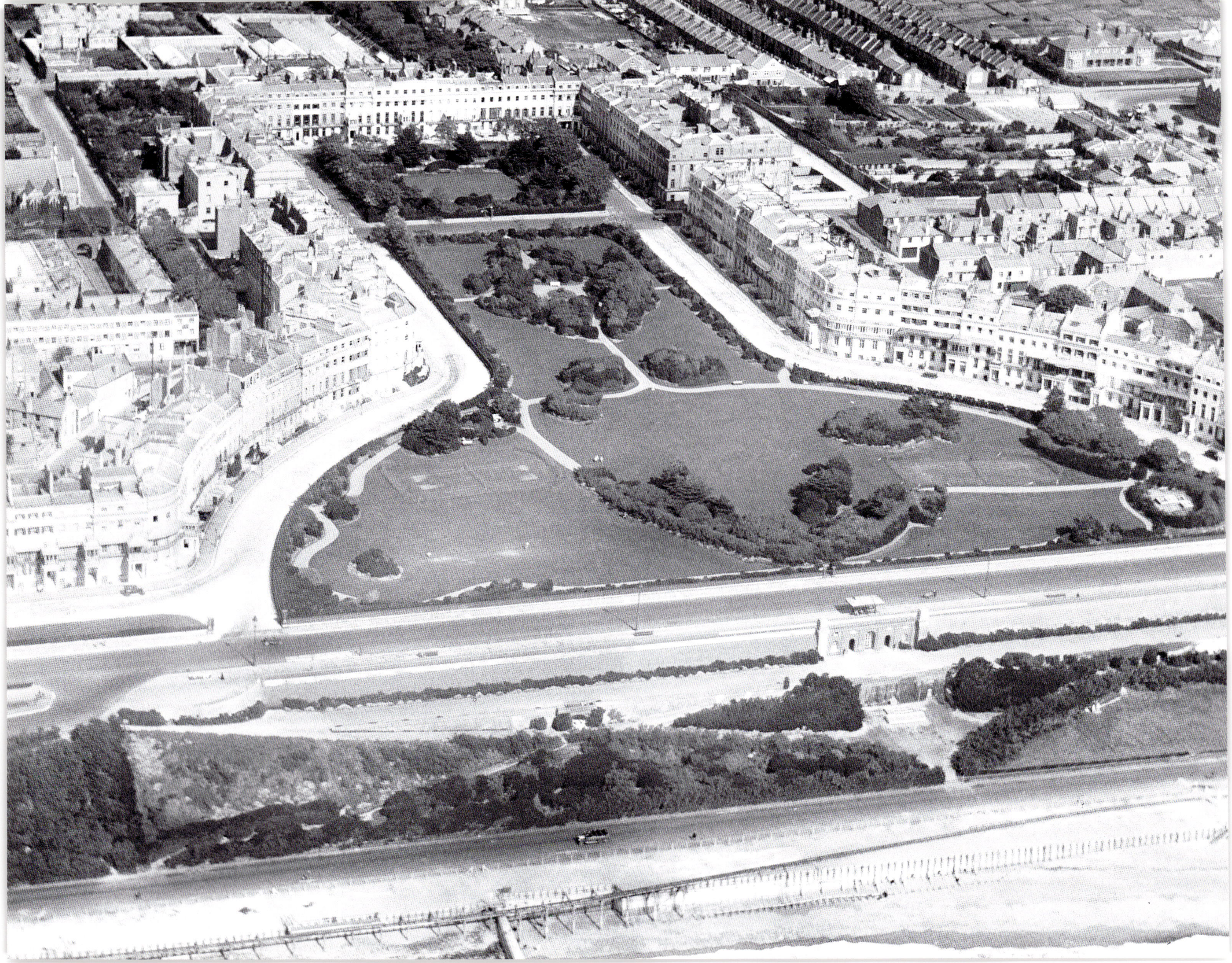

Kemp Town, Brighton, East Sussex
August 1926

By the early 19th century, the number of people, specifically wealthy people, who wished to spend time at seaside resorts had grown sufficiently large to prompt major new schemes of housing development. Some of the houses were for people to live in throughout the year, but many, if not most, were intended to provide lodgings for affluent visitors during the summer months.

The pioneering schemes were erected at Brighton, with Kemp Town being erected to the east of the rapidly growing town and Brunswick Town to the west. In 1823, Thomas Read Kemp embarked on the construction of a large estate on his land to the east of Brighton and most of the development was completed over the next two decades. The central part of Kemp Town is the elaborate, high-status housing in Sussex Square, with the quadrants of Lewes Crescent attached to its seaward ends, while along the seafront there are two flanking terraces. Just over 100 houses were eventually erected, whereas its ultimate inspiration, the Royal Crescent at Bath, only provided 30 houses. Originally, Kemp Town was intended to have 250 homes; these additional houses were to have been constructed behind the seafront terraces.

At the other end of Brighton and in neighbouring Hove, Brunswick Town was built from 1825 on land owned by the Scutt family. Amon Wilds and Charles Augustus Busby were responsible for the design of both schemes, though most buildings in Brunswick Town were probably designed by Busby alone (*see* p 207). In both schemes the large terraced houses ranged in size from three to five storeys, and their inspiration was developments in London such as John Nash's Regent Street and Regent's Park, or Thomas Cubitt's Eaton Square.

EPW016880

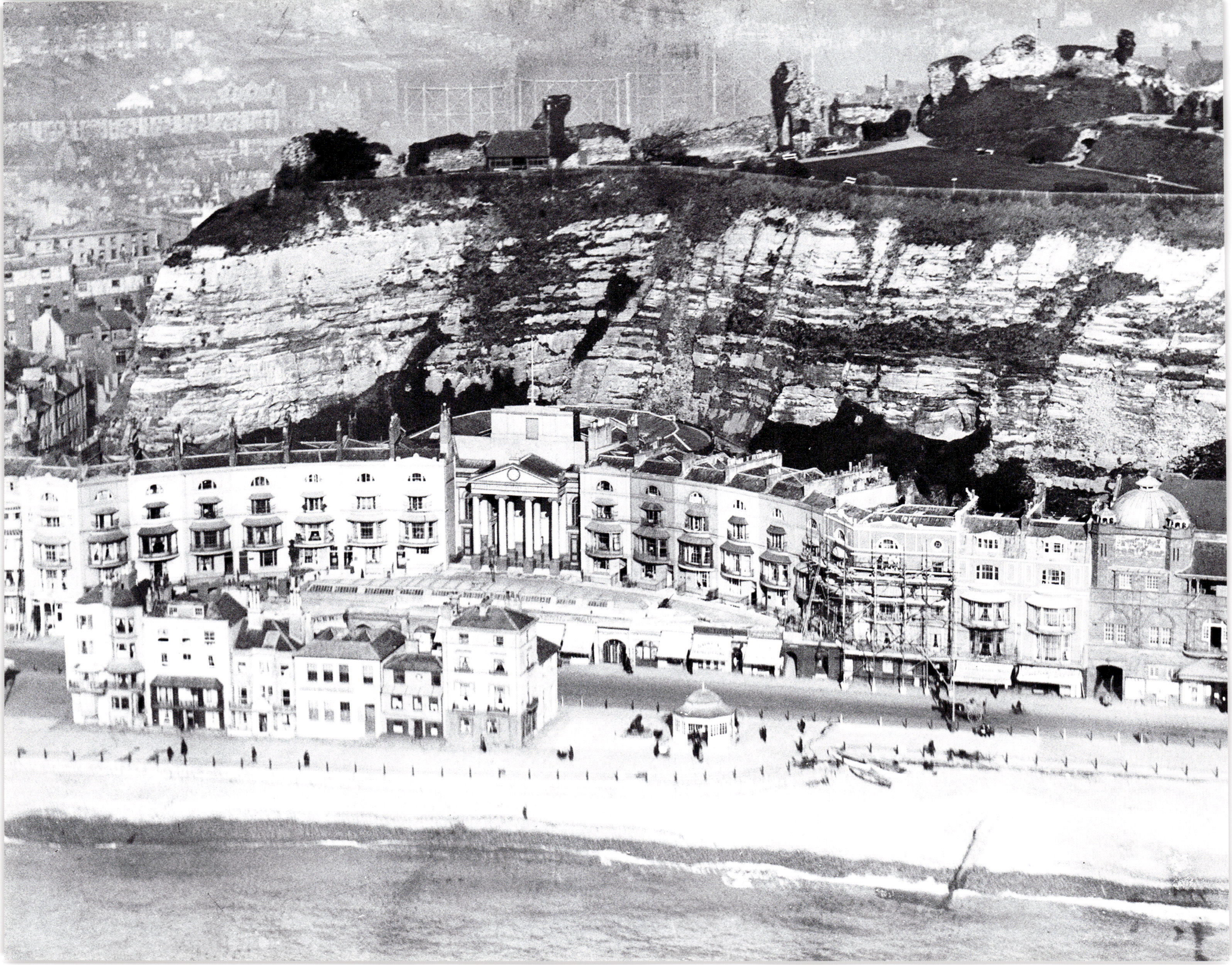

Pelham Crescent, Hastings, East Sussex
February 1920

Between 1824 and 1828, Thomas Pelham, Earl of Chichester, employed Joseph Kay to build a seafront crescent of houses with a large parish church at its centre and a large bazaar in front. Churches are rarely found on the seafront of seaside resorts. This may be because it was felt that some activities taking place might be at odds with polite churchgoers, but perhaps more significantly, there was no money to be made from a church as developers sought to maximise their profits from the most valuable seafront sites in a resort. However, Pelham Crescent has a central detached chapel separating the two quadrants of the crescent. The foundation stone of the church, St Mary-in-the-Castle, was laid on 21 September 1825.

Also included in the scheme was a lavish bathhouse containing 11 warm baths and octagonal saloons decorated with Chinese scenery. Pelham Arcade in front contained about 20 shops in two rows flanking a central, top-lit corridor, and on summer evenings it was converted into a musical promenade. This scheme was more than just a housing development, as the presence of the church, a shopping bazaar and baths demonstrate. In fact, it seems like a small-scale version of the Kemp Town and Brunswick Town developments at either end of Brighton, which began to be constructed shortly before Pelham Crescent.

To the right of Pelham Crescent can be seen the former Palace of Varieties, constructed by Ernest Runtz in 1897–9 for music hall, a form of popular entertainment that had emerged from the back rooms of pubs to be housed in some of the grandest buildings on the seafront. The eclectic mixture of classical forms with some lively detailing is typical of major entertainment buildings erected *c* 1900 around the coast. This building later became a cinema, a bingo hall and an amusement arcade.

This 1920 photograph also shows Beach Terrace in front of Pelham Crescent. It appears to be a mixture of 18th- and 19th-century buildings in a haphazard arrangement similar to groups of buildings found further to the east on the seafront of the old town. This terrace survived until Sydney Little's wholesale reconfiguration of the seafront in the early 1930s, in which a single major road was created along the whole length of the resort. The site is now a car park. Behind Pelham Crescent can be seen the ruins of Hastings Castle, which dates from the late 11th century onwards (*see* p 1).

EPW000111

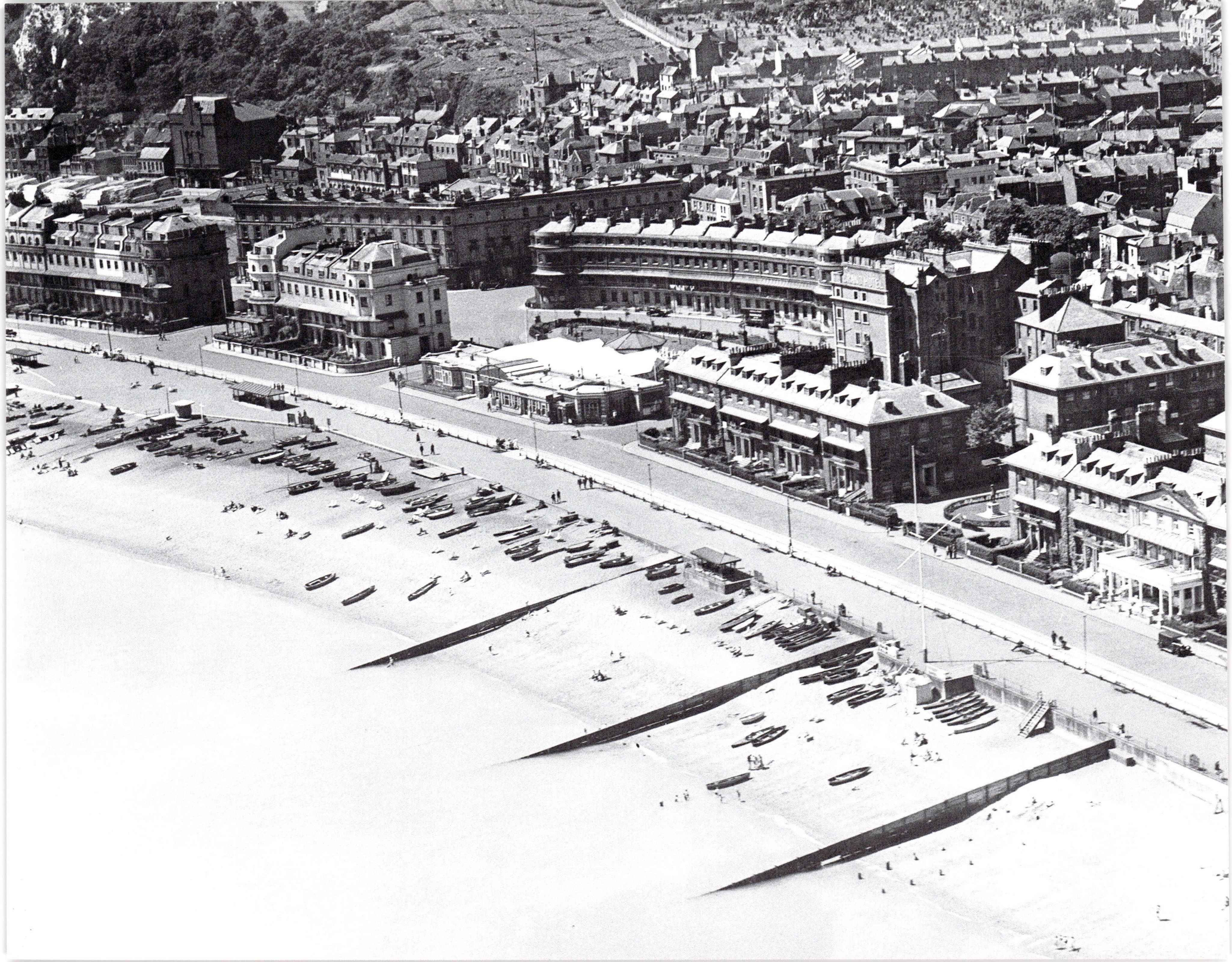

Camden Crescent, the seafront and the town centre, Dover, Kent

August 1932

In the 1820s, Kemp Town and Brunswick Town at Brighton and St Leonards beside Hastings set a new benchmark for domestic architecture at the seaside and their influence is obvious in a number of projects in the late 1820s and 1830s. In 1828, Thomas Ellis Owen designed Crescent Road at Alverstoke near Gosport (Hampshire) as the centrepiece of a new settlement, Anglesey. At the eastern end of the crescent was a large hotel, while a series of detached and semi-detached villas were built to the west. The crescent was three-storeyed, with attics and basements, and with a Doric colonnade running along the front between the end and central pavilions, which are decorated with Ionic columns. In 1829, Amon Henry Wilds designed Park Crescent at Worthing (West Sussex), a scheme of 22 three-storey houses, though only 14 were built. The houses were built in threes, with the central one of each group being treated with pilasters with Corinthian capitals with honeysuckle leaves. The crescent and its gardens are entered through a large gateway designed in the form of a triumphal arch.

On the seafront at Dover, Waterloo Crescent was built in 1834–8 by Philip Hardwick. It was built in three parts, a central block of 19 houses flanked on either side by a pair of blocks containing 5 houses. The individual houses are three-storeyed with two storeys within the roofs and a basement, while the ends of each block were treated as four-storeyed with an attic and a basement with giant-order Corinthian pilasters. This development can be seen at the left of the photograph and still survives today following significant rebuilding and restoration after the Second World War. The rest of the seafront in this photograph fared less well. The damage caused by bombing and shelling from long-range guns on the French coast meant that this part of the seafront was entirely cleared, and the monumental, modern Gateway block of flats was completed in 1959 (*see* p 279).

EPW039375

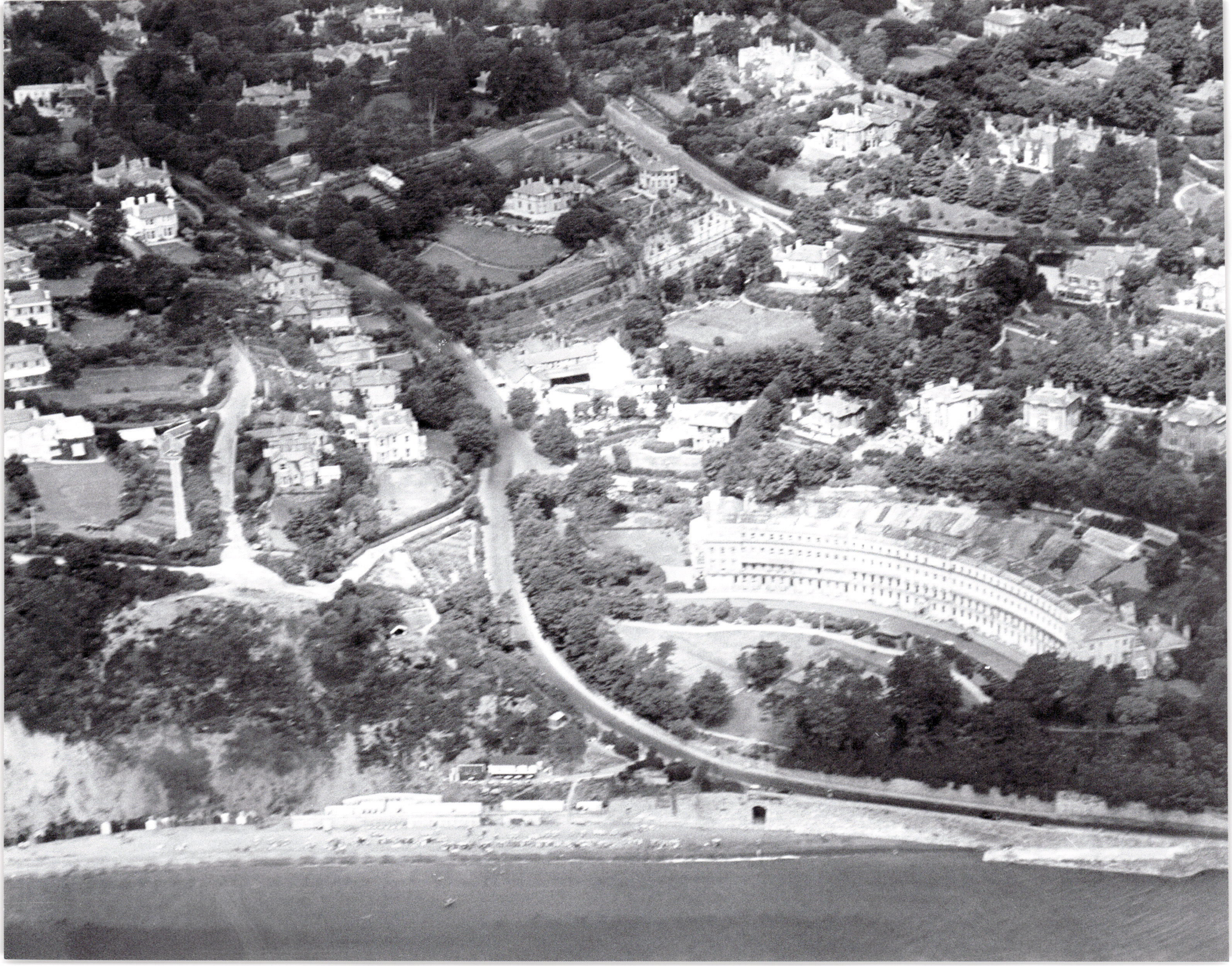

The Osborne Hotel and environs, Torquay, Devon
July 1930

Most of the grand housing schemes of the second quarter of the 19th century that were inspired by Brighton can be found in the south-east of England, the most prosperous part of the coast at this period and the one with most resorts. However, by the mid-19th century, some large developments can be found in the north of England, such as at Scarborough or at Fleetwood. In the south-west, Torquay was becoming more popular and to accommodate its growing number of wealthy visitors, Hesketh Crescent was constructed. Originally called Meadfoot Crescent, it is a crescent of 15 houses with three-bay-wide end pavilions and a five-bay centrepiece with Corinthian pilasters, a type of design known as palace-fronted. Built in 1845–8 by the speculative builder Jacob Harvey (1783–1867) with his sons William and John Harvey, the scheme was the brainchild of the local landowner Sir Lawrence Palk, later Lord Haldon. He originally occupied the central, largest house, which is now the Osborne Hotel.

The clifftop crescent, with its formal late Georgian form, is in marked contrast to the surroundings with the dozens of high-quality villas for prosperous residents and retirees set within their own grounds, the most distinctive form of domestic architecture of Torquay.

EPW033404

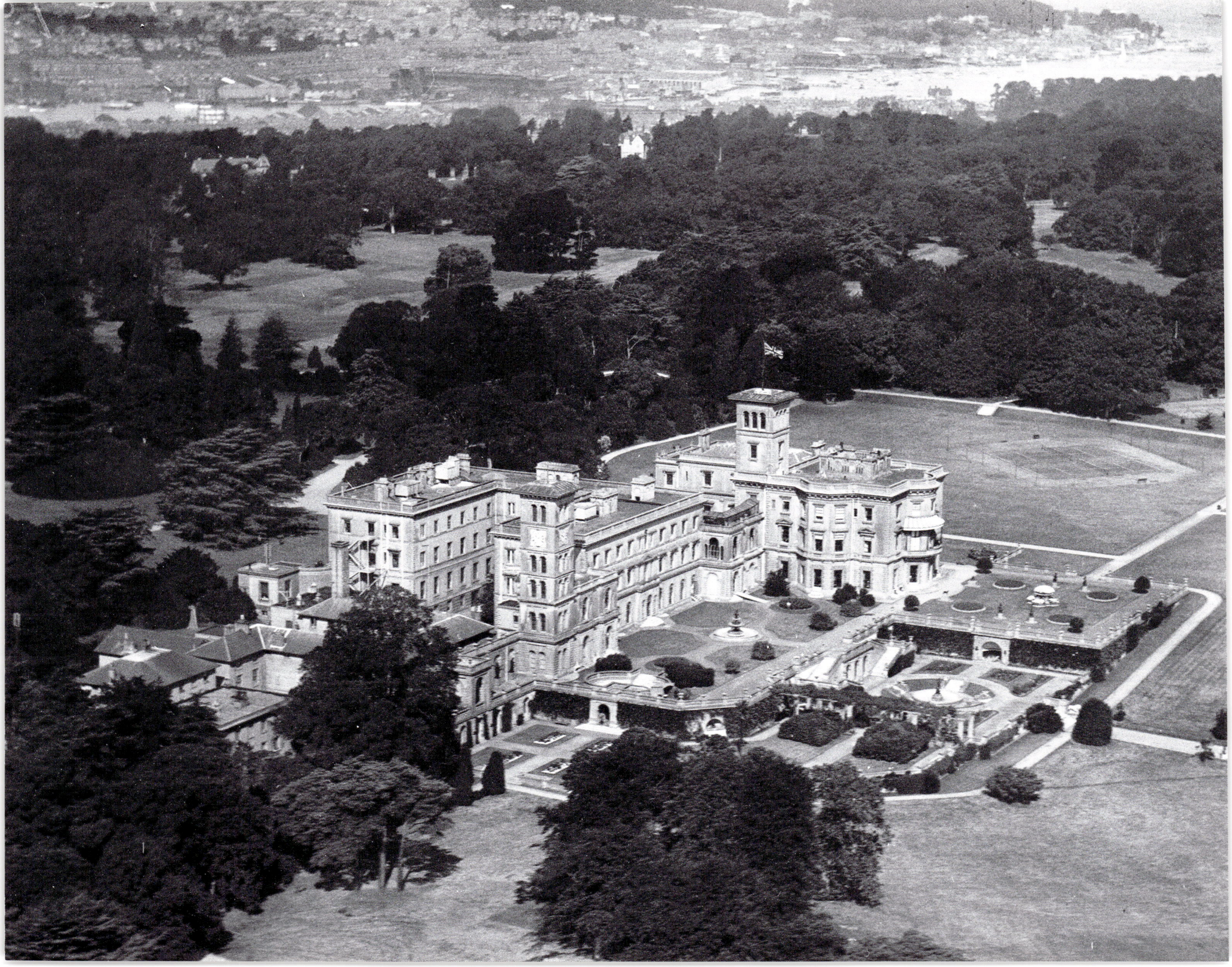

Osborne House from the south, East Cowes, Isle of Wight
1923

The main location for reigning monarchs to enjoy time by the seaside on England's south coast was initially at Weymouth and at Brighton, where the Prince Regent, who became George IV in 1820, created the opulent Royal Pavilion. Queen Victoria continued to use this building during the early years of her reign, but she soon wanted something larger, less urban and more private, as her family grew in size.

In 1845 Queen Victoria and Prince Albert bought Osborne House from Lady Isabella Blachford and demolished the existing 18th-century house. A new, larger house was designed by Prince Albert, but Thomas Cubitt was the builder and probably to some extent the architect. The large house, with a deliberately irregular plan, was built in an Italianate style, with the Main Wing (right) and Pavilion Wing, featuring its distinctive tower, to the north (top of photo) being completed in 1846, followed by the Household Wing (left) in 1851. The Pavilion Wing contained the main royal apartments, with grand public rooms on the ground floor and more private, homely suites of rooms on the first floor. The Household Wing contained the household accommodation, as well as audience chambers.

In the early 1890s, the Durbar Wing (hidden behind the house), including the very elaborate Durbar Room, was added, built by Bhai Ram Singh and John Lockwood Kipling, Rudyard Kipling's father. The architect was J R Mann. This wing celebrated Queen Victoria being the Empress of India and was designed to contain all the Indian gifts presented to the Queen at her Golden Jubilee in 1887 and later her Diamond Jubilee in 1897. Queen Victoria died at Osborne House on 22 January 1901. Her son, Edward VII, presented the house to the nation on his Coronation Day in August 1902, and the royal apartments on the upper floors of the pavilion wing were turned into a private museum accessible only to the royal family.

The house is set within extensive grounds and below the gardens on Osborne Bay to the north-east was a private beach where the Queen kept her own private bathing machine, which was large enough to contain its own water closet. Osborne House is now looked after by English Heritage.

EPW009059

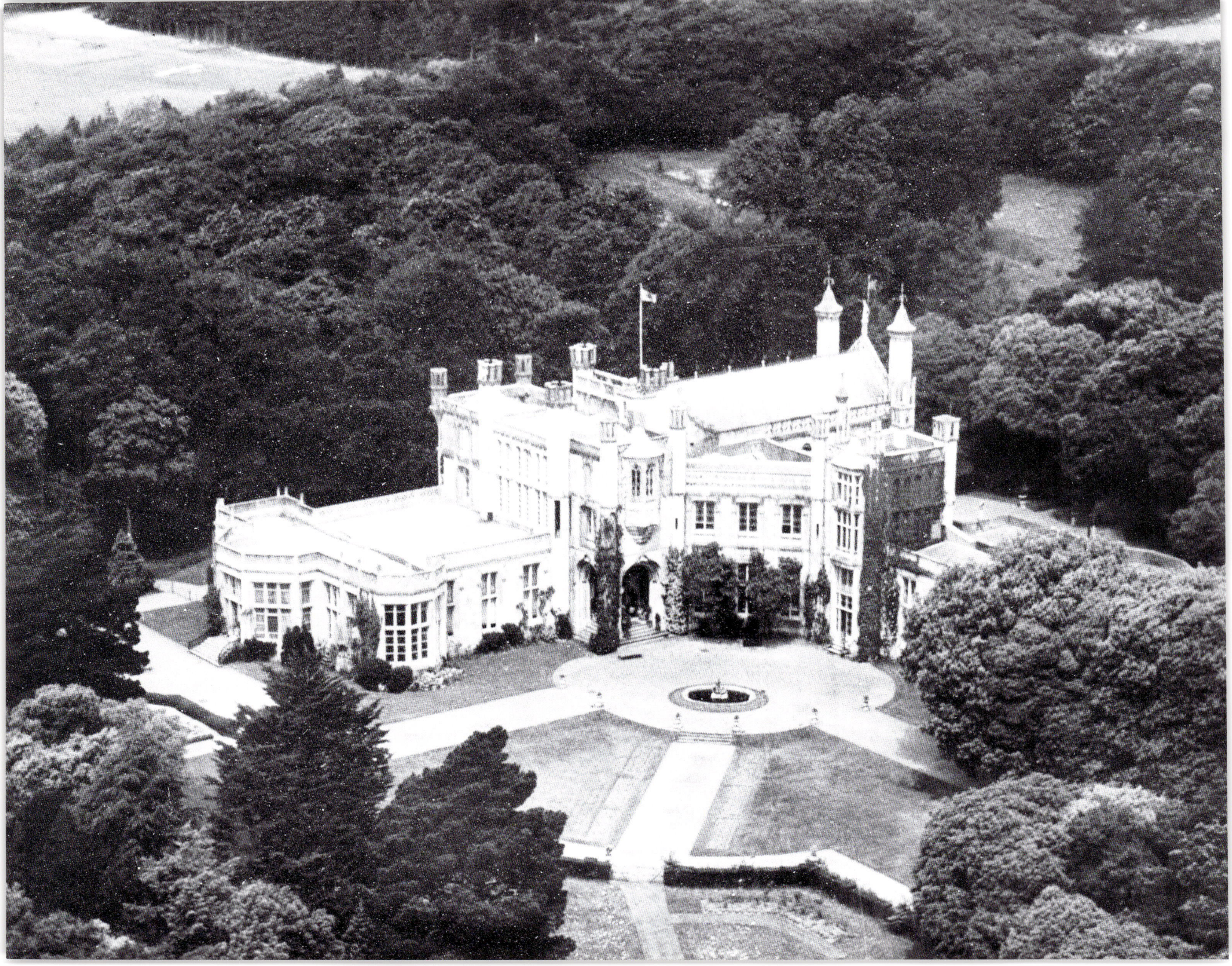

Highcliffe Castle, Highcliffe, Dorset
June 1927

It was not only royalty who wished to have a house beside the seaside. The original house at Highcliffe was built near this site in about 1775 for the third Earl of Bute, but was demolished in 1794. Its successor was demolished in 1830, and the present Highcliffe Castle was built by Lord Stuart de Rothesay in 1830–4. He had been the British Ambassador to France until his retirement in 1830, and while returning to England he saw the Hotel des Andelys near Rouen in Normandy being demolished. This house was where Antoine de Bourbon, the father of Henri IV, had died in 1562. Lord Stuart de Rothesay purchased the materials, along with other architectural sculpture that he appears to have been able to collect in northern France, including fragments from St Pierre at Jumieges.

In England, Lord Stuart de Rothesay commissioned the architect William Donthorne to build a grand house looking out across the sea that incorporated the fragments that he had collected. The largest single item that he got from France was the polygonal oriel window, which is a key feature of the central part of the house. Donthorne's main inspiration was clearly French châteaux, but the plan form and general style is also reminiscent of the extraordinary Fonthill Abbey in Wiltshire. It was built by William Beckford between 1796 and 1813, and at its centre was a 90m-tall (295ft) tower that collapsed in 1825. Lord Stuart de Rothesay's house echoed Fonthill's general form, but wisely omitted the perilously tall tower.

In the 1950s, Highcliffe Castle was used as a children's convalescent home and later as a training centre for student priests of the Claretian Order of the Roman Catholic Church. The Claretians moved out in 1966; shortly after, two fires badly damaged the building and a long period of vandalism and neglect followed. Fortunately, the building has been saved and major repairs were carried out during the 1990s.

EPW018174

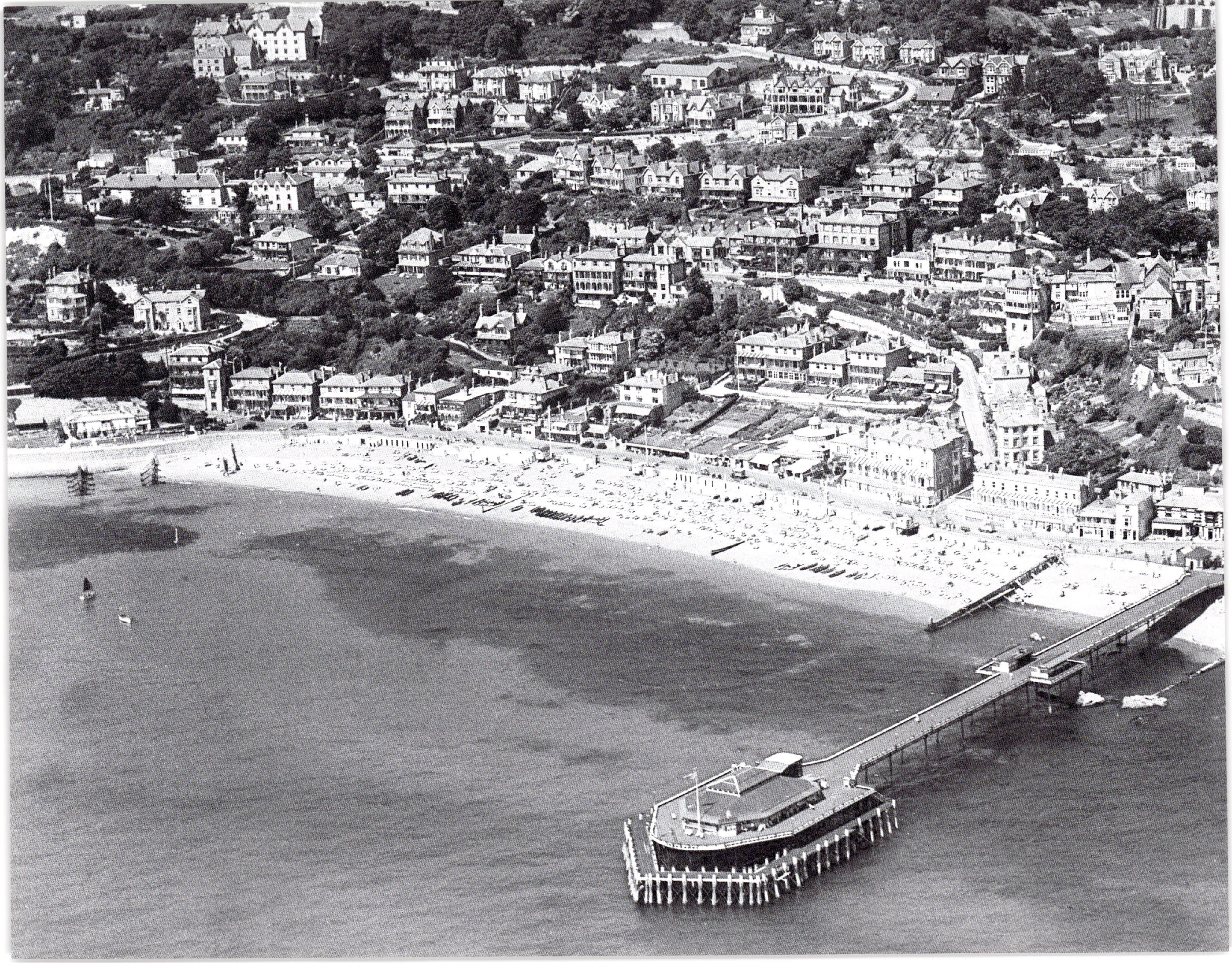

The Royal Victoria Pier and the town, Ventnor, Isle of Wight
12 August 1932

The terraced house seen at Kemp Town and Brunswick Town formed part of a grandiose architectural scheme and this form of house, along with the more humble and more common terraced house in ordinary streets, remained the dominant architectural form in seaside towns through the 19th century. However, there was also a growing number of villas and substantial semi-detached houses beginning to be built. This shift in taste marked a departure from the intimate character of life in a terrace, even a grand one, to a more private, quasi-rural existence. This clear reaction to the Picturesque had even begun to take place in Bath, the home of the grand palatial terrace.

Villas are most common in resorts that were regarded as 'quiet' or 'genteel' during the 19th century. Hence they were not common in the south-east, where much of the development in the heart of resorts had first taken place, but they were popular further west at resorts such as Torquay, Bournemouth, Sidmouth and here at Ventnor. In the north-west, Blackpool was a magnet for working-class tourists and much of its housing reflected this clientele. However, the area around Stanley Park grew during the course of the late 19th century through the addition of villas, and at nearby Southport, Hesketh Park has a similar arrangement of villas. This demonstrates that villas were being constructed in the most prestigious resorts and at the most exclusive locations.

Stylistically, seaside villas followed current tastes as they changed during the 19th century and make the standard allusions to their 'elders and betters'. For instance, it is not uncommon to see references in suburban villas to Osborne House, Queen Victoria's Isle of Wight retreat, the ultimate seaside villa (*see* p 179). These homes were intended for the growing numbers of genteel residents, including many retired people, who wished to live by the sea but were in search of more peace and quiet than could be achieved in a street of terraced houses. Therefore, most villas stand within their own secluded grounds and are usually set within discrete areas of a resort, usually high above the bustle of the town and, trees permitting, with a sea view. However, here at Ventnor, which was a renowned genteel resort, villas can be seen spreading up the hillside behind the seafront.

Discussions first took place regarding the construction of two piers at Ventnor to form an enclosed harbour in 1861, but this initiative came to nothing. However, the Ventnor Pier & Esplanade Company was formed in 1870 and a new 478ft-long (144m) pier was completed in 1873. This was destroyed by storms in 1881 and a longer replacement one opened in July 1887. The pavilion was added to the pier in 1906, but the entire structure was replaced after the Second World War.

EPW039653

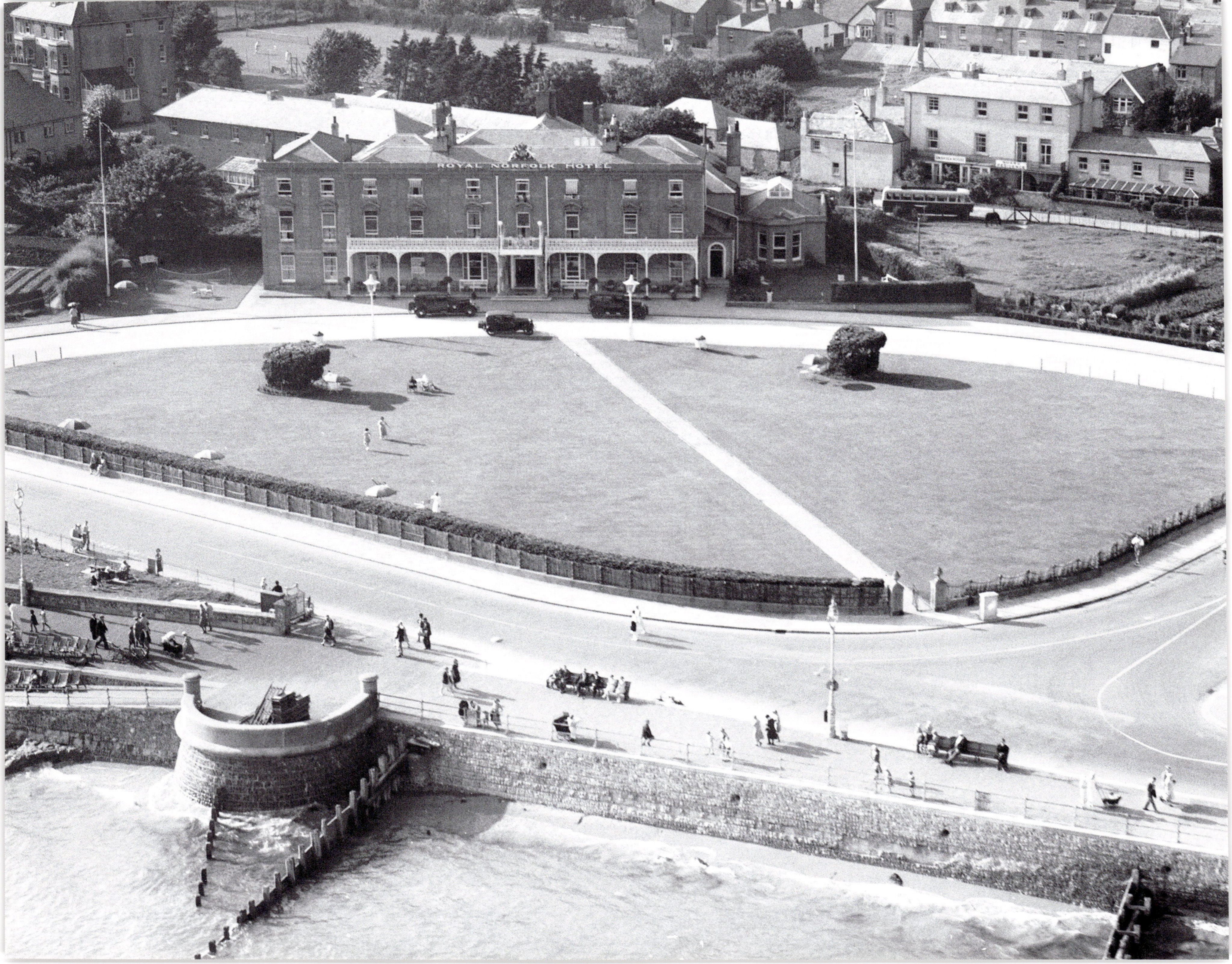
ROYAL NORFOLK HOTEL

The Royal Norfolk Hotel, Bognor Regis, West Sussex
August 1932

The construction of Kemp Town and Brunswick Town at Brighton and the development of St Leonards at Hastings were due to growing numbers of wealthy residents and visitors wishing to enjoy some privacy and separation from the increasingly busy hearts of seaside resorts. At the same time as this was occurring, hotels as purpose-built building types began to appear at seaside resorts to achieve a similar aim. Hotels, at least in name, existed prior to this; for instance, in 1769 a large assembly rooms was built as part of Fox's Tavern in Cecil Square in Margate, but in 1794 it was renamed the Royal Hotel in honour of the visit of George, Prince of Wales, who was meeting his intended bride Caroline of Brunswick. There is no indication of physical changes to the building, simply a renaming to suggest a higher status and greater comfort.

The word 'hotel' was in use by the 1760s, for example on the Lincolnshire coast where it was applied to the large houses providing lodgings and meals, but the first full-scale, purpose-built hotel was probably the Royal Hotel at Plymouth, which was completed in 1819. One of the first, substantial, purpose-built seaside hotels is the much extended and altered Royal Victoria Hotel, which was part of James Burton's development at St Leonards in the late 1820s.

Another contender for the title of the first substantial, purpose-built seaside hotel is the Norfolk Hotel at Bognor. In June 1826 a fire destroyed the existing hotel, and on its site a new, large hotel was constructed. While the original Royal Victoria Hotel at St Leonards resembled a large house or London club, the Norfolk Hotel, prior to its extension, was more reminiscent of a large Georgian vicarage or a short terrace of houses.

At the time that the Norfolk Hotel was built at Bognor, this was just a small settlement. An attempt to establish a new resort here had taken place in the late 18th century, but had been largely unsuccessful. Sir Richard Hotham, a successful London businessman and former MP, invested up to £160,000 in a prestigious new development for wealthy visitors. Hothamton was located near the inland village of South Bersted, which is now part of Bognor Regis, and welcomed its first guests in 1791. As well as accommodation inland, a bathing facility and a small hotel were created on the seafront; the hotel succumbed to fire in 1826. The aim of Hotham's scheme was to attract aristocrats and perhaps even royalty, but the economics of his investment proved unsustainable, and on his death in 1799 the estate was sold, leaving his heir a mere £8,000.

EPW040096

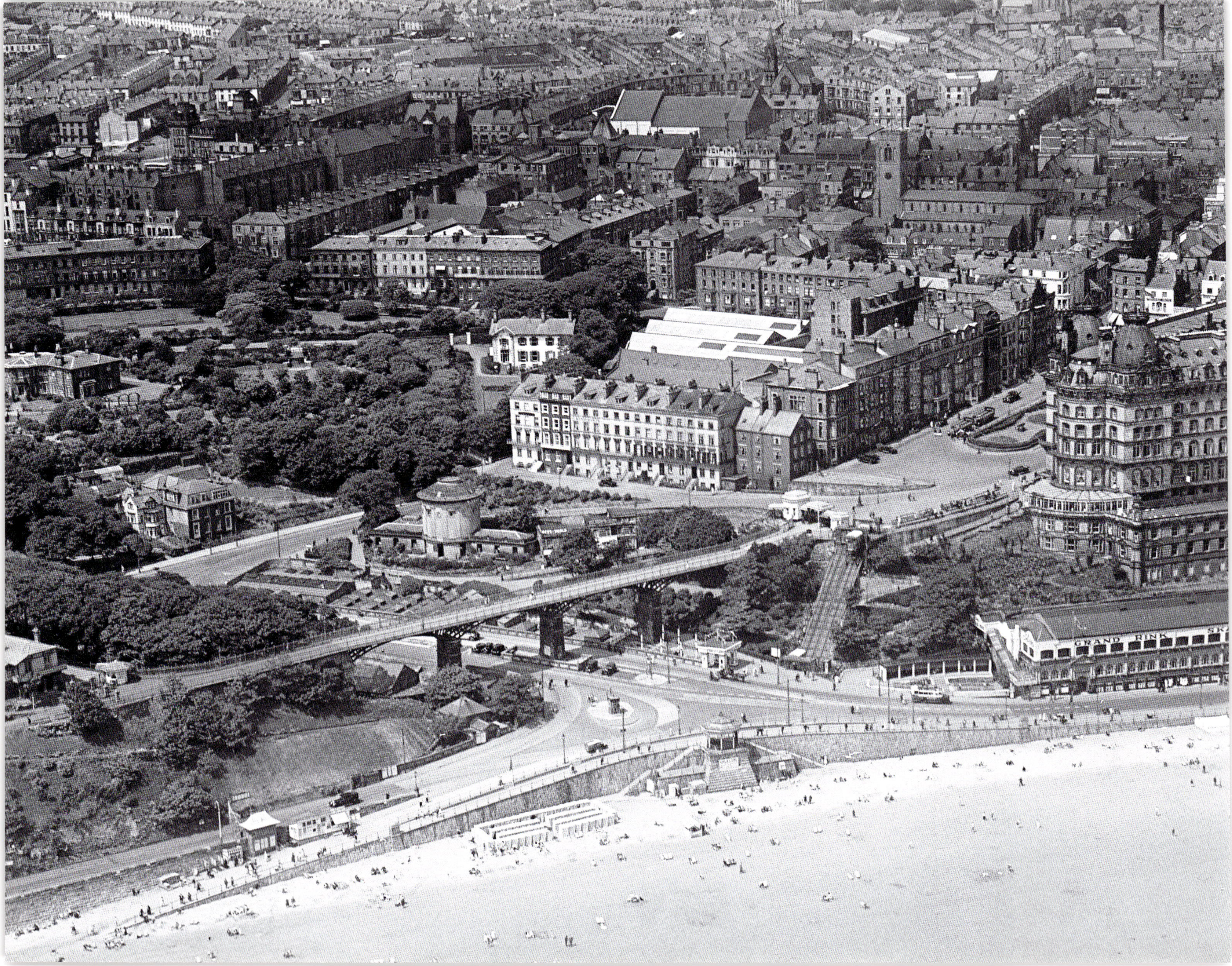
GRAND RINK

The Grand Hotel, Rotunda Museum and Spa Bridge, Scarborough, North Yorkshire
July 1932

This photograph shows the central part of the seafront of the South Bay at Scarborough, with the Grand Hotel to the right, the cylindrical-shaped museum and Spa Bridge, also known as the Cliff Bridge, in the centre, and the beginning of the South Cliff on the left. In 1828–9 the central, stone rotunda of the Museum was constructed by William Smith, often described as the father of English geology. The architect was R H Sharp. Low wings were added in 1860. The completion of the Spa Bridge in 1826 helped to link the old town to the South Cliff on the left and stimulated the construction of new accommodation in this previously undeveloped part of the resort. Behind can be seen the town, including the Crescent, built between 1832 and 1833 and 1856–57, using designs created in 1832 by the architects R H and Samuel Sharp of York.

The most prominent building in this photograph is the Grand Hotel, on the right, a grand structure both in name and scale. The first hotels at the seaside resembled terraces or large Georgian houses, but by the 1860s, the largest hotels were emulating the grandest, palatial hotels of London and Paris. In the late 1850s and 1860s, London was provided with a new group of huge hotels that are still among the most prestigious hotels of the capital today. The Grosvenor, the Charing Cross Hotel and the Langham introduced a new scale of construction and helped to establish a version of the style being adopted in Deuxième Empire Paris as the preferred choice for grand hotels, combining elements of the Italian Renaissance with French detailing, particularly in the rooflines. Brighton's Grand Hotel, which opened in 1864, was the first to adopt the name that would associate it with the Grand Hotel du Louvre in Paris (opened 1855). It originally had 260 bedrooms served by a tall open-well stairway and hydraulic lifts. The Grand Hotel at Scarborough was even larger; when it opened in 1867 it was constructed using around 6 million bricks and contained 300 bedrooms, making it apparently the largest hotel in Europe at that date. Reputedly, the architect Cuthbert Broderick designed the hotel around the theme of time, the four corner towers representing the seasons, 12 floors for the months, 52 chimneys for the weeks and 365 rooms for the days of the year.

EPW038932

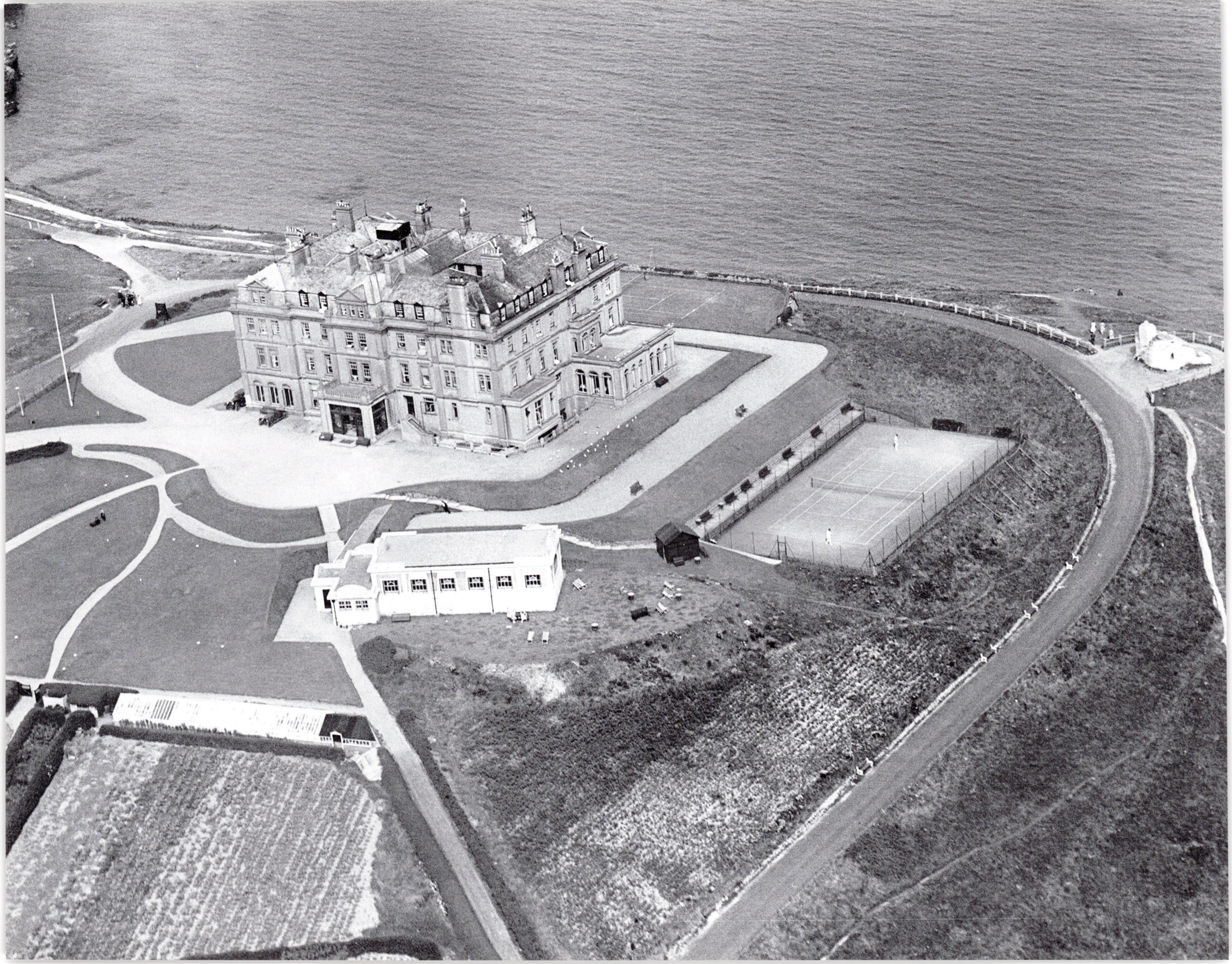

The Atlantic Hotel, Huer's Look-out House and the war memorial, Newquay, Cornwall

August 1932

The Atlantic Hotel stands on a headland to the north of Newquay, and when it was constructed at the end of the 19th century, it stood almost alone. The Cornish Hotel Company acquired a lease for 10 acres of land in 1890 and the hotel that opened in 1892 was designed by Silvanus Trevail and contained more than 100 rooms. During the Second World War the hotel was used as a hospital, but returned to being a hotel after the war, and in 1967 the Beatles stayed there while filming *Magical Mystery Tour*.

By the end of the 19th century, the local council was aware of the impact on the town's economy of the decline of the pilchard fishing industry and the need to stimulate tourism as an alternative source of income. To the right of the hotel can be seen a small white structure, Huer's House. This late 18th- or early 19th-century building was used as a lookout to alert fishermen when shoals of migrating pilchards were nearby. The town's fishing fleet would then put to sea to catch what might be millions of fish at a time.

To the left of the hotel (just beyond the edge of the photograph) is the town's war memorial. It was unveiled on 24 May 1921 by HRH Prince of Wales, Duke of Cornwall, and cost £1,000. It was constructed on the site of a Napoleonic lookout; a watchtower is recorded in this location on the 1840 Tithe Map and was still there when the Ordnance Survey map was published in 1880.

EPW039795

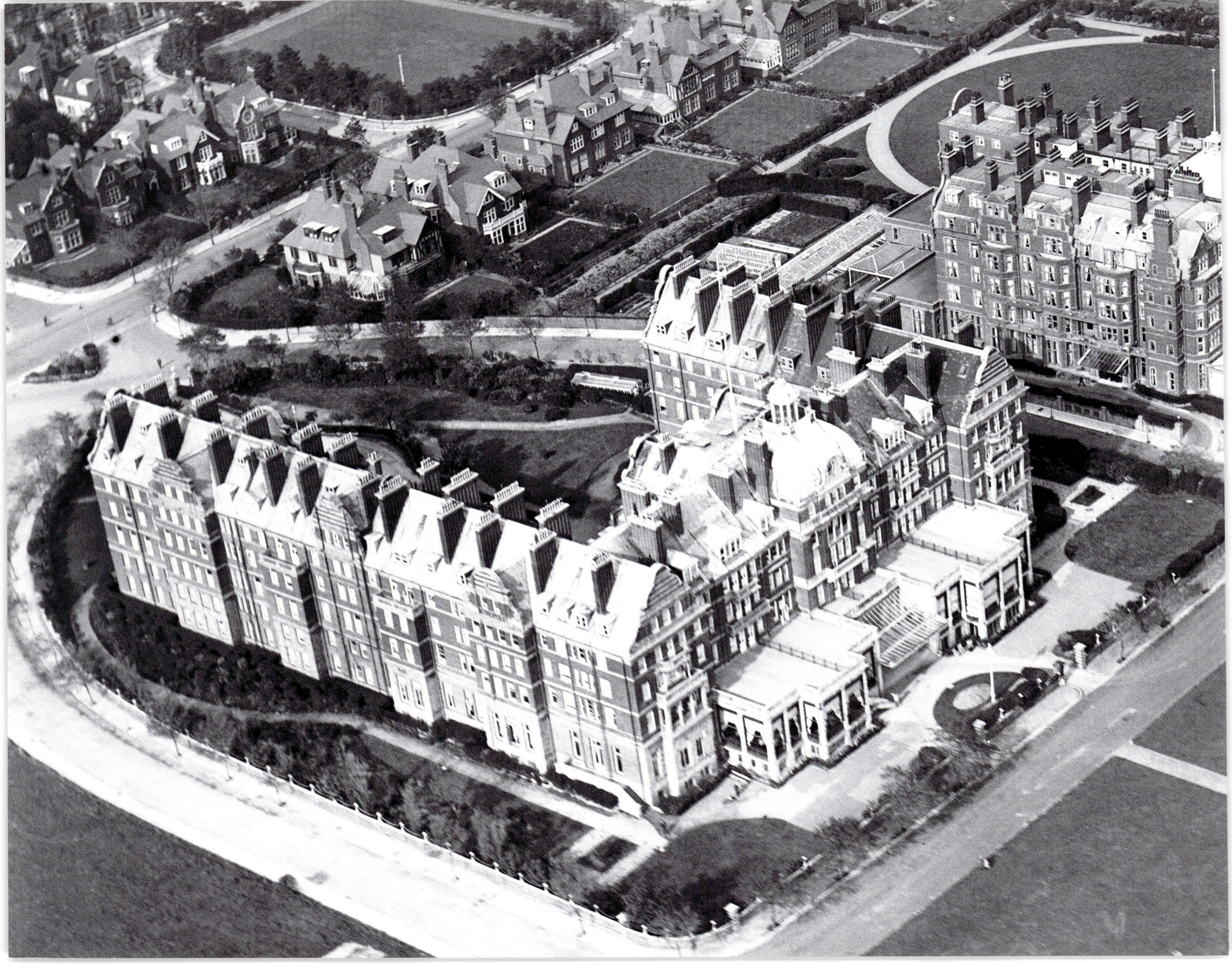

The Hotel Metropole and the Grand Hotel, Folkestone, Kent

April 1920

This photograph shows the present Grand Hotel at Folkestone, the smaller building that began life in 1903 as a block of flats. The Grand could easily be mistaken for a conventional hotel and it is indeed very similar to the adjacent, larger, Metropole Hotel, which, for the sake of confusion, has now been converted into flats. Both are located on the clifftop Leas, an exclusive and prestigious area, where the wealthier residents and visitors to Folkestone congregated.

The Metropole was built in 1895–7 by T W Cutler, and it is U-shaped in plan. It has four storeys, with basements and attics, and its roofline is dominated by Dutch gables and a central dome with a cupola. The basement contained all the below-stairs rooms that might be expected in a country house, as well as a hairdresser's room. On the ground floor there was a dining room, ballroom, lounge, drawing room, smoking room, reading room and billiard room. The first and second floors had a mixture of bedrooms (33), dressing rooms (7) and 3 rooms that could be used as either bedrooms or sitting rooms. There were also four suites of rooms, two with WCs and two without. Compared to modern hotels, the toilet and bathing facilities were small. They were located flanking the stair at the centre of the building and at the rear ends of both wings. On the third floor the arrangement was broadly similar to the two floors below, but rooms that could be used as either bedrooms or sitting rooms were now exclusively used as bedrooms. The top floor had solely bedrooms, tucked into the roof and may have been staff bedrooms. In total there were 106 bedrooms, 60 probably staff bedrooms, 9 dressing rooms, 6 rooms that could be used either as sitting rooms or bedrooms, and 12 suites. The hotel is now a health club, gym, restaurant, bar, art gallery and flats.

During the early 20th century, the earliest purpose-built blocks of flats were beginning to be built in seaside towns. The Grand is now a hotel, but was built as a block of 'gentleman's residential chambers'. It was built by local builder Daniel Baker and opened on 12 September 1903. In plan the block had communal facilities on the ground floor and apartments on the upper floors. Gentlemen had the rooms around the outside of the building, while their servants were in rooms around an inside courtyard, across the corridor from their masters. The Grand has four storeys and attics, and there is a long palm court in front of the building. In style it is designed to be sympathetic to, yet distinctive from, its larger neighbour the Metropole, and its central dome is a clear echo of the adjacent hotel. The building used one of the earliest steel frames and was reputed to be the first to infill its frame with reinforced concrete. Suspended ceilings were included for improved soundproofing, and insulation filled the cavity curtain walls. A new ballroom was opened in 1909 by King Edward VII and was apparently the first sprung dance floor in Europe.

EPW000594

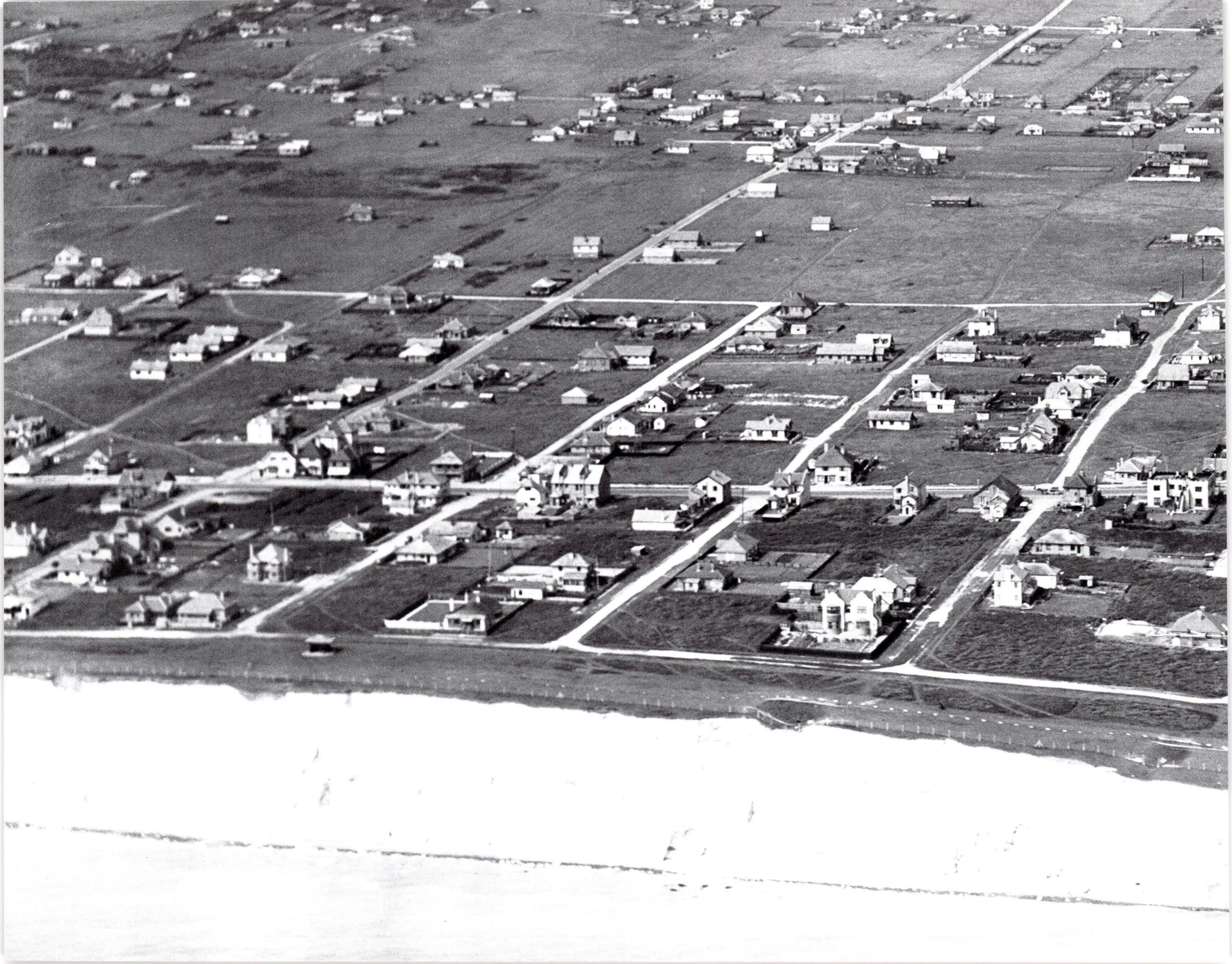

Horsham Avenue and environs, Peacehaven, East Sussex
1933

The growth of motor car ownership created new types of problems and opportunities for seaside resorts. The new freedom changed the pattern of travel within towns and allowed more people to travel to, and live in, settlements without a railway station. Towns and cities began to spread rapidly as people were able to live further from the centre, and in greater degrees of isolation from one another, so creating suburbia.

Most towns developed extensive suburbs, but the seaside acquired its own particular variation as a direct consequence of the car, a form of suburbia independent of an existing resort. Plotlands allowed people who could not afford to purchase a property in the heart of a resort, or did not wish to live in the more formal environment of a seaside town, the opportunity to reside, temporarily or permanently, at the seaside. Keeping costs down inevitably brought a poor standard of architecture and design, and although to the modern eye these settlements have a certain charm, some contemporaries felt they were an abomination.

Plotlands were established, particularly on the south and east coasts, for a variety of reasons and through various mechanisms. Peacehaven, perhaps the most famous plotland development, was conceived as a commemoration of the horrors of the First World War and was originally to be named Anzac-on-Sea. It was established in 1916 by the entrepreneur Charles Neville, who had purchased land and set up a company to develop the site. Peacehaven was intended to house retiring war veterans seeking to escape, and recover, from the effects of war. Many of the original houses were modest, temporary structures, sometimes formed by reusing old railway carriages or army huts. Contemporary commentators thought it was far from being a fitting memorial. C E M Joad in 1927 described it as 'a pigsty of hideously coloured bungalows, shacks and even tents, set down, without rhyme or reason, in a fair, green land'.

EPW041387

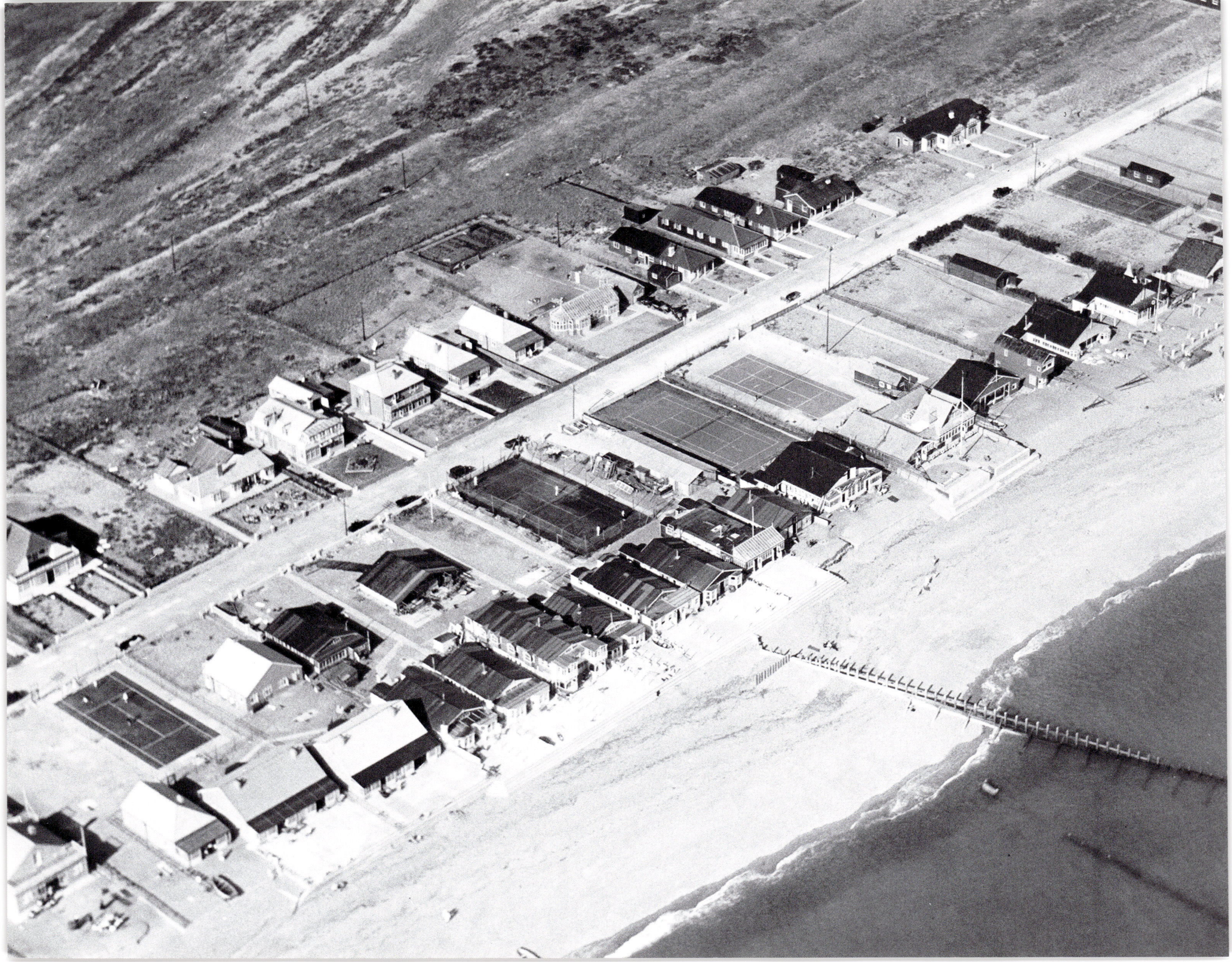

Old Fort Road, Shoreham-by-Sea, West Sussex
July 1924

Some plotlands used former railway carriages as houses and examples survive today at Sutton-on-Sea in Lincolnshire. Old boats and railway carriages were once common at Bungalow Town, established at Shoreham-by-Sea between Brighton and Worthing. However, in this photograph of 1924, the houses in the most prestigious location on Shoreham Beach overlooking the sea, rather than the industrial harbour behind, are already fairly substantial structures, if nevertheless fairly cheaply built.

Old Shoreham on the mainland is an ancient settlement and during the Victorian period it grew into a prominent seaport with shipyards and an active harbour, which remains in use today. Shoreham Beach, to the south of the town, is a shingle spit that blocks the southerly flow of the River Adur, which is forced to turn eastwards. This was where the harbour was established, between the spit and the mainland.

The first settler on Shoreham Beach was reputed to have been a lone camper who erected a disused railway carriage on the beach at the end of the 19th century. Converted railway carriages began to be used as summer homes in the early 20th century, and 'Bungalow Town', as it was then known, became home to the early British film industry. In 1900, Marie Loftus, the 'Sarah Berhnardt of the Music Halls', arrived, and in the following years she and her friends had bungalows built, creating a thriving artistic community. Francis L Lyndhurst founded the Sunny South Film Company, which made its first commercial movie on Shoreham Beach in 1912 and built a film studio there. Much of the housing in the area was cleared for defence reasons during the Second World War.

EPW011521

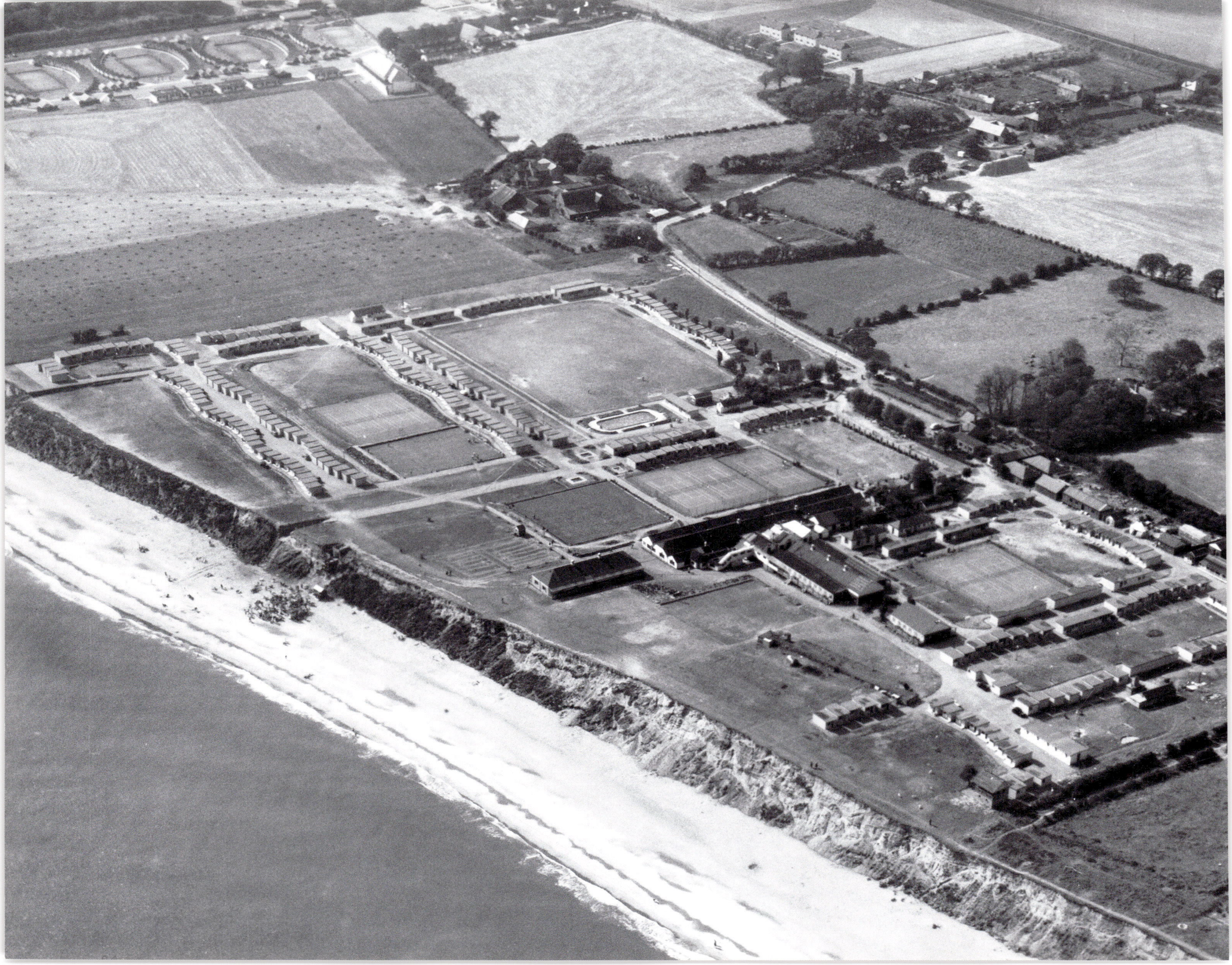

The Constitutional Holiday Camp, Hopton-on-Sea, Norfolk
16 September 1949

By 1939 there were 116 permanent holiday camps and 59 temporary ones. These were a mixture of philanthropic foundations, local government sites and growing numbers of commercial holiday camps that were beginning to be established. In 1920, Herbert Edward Potter and his brother Arthur opened a camp at Hemsby, and it moved to its present site at nearby Hopton-on-Sea near Great Yarmouth in 1925. The coastline around Hopton proved a fruitful location for holiday camps, with five being created during the interwar period, including the Constitutional Holiday Camp in 1928 by A Edgar Simmons, a site that covered 26 acres (10.5ha). In this aerial photograph, as at many other holiday camps, the accommodation is in small chalets or huts, while the larger buildings held the entertainment facilities and dining areas. The largest camps, particularly those operated by Billy Butlin, had industrial-scale buildings at their heart (*see* p 199).

Around the coast there were a number of clusters of holiday camps. Beginning with a single camp that proved successful, investors who could identify a suitable site and a market for their enterprises would create new holiday camps. The Isle of Wight is another of these clusters of holiday camp development. In 1939 there were 12 camps operating, and in the 1950 Holiday Camps Directory and Magazine, 11 camps were listed. Hayling Island was home to another cluster. The success of the first Civil Service Holiday Camp at Corton led to the creation of a second one on Hayling Island in 1930 (*see* p 31).

In 1925 Captain Harry Warner retired from the Royal Artillery and rather implausibly opened a seaside restaurant. He opened his first holiday camp at Northney on Hayling Island in 1931, where the CSCA camp already existed, and by the outbreak of the Second World War, he owned four camps. After the war, the company expanded until it had 14 camps. Other camps followed on Hayling Island, including the Sunshine Camp in 1936 and the Coronation Camp in 1938.

EAW026607

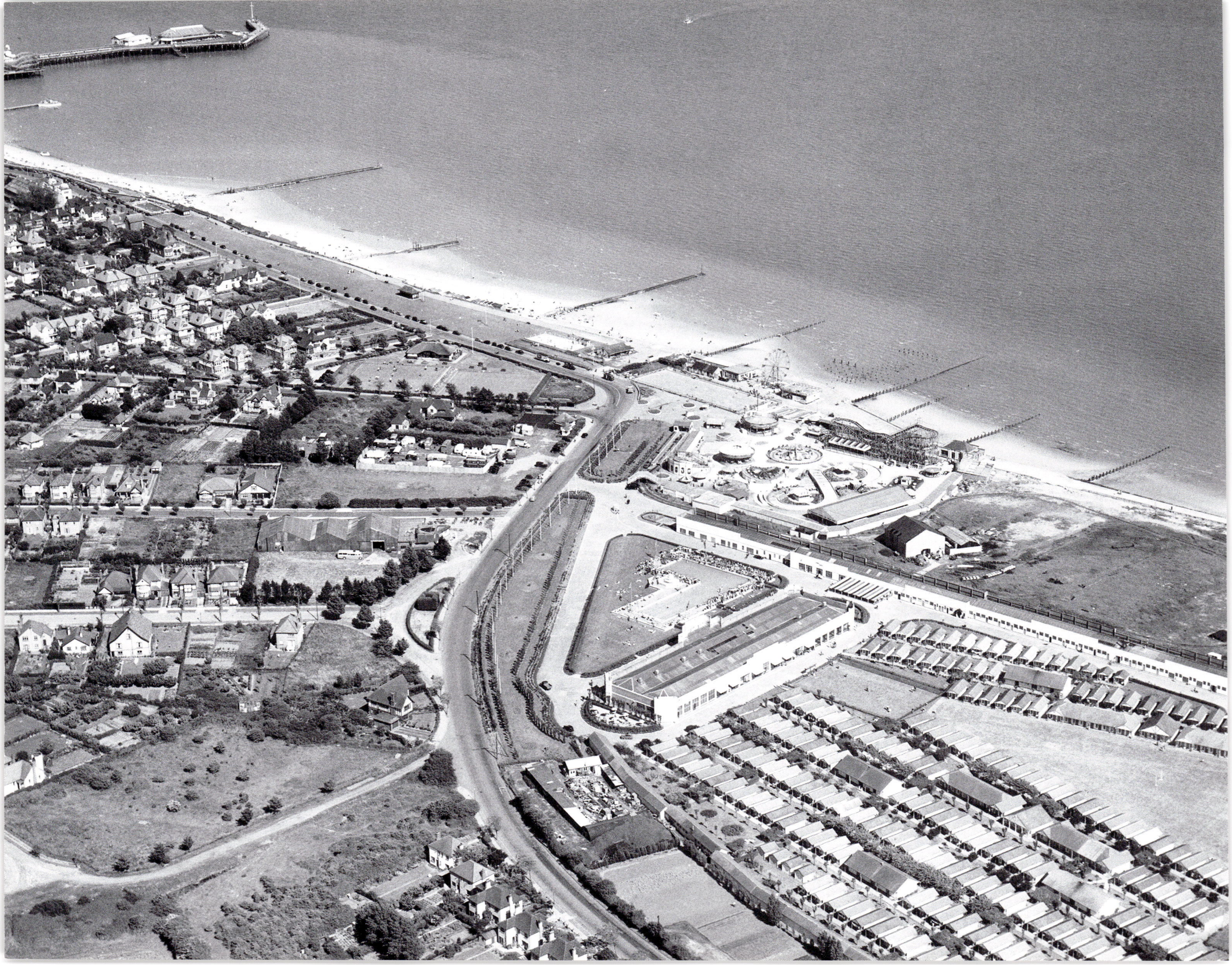

Butlin's Holiday Camp, Clacton-on-Sea, Essex
1952

William 'Billy' Butlin (1899–1980) began his career in 1921 with a single hoop-la stall and in 1928 he took a huge gamble by investing £2,000 in the first batch of Dodgem cars to arrive in Britain. By 1934 he ran eight seaside amusement parks and operated most of the attractions at several big Christmas fairs.

In the mid-1930s he decided to diversify into holiday camps. He visited Joseph Cunningham's pioneering holiday camp on the Isle of Man to learn about the practicalities of the business, and although the family who ran it could not prevent him from seeing the camp, they barred him from witnessing the secrets of their kitchens. Holiday camps had existed since the early 20th century, with Cunningham having led the way in 1904, but Butlin saw the potential of creating a self-contained holiday village for middle-income families, with chalets set in landscaped gardens and a range of sports and entertainment facilities.

Building work began on his first camp in October 1935 at Ingoldmells, near Skegness, and it opened to its first 500 visitors on Easter Saturday 1936. The site was to accommodate 1,000 people in 600 chalets and 250 bathrooms. Set within the landscaped grounds were what he described as all the amenities of a first-class hotel, as well as free golf, tennis, bathing, bowling, dancing and concert parties, and a boating lake.

A key to the success of Butlins was the creation of a strong brand. During the 1920s he had issued his staff with coats with an embroidered 'B' badge, and his stalls and lorries bore the slogan 'Hurrah! It's Butlin's'. This was superseded at Skegness by the slogan on the reception block 'OUR TRUE INTENT IS ALL FOR YOUR DELIGHT', a slight misquote from *A Midsummer Night's Dream* lifted from the side of a fairground organ. Butlin was convinced that he had provided the infrastructure to guarantee a happy holiday, but he sensed that something was missing. Bored campers, keeping to their own family groups, were not getting involved with activities. A new type of culture was needed and to achieve this, the legendary 'redcoats' were created to encourage the holidaymakers to participate in the activities. Butlin and Norman Bradford, one of his staff, were behind this innovation, and it was Bradford who first uttered the immortal, pre-breakfast greeting 'Good morning campers'.

By 1939, Butlin had two camps and a third was being built at Filey when war broke out. This site at Clacton was Butlin's second camp, opening on 11 June 1938 originally for 1,000 campers, with a further 500 being catered for during the following year. In this aerial photograph, the ranks of small chalets can be seen arranged around a central green. At the top of the site is a large, almost industrial-looking building, which contained all the entertainment facilities for the visitors and beyond it there is a large open-air swimming pool. The adjacent amusement park was another creation of Billy Butlin, and it opened in 1937.

The camp closed on the outbreak of war in 1939 and was taken over by the army. It reopened as a holiday camp in April 1946. This photograph was taken shortly before the camp was enlarged in 1955, raising the capacity of the site to 6,000 guests. In October 1983, Butlin's announced that the Clacton camp would be closed. The site is now a housing development.

EAW043668

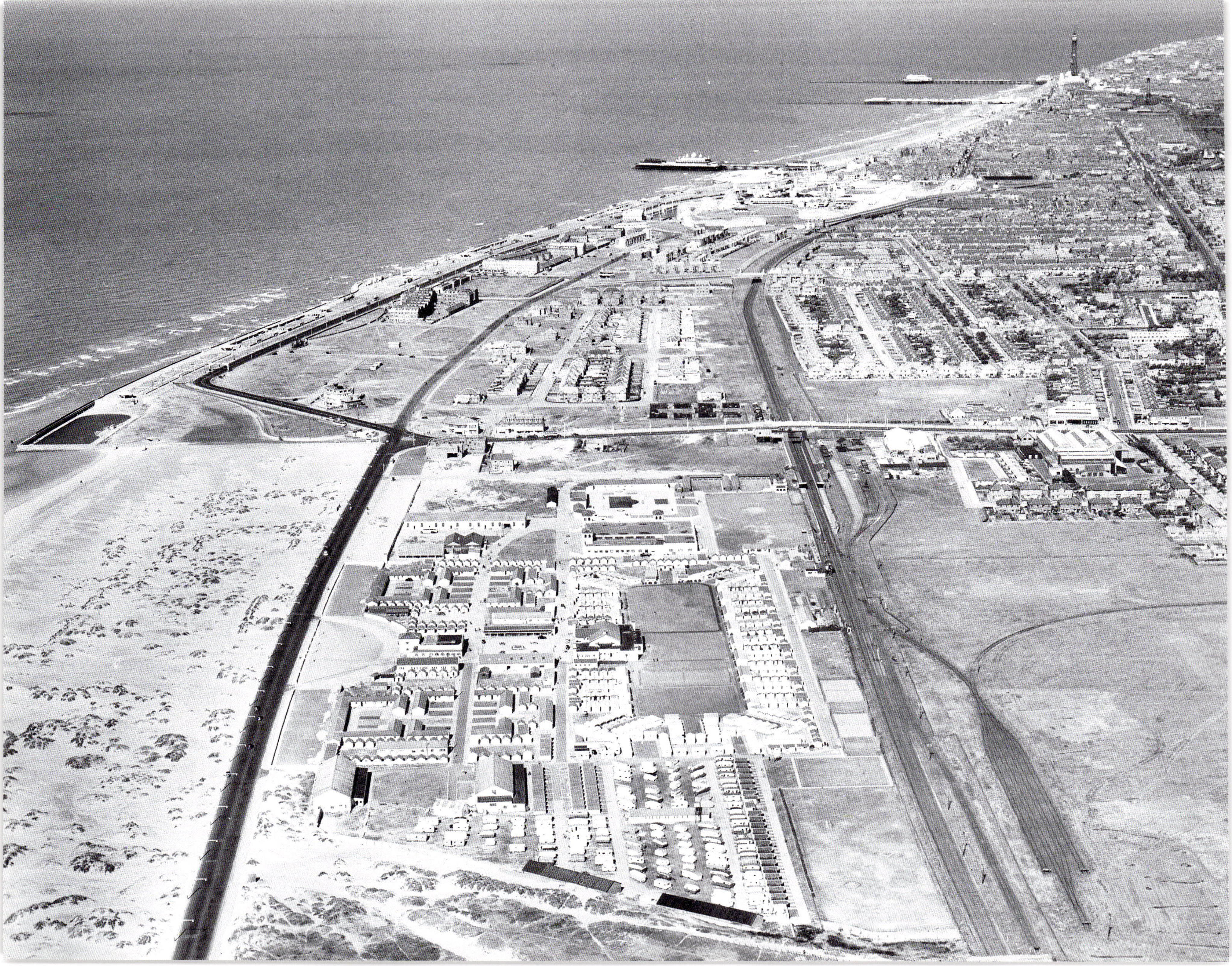

Squires Gate Holiday Camp looking towards Blackpool Tower and the seafront, Lytham St Annes, Lancashire

18 September 1952

Set behind the sand dunes at the southern end of Blackpool was a substantial holiday camp that was latterly run by Pontins, but was set up before the Second World War. An advertisement for Squires Gate Holiday Camp in April 1939 described how Blackpool's magical sands were reminiscent of California. The 40-acre site was covered with chalets, ballrooms, games and dining halls, and there were plans to add a new swimming pool during the year. Prices ranged per person per week from 55s to 79s at the height of the season, and the advertisement trumpeted that there was nothing to pay for any extras.

This holiday camp was subsequently taken over by Pontins. Its founder Fred Pontin was born in 1906 in the East End of London, and after a career in the Stock Exchange between the wars, he established hotels for construction workers during the Second World War. It was this experience that inspired him to go into the holiday business. In the years immediately after the war he began to open holiday camps, and by 1947 he ran six camps that could house 1,300 visitors. Compared to the Butlin's camps of the same date, Pontin's sites were much smaller; the five Butlin's camps open in 1947 could accommodate over 30,000 guests. By the 1960s, Pontin's business had grown to include 16 camps and by the mid-1970s it had 24, as well as accommodation in Jersey and in the Mediterranean.

As well as the chalets and huts, at the southern end of the site, at the bottom of the photograph, there was space for caravans. The Squires Gate site closed on 2 October 2009 and was subsequently demolished and cleared to make way for housing.

EAW047519

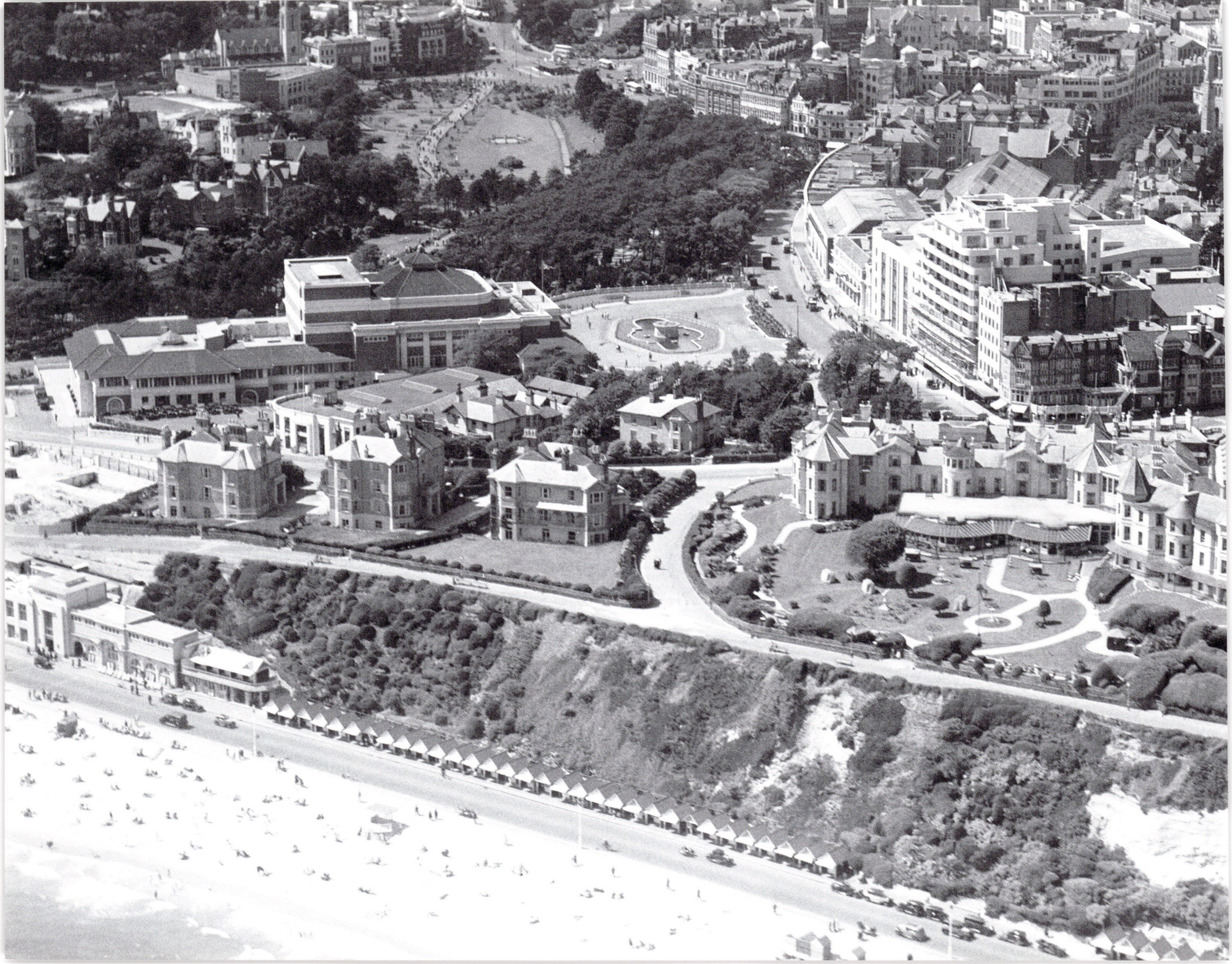

The Royal Bath Hotel, Pavilion and the town centre, Bournemouth, Dorset
26 June 1935

This photograph shows two contrasting visions of hotels at the seaside. On top of the cliff on the right-hand side of the image can be seen the Royal Bath Hotel. It originated in 1837–8 as part of the development of this side of Bournemouth for Sir George Tapps-Gervis. The architect of the original structure was Benjamin Ferrey, and it was substantially extended in 1878–80 by C C Creeke.

This meandering collection of structures in classical and Italianate styles is in marked contrast to the modernity and unified design of the Palace Court Hotel behind. Opened in the mid-1930s, and designed by A J Seal and partners, this steel-framed structure with reinforced concrete walls consisted of shops on the ground floor, with the hotel on the lower floors and service flats between the fifth and ninth floors. Its façade is marked out by the large windows and curving balconies. It is still a hotel today. Behind it were the Palace Court Theatre and the 1932 Motor Mac car park, the earliest multi-storey car park in the modern sense built at a seaside resort.

The large structure in the centre-left of the photograph is the Pavilion Theatre. This large entertainment complex, consisting of a theatre with a ballroom and supper rooms, was built in 1928–9 by G Wyville Home and Shirley Knight, who were winners of a competition in 1923. It was officially opened by the Duke of Gloucester on 19 March 1929. The building was remodelled in 1934 and in the 1950s, but the original interiors survive in a variety of styles reflecting the importance of Grecian and Egyptian influences in the late 1920s.

On the seafront can be seen the extensive bathing chalets and beach huts that had been constructed during the interwar years.

EPR000663

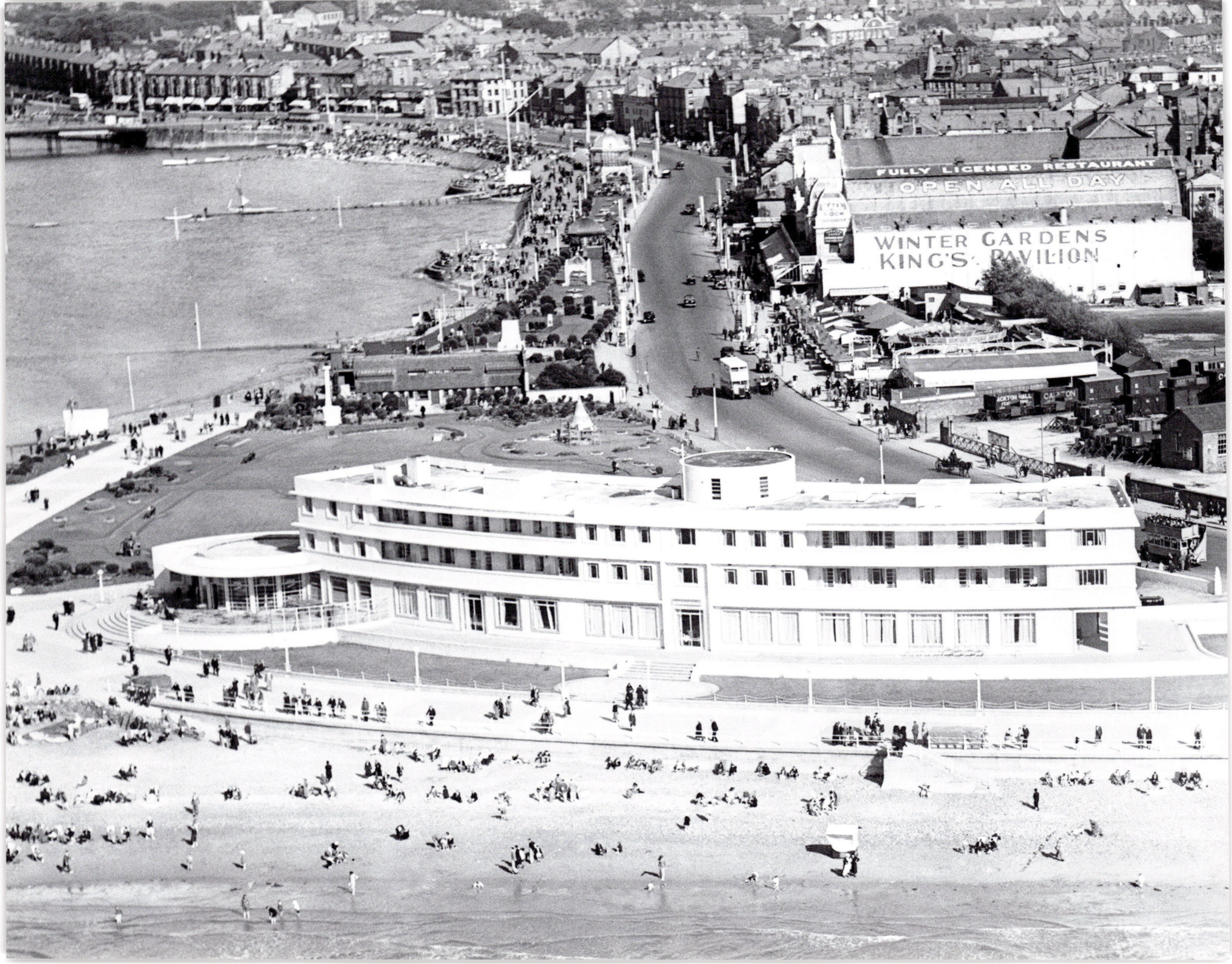
FULLY LICENSED RESTAURANT
OPEN ALL DAY
WINTER GARDENS
KING'S PAVILION

The Midland Hotel and the seafront, Morecambe, Lancashire
30 August 1934

The North Western Hotel opened in 1848, when Morecambe was just beginning to develop as a seaside resort, and it was renamed the Midland Hotel in 1871. The leading modernist architect Oliver Hill was commissioned by the London Midland and Scottish Railway to design a hotel in a contemporary style to replace the company's existing hotel, and Lord Clonmore described in *The Architectural Review* in September 1933 how its construction meant that Morecambe would be 'well emancipated from Victorian gloom'.

The Midland Hotel was built in 1932–3 in a striking, modernist form, and avant-garde art and design were incorporated into the building. Eric Gill was responsible for the seahorses on the exterior and carved a stone relief entitled 'Odysseus being welcomed from the sea by Nausicaa' in the entrance lounge. Gill and Denis Tegetmeier created a ceiling panel featuring Triton above the main spiral staircase and a painted map on the wall of the Children's Room. There were wave-patterned rugs by Marion Dorn and the circular café at the north end of the hotel included a seaside-themed mural by Eric Ravilious. Here modern art was included to replace the opulence of Victorian interiors. During the late 20th century, the Midland Hotel was almost a symbol of the decline in the fortunes of the English seaside resort and it was forced to close in 1998. It stood derelict for a number of years, but was refurbished and reopened in June 2008.

Behind the Midland Hotel on the seafront can be seen the Winter Gardens. Its façade contained a mixture of features and styles with mainstream, red-brick Edwardian forms intermingled with some Italianate arcading and topped with a line of pepper-pot finials inspired by Indian temples. This is a great example of the type of architectural eclecticism that dominated the period around 1900, against which the new Midland hotel was consciously reacting (*see* p 85).

EPR000309

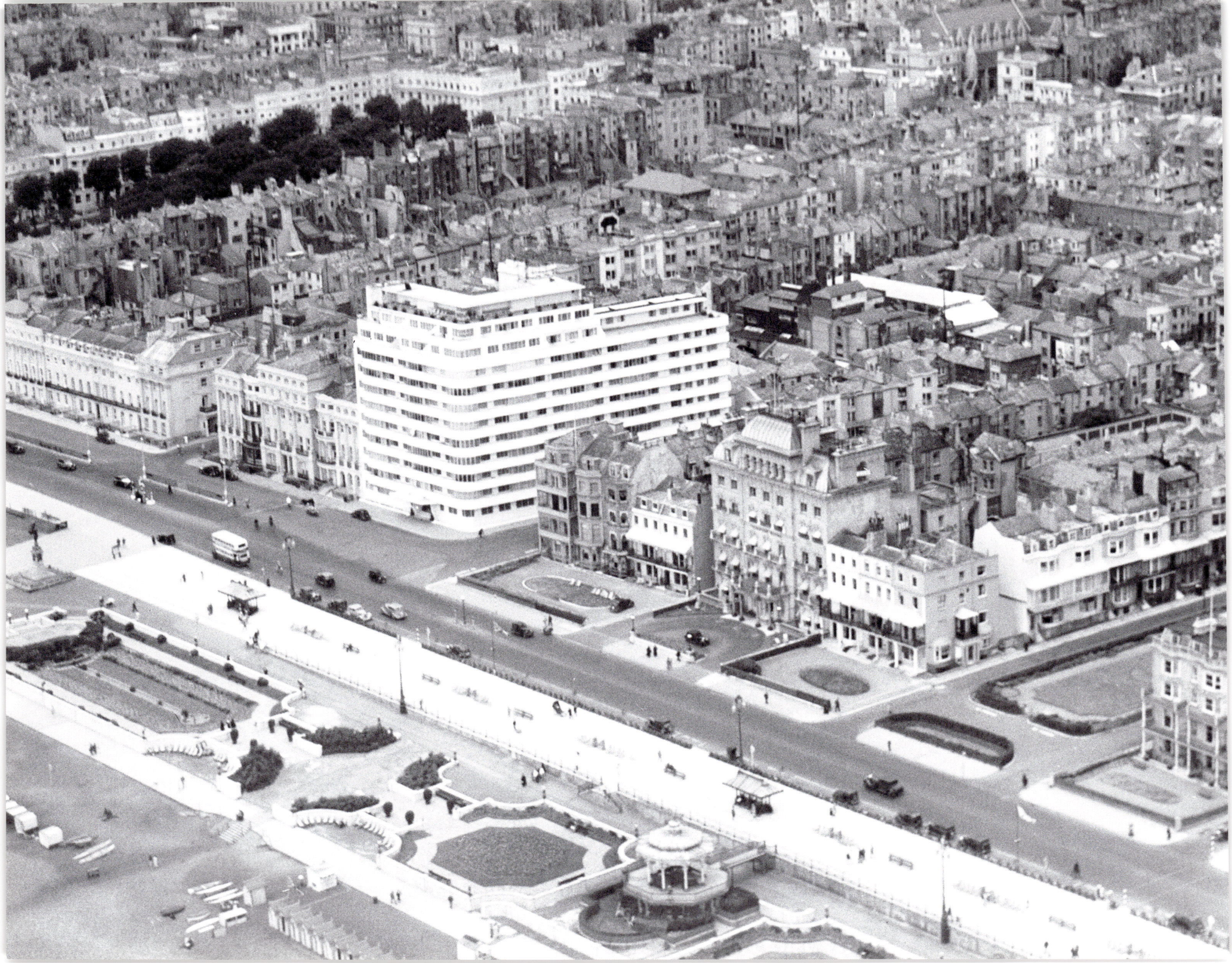

Embassy Court and Brunswick Town, Brighton and Hove, East Sussex
June 1937

This photograph shows an area of the city including the legal boundary that once existed between Brighton and Hove. To the left of the prominent modern block of flats is Brunswick Town, built from 1825 on land owned by the Scutt family. These large terraced houses were created behind the grandest type of palatial façade found at the seaside. They used a variety of forms, ranging in size from three to five storeys, and embellished with Ionic and Corinthian pilasters and engaged columns.

The large block of flats is Embassy Court, which was built in 1934–6 by the leading architect Wells Coates. Whereas Brunswick Town took prestigious and expensive seaside accommodation along the seafront, Embassy Court took it upwards. The building incorporated features such as sun lounges and large, sliding, folding windows that accorded with prevailing views about healthy living. These flats were designed for an up-market, modern clientele; therefore, the basement included a car park and lock-up garages, and the interiors featured works of art, textiles and furniture by leading designers. The prominent local solicitor and politician Herbert Carden wanted to turn Brighton into a modern, forward-looking city, and was willing to sacrifice much of the resort's historic townscape to do so. He cited Embassy Court as the model building, and if Carden's plans had been realised, the Royal Pavilion would have been replaced by a conference and entertainment centre and the Lanes, the historic centre of Brighton, would have disappeared.

EPW054034

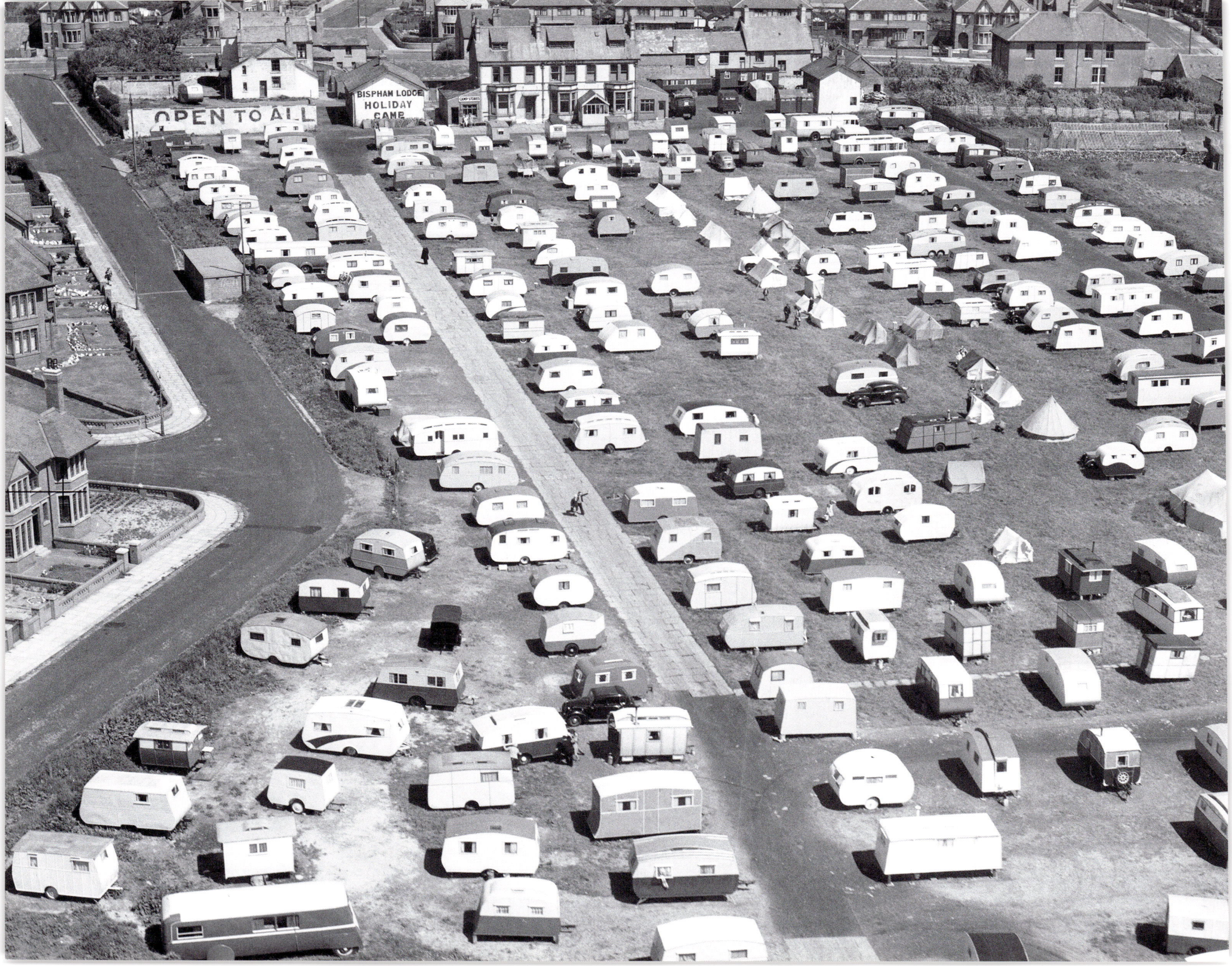
OPEN TO ALL
BISPHAM LODGE
HOLIDAY
CAMP
CAMP STORES

Caravans at the Bispham Lodge Holiday Camp, Norbreck, Blackpool, Lancashire
3 June 1946

This photograph shows a busy caravan site at a holiday camp at Bispham to the north of Blackpool. Before the Second World War, photographs show most of the occupants were staying in tents, but after the war caravans seem to have dominated, though within a few years the site had been redeveloped for housing. At the top of the photograph can be seen what are presumably the limited facilities provided for campers. A huge variety of caravans can be seen, as well as one or two large motorhomes, easily recognisable as they have four wheels.

Horse-drawn carriages as homes, described as 'caravans', have existed since at least the 17th century, and during the 19th century they were used by travelling menageries, circuses and gypsies. As a boy in the 1830s, the circus proprietor 'Lord' George Sanger had travelled around fairs with his family in a caravan, and by the end of the 19th century many private citizens were using horse-drawn caravans for leisure.

The first motorhomes resembling a caravan on a lorry chassis had appeared by the outbreak of the First World War, but the first motor-towed caravans had to be small as the cars that towed them were not particularly powerful. Between the wars caravans became increasingly sophisticated and more comfortable, but they remained an expensive item restricted to wealthy travellers, though an extensive trade in hiring caravans developed. By the mid-1930s, there were about 3,500 caravans in use and the first caravan rallies were taking place. At this time there were not yet designated caravan sites and people had to negotiate with a friendly farmer for the use of a corner of a field.

Caravan numbers grew rapidly after the Second World War. In 1939, 2,500 were produced each year, but by 1966 this had risen to 65,000. Formal caravan sites only began to appear after the Second World War and in 1960 these became regulated by the Caravan Sites and Control of Development Act. Before the war, the caravan holiday was confined to people able to afford a car, but by the mid-1950s static caravans to rent had been established at many resorts.

EAW001054

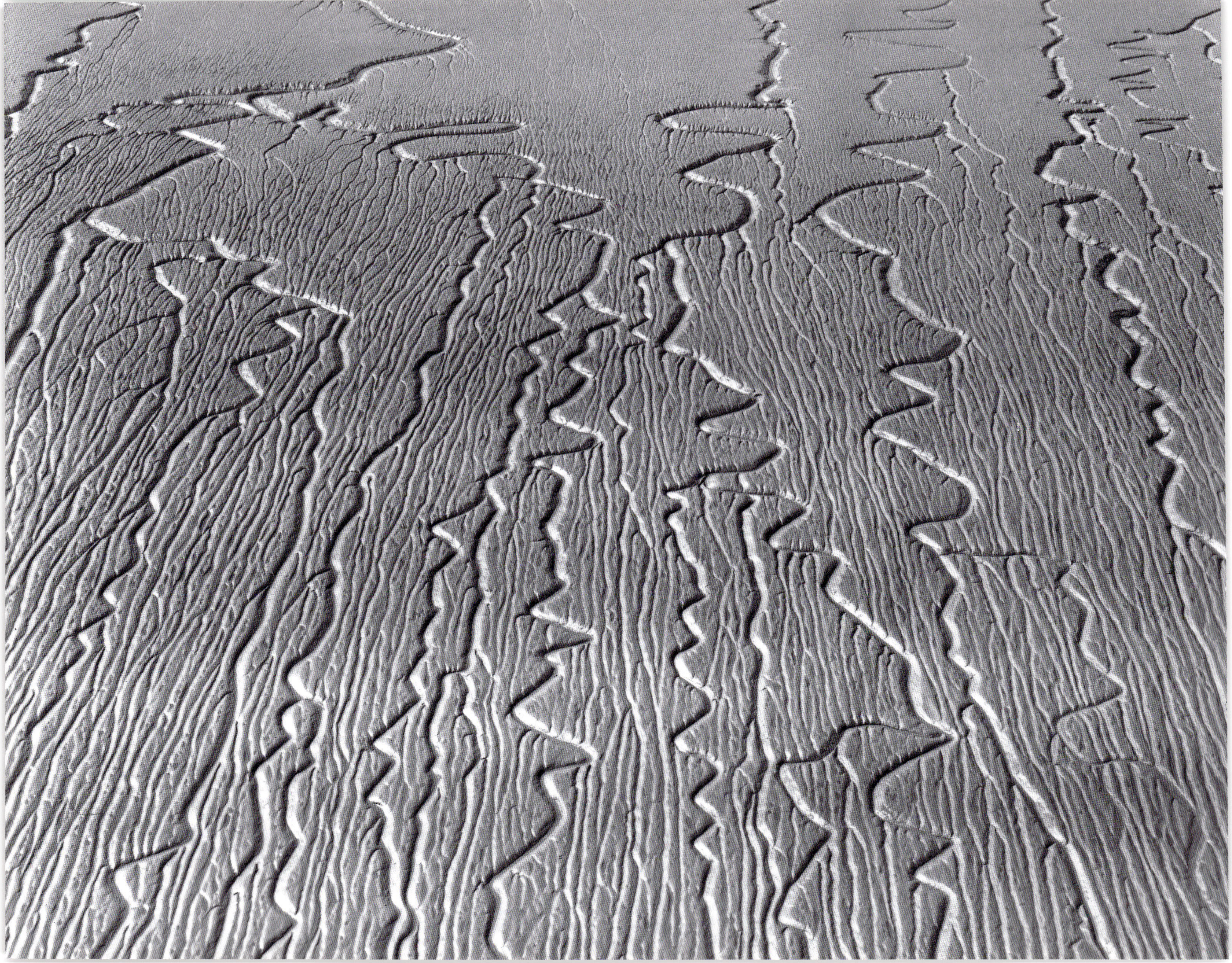

Patterns in the mud off Weston-super-Mare, Somerset
26 May 1948

In this particularly artistic image of patterns in the sand, which resemble the craquelure pattern on the surface of an oil painting or a ceramic pot, the Aerofilms photographer has captured an image of what was captioned as the mud at Weston-super-Mare, though more charitably it might be described as a wealth of fine sand.

Located on the River Severn estuary, Weston-super-Mare enjoys, or perhaps endures, the second largest tidal range in the world. The difference in height between high tide and low tide can be up to 12.3m (40ft), the height of a four-storey building. The Bay of Fundy on the east coast of Canada is the only place in the world that exceeds this, with a tidal range of about 13m (43ft); the average tidal range worldwide is about 1m (3ft). Because Weston-super-Mare has a shallow, sandy beach, the sea can appear very distant at low tide and the area of the beach increases dramatically, though much of the land uncovered is unsuitable to walk on. A 1913 guidebook noted that the beach was Weston's chief attraction, but it then went on to record that 'Beyond the sand is a considerable expanse of exceptionally sticky mud'.

Although Weston is an attractive town in a sheltered location, the absence of the sea for much of the day has caused it a number of problems. In the Georgian period, sea bathing took place in the morning on medical advice, predominantly through the use of bathing machines. However, an 1822 guidebook for Weston-super-Mare, which referred to the three bathing machines on the sands, noted that the time of their use was regulated by the tide, rather than by medical opinion. Additional arrangements had to be made at Weston-super-Mare, and as well as providing a bathhouse, there was an area reserved for ladies, where the sea was slightly more accessible. During the interwar years, the Marine Lake and an open-air bathing pool were constructed by the local authority to cater for the growing number of visitors who wished to swim and play in the sea, irrespective of the level of the sea (*see* p 81).

The other problem caused by the wide tidal range was that it severely restricted the development of steamer services, and this is the reason that Weston undertook the construction of a pier as early as 1847. This proved unsuccessful, but by the 1860s Birnbeck Pier had opened and projected a sufficient distance into the Severn Estuary to allow steamers to land passengers (*see* p 129).

EAW014929

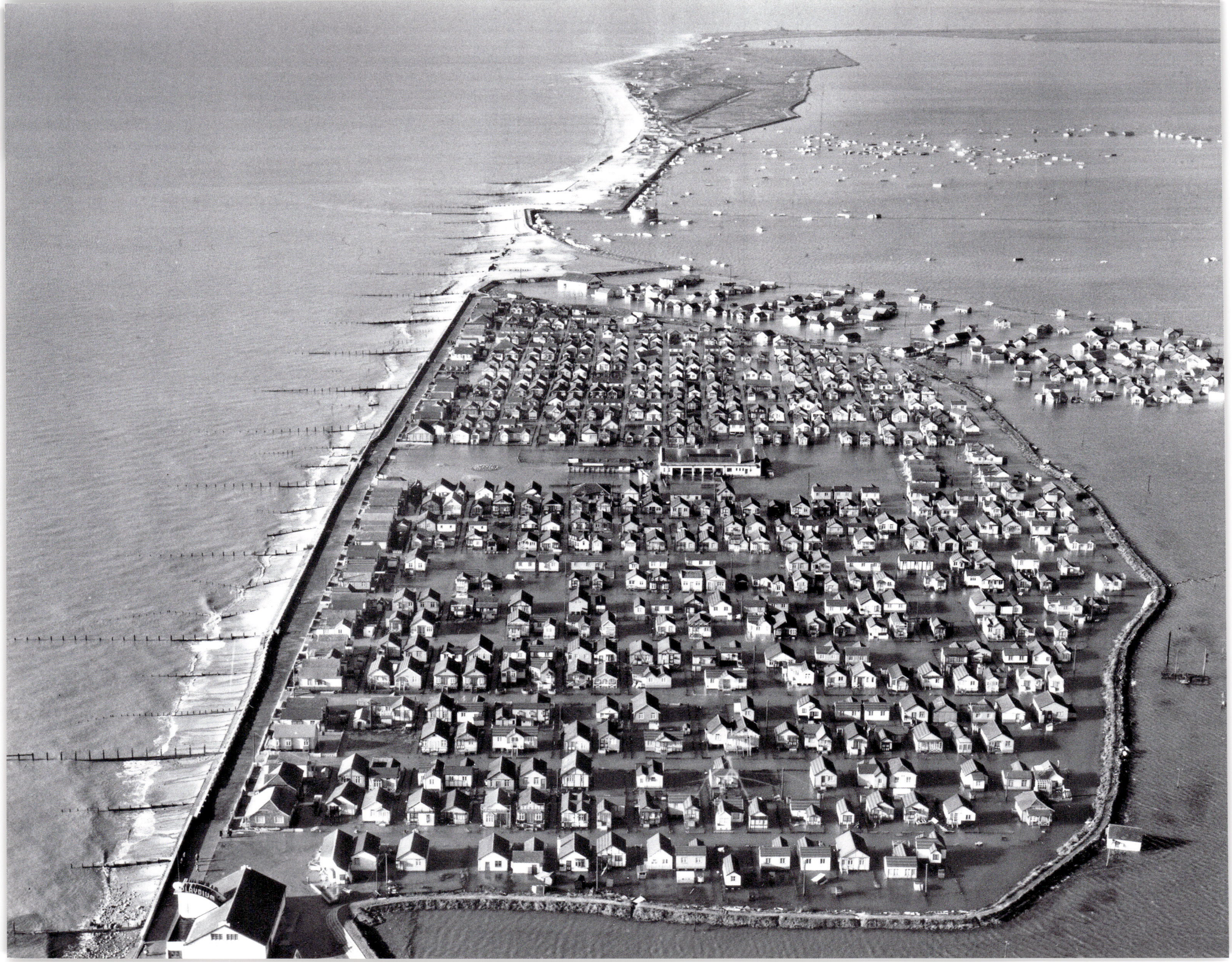

Damaged sea defences and flooding along the Essex coast, Jaywick, Essex
2 February 1953

This photograph shows the small coastal town of Jaywick in the immediate aftermath of the huge storm surge of 31 January and 1 February 1953. Storm surges in the North Sea occur when high tides, low barometric pressure and strong winds from the north combine to force water southwards down the North Sea. Its shape, with the wide northern gap between Scotland and Norway, but the narrow English Channel at the south, builds up pressure that has to go somewhere, and therefore seawater inundates wherever there is a low-lying or poorly defended coastline.

In 1953, the height of the southern North Sea rose by between 2.7m and 3.4m (9–11ft), leading to 800km^2 (309 square miles) of land being inundated, and causing damage costing £900 million. The east of England was worst affected, especially Essex, where 112 people died. The village of Jaywick was inundated by 9 billion litres of water, causing flooding up to 1.8m (6ft) deep in places and leading to 35 deaths. Gaps were torn in the concrete facing of the promenade at Margate, the railway line flooded, boats were washed into the streets of the Old Town, and the lighthouse at the end of the pier fell into the sea. Further north, in Lincolnshire, an estimated 860,000 tons of sand was washed into Mablethorpe, stripping the beach back to its black clay, while near Skegness sea defences were destroyed. Twenty people died in the Skegness area while a further 16 perished in the Mablethorpe to Sutton area. In total, 307 people died and 24,500 houses were destroyed or damaged. Prime Minister Winston Churchill called it a 'National Disaster'.

EAW048263

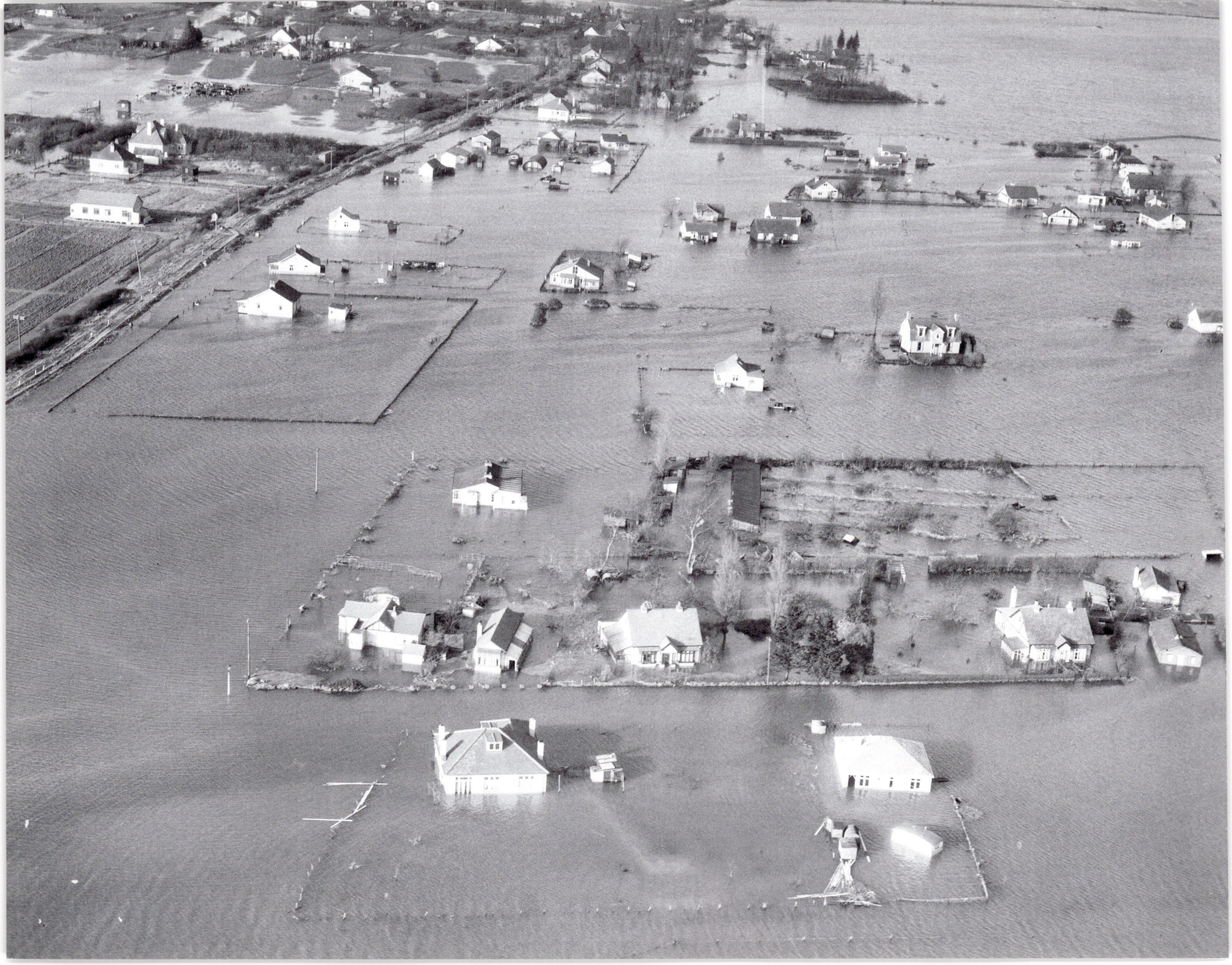

Flooding around Terschelling Avenue and Somnes Avenue, Canvey Island, Essex
2 February 1953

Canvey Island, like Jaywick, was another low-lying settlement on the Essex coast that suffered dramatically during the 1953 storm surge. There were 58 deaths and some of its victims drowned while in bed.

After the Second World War, England's coastal defences had been neglected; Hunstanton actually had a hole in its sea wall in 1950 and Canvey Island had no adequate protection for its housing and industry. Sea wall design was poorly understood. Defences were too low in some places and not well built, and many were too vertical to be effective. In many places, bungalows, beach huts and industrial facilities were low-lying and in the way of defences. Additionally, long stretches of natural defences, including beaches and sand dunes, had not been maintained. There was also a lack of coordination; in 1953 defences were looked after by local authorities, river boards and government departments, as well as private people, and there was no single chain of command to react to events taking place.

This photograph was taken a day after the storm surge and Canvey Island was still inundated with water. Once the waters receded, new, substantial concrete sea defences were installed here and at Jaywick.

EAW048243

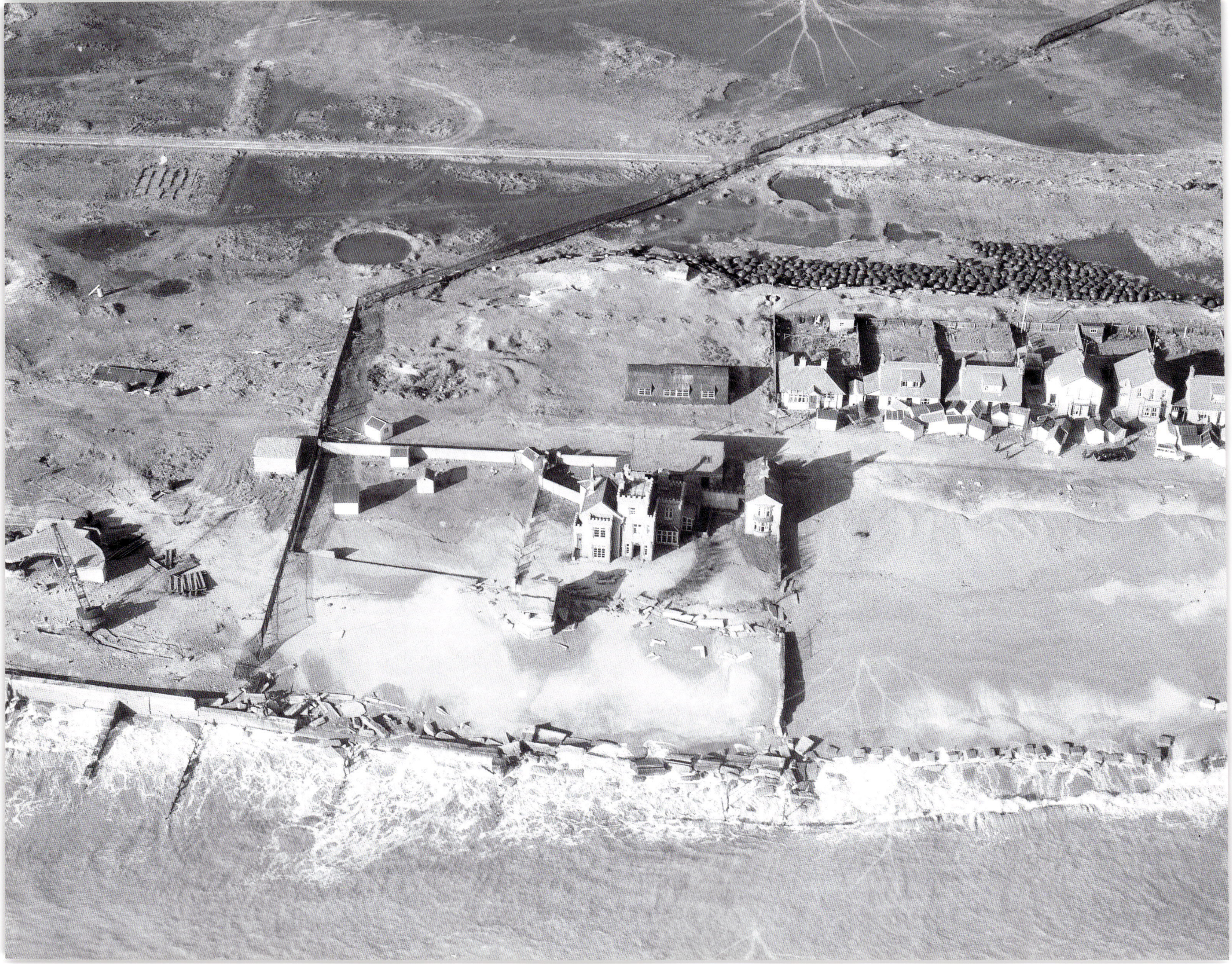

Damaged sea defences near Landguard Lodge, Felixstowe, Suffolk

2 February 1953

This photograph was taken on the same day, and presumably on the same flight, as the photographs of Jaywick and Canvey Island, and shows the coastline further to the north. This stretch of coast is a short distance south of Felixstowe and close to Landguard Fort, a substantial, square fortification built during the reign of James I.

This photograph shows how the power of the sea had smashed the sea defences, pushed inland and demolished the wall in front of Landguard Lodge, which was built around 1900 and resembles a miniature castle. The beach huts that once lined the shore can be seen washed up against the line of 1930s houses, which have presumably suffered significant damage as well. What is interesting is that there seems to have been very little in the way of the sea wall in front of these houses compared to the quantity of demolished structures in front of the lodge. Landguard Lodge now sits in the midst of a large caravan site and there are rows of caravans on the land in front of the line of interwar houses.

The 1953 storm led to both immediate and longer-term responses. Remedial works took place quickly, including creating new sea walls and improved defences along the East Anglian coast. However, perhaps the longest-lasting legacy of 1953 was a growing appreciation that sea defences should be a national responsibility. The Waverley Committee was established to consider the country's coastal defences and concluded that the height of the surge was higher than had been expected and planned for. Therefore, the 1953 storm became the new minimum height to which future defences were designed to respond. After 1953, around 1,200 beaches were replenished with sand to make them more resilient, hundreds of kilometres of defences were repaired and improved, walls were raised where needed and early warning measures were put in place.

EAW048292

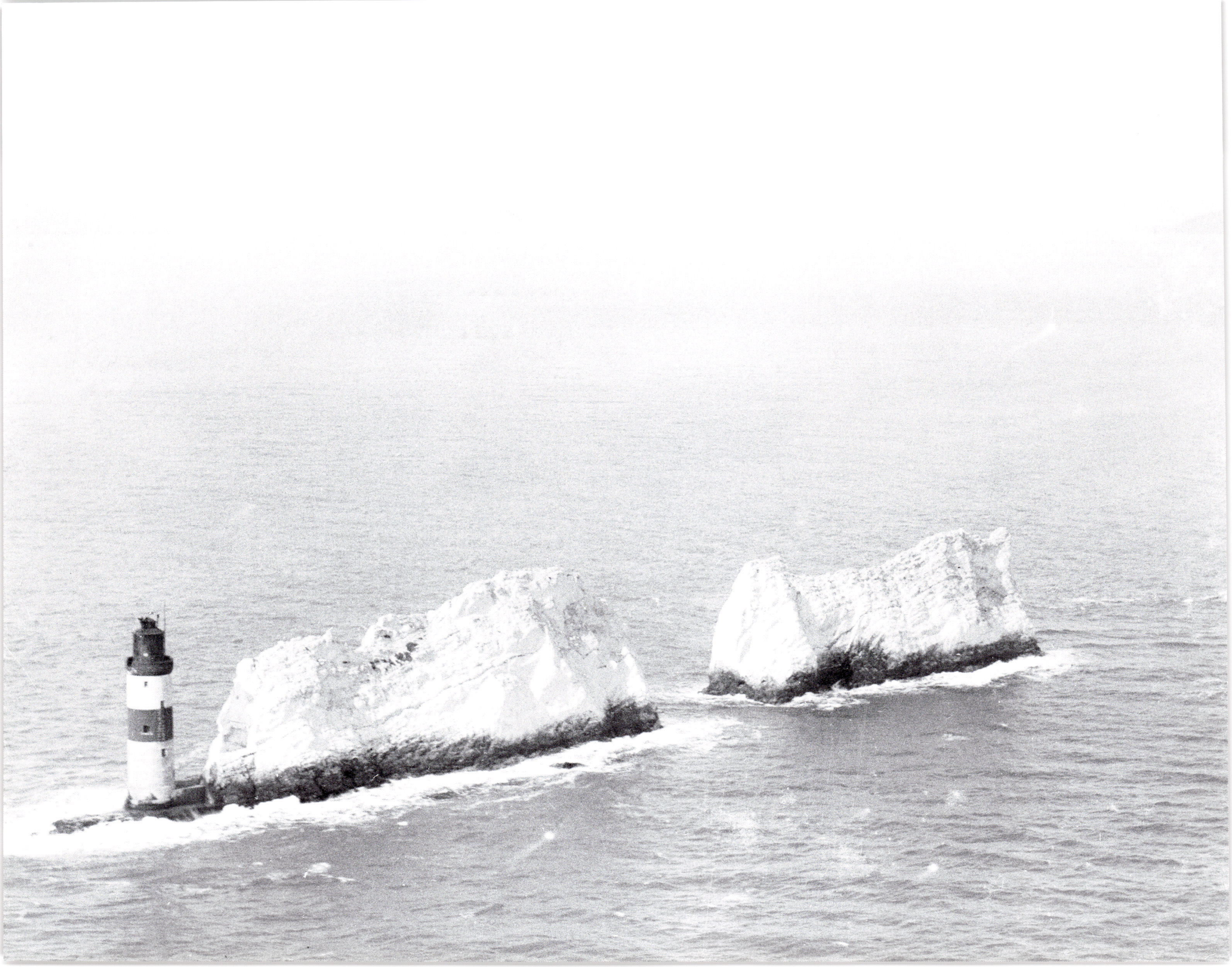

The Needles Lighthouse, Isle of Wight
May 1920

To allow people to safely travel out to sea around the coast, a range of lighthouses and day marks have been created over the centuries. These are designed to aid navigation and to warn of hazards at sea. Lighthouses are the inspiration for numerous seaside souvenirs, as well as serving as obstacles on crazy golf courses and, perhaps most poignantly, the inspiration for a gravestone in the cemetery overlooking the sea at St Ives commemorating a person who died at Longships lighthouse. In fact, most seaside resorts do not boast an iconic lighthouse, the tall tower set on a lonely rock out at sea, as seen here at the Needles. Instead, most lighthouses at seaside resorts are more modest structures, providing guidance and location information to direct ships into a port or harbour. For instance, a small lighthouse on the seafront at Teignmouth alerts boats to the location of the adjacent harbour, while many harbours have small lighthouses at the ends of their piers to guide ships in safely.

Where larger lighthouses are constructed at seaside resorts, they often take advantage of a suitable clifftop location to raise the height of their light, and therefore the distance they can be seen out to sea. A chapel on the clifftop at Ilfracombe had a light in its window to serve as a simple form of lighthouse at least from the 16th century, while at Lowestoft there is a small, mid-19th-century lighthouse on the clifftop behind the seafront.

The Needles is a row of three (formerly four until 1764) chalk stacks that rise about 30m (98ft) out of the sea at the western end of the Isle of Wight. At their outer end is the 1859 lighthouse by James Walker, who was the consultant engineer to Trinity House. This structure replaced an earlier lighthouse that stood on the clifftop. It is built of granite masonry and at 33m (108ft) high it therefore projects just above the highest points of the adjacent chalk stacks.

On the Isle of Wight, beside the Needles, there were two gun batteries. The first was built between 1861 and 1863, following the Royal Commission Review into the state of Britain's defences after France's first ironclad warship *La Gloire* was built. The old Needles Battery was one of a series of fortifications designed to protect the strategically vital ports of Portsmouth and Southampton. The gun emplacements were enlarged to receive larger guns in 1869–75, but in 1893 a new battery was built nearby to take three larger, more up-to-date artillery pieces. This was decommissioned in the 1950s, but a nearby site was employed in the testing programme for strategic rockets.

EPW000793

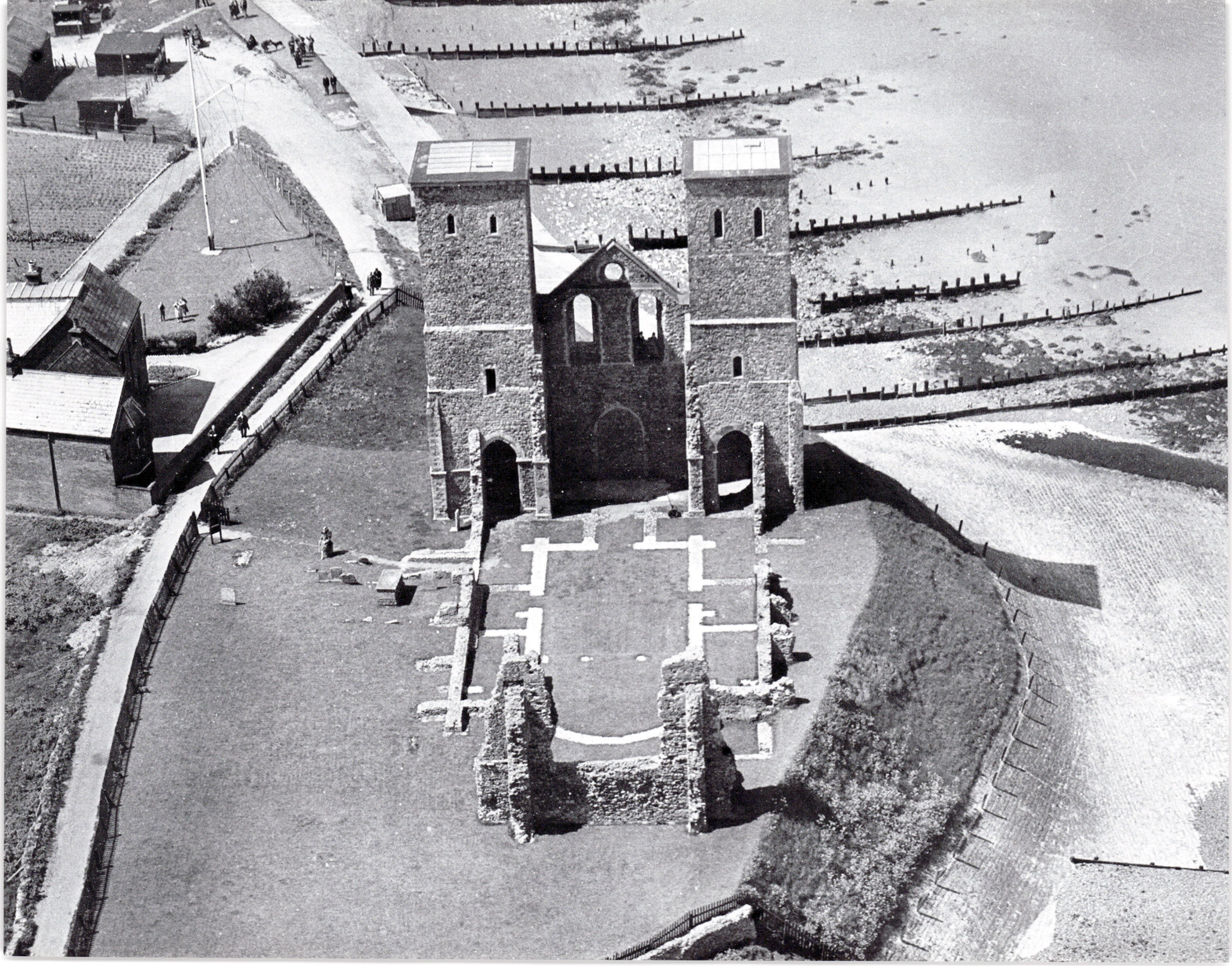

The ruins of St Mary's Church, Reculver, Kent

May 1931

The distinctive silhouettes of the seafronts of seaside resorts, and some of their larger buildings, have served on charts to aid navigation. A number of seaside resorts also have buildings that incorporate time balls. This involves providing a large ball on a shaft that is dropped at a predetermined time to allow navigators on ships to check their marine chronometers. The seafront Jubilee Clock Tower at Margate of 1889 incorporates a time ball, as does a building on the seafront at Deal. Like the Greenwich time ball, it was programmed to fall at 1pm, triggered by an electric signal sent directly from the Royal Observatory.

At some coastal locations, away from the hearts of seaside resorts, day marks may be provided on prominent headlands to assist navigation. For instance, the twin west towers of the medieval church at Reculver near Herne Bay have been maintained to serve as a navigational aid after most of the church had been demolished in 1805. In 1809, the ruined church was bought, repaired and underpinned by Trinity House.

The Anglo-Saxon monastery of Reculver was founded in *c* 669 and was created within the walls of a Saxon Shore Fort. These were built by the Romans in the south-east of England during the 3rd century, to provide protection against sea-borne Saxon raiders. Much of the original extent of Roman fortification and the Anglo-Saxon monastery has been lost to coastal erosion, but the plan of the medieval church can still be discerned. The surviving towers date from a substantial remodelling of the western end in the early 12th century, while the chancel was built during the 13th century. The towers, minus their original wooden steeples, still stand on the cliff edge and survive today, thanks to substantial sea defences designed to prevent further coastal erosion.

EPW035490

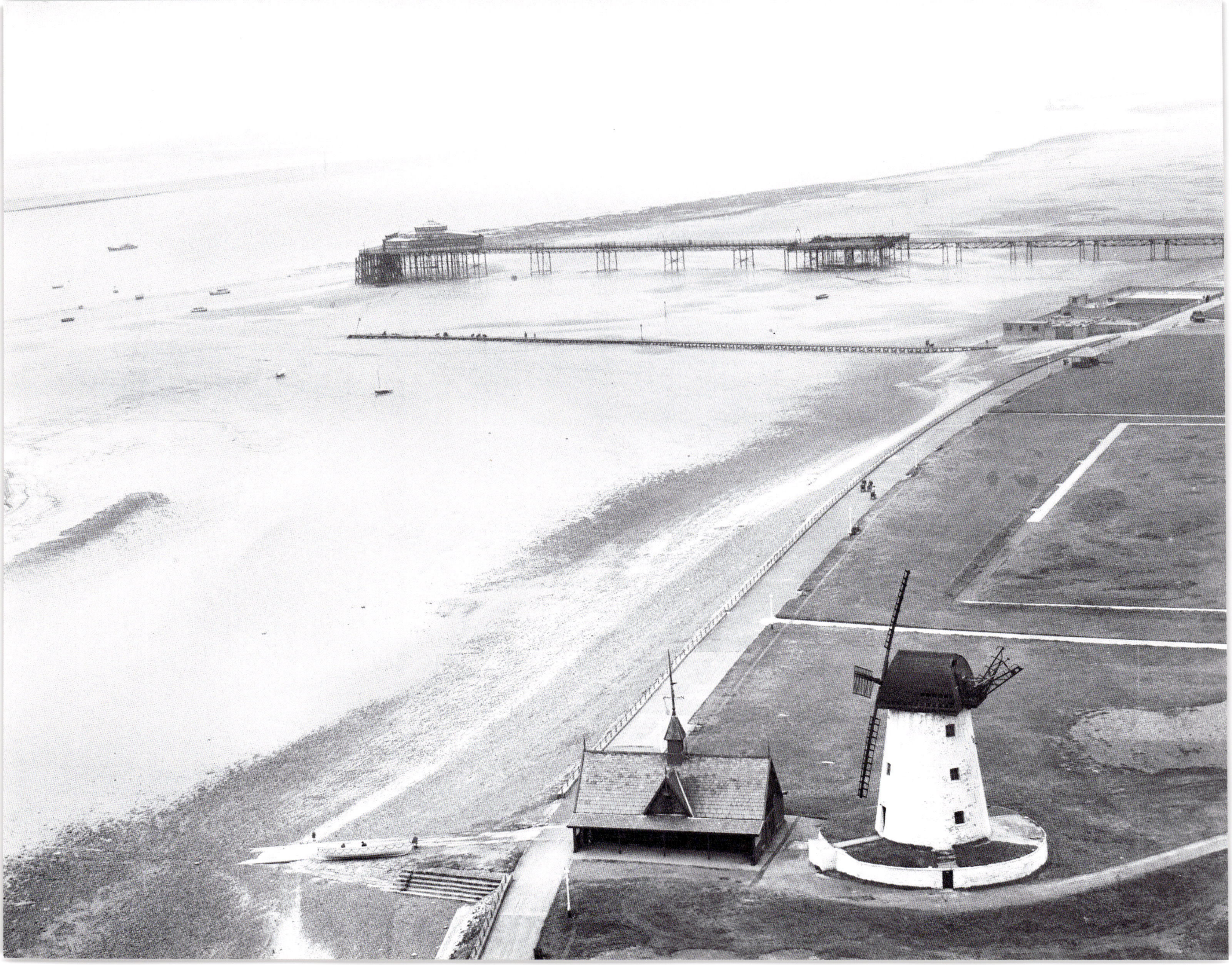

Lytham windmill and lifeboat house with the pier in the distance, Lytham, Lancashire

21 May 1948

The earliest dedicated lifeboat was based at Formby in the 1770s, but the first purpose-built boat for lifesaving was built by Henry Greathead at South Shields in 1790. Greathead was the foremost lifeboat builder in his lifetime and his boats were in demand around the coast, leading to the construction of 31 boats of this design. The only surviving example is the 1802 *The Zetland*, which is housed in a dedicated museum at Redcar.

Leaving the provision of lifeboats to local communities inevitably led to a haphazard deployment of boats around the coast and therefore, in 1824, the Royal National Institution for the Preservation of Life was established, its name being changed to the Royal National Lifeboat Institution (RNLI) 30 years later. By 1851, it was operating 95 boats around the coast, many of which were in need of buildings to house them. In 1858 Charles Cooke was appointed as the RNLI's first architect, leading to the creation of a distinctive building type resembling a church hall with large doors. As the first lifeboats were relatively small and unpowered, the buildings housing them did not have to be very substantial. The lifeboat house at Teignmouth of 1862 is a simple stone building with substantial doors in the gable end, but little lighting of the interior. During the following year the lifeboat station at Lytham St Annes was built and, like the example at Teignmouth, it had a lack of natural light when the main doors were closed. In keeping with the quasi-ecclesiastical style employed by Cooke, it has an elaborate gabled roof line.

Many of the older, smaller, lifeboat stations have been superseded by larger, more modern structures as lifeboats became larger and powered, rather than rowed. However, with the appearance of smaller, inshore lifeboats, some of the older lifeboat stations have continued in use or have returned to use; at Teignmouth the 1862 lifeboat house closed in 1940 and was sold off for use as a cafe, but in 1991 it was reacquired by the RNLI and renovated to house a new inshore lifeboat.

Behind the lifeboat station at Lytham is a windmill, an unusual feature on a seafront at a seaside resort. This brick tower mill was built in the early 19th century and remained in use until it was damaged by fire in 1918. It is perhaps slightly puzzling why the lifeboat station was built in this location, where it might impede the wind reaching the sails of the windmill. In the distance can be seen St Annes Pier, designed by Alfred Dowson; it opened on 15 June 1885. The pierhead was enlarged to allow the construction of an onion-domed Moorish-style theatre, which opened on 2 April 1904, and an 850-seat Floral Hall was added in 1910 on the pier's northern flank.

EAW014623

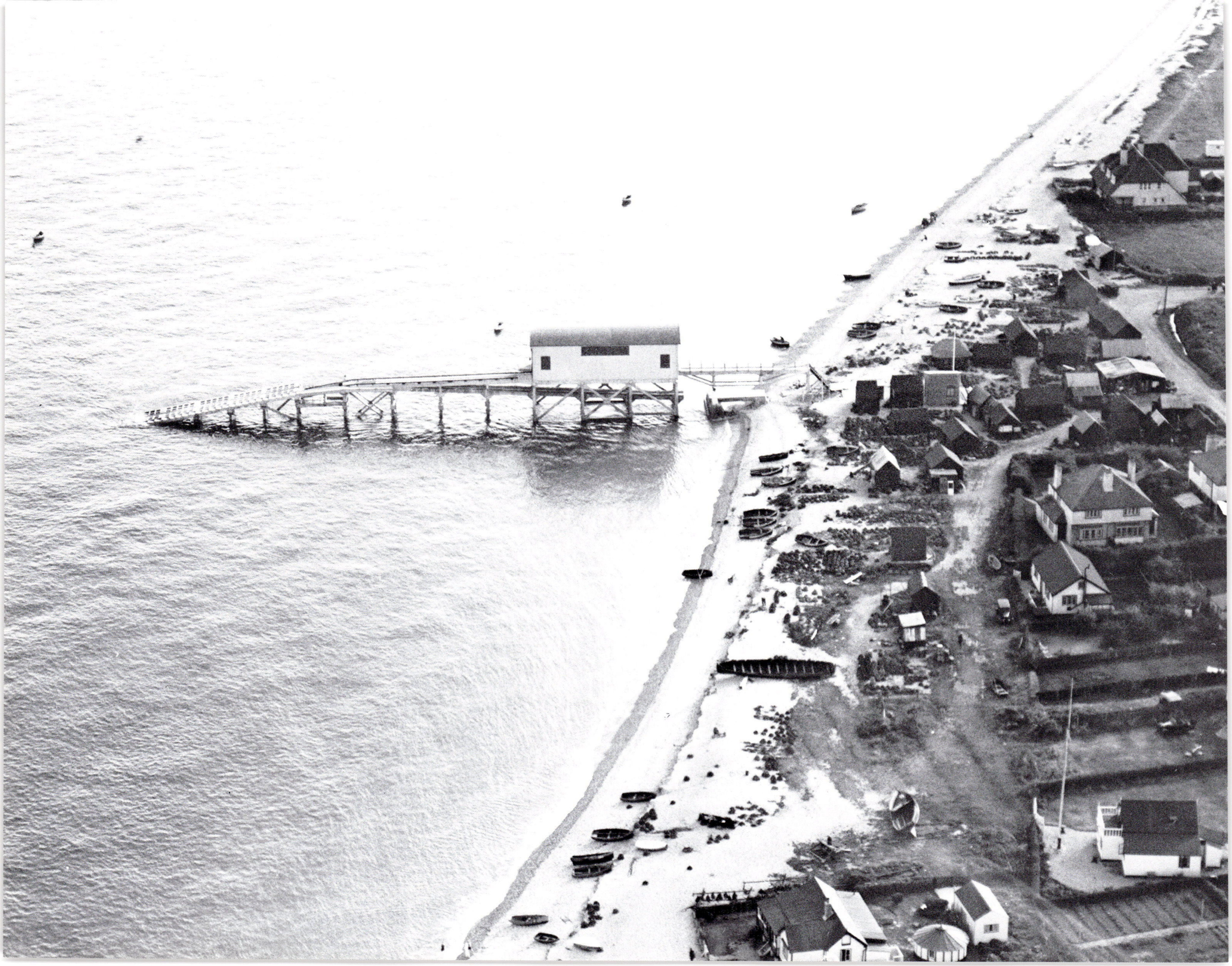

The lifeboat house, Selsey, West Sussex
October 1928

Today, Britain has a complex, comprehensive search and rescue infrastructure that involves a number of bodies ranging from government agencies and military personnel and assets to charities and volunteer organisations. The Royal National Lifeboat Institute (RNLI) is responsible for saving lives at sea; it has a fleet of more than 340 lifeboats, ranging from just under 4m (13ft) to over 17m (56ft) in length, as well as a relief fleet and seven hovercraft. The type of rescue likely to be required determines the type of boat and therefore the size and form of any lifeboat station.

The story of the evolution of lifeboat houses reflects the increasing size and the improved technology of the lifeboats. Therefore, in most cases the historic lifeboat stations have been replaced by more recent, larger structures, though some have remained in use as the bases for smaller inshore lifeboats. The first steam-powered lifeboat was introduced in 1890, followed by petrol engines being added to existing boats in 1904, and purpose-built, internal-combustion-engined boats in 1908. Therefore, at Blackpool, the original lifeboat station of the 1860s was replaced in 1937 by a larger one and this one was demolished when the new sea defences were created between 2005 and 2012, having been succeeded by a modern building.

Most lifeboat stations at seaside resorts are to meet local safety needs; they will be located on or very near the seafront, with the lifeboat being launched from a slipway or towed out into the sea by a tractor. However, at some seaside resorts large lifeboats are now kept at moorings in harbours, such as at Weymouth and at Hugh Town in the Isles of Scilly. In both instances, the modern lifeboat is too large for the historic lifeboat station, which is now used as a base for the lifeboat crew. At Cromer and Southend-on-Sea, the lifeboat stations are at the end of the pier, an arrangement that still exists at Birnbeck Pier in Weston-super-Mare, though the dilapidation of the pier means that it can no longer be launched from there.

The first lifeboat at Selsey was established in 1861 and was launched from the beach. In 1925, work began on the construction of a boathouse built on a piled platform with a gangway leading to it from the shore. Two years later, the boathouse was rebuilt to house the station's new lifeboat and subsequently rebuilt in 1958 as the old structure had become unsafe and unserviceable. This jetty and lifeboat station were demolished in 2017 once a new facility had been built nearby onshore.

EPW024674

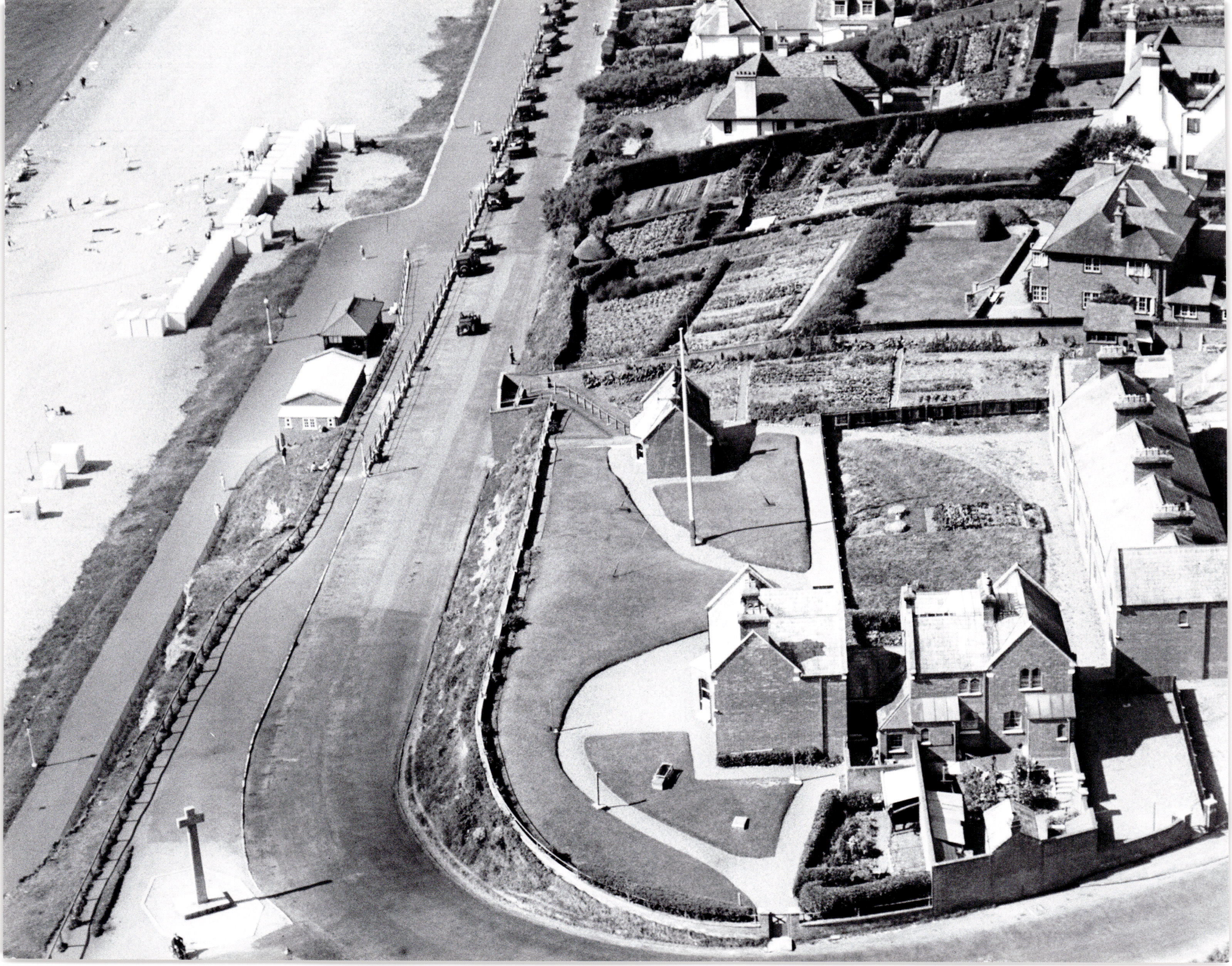

Coastguard station and the war memorial, Budleigh Salterton, Devon
September 1928

As well as the Royal National Lifeboat Institute (RNLI), which is charged with saving lives at sea, HM Coastguard is also a crucial part of the search and rescue infrastructure, particularly for emergencies on and near the coast. In 1809, the Preventative Water Guard was established to combat smuggling, but with this activity decreasing during the mid-19th century, the organisation began to function like an auxiliary naval service. Therefore, under the Coastguard Service Act of 1856, control passed from the Board of Customs to the Admiralty. Although responsibility for revenue protection was retained, rescue services began instead to be undertaken by Volunteer Life Brigades and by the lifeboats of the RNLI, with the Coastguard acting in a support role.

In 1923 the Coastguard was re-established as a coastal safety and rescue service, and also dealt with salvage from wrecks and the administration of the foreshore. By 1931, there were 193 stations and 339 auxiliary stations in England. However, from the 1960s onwards, the service's priority shifted again from maintaining coastal lookouts to the provision of co-ordinated search and rescue services. Old watch houses, with their on-site accommodation and annexed boathouses, were superseded by fewer, purpose-built Maritime Rescue Co-ordination Centres. During the 1990s, HM Coastguard became a government executive agency, and in 1998 the Marine Safety Agency and the Coastguard Agency were merged to become the Maritime and Coastguard Agency (MCA). Today, the agency is not only responsible for search and rescue, but also for much of the regulation and licensing of shipping and maritime activity.

In the past coastguards operated from watch houses, some of which survive, such as the small octagonal lookout hut on the headland at Newquay. While these are normally on a clifftop to maximise the area of sea that can be observed, any boathouses that the service used were inevitably at sea level. Coastguards also re-employed other suitable coastal structures, such as Martello towers at Felixstowe and Folkestone.

The service also provided its staff with housing, which would not necessarily be located on the seafront. One of the most ambitious sets of coastguard cottages can be found on the cliffs at Ramsgate, where three terraces of two-storey brick houses of 1865 are placed around an open courtyard, an arrangement comparable to contemporary almshouses. The coastguard station at Budleigh Salterton was slightly less ambitious, but nevertheless is an impressive complex. It was built to designs dated 1873 by John Haite, assistant civil engineer to the Admiralty, and was located on the cliffs overlooking the Budleigh Salterton coastline. The facility consisted of a row of eight terraced coastguard cottages, a pair of Petty Officer's cottages, an Officer's House, the single-storey rocket cart house and wash house, and steps providing access down to the boathouse. As some of the rescues in which the coastguards participated took place close to shore, rockets were often used to fire lifelines to wrecked ships. In 1890, 11 men and 1 officer manned the coastguard station.

EPW023989

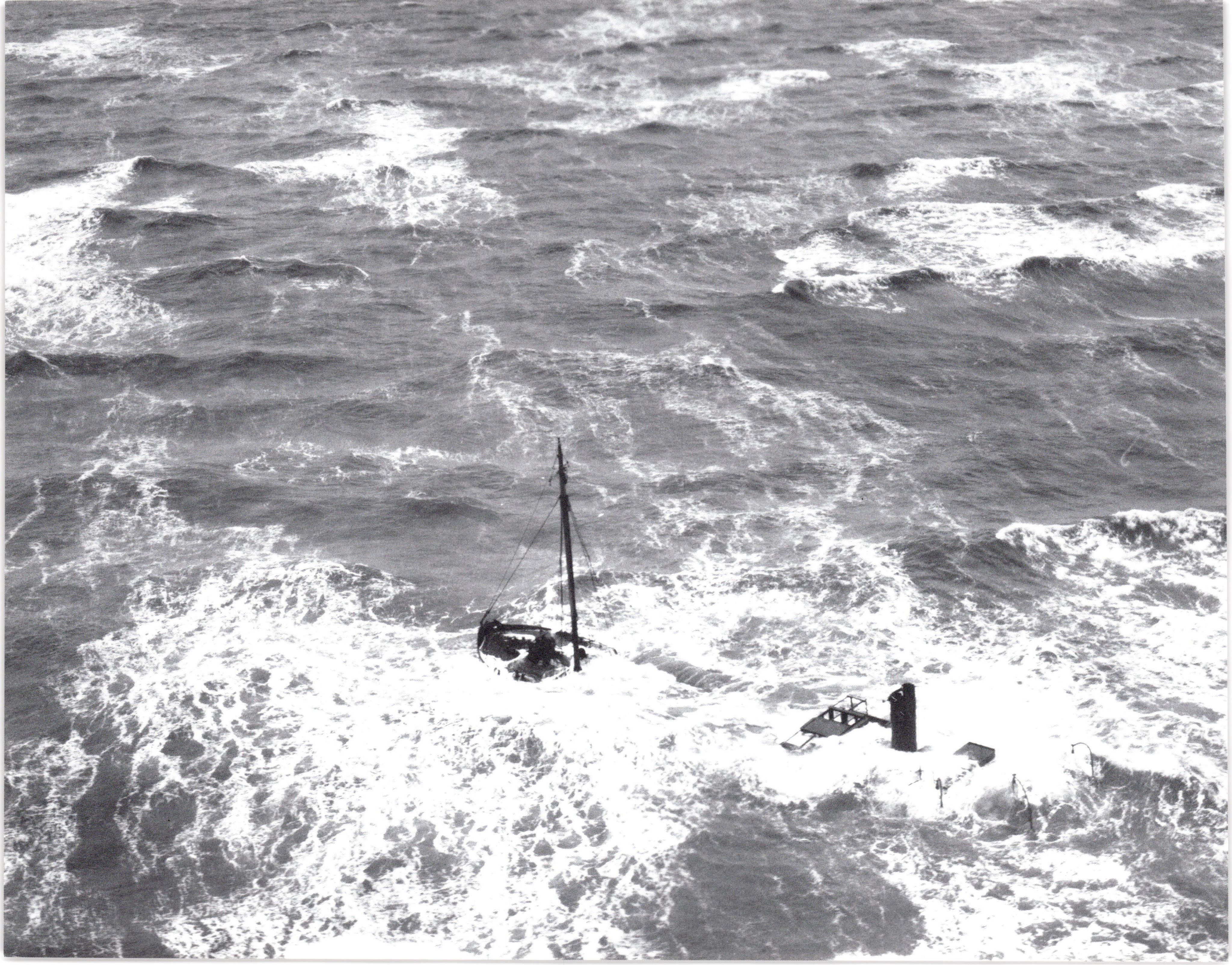

A wreck on the Duddon Sands (possibly the *Anastasi*), Walney Island, Barrow-in-Furness, Cumbria

15 October 1948

The ultimate proof of the power of the sea is its ability to destroy ships of all sizes. This photograph shows a wreck on Duddon Sands, which is located a short distance off Walney Island at the western end of Morecambe Bay, separated from the mainland part of Barrow-in-Furness by the Walney Channel. Duddon Sands is now the site of an offshore wind farm.

The ship is thought to be the SS *Anastasi*, which was wrecked on 25 December 1946 en route from Barry for Kilkeel. It was built in 1909 and was a steam-powered coastal cargo ship, measuring 40m (131ft) in length and weighing 283 tons. Fragments of the ship can still be seen at low tide on the sandbank.

EAW019740

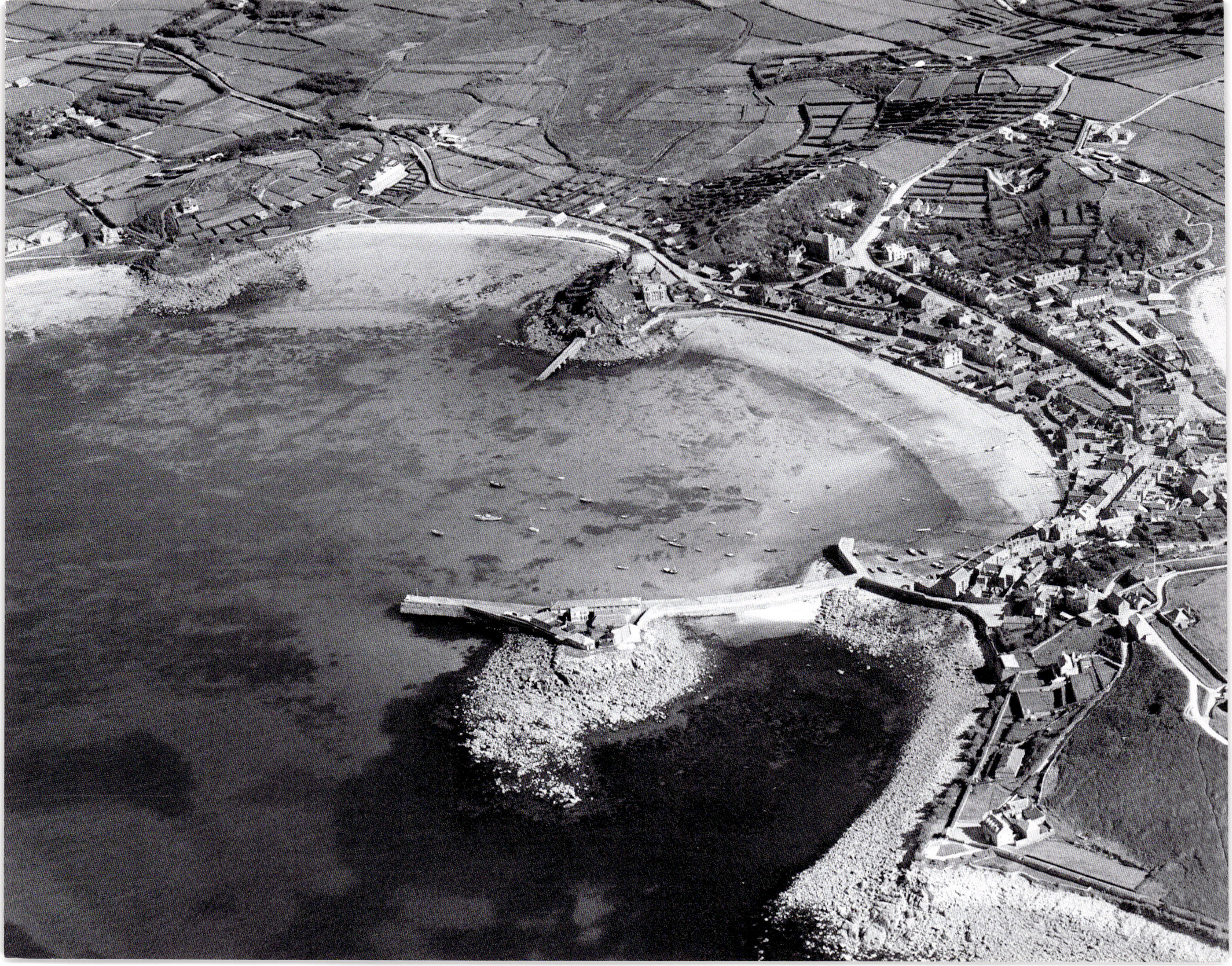

St Mary's Pool, Rat Island and Hugh Town, St Mary's, Isles of Scilly

15 September 1938

Around the English coast, there are a number of islands and groups of islands that are holiday destinations or places that tourists might visit for a day trip. The Isles of Scilly are a destination for lovers of flowers, for bird watchers in search of rare feathered visitors blown on to the islands by Atlantic winds, and for people in search of serene, natural beauty. This group of five inhabited islands, or six at high tide, are located 45km (28 miles) south-west of Land's End and are connected to the mainline by scheduled air services, the *Scillonian III* ferry in the middle months of the year when the sea is calmer, and by helicopter, a new service launched in 2020.

In a number of places around the archipelago, sandbanks connect two islands; St Agnes is joined to the Gugh with its three houses, except at high tide, hence the count of inhabited islands rising from five to six. St Mary's, the largest island in the group, and the one that is home to the majority of Scilly's population, was once two islands linked by a sandbank. This can be seen in the centre-right of the photograph, now largely obscured by the houses of Hugh Town, the largest settlement in the islands. On the right-hand side of the photograph, to the right of the harbour, can be seen part of the smaller island, now known as the Garrison because this was where most of Scilly's military defences were constructed. These idyllic islands have been in the frontline of England's, and later Britain's, defences since the 16th century and the star-shaped Star Castle, now a hotel, can be seen on the hilltop, with 18th-century walls running around the edge of the Garrison.

The harbour at St Mary's has developed over the past 200 years and includes Rat Island, its presence allowing the construction of substantial buildings to serve users of the harbour, including holidaymakers arriving at the quay. The island is covered with small fields, which have variously been used to grow potatoes and now more often flowers. Scilly's climate means that flowers can be cultivated for most of the year, at a time when similar cut flowers would not be available on the mainland, and while this brings in valuable income, tourism now dominates the Scillonian economy.

EPW059643

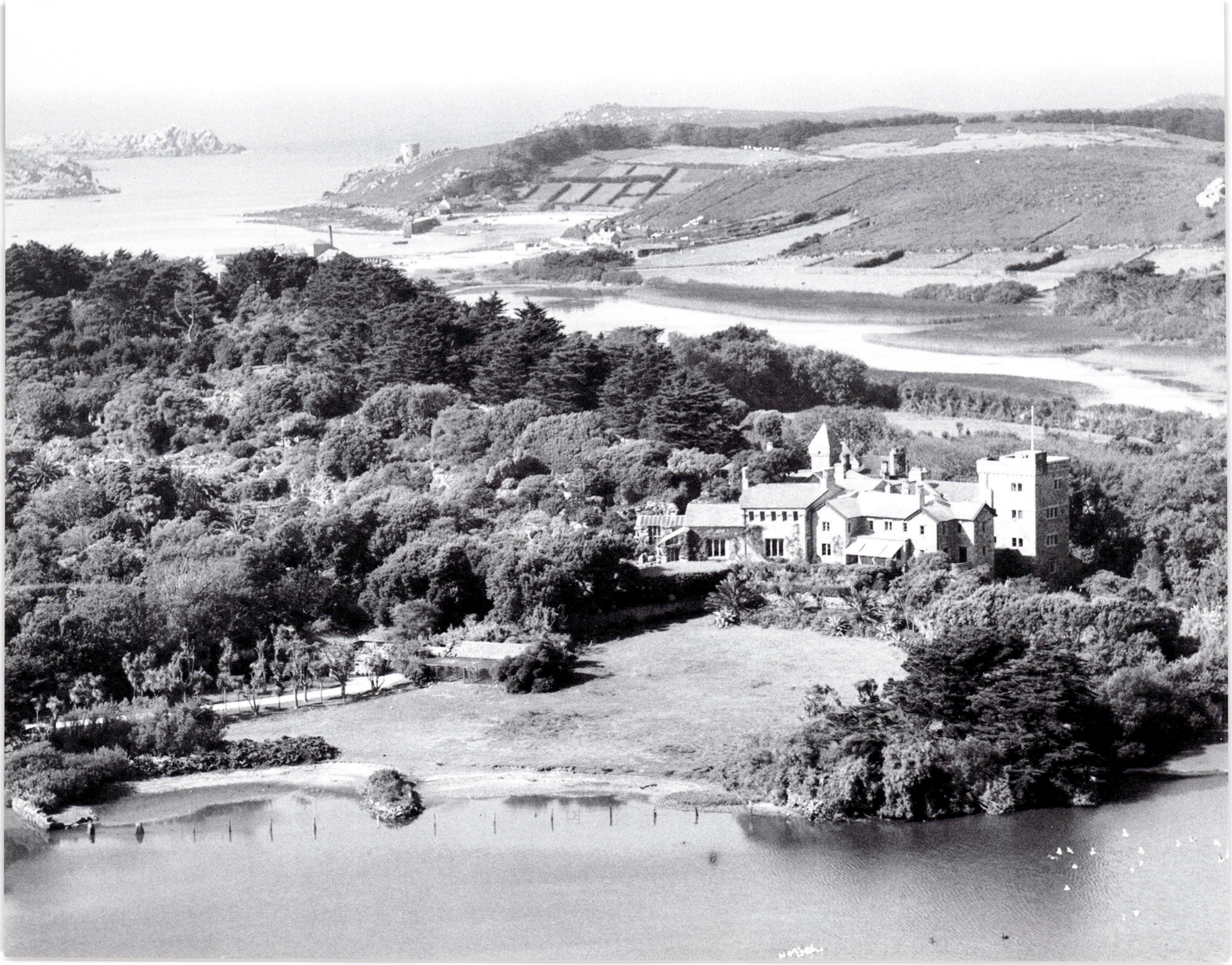

Tresco Abbey and Gardens, Tresco, Isles of Scilly
15 September 1938

Most visitors to the Isles of Scilly stay on St Mary's and take a day trip on one of the boats that connect the island to the others in the group, St Agnes, Bryher, St Martin's and Tresco. There are also occasional boat trips to some of the now uninhabited islands, opportunities to look for seals and a chance to see the most southerly built structure of England, the now-automated Bishop Rock lighthouse.

Tresco is by far the most popular island to visit and is also a magnet for people who have a brief visit to the islands on cruise liners. This is due to Tresco Abbey Gardens, renowned for its tropical and sub-tropical plants and, in recent years, reintroduced red squirrels.

In 1834, Augustus Smith obtained a lease from the Crown of the Isles of Scilly and embarked on a lifelong programme of reform, reconstruction and improvement of the islands and their buildings. He chose to build his own home beside the remains of the priory church on Tresco and oversaw the initial creation of the gardens. Since the 1850s, they have been a magnet for tourists, and in the early 20th century one of his descendants, Arthur Algernon Dorrien-Smith, undertook a major expansion of the collection, making a number of trips to South Africa in search of suitable trees and plants. He also visited New Zealand and Australia and by 1909 he had amassed a collection of over 2,000 plants and seeds that would thrive in the climate of Tresco. Today, the gardens contain exotic plants from around the world, including from the Mediterranean and South America, as well as South Africa and Australasia.

EPW059641

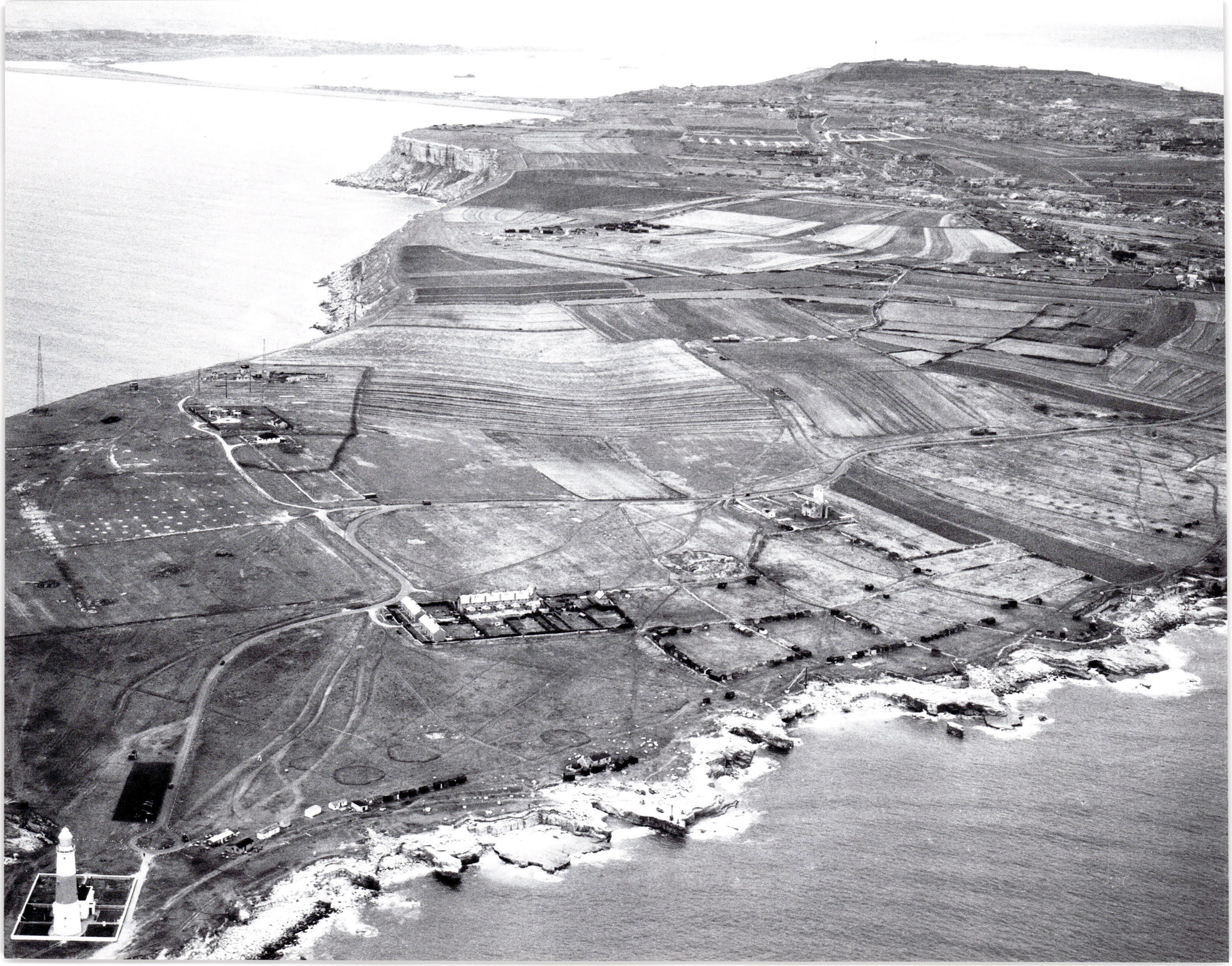

The Island, Portland, Dorset
3 October 1946

Many people on holiday at Weymouth will venture south past Portland Harbour at the top of the image to the Isle of Portland, which is linked to the mainland by Chesil Beach. The island is 4 miles (6 km) long by 1.7 miles (2.7 km) wide, and the central part of it rises steeply from the sea, making it a prominent landmark for navigators. At its southern tip is Portland Bill; this is the site of a lighthouse, a former one and a daymark that is now perilously close to falling into the sea. It is also the location for coastguard cottages and a coastguard station.

Portland Harbour is also of strategic military significance (*see* p 285), as is the island, hence the presence of an 11th-century castle, rebuilt in the 15th century, and Portland Castle of 1539, one of the coastal defences erected by Henry VIII. The island also has a large Victorian military fortress, which is now a prison, HMP The Verne. The island's naval base closed after the end of the Cold War in 1995 and the Royal Naval Air Station followed in 1999.

Portland is perhaps most famous for its stone, and small-scale quarrying activity is clear along the coast at the bottom of this aerial photograph, though the larger quarries are in the heart of the island. Inigo Jones, Surveyor of the King's Works, surveyed the area and introduced the local Portland stone to London, using it in his Banqueting House in Whitehall and for repairs to the old St Paul's Cathedral. Sir Christopher Wren, his successor and the Member of Parliament for nearby Weymouth, used six million tons of Portland limestone to rebuild destroyed parts of the capital after the Great Fire of London in 1666, including the new St Paul's Cathedral. The presence of such substantial quantities of good building stone led to the opening of the convict prison HMP Portland in 1848, whose inmates quarried stone for the Portland Breakwaters. HMP The Verne opened after the Second World War and briefly the island was also home to Britain's only prison ship, HMP *Weare* in the harbour from 1997 to 2005–6.

Portland Harbour can be seen at the top of the photograph, along with the link between the island and the mainland. Chesil Beach is the 29km-long (18 mile) tombolo made up of shingle. Portland is situated approximately halfway along the UNESCO Jurassic Coast World Heritage Site.

EAW002985

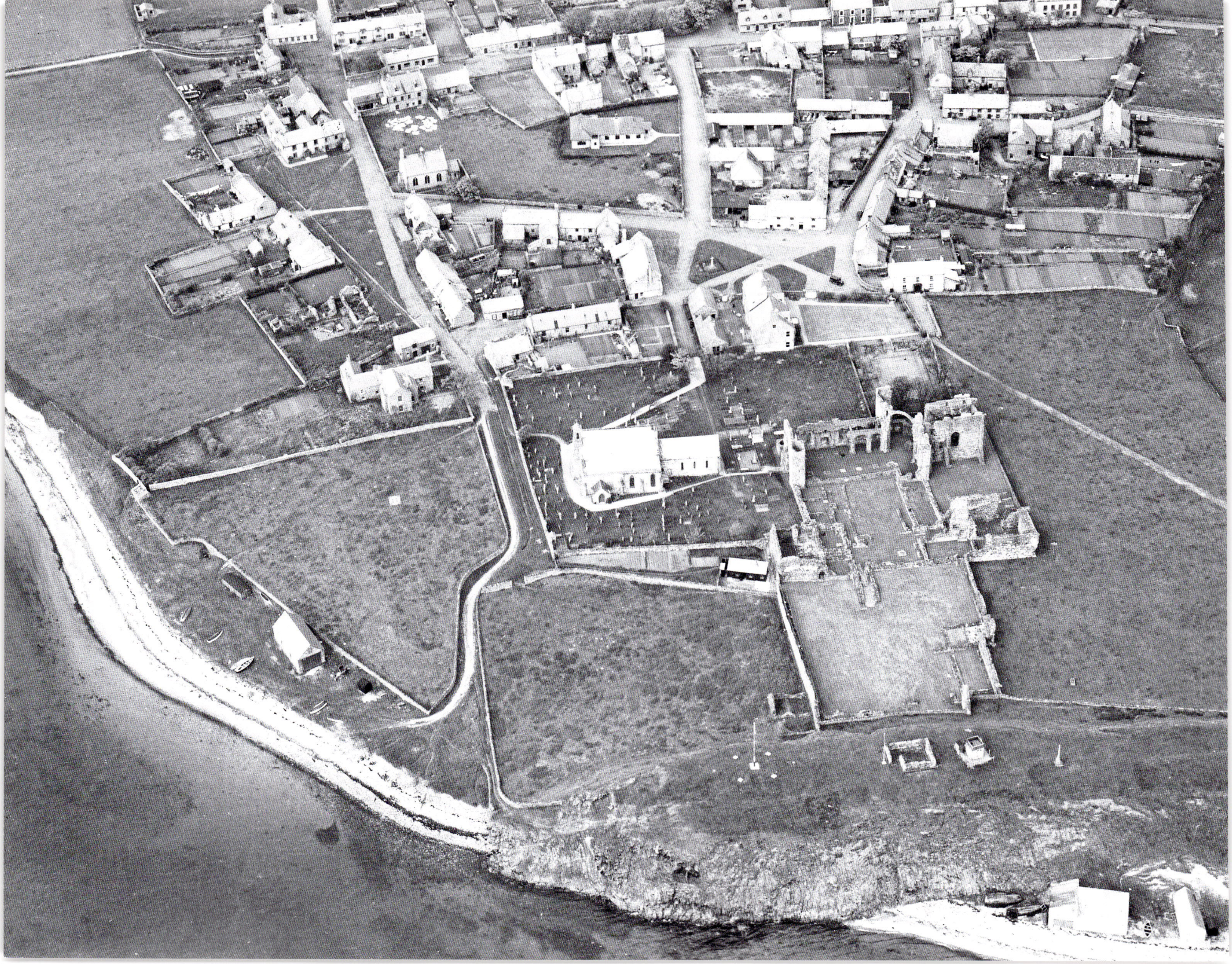

Lindisfarne Priory and the village, Holy Island, Northumberland
21 May 1947

This image shows the southern end of Holy Island, with the remains of Lindisfarne Priory in front with the village behind. The island is the final destination of long-distance walking routes and one of Scotland's Great Trails, the St Cuthbert's Way, a 62-mile (100km) long-distance trail between the Scottish Borders town of Melrose and Lindisfarne. The walk is named after Cuthbert, a 7th-century saint who started his religious life in 651 and later came to Holy Island, his eventual resting place and the site of his original pilgrimage shrine.

The monastery of Lindisfarne was founded *c* 634 by St Aidan, an Irish monk who had been sent from Iona off the west coast of Scotland to Northumbria at the request of King Oswald. It became an important base for Christianity in the north of England, and among the community was St Cuthbert, who later became the first Bishop of Lindisfarne.

Cuthbert was elected to the see of Lindisfarne on 26 March 685. He was at Lindisfarne at Christmas 686, but he then returned to his hermitage on the Inner Farne and died there on 20 March 687. Cuthbert was buried on Lindisfarne, but to escape the attention of raiding Vikings in 793, his remains were later moved to Durham Cathedral, where his shrine became a major pilgrimage centre. As well as being famed for its association with St Cuthbert, the monastery was where the Lindisfarne Gospels were created in the early 8th century.

The ruined church that can be seen today was begun in 1093, the same year as Durham Cathedral's reconstruction was begun. It was largely completed by the early 12th century, but was lengthened and given a square east end in *c* 1140–50. The influence of Durham is obvious, including in the use of stone vaults throughout. The monastery continued in use with limited modifications until its suppression in 1536.

EAW006094

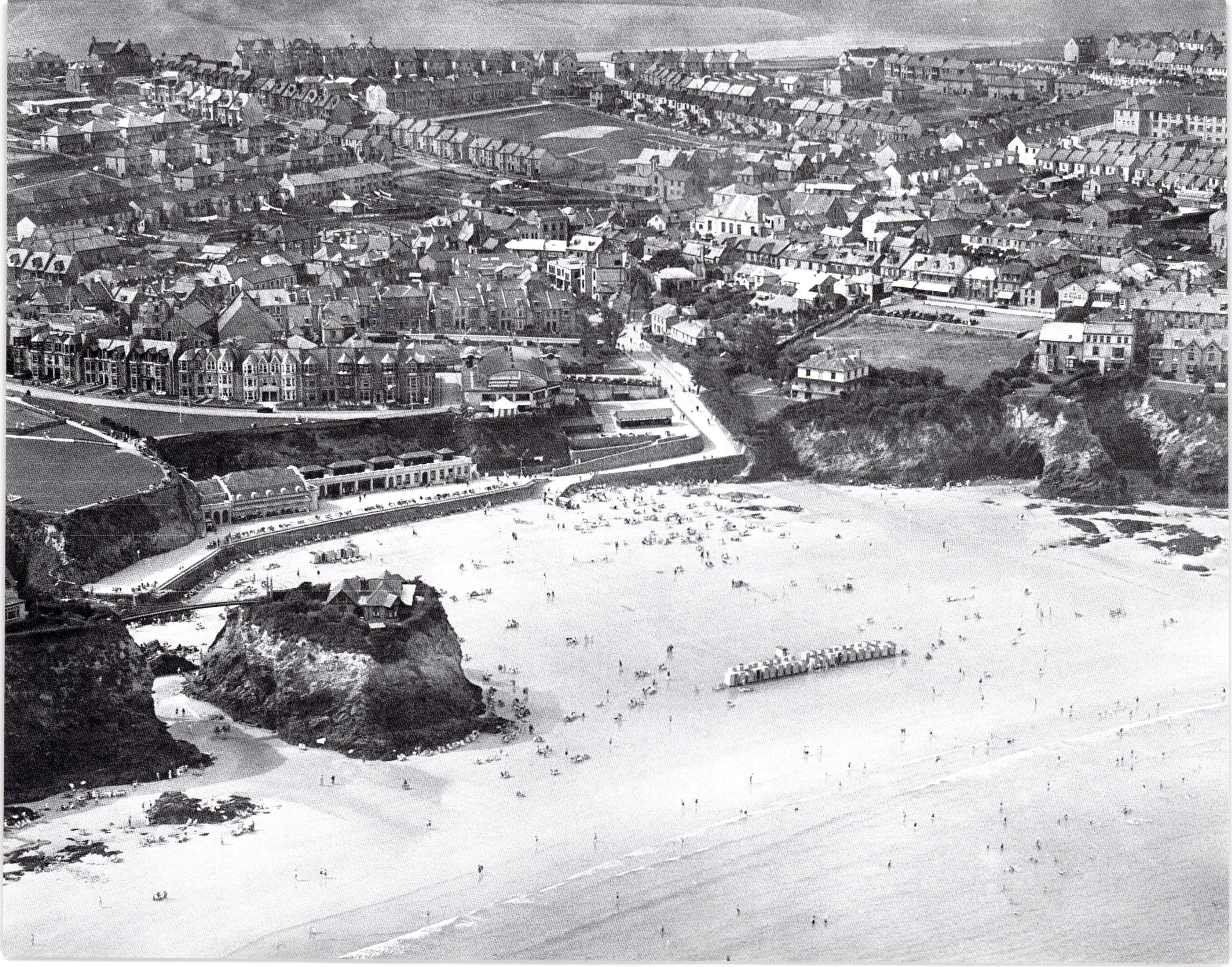

The Island and Towan Sands, Newquay, Cornwall
August 1932

Some stretches of coastline at seaside resorts set developers geographical challenges or opportunities. At Hastings, Dymchurch and Swanage, streams that flowed into the sea required the creation of conduits or outflows running across the beach. Large rocks might also complicate access to the sea for holidaymakers, though some were also celebrated as landmarks. A major storm on 22 November 1824 destroyed the Chit Rock at Sidmouth, a prominent landmark for returning fishermen seeking the beach. The White Rock at Hastings was seen as a barrier to expansion and the unification of Hastings with St Leonards, and therefore in 1834 it was cut away.

At a number of seaside resorts, islands exist close to the seafront. Knightstone Island at Weston-super-Mare has been a focus for health activities since the 1820s, when the first bathhouse and accommodation were created there, while it was still only accessible at low tide. Further to the north, Birnbeck Island lies a little further off the coast and in 1867 it became the ingenious destination for a pier designed by Eugenius Birch (*see* p 129).

In this photograph of one of the main beaches at Newquay, Towan Island can be seen towering above the beach below. A dramatic suspension bridge links the island to the mainland, allowing the inhabitants of its single house an unrivalled sense of privacy in the heart of a busy seaside resort. Meanwhile, on the beach, a series of bathing cabins can be seen drawn down towards the water's edge.

EPW039799

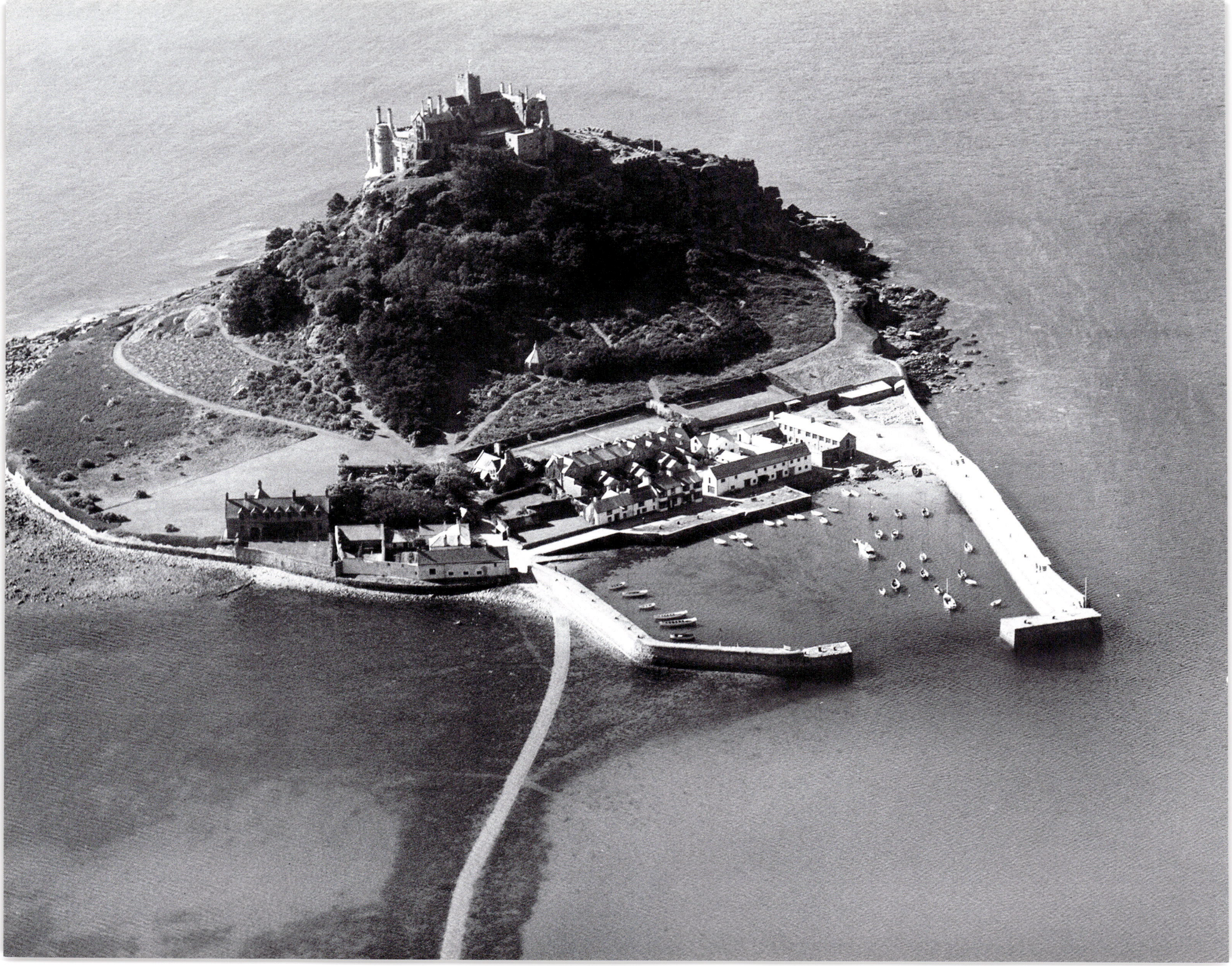

St Michael's Mount, the harbour and causeway, Cornwall
24 September 1938

St Michael's Mount is a small island off the south coast of Cornwall near Marazaion and Penzance. It measures 57 acres (23ha) in area and is home to a village and a harbour in the foreground, and a castle and the remains of the priory behind. Most of the island was given to the National Trust in 1954, but the St Aubyn family, who had owned the castle since 1659, retained a 999-year lease to continue living in the castle while allowing the public to visit it. At low tide the island can be visited on foot via the causeway seen at the bottom of the photograph.

There may have been a monastery on the island from the 8th to the early 11th centuries, but Edward the Confessor granted the site to the Benedictine monastery of Mont Saint-Michel, the larger island off the Norman coast that also hosted a religious community. The priory church was built in *c* 1135, but was substantially remodelled and mostly rebuilt in the 14th century following damage by an earthquake in 1275. It was restored by Piers St Aubyn in the late 19th century. The adjacent castle was also begun *c* 1135 and similarly reworked after the earthquake. It was remodelled and extended in the late 19th century by Piers St Aubyn.

The village consisted of a few fishermen's cottages, but after improvements to the harbour in 1727, St Michael's Mount became a busy port. By 1811, the village consisted of 53 houses on four streets. A decade later, the pier was extended and the island's population rose to 221, the highest number of residents ever recorded. Today, visitors can enjoy the village, its cemetery and pub; to make life possible on the island an underground narrow-gauge railway was constructed *c* 1900 to supply the islanders with their needs. The former engine house and workshop survive on the island.

EPW059663

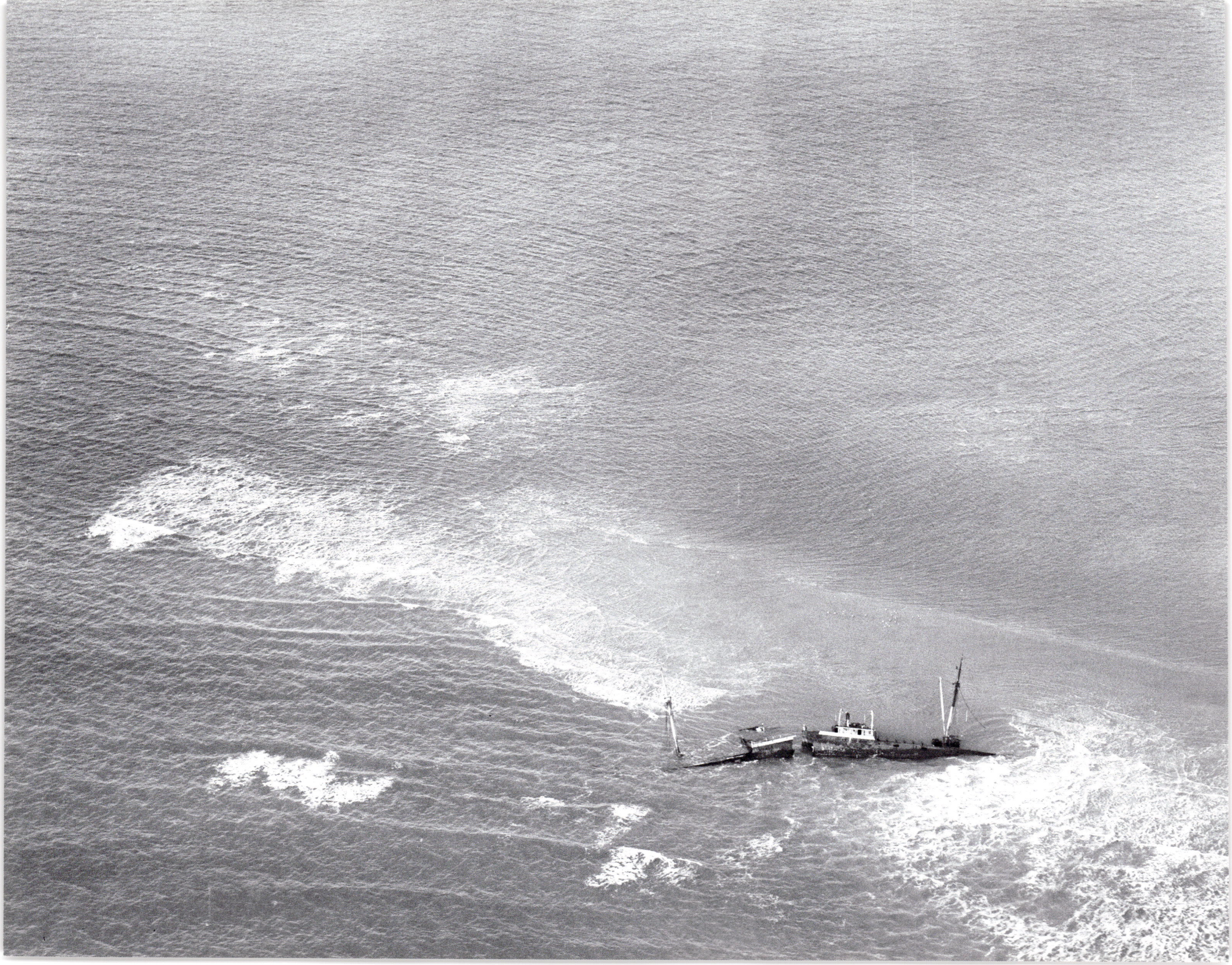

A wreck on the Goodwin Sands, Kent, possibly the *Silvia Onorato*
9 November 1948

Why a wreck far out to sea off the Kent Coast in a section of a book about islands? The Goodwin Sands has historically been associated with the once fertile low-lying island of Lomea, which may have existed until the late 11th century, though geologists today are sceptical of the historical evidence. Although it is now simply a hazardous sandbank, since 1824 it has been the venue for a rapid cricket match at low tide.

The Goodwin Sands is a 10-mile-long (16km) sandbank off the Kent coast near Deal. It has been a notorious hazard for shipping over the centuries as the banks lie between 0.5m (1.6ft) above the low water mark to around 3m (10ft) below low water. In the Great Storm of 26 November 1703, at least 13 warships and 40 merchant vessels were wrecked in this area, with the loss of more than 2,000 lives and over 700 guns. In January 1740, the Dutch merchant ship *Rooswijk* sank without survivors en route to Cape of Good Hope and the East Indies. This was one of hundreds of victims of this sandbank, but it made headlines in recent years when it was discovered surprisingly intact, and in 2017 it was excavated and salvaged by Historic England and the Cultural Heritage Agency of the Netherlands.

The ship seen foundering on the Goodwin Sands appears to be the 2,300-ton Italian cargo ship *Silvia Onorato*. Built in 1916 by John Priestman & Co, and owned by Achille Onorato, it was on a voyage from Rijeka to Rotterdam with a cargo of lead ore when it was wrecked off the East Goodwin Sands on 2 January 1948. Thankfully, all 30 of its passengers and crew were rescued successfully.

EAW020496

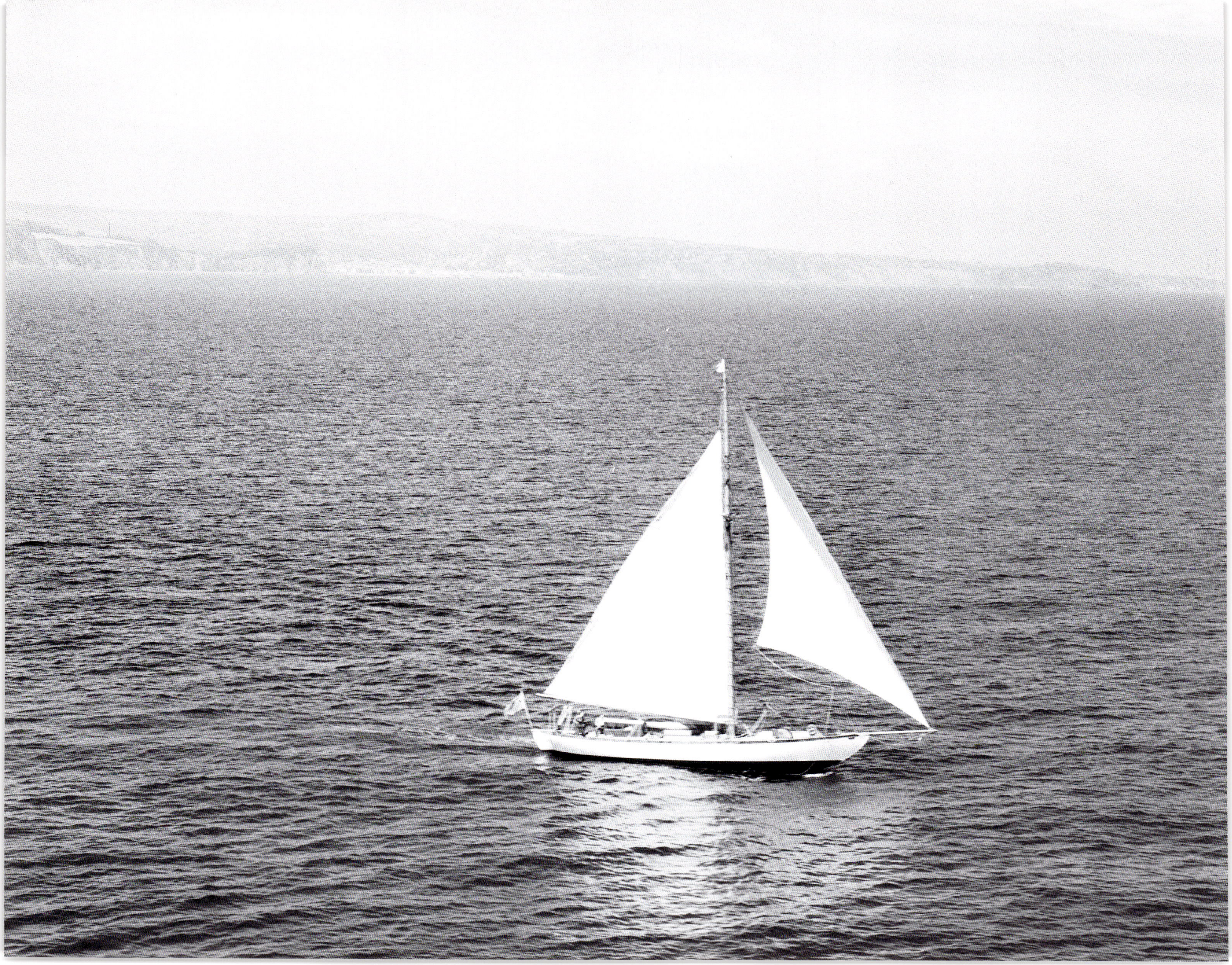

A yacht at sea off Teignmouth, Labrador Bay, Devon
25 June 1947

This photograph shows a majestic yacht sailing off the Devon coast to the south of Teignmouth on a calm June day. An almost timeless scene, the year 1947 saw around 8,000 yachts registered with Lloyds of London, but the owners of these craft and pleasure cruisers faced particular difficulties in the years immediately after the war in the form of residual minefields and strict petrol rationing. Nevertheless, there were more than double the number of yachts at sea than had been registered at the outbreak of the First World War.

The yacht was a Dutch invention and the name *jacht*, meaning hunt, came from the small, fast boats used to chase smugglers, pirates and criminals in the waters around the Low Countries. It arrived in England as a pleasure vessel with Charles II, following his exile in Holland and his Restoration in 1660. He regularly sailed his 60ft (18m) yacht *Mary* on the Thames and his passion was shared by his brother James, Duke of York.

Yachting was initially a largely royal or aristocratic pursuit, but gradually it spread down the social scale, though until the 20th century it remained in the hands of the wealthiest. The first yacht club in the world, called the Cork Water Club, was established in Ireland in 1720. Probably the most famous of all the English yacht clubs, The Royal Yacht Squadron, was founded in 1815 by 42 gentlemen interested in yachting (*see* p 249).

EAW007584

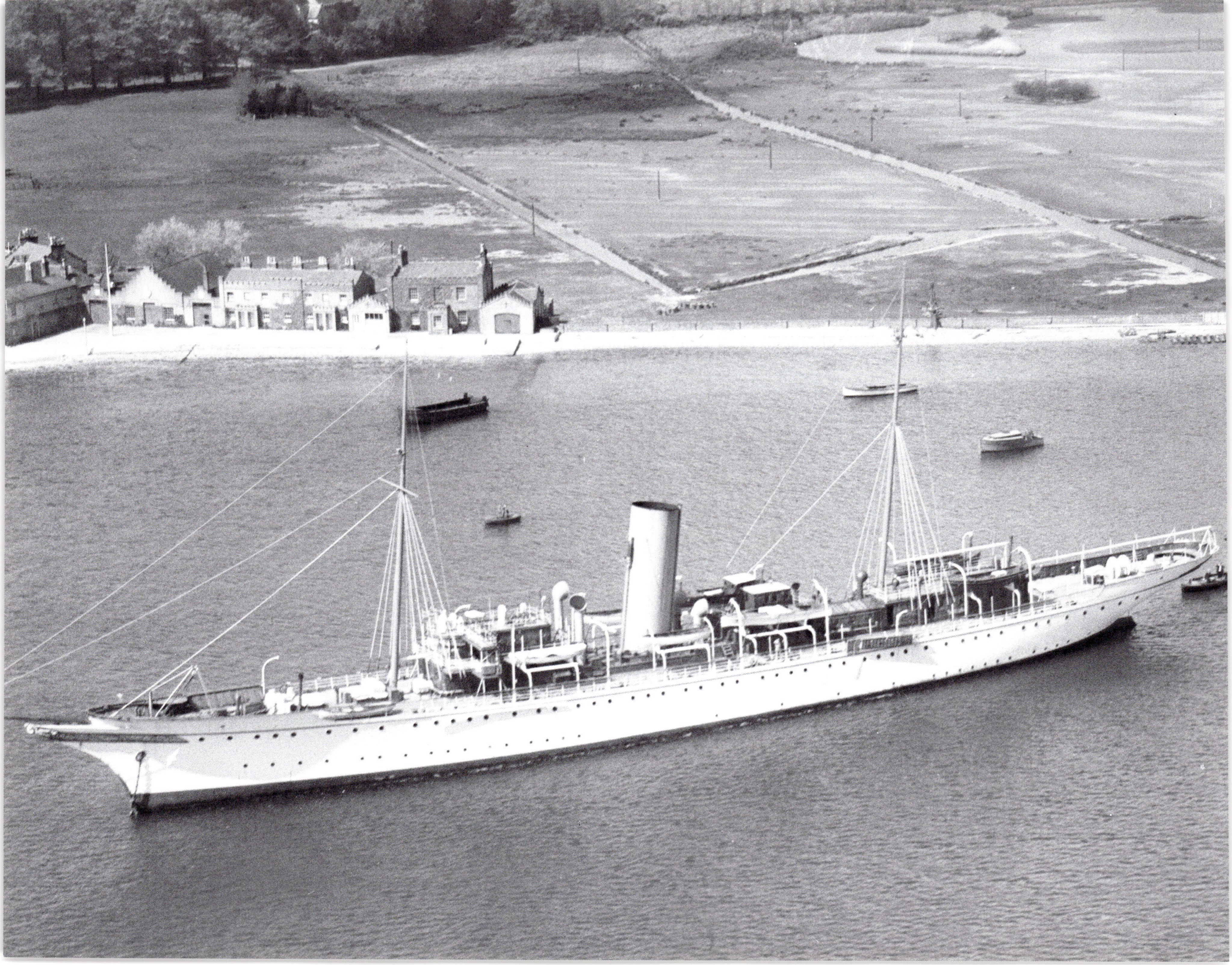

Montague Grahame-White's steam yacht *Alacrity*, Brownsea Island, Dorset
April 1933

If you wanted to mess about in a boat between the wars, perhaps you might dream of being Montague Reginald Grahame-White (1877–1961), a famed racing driver who liked to travel in style. In 1898, he learned to drive and joined Daimler; in the same year, he is thought to have bought his first boat, *MiLadye*, the first 4-cylinder petrol launch on the Thames and one of the fastest pleasure steam launches around. In the years before the First World War, he became a successful car, yacht and aeroplane broker, with clients in the British aristocracy, as well as a number of Indian rulers, including the Maharajah of Cooch Behar. The Maharajah ended his life while recovering from illness in Bexhill-on-Sea, in a seafront cottage near the site of the future De La Warr Pavilion.

Montague Grahame-White also managed to combine this interesting career with becoming a Lieutenant-Commander in the Royal Navy. Therefore, it may explain why he had such a high-class steam yacht at his disposal. It was constructed by Scotts of Greenock and launched on 30 April 1900 as the private steam yacht *Margarita* for an American Banker. It was 341ft (104m) long and its gross register tonnage was 1,830 tonnes. Work was completed on the yacht on 28 December 1900 and by 1910 it was owned by the Marquess of Anglesey and renamed *Semiramis*. It had passed by 1913 to Princess Schahovskoy Gleboff Strechneff of Russia, and following the Russian Revolution it became attached to the Arctic Ocean Flotilla, based in Petrograd. As an armed yacht, *Mlada* was hired for conversion to an Armed Boarding Steamer and in March 1919 it was purchased by the Royal Navy and commissioned as HMS *Alacrity* in August 1919, serving briefly as an Admiralty Yacht for the Commander-in-Chief Far East based in China. By 1926, it had been sold to Lt Cdr Montague Grahame-White and it was registered at Southampton.

This photograph shows *Alacrity* moored off Brownsea Island, the largest island in Poole Harbour and now owned by the National Trust. It was the site in 1907 of an experimental boys' camp that led to the foundation of the Boy Scout movement by Robert Baden-Powell. The island is also celebrated as one of the few places in southern England where native red squirrels can still be seen.

EPW041057

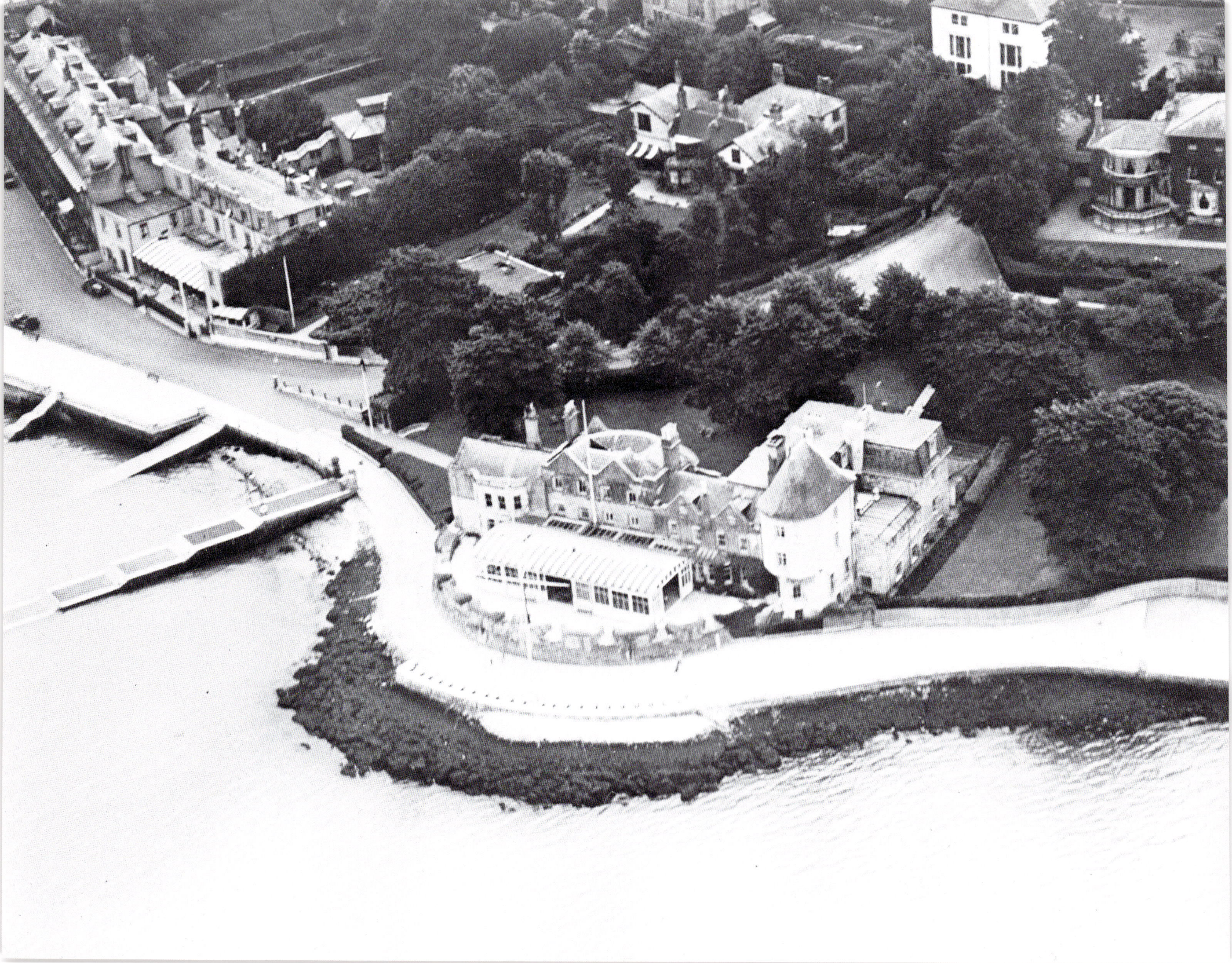

Cowes Castle (Royal Yacht Squadron Club House), Cowes, Isle of Wight

August 1928

The Royal Yacht Squadron is one of the most prestigious yacht clubs in the world and this photograph shows its clubhouse, Cowes Castle on the Isle of Wight. Member yachts bear the suffix RYS and are allowed to fly the White Ensign of the Royal Navy, rather than the Red Ensign of the Merchant Navy. HM Queen Elizabeth II is the club's patron and the club's admiral is Prince Philip, who is also a former club commodore.

The Royal Yacht Squadron, originally just the Yacht Club, was founded on 1 June 1815 at the Thatched House Tavern in St James's, London, for gentlemen owning a vessel not under 10 tons. In 1817, the Earl of Yarborough, later first Commodore of the Yacht Club, welcomed the Prince Regent as a member and in 1820, when he became George IV, Royal was added to the club's name. In 1826 the club began to organise yacht racing as part of the annual regatta at Cowes, and in 1833 the Club became the Royal Yacht Squadron.

In 1851 Commodore Jon Cox Stevens of the New York Yacht Club competed for the Squadron's £100 Cup for a race around the Isle of Wight. The victory of the yacht *America* led to the RYS £100 Cup being renamed the America's Cup. It was donated to the New York Yacht Club, which makes the cup available for the international sailing competition held every few years.

The club's present home, West Cowes Castle, was built in 1539 as part of Henry VIII's chain of coastal defences, along with East Cowes Castle on the other side of the River Medina. It became a private house in the 18th century and in 1856 it was bought by the Royal Yacht Squadron. Most of the present structure belongs to the 18th and 19th century.

EPW023049

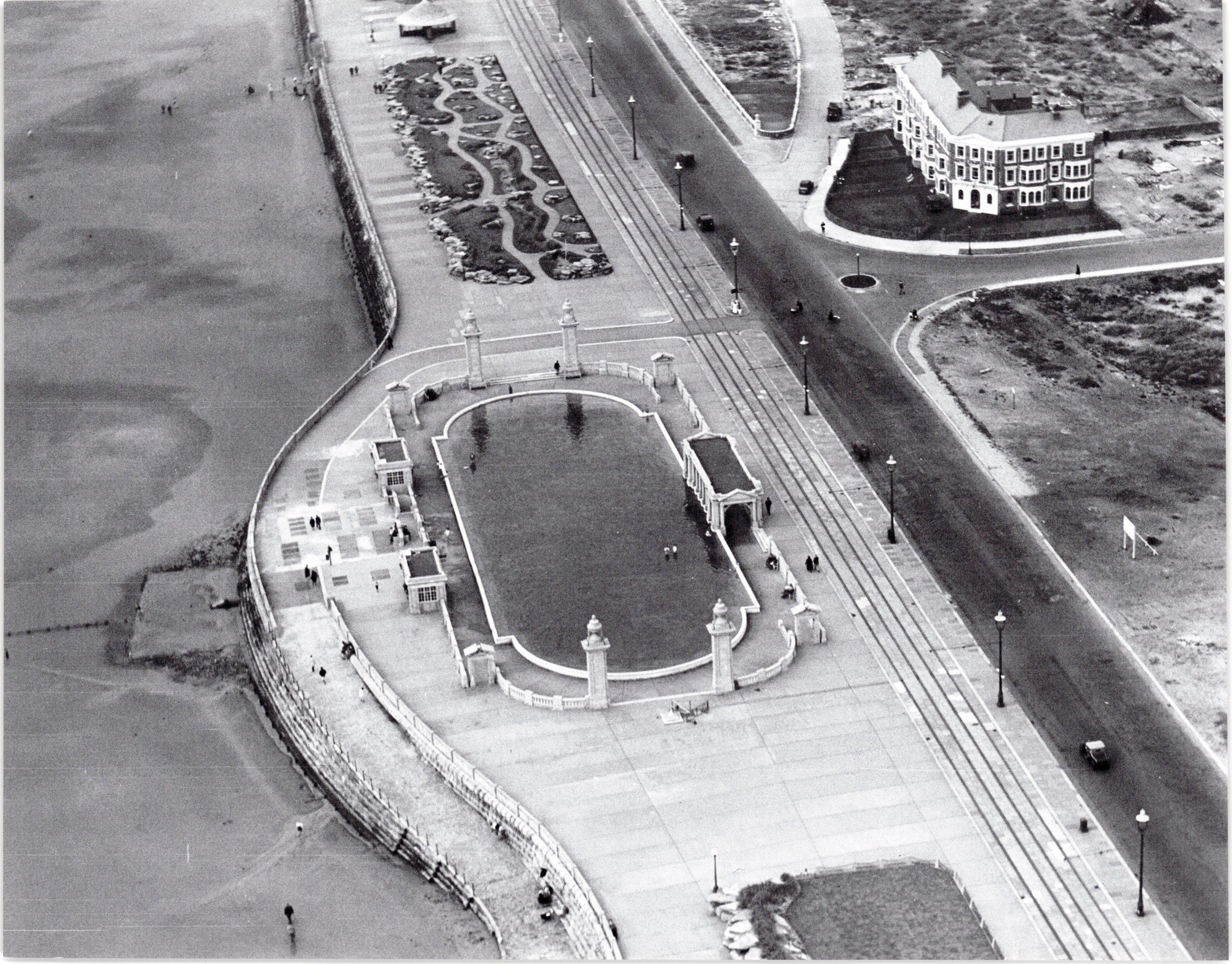

The model yacht pond on the South Promenade, Blackpool, Lancashire
July 1932

Yachting was once described by a comedian as being like setting fire to £5 notes in a shower, alluding to the fact that it was an expensive hobby. Today's most expensive yachts can cost over £1 billion, but for most people their fun comes from sailing out for the day in a more modest dinghy.

Some of the pleasure of sailing can also be found in the making and sailing of pond yachts, ranging from classical sailing yachts to some modern remote-controlled vessels in the form of a submarine or an aircraft carrier. Far from being toys to play with in the bath, the creation and care of pond yachts is a serious hobby, and the Model Yachting Association (MYA) was formed in 1911 as the Model Yacht Racing Association, changing its name to its present title in 1923.

At a number of seaside resorts there are shallow pools created on the seafront for children to play safely, but also for people to sail model yachts. Before the First World War, the area south of the Pleasure Beach at Blackpool remained largely in its natural state, but the extension of the promenade and the tramway southwards to the borough boundary was a logical decision for a booming resort that required extra seafront space. Between 1922 and 1926, work took place on the new roadway, tramway and sea defences and the scheme included elaborate sunken gardens complete with rockeries and flowing streams, along with a large model yachting pond and stylish circular shelters. As can be seen in this photograph, this pool was no simple concrete basin, but an ornate structure reminiscent of a classical pool.

This photograph also shows the new tram tracks, and beyond is the area of former sand dunes waiting to be developed with housing and other structures. This included the Harrowside Sun Parlour in 1938, a solarium that would be constructed opposite the model yachting pond.

EPW038915

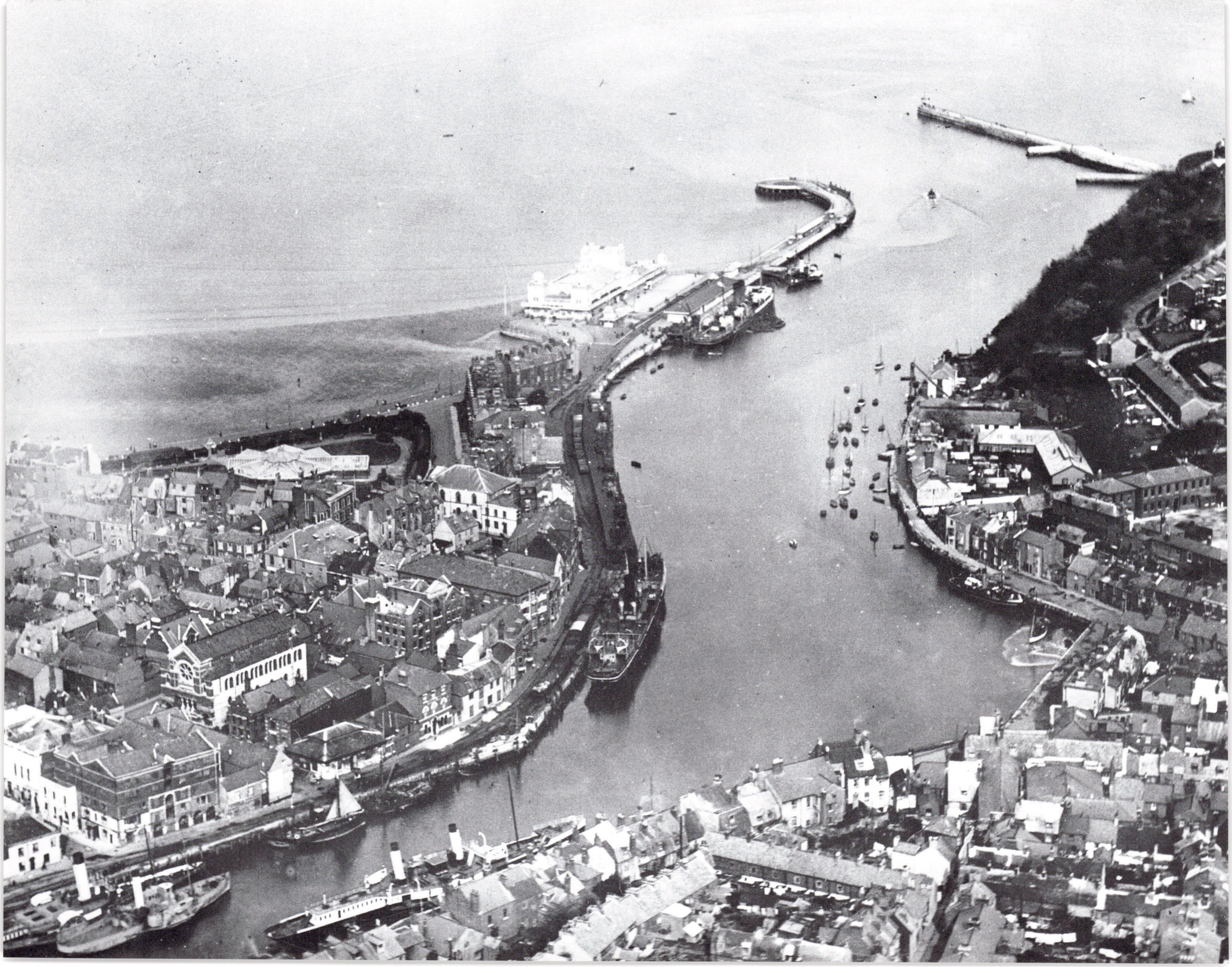

The harbour, Weymouth, Dorset
April 1920

Many of England's seaside resorts are located at coastal towns with harbours. This was because the first sea bathers needed somewhere to stay and at least rudimentary entertainment facilities while they were on holiday. At some seaside resorts the harbour today is little more than a place for a few pleasure craft to be moored, but some resorts such as Scarborough and Weymouth still have an active fishing fleet that moors alongside modern yachts, cabin cruisers and dinghies.

During the Middle Ages, Weymouth consisted of two distinct settlements each with their own local government and Members of Parliament. Weymouth was the name of the older settlement on the south side of the harbour, seen here on the right-hand side, while the larger town, on the north side, was Melcombe Regis. Two towns sharing a harbour led to a series of heated, sometimes violent, disputes and Parliament forcibly amalgamated the two settlements in 1571.

When the first visitors arrived at Weymouth to bathe in the sea, they stayed in houses constructed around the harbour, and there was also a bathhouse and floating bath in the harbour. Although the income from visitors was of growing importance from the late 18th century onwards, the harbour still lay at the heart of Weymouth's economy and identity. The north side of the harbour, the Melcombe Regis side, contains the main working buildings of the harbour, including the old fish market, the former Custom House, the Harbour Master's Office, warehouses and the current Royal Dorset Yacht Club, which was built in 1866 as a Christian Institute for Seamen. The south side of the harbour in the 18th century was predominantly occupied by domestic buildings, the most famous being the house used by Ralph Allen from Bath; his presence attracted other aristocrats and in due course members of the Royal family.

As well as being a working quay and an attractive place to stay for fashionable people, the harbour was also the departure point for ferry services to the Channel Islands and France.

In 1794, a packet service began to Guernsey and Jersey, and in 1827 a steam packet was introduced. The Pile Pier was created in 1840 on the north side of the harbour, but with the opening of the railway from London to Southampton in the same year, Weymouth lost its advantage and the ferry service closed in April 1845. However, a new service opened in 1850 from Weymouth to St Malo, with stops in the Channel Islands, and with the opening of the railway to Weymouth in 1857, a new regular ferry service was inaugurated.

A new pile pier was erected in 1859 and in 1878 a new landing stage was completed. Further developments took place following an agreement in 1889 between the Great Western Railway and the Weymouth Corporation. The Corporation agreed to improve the harbour and build new facilities in exchange for the railway company introducing an improved steamer service. The most obvious change to the form of the harbour in the late 19th century was at Hope Cove, where some of the land reclaimed in the 1780s was removed, along with the houses on it. Seen here on the right-hand side of the harbour, this was to make room for new, larger steamers to turn inside the harbour.

At the top of the photograph, near the mouth of the harbour can be seen the Edwardian Pavilion constructed in 1908. It had an auditorium that could seat 1,200, but was destroyed by fire in 1954 and the present Pavilion Theatre opened in 1960 (*see* p 111).

EPW000316

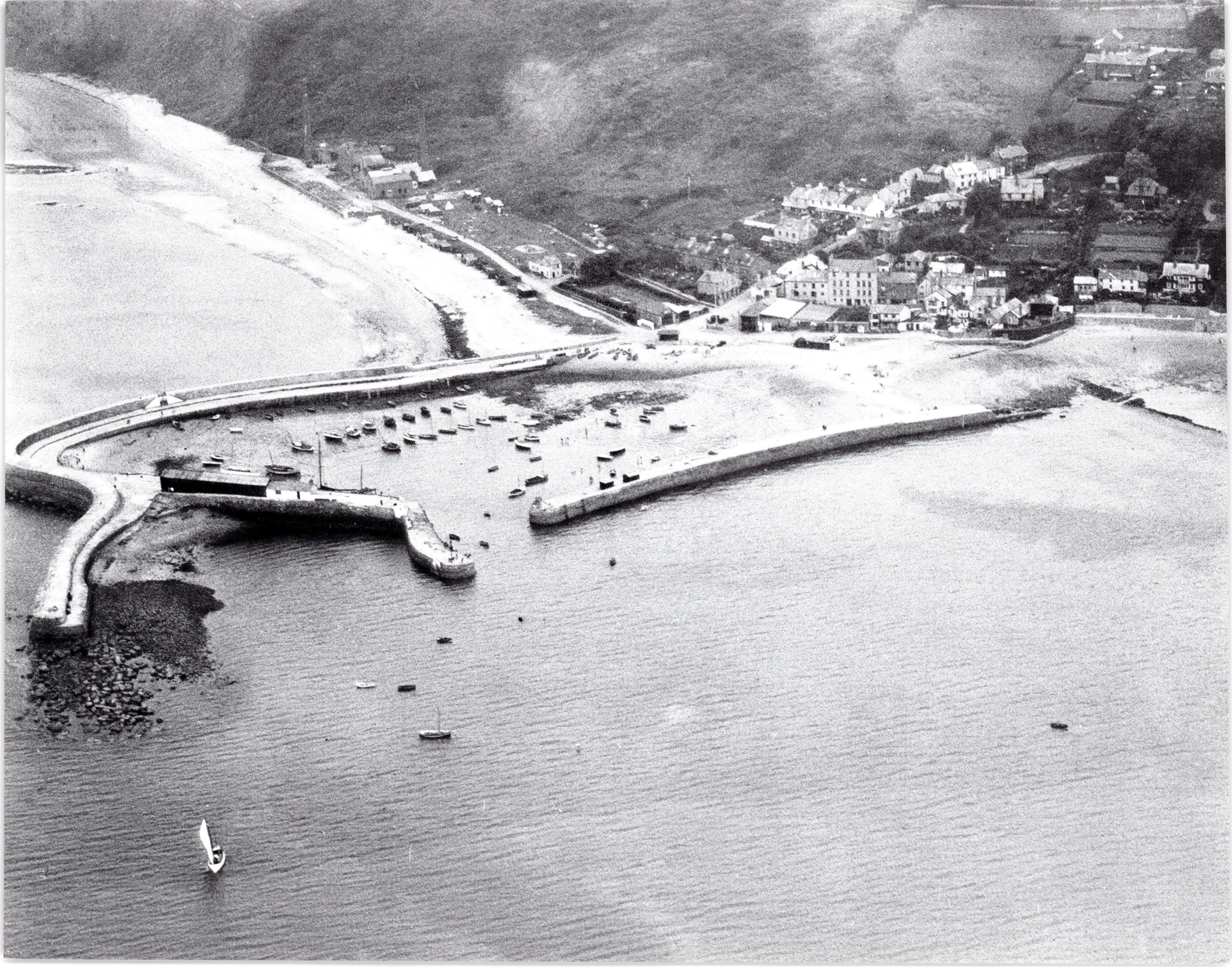

The Cobb, Lyme Regis, Dorset
August 1932

At Lyme Regis there was no natural harbour or suitable river in which boats could shelter, and therefore the Cobb, the town's harbour wall, was created. It is first mentioned in 1328 when it was described as a structure of oak piles driven into the seabed with boulders between. It was swept away during a storm in 1377, but as the centuries progressed, the structure became more substantial and its southern arm was added in the 1690s and rebuilt in 1793 following a storm during the previous year. During the 1750s it became fully connected to the mainland, resulting in the interruption of the local longshore drift, leading to the accumulation of sand forming Monmouth Beach on its western side. The Cobb was reconstructed as a more substantial structure in 1820 and serves as a breakwater, protecting the town and boats in the harbour from storms.

The Cobb featured prominently in literature; Jane Austen visited it while on holiday and she used the location in her novel *Persuasion*. The local writer John Fowles employed it as a central location for his novel *The French Lieutenant's Woman* and in the subsequent film. It is now a popular place to promenade and look out to sea.

EPW039714

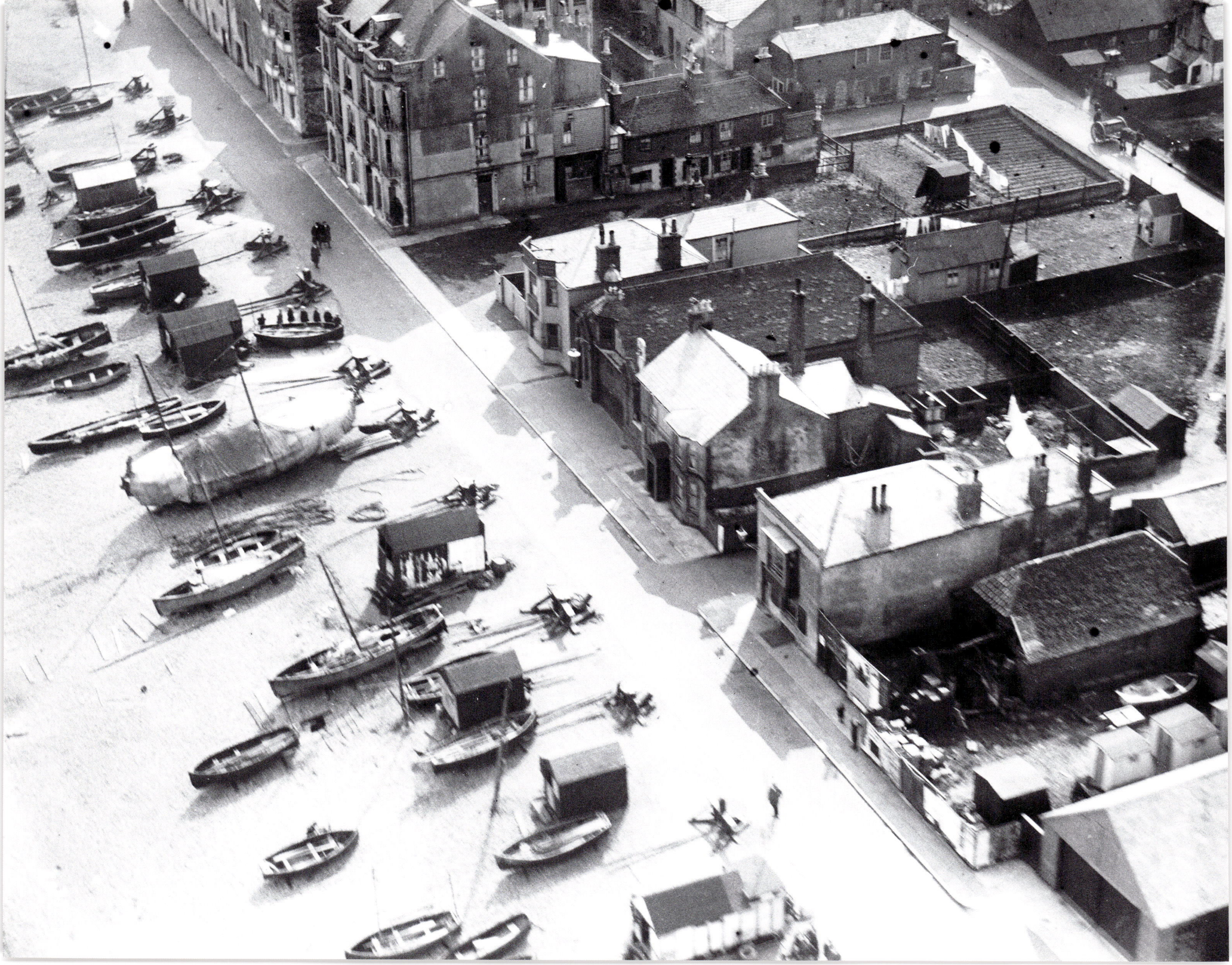

The Marina, Deal, Kent
April 1920

Fish and seaside holidays are inextricably linked, not only geographically, but also gastronomically. The origins of fish and chips can be traced back to two unconnected and geographically separate traditions that seem to have come together at Blackpool. Businesses selling pieces of fried fish appeared in London as early as the 1830s, while the chipped potato became popular in Lancashire during the mid-19th century. By the 1870s, the fortuitous geographical coincidence of fine, plentiful fresh fish from the Irish Sea and good crops of potatoes from the Fylde in Lancashire soon combined to create Blackpool's celebrated fish and chips.

At many seaside resorts, there are still harbours from which fishing fleets operate, though often they jostle for position more or less uneasily with pleasure craft. Where natural or man-made harbours do not exist, for instance on parts of the south coast of England, fishing fleets once operated from many beaches, the largest probably being at Brighton, though today only vestiges of this heritage survive. The largest beach-launched fleet today is at Hastings and a smaller one still operates from the seafront here at Deal. This photograph shows the capstans used for drawing boats up from the sea.

On the right-hand side of the photograph can be seen a large yard in which a number of bathing machines are being stored, as this photograph was taken in April 1920, before many visitors would have arrived. Another noteworthy feature is the absence of any sea defences beyond simply the sloping beach; in modern times when climate change and rising sea level dominate so much of our lives, such exposure to the power of the sea would be unthinkable, and along much of the seafront at Deal today there is a low sea wall.

EPW000382

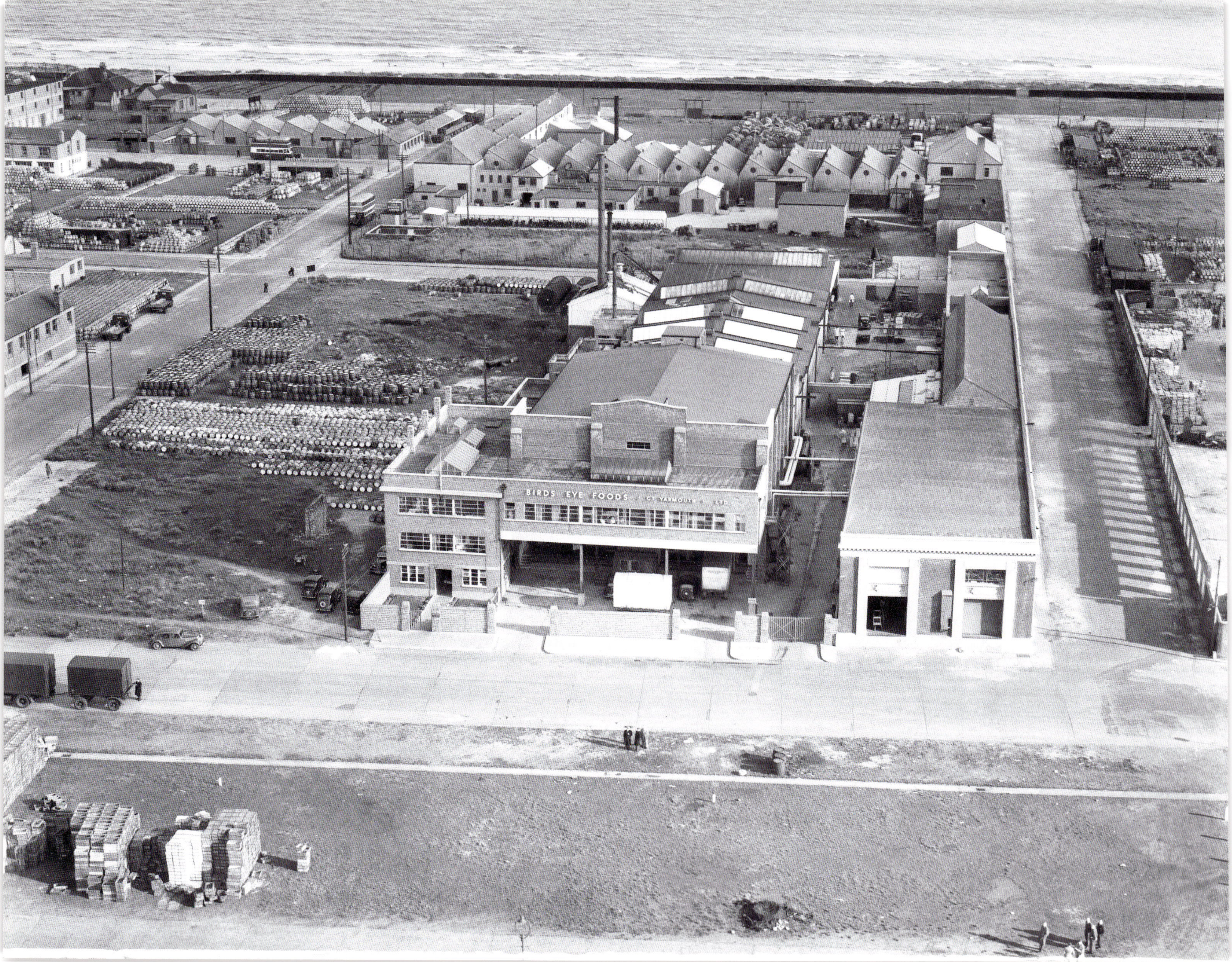
BIRDS EYE FOODS (GT YARMOUTH) LTD

The Birds Eye Foods Ltd canning factory on South Denes Road, Great Yarmouth, Norfolk

31 October 1949

Having caught fish, a boat would return to its home port to discharge its cargo for sale. Old maps and photographs show that there were a number of fish markets on seafronts, such as at Hastings and at Brighton, and the last vestige of this function can be seen in the stalls selling freshly caught fish at Hastings. There are also fish markets set in the harbours of many towns around the coast, providing fresh fish for takeaway chip shops and fish and chip restaurants. There are also now many celebrated fish restaurants around the British coast that rely for their reputation on the catch being landed every day; Padstow has become famed for its connection with the chef Rick Stein, and the quality of the catch arriving in its harbour has attracted other restaurateurs to the town. Whitby, where there is also a large fishing fleet, has become renowned for its fish and chips.

Fishing is now predominantly an industrial rather than an artisanal function at most ports; for instance, there is a large Birds Eye processing plant on the seafront at Lowestoft to the north of the harbour. This photograph shows the company's rather more modest facility that existed at Great Yarmouth in 1949, seemingly with offices to the front and production facilities behind. Thousands of barrels of fish can be seen in the yards around the complex. The factory lay inland from the seafront to the south of the resort, a short distance from the tall memorial to Admiral Lord Nelson (*see* p 291).

Clarence Frank Birdseye II of Montclair, New Jersey, in the United States, at the beginning of the 20th century developed improved methods to freeze fish for commercial production, and in 1922 he formed Birdseye Seafood to sell freeze-dried fish. Two years later he developed a new process for quick-freezing fish in cartons and 30 years later, Britain's favourite, the fish finger, was born in 1955, here at Great Yarmouth. Captain Birds Eye, the sailor with a large white beard and strong rustic accent, became Birds Eye's advertising mascot and the character was played by one actor for over 30 years.

EAW027509

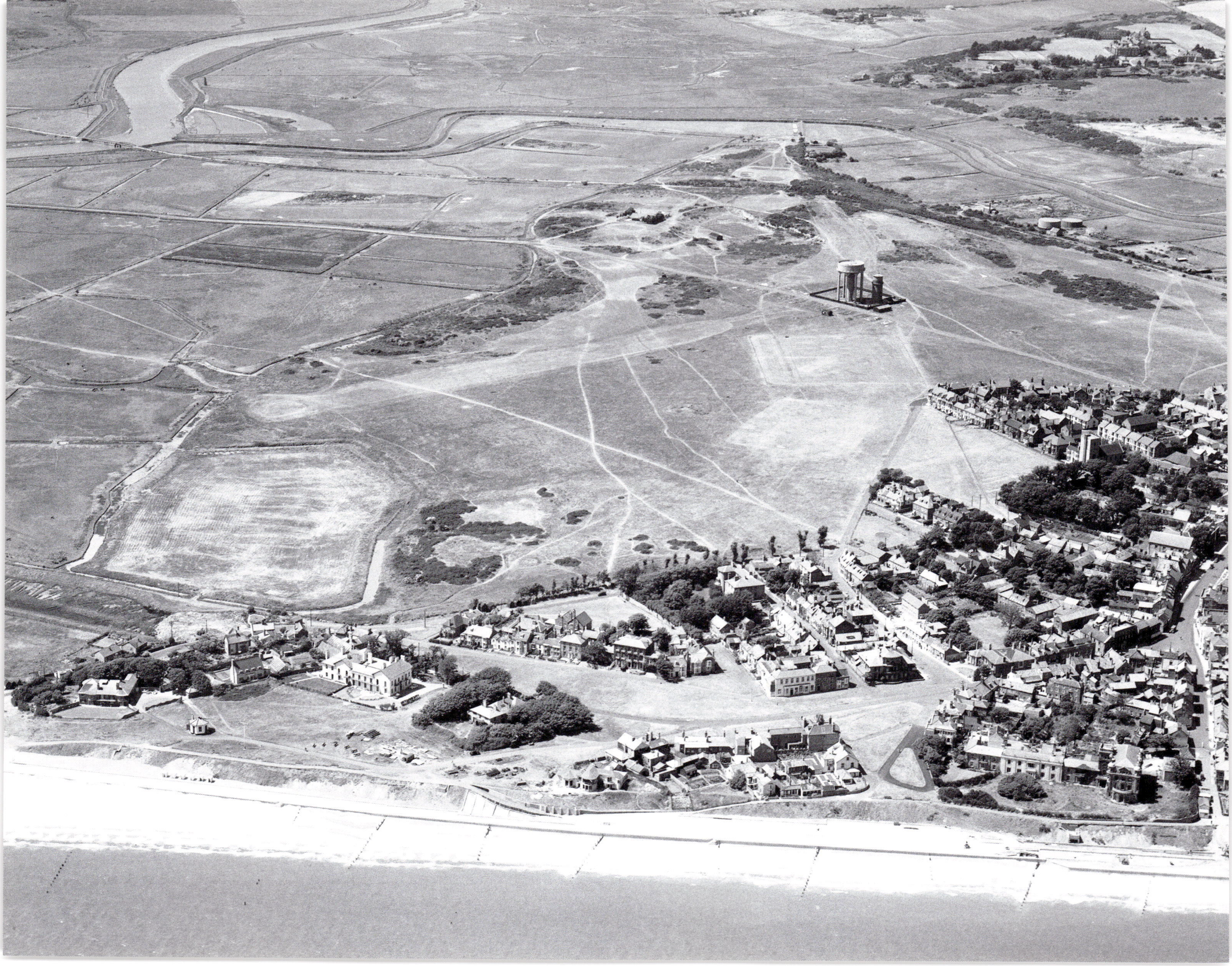

Southwold Common, Southwold, Suffolk
4 July 1949

No seaside holiday would be complete without fish and chips! A vital accompaniment to any such meal is salt, which is one of England's oldest coastal industries. Salt-water baths were a prominent feature of many seaside resorts, and at Southwold a seawater bathhouse was erected in 1766 and used waste heat from the salt pans to warm its water. The 1884 Ordnance Survey map shows that these were a short distance inland at the south end of the resort, in the undeveloped area seen in this photograph. However, as salt production had ceased there in 1894, there is perhaps little to indicate the presence of this industry beyond hints of the regular, rectangular forms in the field in the left of the photograph, beside the former wide drainage ditch.

To the right of the large domestic building on the left side of the photograph is a small polygonal building. On the 1904 Ordnance Survey map, it is rather puzzlingly described as 'Casino (Reading Room)', its small size being rather in conflict with its purported function. Interestingly, Southwold is famous for its Sailors' Reading Room, built in 1864 as a place for fishermen and mariners to read, as an alternative to drinking in pubs and also to encourage the pursuit of Christian ideals. Today, the room nearer the centre of the resort has a number of historic displays of model boats and other maritime objects in glass cabinets for visitors to enjoy.

In the vicinity of the water tower can be seen the remains of some of the accommodation and administration buildings for a heavy anti-aircraft battery deployed at Southwold on 24 November 1944 to counter the threat from V1s. It was armed with four 3.7-inch Mark IIc guns and was manned by 401 Battery of 122 Anti-Aircraft Artillery Regiment.

EAW024300

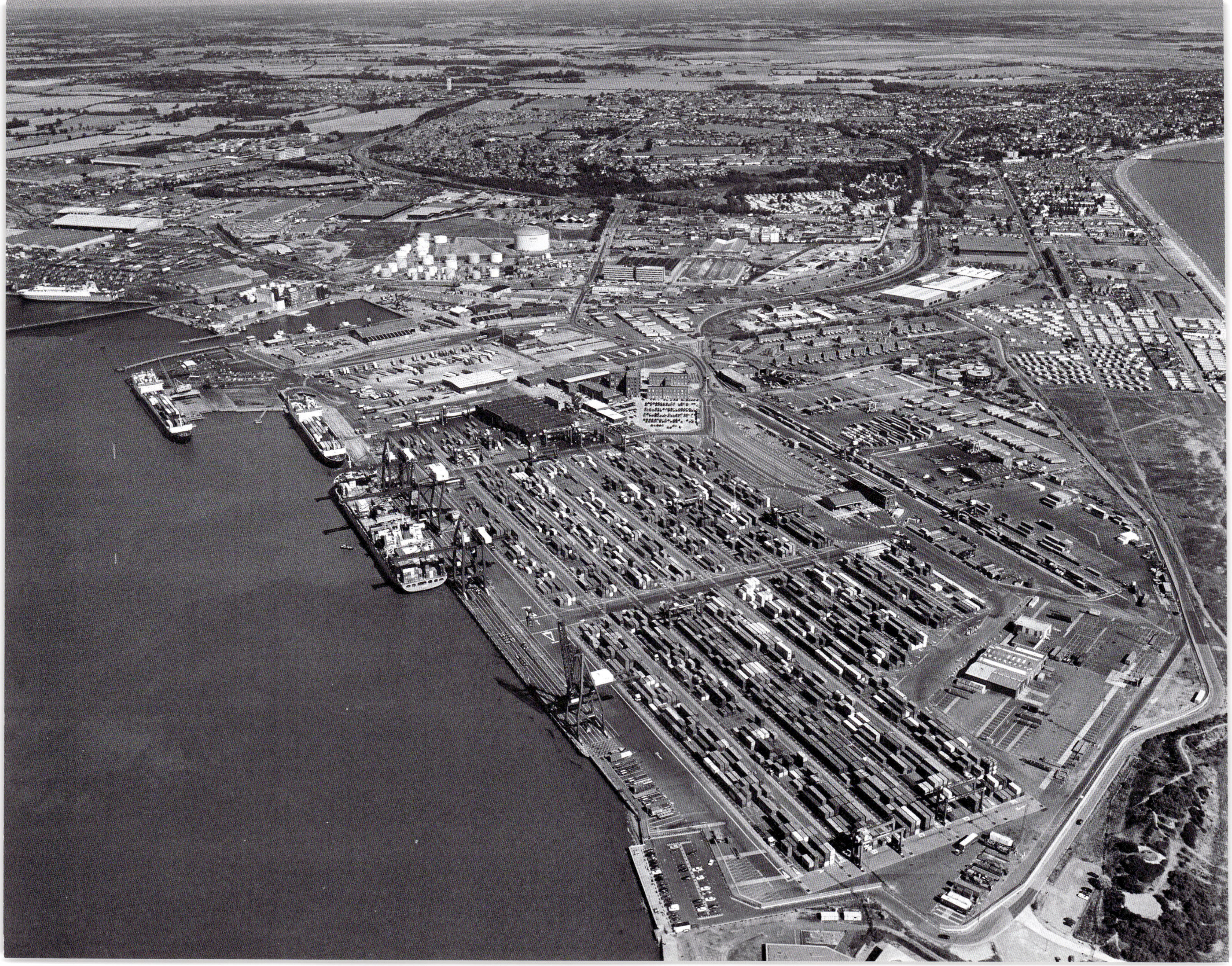

The Port of Felixstowe, Felixstowe, Suffolk
2 July 1997

Think of a harbour at the seaside resort, and the image that may come to mind is one with a few quaint fishing boats and yachts, where visitors walk along the quayside to buy some fresh fish and enjoy a bag of chips. Harbours as different as Scarborough and Bridlington or Weymouth and Whitstable may come to mind, but at some former and current seaside resorts there are now port facilities on an industrial scale. Inevitably, these are not places that can be visited by a holidaymaker, though at Felixstowe it is possible to stroll along the seafront to peer through the fence at the vast numbers of containers.

Containers were first used for freight during the early 20th century in the United States and spread gradually through Europe during the interwar years. However, it was during the later 20th century that containerisation transformed the landscape of freight transportation, leading to the closure of many smaller harbours and the creation of vast new complexes to handle the growing worldwide trade in goods. In 1967, the Port of Felixstowe became Britain's first container terminal, leading to it soon becoming the UK's largest container port, dealing with over 40% of Britain's containerised trade. In 2017, official statistics show that it was Britain's sixth busiest port, handling 29 million tonnes of freight.

EAW670704

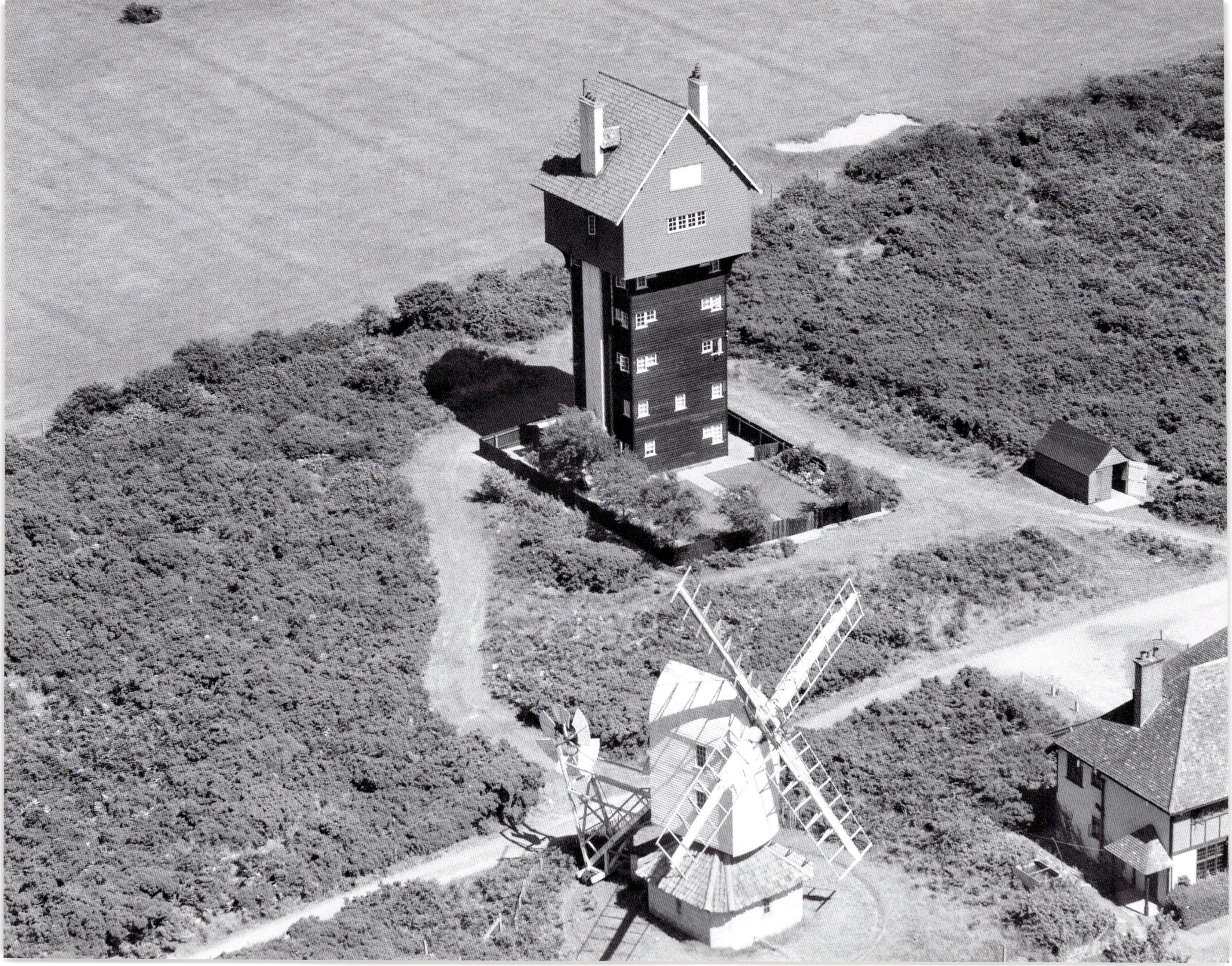

The House in the Clouds and Thorpeness Windmill, Thorpeness, Suffolk

3 August 1951

Seaside resorts, like any other town or city, need to supply their population with basic services such as electricity, telephone lines and water. Often the seafront of a seaside resort will be home to major water works, and perhaps the town's main sewer, almost all of their infrastructure for these services being beneath the ground. However, at some seaside resorts water towers can be seen; there is an impressive 1930s concrete structure a short distance inland at Blackpool and a similar structure can be seen in a photograph of Southwold in 1949 (*see* p 261). However, there is one unique, even eccentric water tower at a seaside resort: the House in the Clouds at Thorpeness in Suffolk is an unusual house, which was converted from a water tower that had been built in 1923.

The village of Thorpeness began life as a small fishing hamlet in the late 19th century; in the early 20th century, Glencairn Stuart Ogilvie, a Scottish barrister, increased the size of his family's local estates and developed Thorpeness into a fantasy holiday village for his friends' and colleagues' families to enjoy during the summer. Many holiday homes were built in a variety of historical styles and the villagers were provided with a country club with tennis courts, a swimming pool, a golf course and clubhouse.

The village needed a water tower, but to disguise the structure so that it fitted in with other buildings, it was clad in wood to make it look like a small house on top of a five-storey tower, with a separate water-pumping windmill beside it. Known as the House in the Clouds, after mains water was installed the old tank became a games room, and the house is now available to rent as a holiday home.

EAW038353

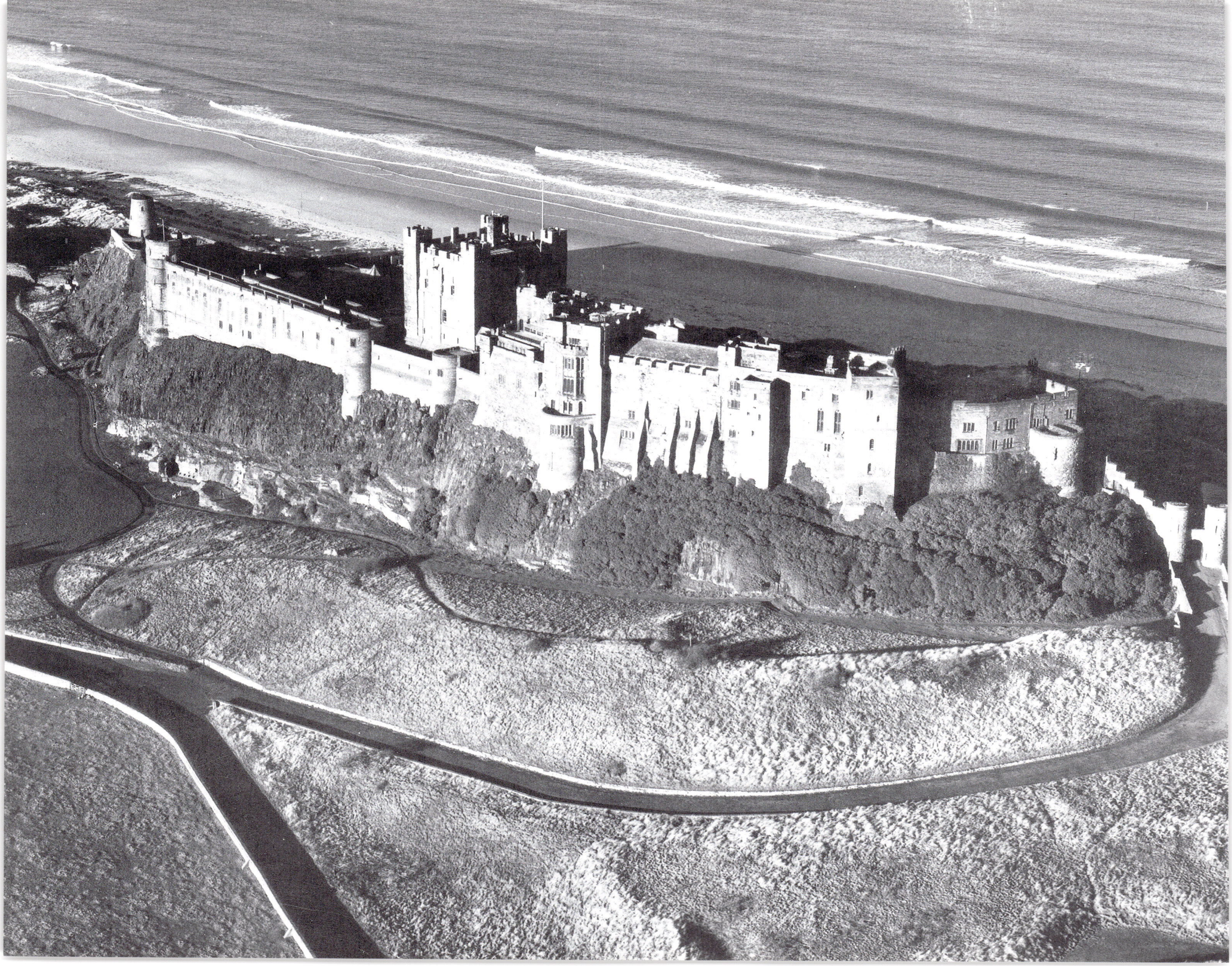

Bamburgh Castle, Bamburgh, Northumberland
25 November 1950

As an island, the British coastline is the key location for military defences to prevent invasion. Before the 16th century, responsibility for any defences near the coast lay in the hands of major landowners, acting to safeguard their own local interests rather than protecting the country. Around the coast there are a number of examples, one of the most impressive being at Bamburgh, perhaps the epitome of a coastal medieval castle and consequently a popular choice with filmmakers.

This was the site of an ancient Celtic fort taken over by the Anglo-Saxons and destroyed by the Vikings in 993. The Normans began the construction of the current castle and, following a revolt in 1095 by its owner Robert de Mowbray, Earl of Northumbria, it became a royal property. Work is recorded as taking place in 1163–4 on the tower of Bamburgh, probably the tall keep in the centre of the complex of buildings. More work was carried out in the late 12th and early 13th centuries, including work by the inveterate castle builder Henry III. In the struggle between the king and Simon de Montfort during the Second Barons' War (1264–7), Bamburgh Castle remained loyal to the monarchy, the only royal castle to do so consistently. Bamburgh's location was significant because of the centuries-long conflict between the English and the Scots, and despite periods of neglect, there were also significant campaigns of construction during the 13th and 14th centuries. Following the defeat of the Scots at the Battle of Neville's Cross in 1346, King David II was held prisoner in the castle. It was the subject of two sieges during the Wars of the Roses, in 1462 and 1464, succumbing on the latter occasion at the end of a nine-month siege, the first time that a castle in England had been defeated using artillery.

Bamburgh Castle is exactly the type of structure that inspires people to build sandcastles while on their seaside holidays. Probably the earliest reference to 'sandcastle' construction comes from Giraldus Cambrensis in the late 12th century, describing how during his childhood he built churches and monasteries while his older brothers built towns and palaces in the sand.

EAW034346

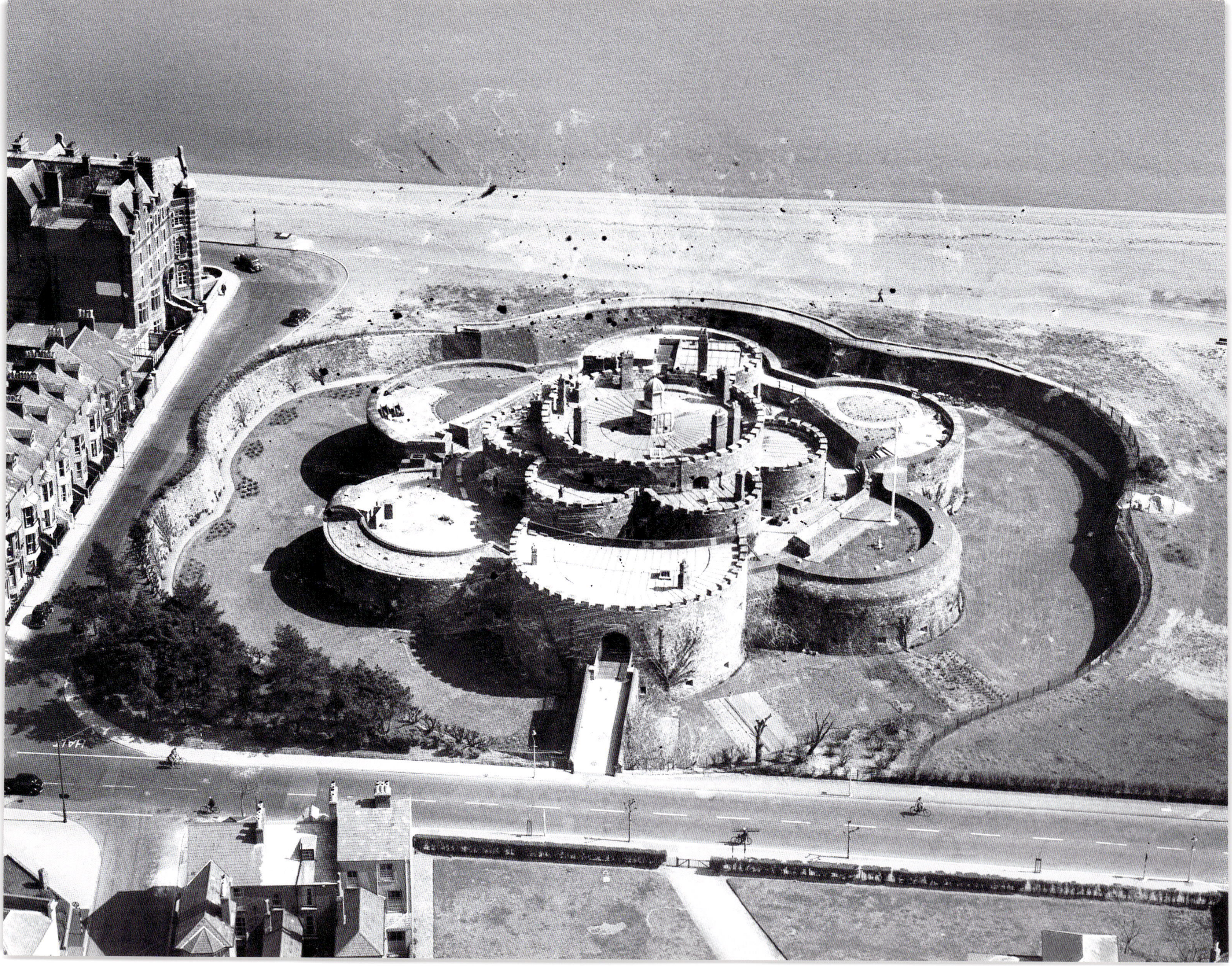

Deal Castle, Deal, Kent
13 April 1948

At the seaside, everybody loves a nice beach, including our enemies, because a stretch of coastline that is great for holidaymaking would also be ideal for an invasion. During the reign of Henry VIII, the Crown began to undertake national initiatives. The reason for this shift in policy was the result of a general change in the philosophy and practice of government, and specifically due to the predicament that resulted from Henry VIII's decision to break from the papacy. England faced invasion in 1538 by the combined forces of the Emperor Charles V and Francis I, King of France, seeking to re-establish papal authority.

The construction of a series of fortifications along the coast of England and Wales, stretching eventually from Hull round to Milford Haven, was undertaken. There was an underlying plan called 'the Device', which was drawn up by February 1539. It envisaged the creation of a series of gun platforms, a form almost transitional in type between the medieval castle and modern fortifications. Unlike their predecessors, these were purely military in character, rather than serving as the domestic and political power base of a nobleman. Although there may have been central direction of sorts, nevertheless there was great variety in the structures built to defend the coast. The smallest were the blockhouses defending the shores of the Thames, which cost from around £500 to just over £1,000 to construct. At some locations on the south coast of England, huge fortifications were built with a tall, central, cylindrical block surrounded by rounded bastions and these cost between £5,000 and £10,000. In terms of their armaments, the firepower ranged from a handful of guns in a small blockhouse up to dozens of gun positions in castles such as those at Deal, Walmer, Sandgate or St Mawes. Although vast sums of money were spent during Henry VIII's reign, these fortifications were not put to the test, as on 7 June 1546 a peace treaty ended the immediate danger of war with France.

Deal Castle remained in use as an official military fortification until the early 20th century, but from the 18th century onwards it was increasingly used, and adapted, as a private house for the captain of the castle, which had become an honorary position. During the Second World War, the castle was used as an observation post for a nearby artillery battery. Following wartime damage, the building was restored during the 1950s and it is now cared for by English Heritage.

EAW014344

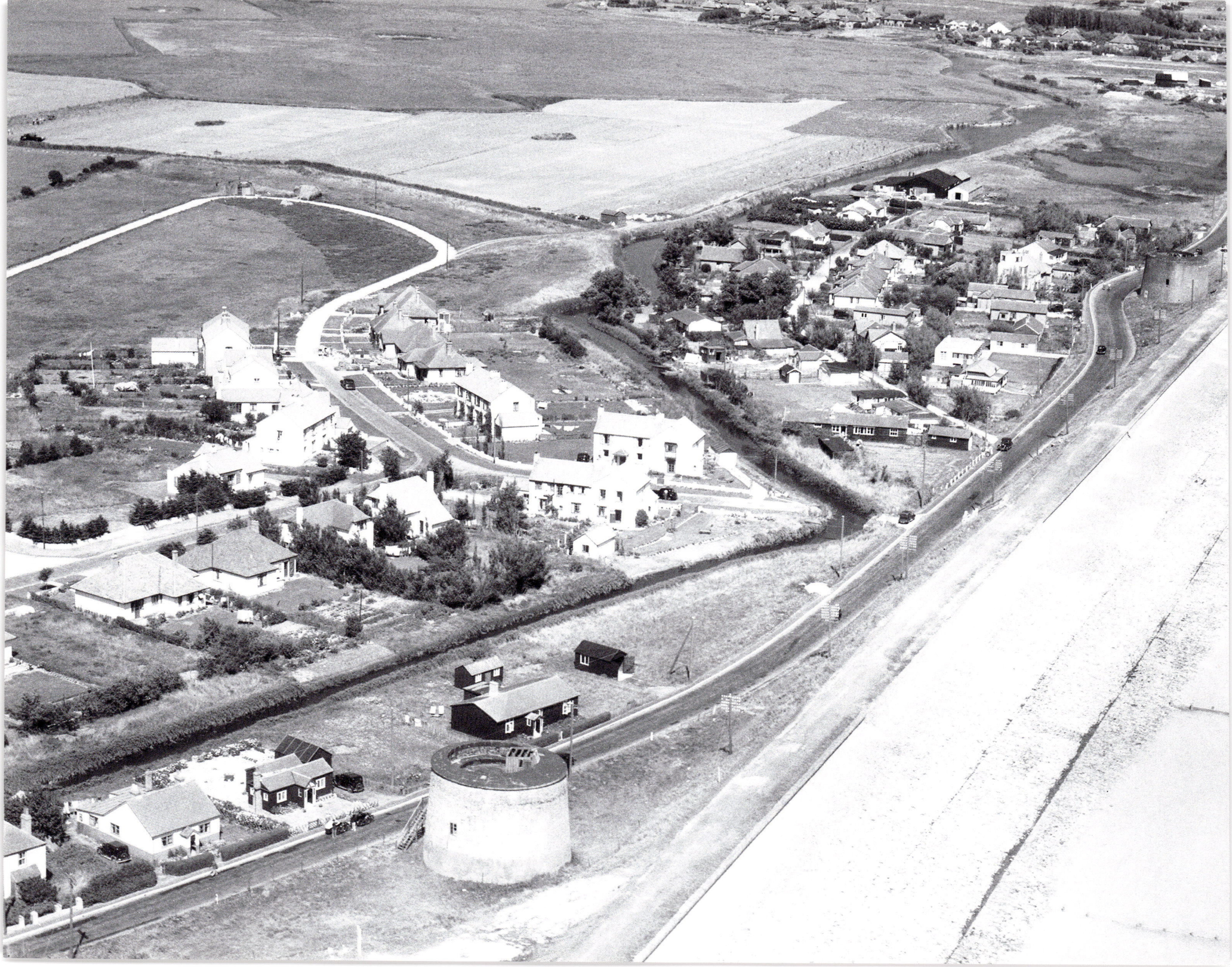

Martello towers No 22 and 23, Dymchurch, Kent

12 August 1947

Through the 18th and 19th centuries, France was the threat to Britain. This prompted sporadic fortification construction in the 18th century and a later, major campaign of Martello tower construction on the east and south coasts. With the outbreak of the Seven Years' War, five new coastal batteries were built in 1759 on the Sussex coast and a new blockhouse at Brighton was built of brick. It was armed with a dozen rather ancient guns, which by 1779 were rusting and their wooden carriages were beginning to rot. The battery succumbed to encroachment by the sea and finally collapsed during a severe storm in November 1786. There were also forts on the seafront at Weymouth – one of which survived until the end of the 18th century – and interrupted the line of the Georgian seafront terraces. In 1793, two new batteries were built at Brighton; the West Battery stood near the site of the present Grand Hotel, and the East Battery was at the southern end of the New Steine overlooking where the Chain Pier would later be built.

In the south and east of England, a more concerted approach to anti-invasion defences was taken at the beginning of the 19th century. The threat of a huge French army assembling near Calais after 1803 prompted the government to build a network of 73 Martello towers on the south coast between 1805 and 1808, followed by 29 on the east coast from 1809 to 1812. The inspiration for their design came from a tower at Mortella Point in Corsica that resisted being besieged by two British warships in 1794. The British examples are up to 12m (39ft) high with two floors designed to house a garrison of one officer and 15–25 men, with a single artillery piece on the roof of the structure. Their cylindrical form and thick masonry walls were designed to resist cannon fire from attacking ships. They were located on stretches of the coastline felt to be vulnerable to enemy forces being landed by ship, and where they were constructed, they were built sufficiently close to each other to be able to give covering fire to the next one along the coast. Most of the towers were constructed under the direction of General William Twiss (1745–1827).

In this photograph of Dymchurch, the Martello towers are located just behind the substantial sea defences needed to protect the low-lying settlement behind.

EAW008992

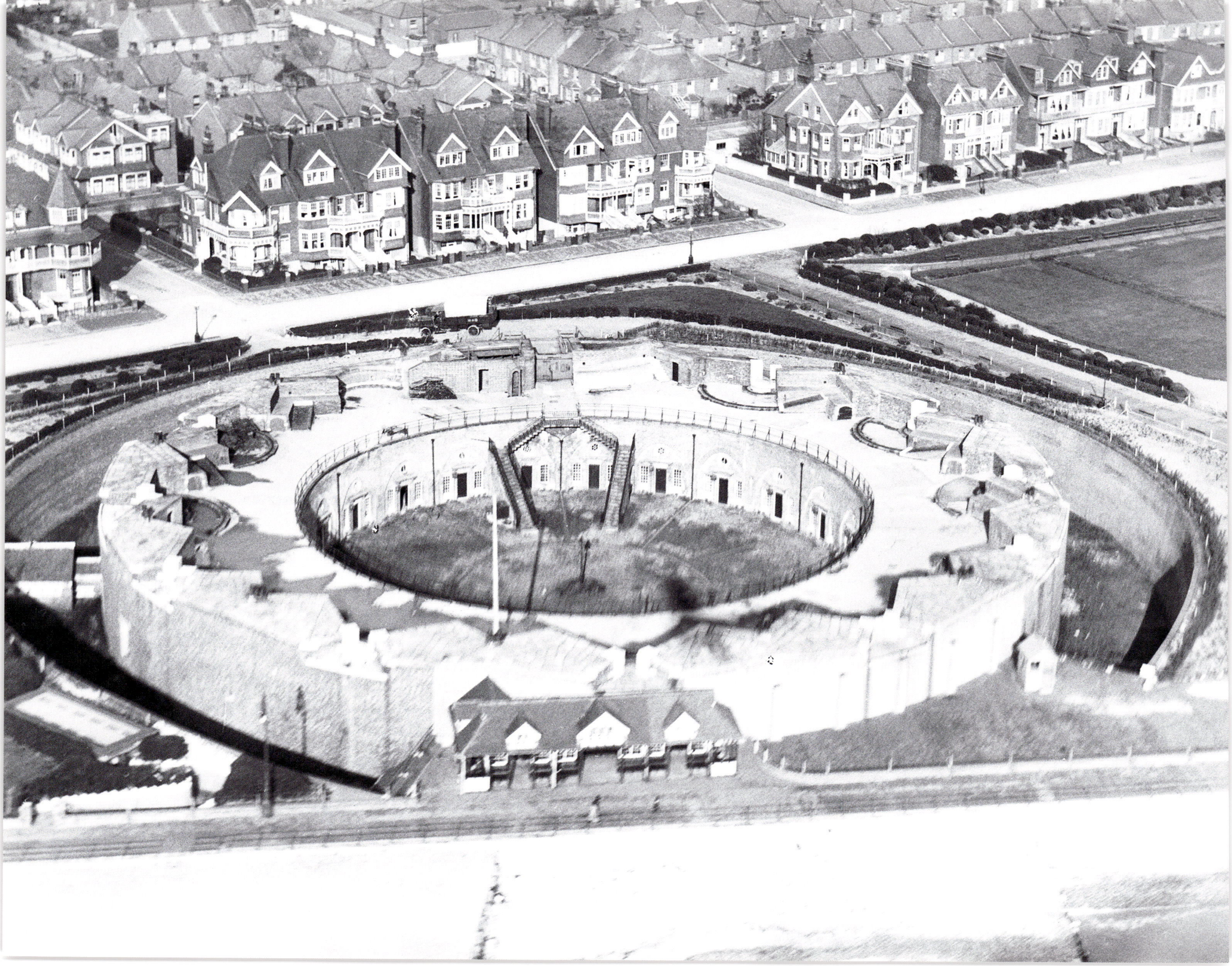

The Redoubt Fort, Eastbourne, East Sussex
February 1920

In addition to the standard, cylindrical Martello towers built on the south and east coasts in 1805–8 and 1809–12, three other, larger forts were built at Harwich, Dymchurch and Eastbourne to serve as control and supply points. The Redoubt at Eastbourne is a circular structure, measuring 68m (223ft) in diameter. Around the lower tier is a ring of 24 casemates that opened into the central, circular parade ground. The upper tier was the gun platform with positions for 11 guns. The Redoubt is surrounded by a dry moat 9m (30ft) deep from the top of the parapet. Access to the main gate of the Redoubt is on the landward side of the fort across a wooden bridge.

Since 1815 the Martello towers have largely been redundant, though some were reused as coastguard lookouts, signal stations and, during the Second World War, as observation positions and radar stations. Today, some of the surviving examples are used as museums, while others have been converted into desirable seafront homes. However, the Redoubt at Eastbourne remained in use during the 19th century as a barracks and its armaments were upgraded during the 1850s and 1870s. During the First World War, the military police used it as a headquarters and a temporary jail. It was purchased by Eastbourne Borough Council after the war and in 1934 a new bandstand was constructed in the gardens beside it. During the Second World War, it was requisitioned for use as a store and in 1944 anti-aircraft guns were placed on the gun platform to try to shoot down V1 flying bombs.

In 1957, the Redoubt was leased to Benjamin White, who created a model village on the parade ground; the earliest example of this type of attraction in the world was Bekonscot in Beaconsfield in Buckinghamshire, which had opened to the public in 1931. The model village was removed in 1975 and today the Redoubt contains two regimental museums.

EPW000101

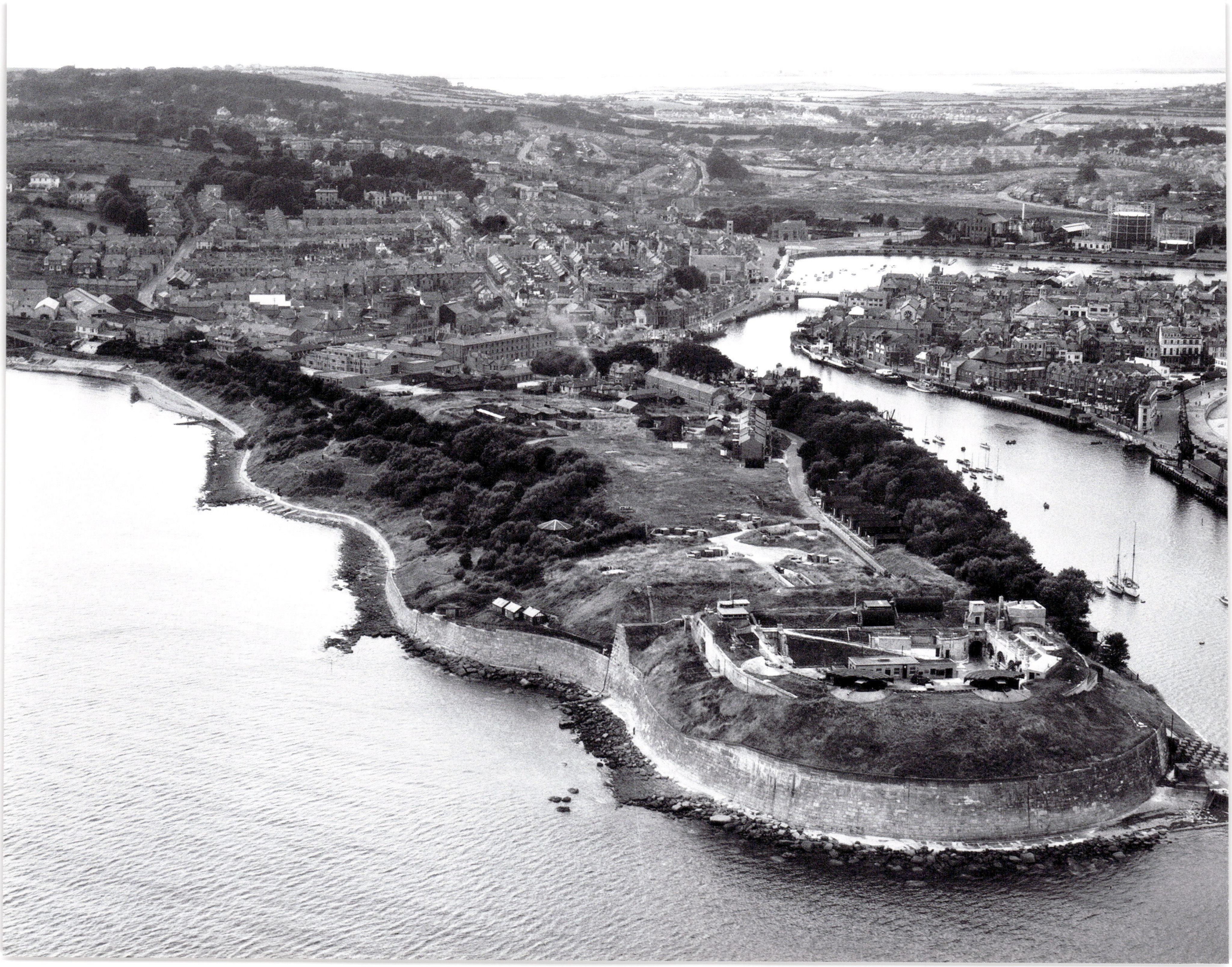

The Nothe, Weymouth, Dorset
24 September 1947

Due to his illness, George III was a regular visitor to Weymouth between 1789 and 1805, a period that coincided with the outbreak of prolonged hostilities with France. Weymouth had become an important base for naval vessels, but also for large numbers of troops stationed in barracks and in tented encampments around the resort. In the distance in this photograph can be seen the Red Barracks, overlooking the Weymouth side of the harbour. It was one of three barracks in the town and was originally a cavalry barracks, though it was used by infantry after its reconstruction in the early 19th century. After the Second World War, the buildings were little used and during the 1980s, they were converted into flats.

In the foreground can be seen the Nothe Fort, one of a number of military defences built on the south coast in response to a perceived, though unrealistic, threat from France. Palmerston Forts, named after Lord Palmerston, who was prime minister at the time, were built as a result of recommendations by the 1860 Royal Commission on the Defence of the United Kingdom, resulting from concerns about the strength of the French Navy.

The Nothe Fort was mainly built between *c* 1860 and 1872 by troops from the Royal Engineers. It is semi-circular in plan with a series of 22 casemates at the upper courtyard level, with 12 original gunports set above a continuous circuit of magazines and stores. In the photograph can be seen guns still in place that would have guarded the entrance to the harbour during the war that ended only two years earlier. Beyond the fort can be seen a series of Second World War concrete structures that survived at least until the 1970s, but disappeared during subsequent landscaping.

The fort remained in active service until 1956. In 1979, Weymouth Civic Society obtained a licence to restore the site, transforming it into a museum that is still open to the public.

EAW010940

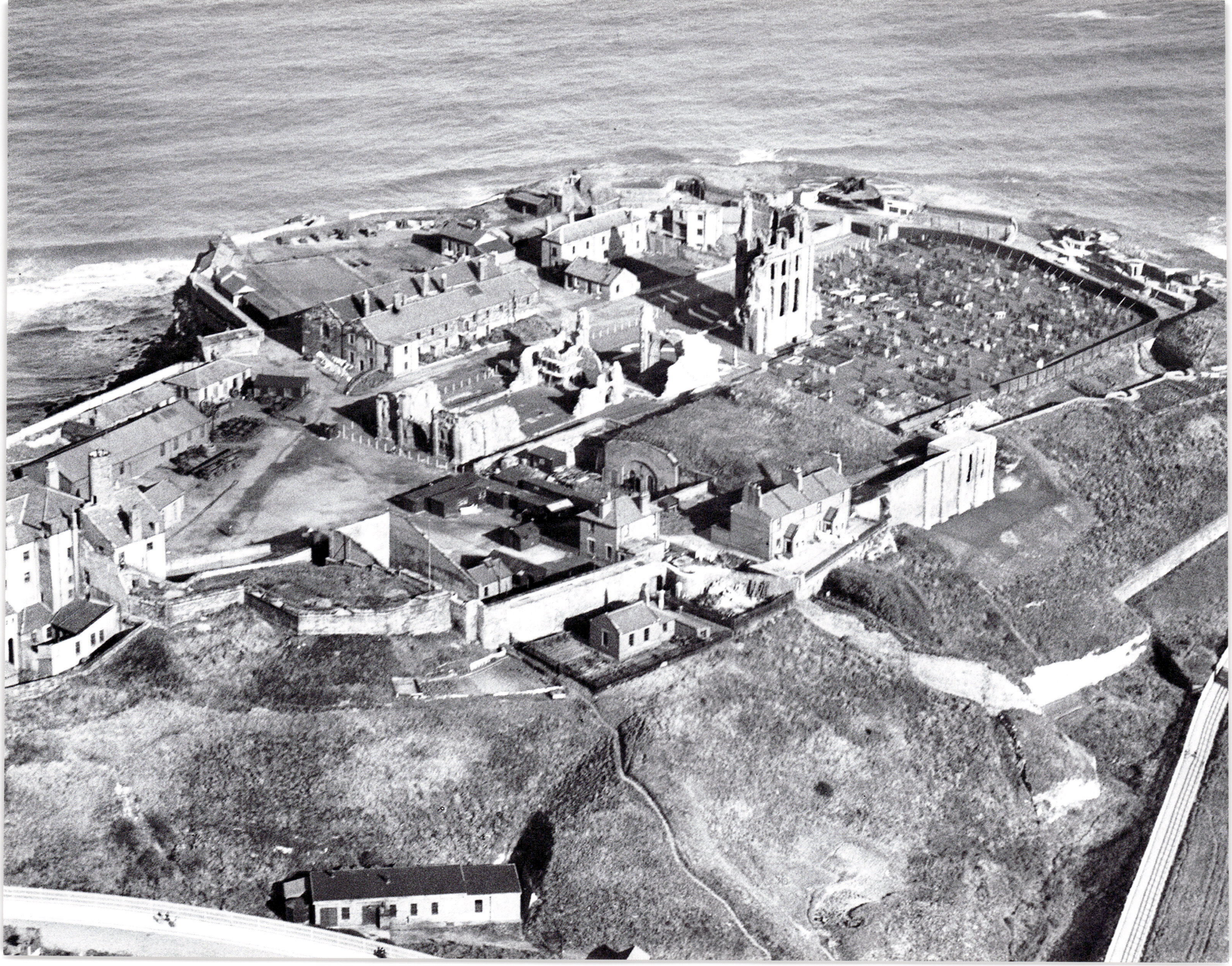

The castle and priory ruins, Tynemouth, Tyne and Wear
18 October 1927

This clifftop site at Tynemouth has a history of more than 2,000 years, beginning as a promontory fort during the Iron Age. A monastery is thought to have been established at Tynemouth by the mid-7th century, when it is believed that the body of St Oswin was interred there. It is thought that the early Anglo-Saxon church was still standing when it was replaced by a post-conquest monastery at the end of the 11th century. The monastery at Tynemouth was refounded by the Earl of Northumberland, Robert de Mowbray, in 1085. It is believed that at the time of Robert Mowbray's capture in 1095 there was a castle on the site consisting of earthwork ramparts and a timber palisade.

The upstanding remains of the priory comprise three main phases; there are ruins dating from the original Norman foundation as well as the more substantial modifications and additions of the early 13th century. There were also alterations and additions during the 15th century. The monks' cemetery was situated to the south and east of the priory church, and the cemetery was reused and extended over the ruins of the church in the post-medieval period. It contains some 700 gravestones, mainly dating from between 1715 and 1856.

In 1296, royal permission was granted to surround the monastery with stone walls, presumably to allow it to be defended against the Scots, and in 1390 a gatehouse and barbican were added on the landward side of the castle. Long stretches of the medieval defences survive, but the north and east walls have fallen into the sea and most of the south wall was demolished.

After the Dissolution, Tynemouth became part of Henry VIII's scheme of national defence and was modified to serve as an artillery castle. Sir Richard Lee, who designed the town defences at Berwick-upon-Tweed, was sent to Tynemouth in 1545 to assess using the site as a military fortress; however, a plan to provide modern defences was not carried out, and instead the existing defences were reinforced.

In 1663, the fortifications were repaired and the lighthouse that had collapsed in 1659 was replaced; it was subsequently rebuilt during the later 18th century, but was demolished in 1859. The defences were adapted to meet changing threats during the 18th and 19th centuries, and at the end of the 19th century, as part of a national programme to improve England's coastal defences, two emplacements for 6-inch breech-loading guns were constructed in 1893. Two 6-inch gun emplacements for close defence were built in 1902 and an emplacement for a 9.2-inch breech-loading gun was constructed in 1904, intended to target large warships. There were also two 12lb quick-fire guns constructed in 1902 to fire on smaller, faster vessels. The remains of this rearmament programme can be seen at the right-hand side of the photograph, between the cemetery and the sea, and between the cemetery and the harbour below the cliffs.

The Tynemouth batteries were updated and were operational during the First World War; additional buildings were constructed including a fire observation post and the Admiralty signal station. These were demolished for the construction of the new Marine Rescue Centre in 1980. At the beginning of the Second World War, the batteries were once again operational and the army remained in residence at the castle until 1960.

EPW019754

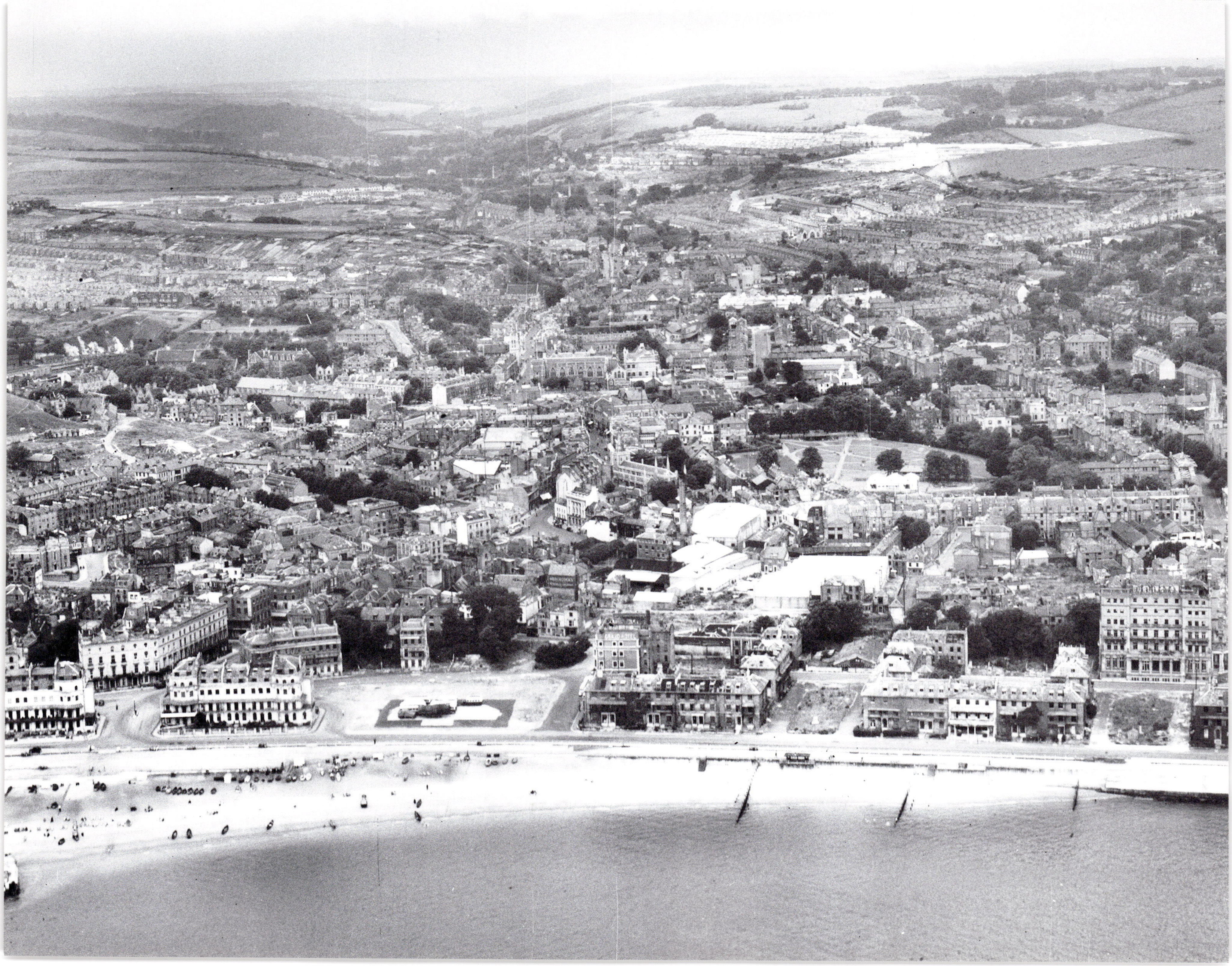

The town and seafront, Dover, Kent

28 June 1947

This photograph was taken just over two years after cessation of hostilities in Europe at the end of the Second World War. For over four years, Dover effectively was in the frontline between Britain and Nazi Germany, and was repeatedly attacked by aircraft and by long-range guns based on the French coast. Therefore, it is no surprise that its seafront was one of the most heavily damaged; apparently the Burlington Hotel at the right-hand side of the photograph was the target that Nazi gunners aimed at. It is perhaps surprising that it had survived when this photograph was taken, though it had lost its distinctive tower on its right-hand side.

Although Dover is considered today to be primarily an important cross-channel ferry port, in the 19th century it was also a seaside resort and a popular place to stay before or after crossing the channel. On the seafront, Waterloo Crescent was built in 1834–8 by Philip Hardwick. It was built in three parts, a central block of 19 houses flanked on either side by a pair of blocks containing 5 houses. The right-hand of the two smaller blocks can be seen beside part of the larger central block, terraces easily recognised by their distinctive curved bay windows (*see* p 175).

These blocks were damaged during the war, but apparently were already repaired and reoccupied by 1947. However, the rest of the seafront in this photograph fared less well and a number of the houses and hotels can be seen to be derelict or certainly in need of repair. Instead of reviving them, most of the area of the seafront in this photograph was cleared and after protracted discussions beginning in the late 1940s, the monumental, modern Gateway block of flats was completed in 1959.

EAW007618

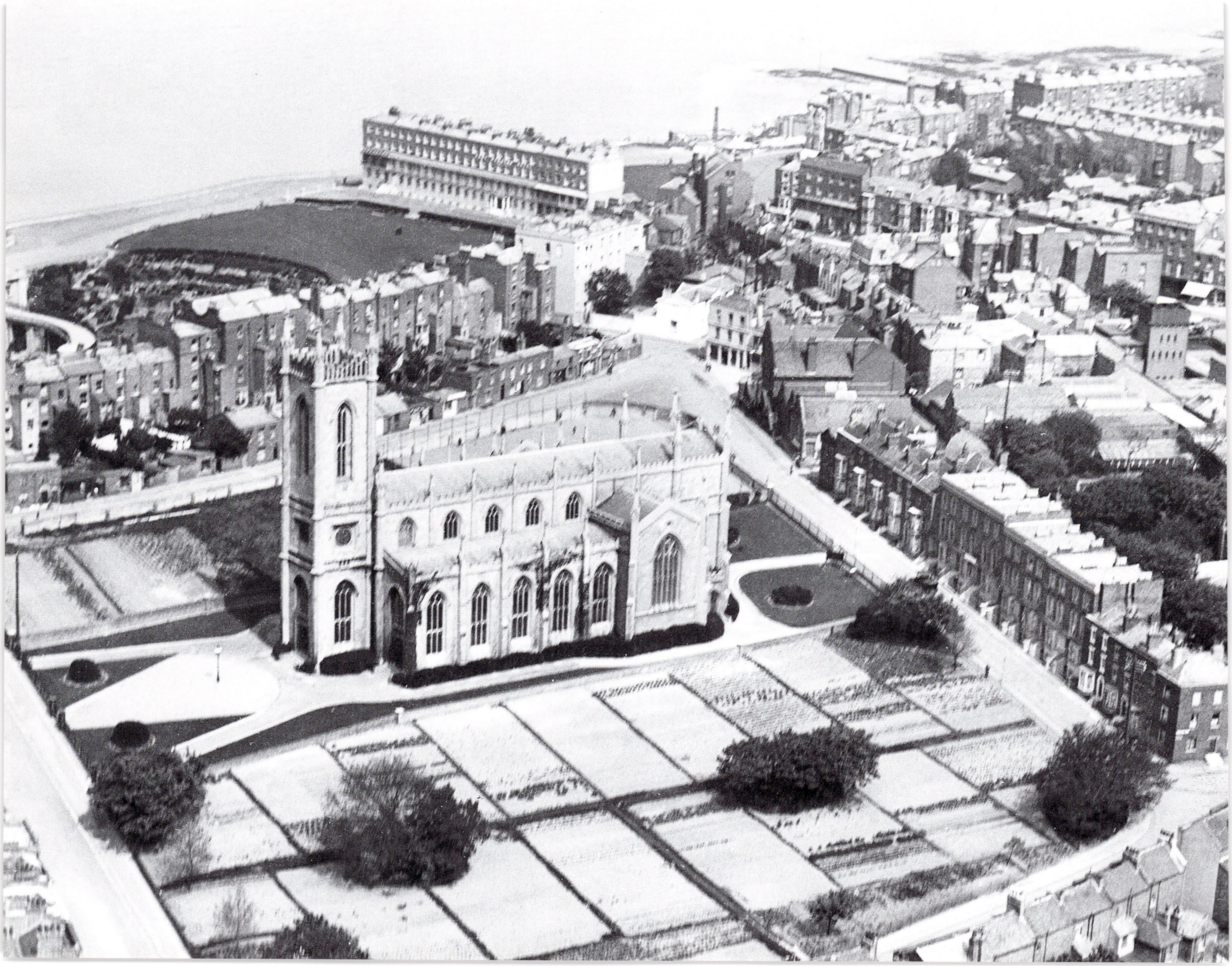

Holy Trinity Church, Margate, Kent
April 1920

Holy Trinity in Margate was not a willing participant in the Second World War, but an unfortunate victim. One of the largest churches built at a seaside resort during the Georgian period, it was badly damaged during a bombing raid in 1943, a consequence of its location close to the town's harbour.

Margate was a booming resort at the beginning of the 19th century; the town's population rose by 65% between 1801 and 1821, from 4,766 to 7,843, while in the same period England's population increased by 35%. In 1800, development was concentrated near the heart of the original town, but by the early 19th century a fundamental shift in this pattern was taking place. Edmund's map of 1821 demonstrates that new developments were being erected on previously undeveloped land along the coast on either side of the historic town. By 1821, the first buildings here in Cliftonville were being erected to the east of Fort Green, the site of the 19th-century fortification created to protect the harbour, which lies just to the left of this photograph.

Trinity Square was a piecemeal development of terraced houses on three sides of an irregular 'square'. Holy Trinity was constructed in the centre of the square. The first stone was laid on 28 September 1825, and the church was consecrated on 11 June 1829 by the Archbishop of Canterbury, Dr William Howley. The church was constructed to hold 2,000 people and had a 17.4m-high (57ft) nave and a tower that rose to a height of 41.5m (136ft). It was badly damaged by a German bombing raid during the afternoon of 1 June 1943, but the tower remained standing for many years; it was eventually pulled down when the decision was made not to rebuild the church.

Margate's location at the eastern tip of the Kent coast made it vulnerable to attack in wartime. During the Second World War, more than 2,700 bombs and shells hit the town, destroying 238 buildings and damaging nearly 9,000 others. With the threat of invasion, the town's population dropped to around 10,000, around a quarter of its pre-war figure. Before the war, there were 30 first-class hotels, 60 smaller hotels, 150 private hotels, 1,300 boarding houses, 1,500 apartment houses and 3,500 private dwellings that took in visitors. An article published in *The Times* on 31 August 1943 noted that there were just two hotels and a handful of boarding houses. A year later visitor restrictions to the Isle of Thanet were lifted and the population rose to around 19,000, but Margate never regained its reputation with the kind of clientele that had frequented the large Victorian and Edwardian hotels of Cliftonville, where Holy Trinity Church had stood.

EPW000636

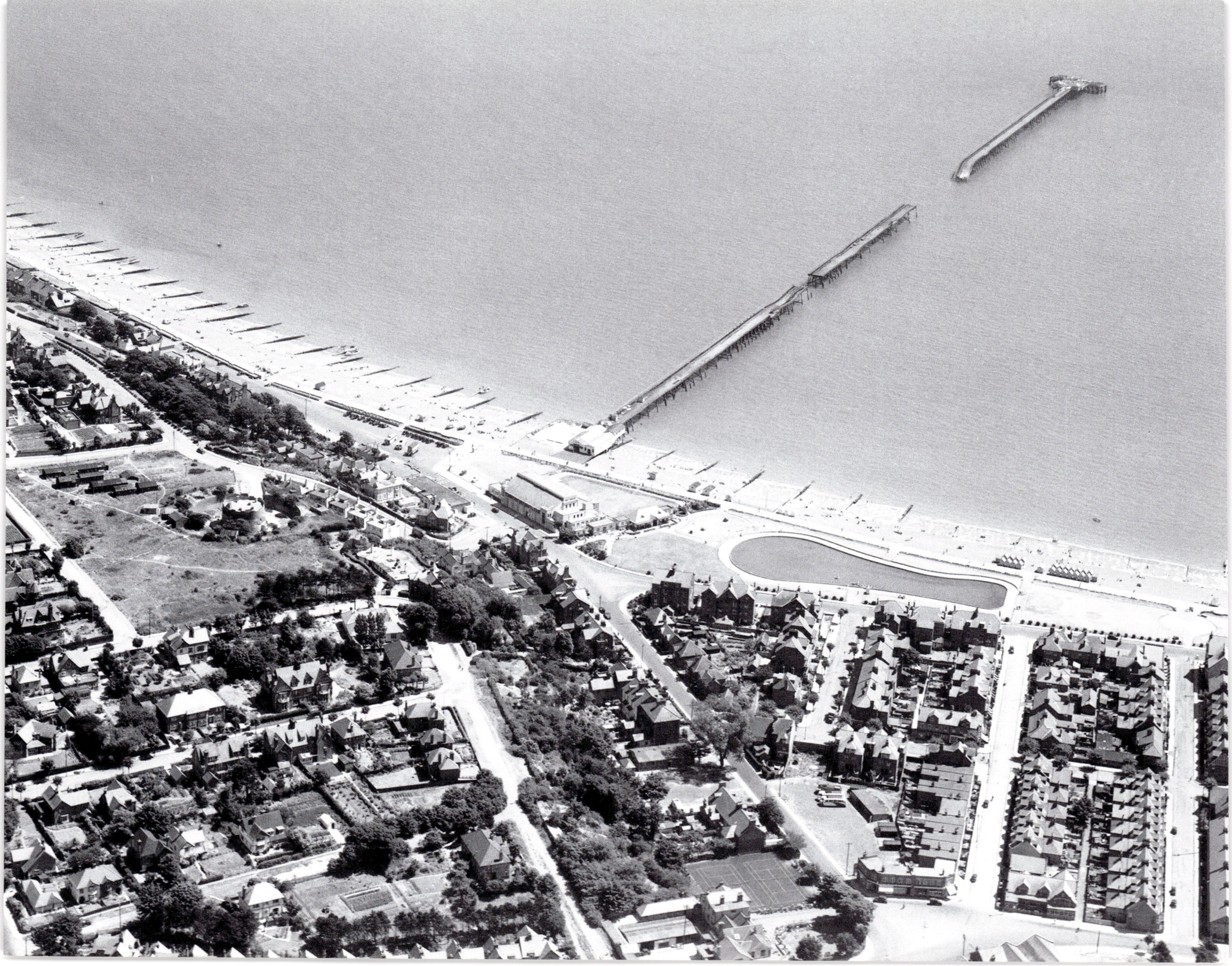

The pier, Felixstowe, Suffolk
4 July 1949

The seaside pier at Felixstowe was another victim of the Second World War, but in this case the damage was inflicted by the British.

Construction of Felixstowe's pier began in 1903 and what was the third-longest in the country at 853m (half a mile) opened in July 1905. Due to its length, tram cars ran on a narrow-gauge track on the east side of the pier, on the left-hand side in the photograph. A café at the pierhead catered to steamer passengers, and by 1912 a large entrance building had also been added, providing a café and amusements. Towards the end of 1939, boats started bringing child evacuees from London, but due to the fear that the Germans might use seaside piers to land their forces, this pier, like many others considered to be in the frontline, was sectioned. This was a euphemism for the removal of a section or sections of the pier, often through the use of explosive charges by the Royal Engineers. The two breaches in the structure can clearly be seen in this photograph taken four years after the war.

After the war, many piers were repaired, but at Felixstowe the outer part was never reinstated, meaning that the only visitors to the shortened head now were fishermen and promenaders. The landward end was rebuilt in concrete. A large entertainment complex known as the Pier Pavilion stood opposite the pier entrance; it was used for shows, dancing and wrestling, but was demolished in 1983 and replaced by a swimming complex. In 1963, the pier was sold to the Felixstowe Property Company and later to Pier Amusements (Felixstowe) Ltd. In 2017, a new structure at the landward end of the pier was opened, offering family entertainments as part of a wider regeneration scheme for the local area.

EAW024305

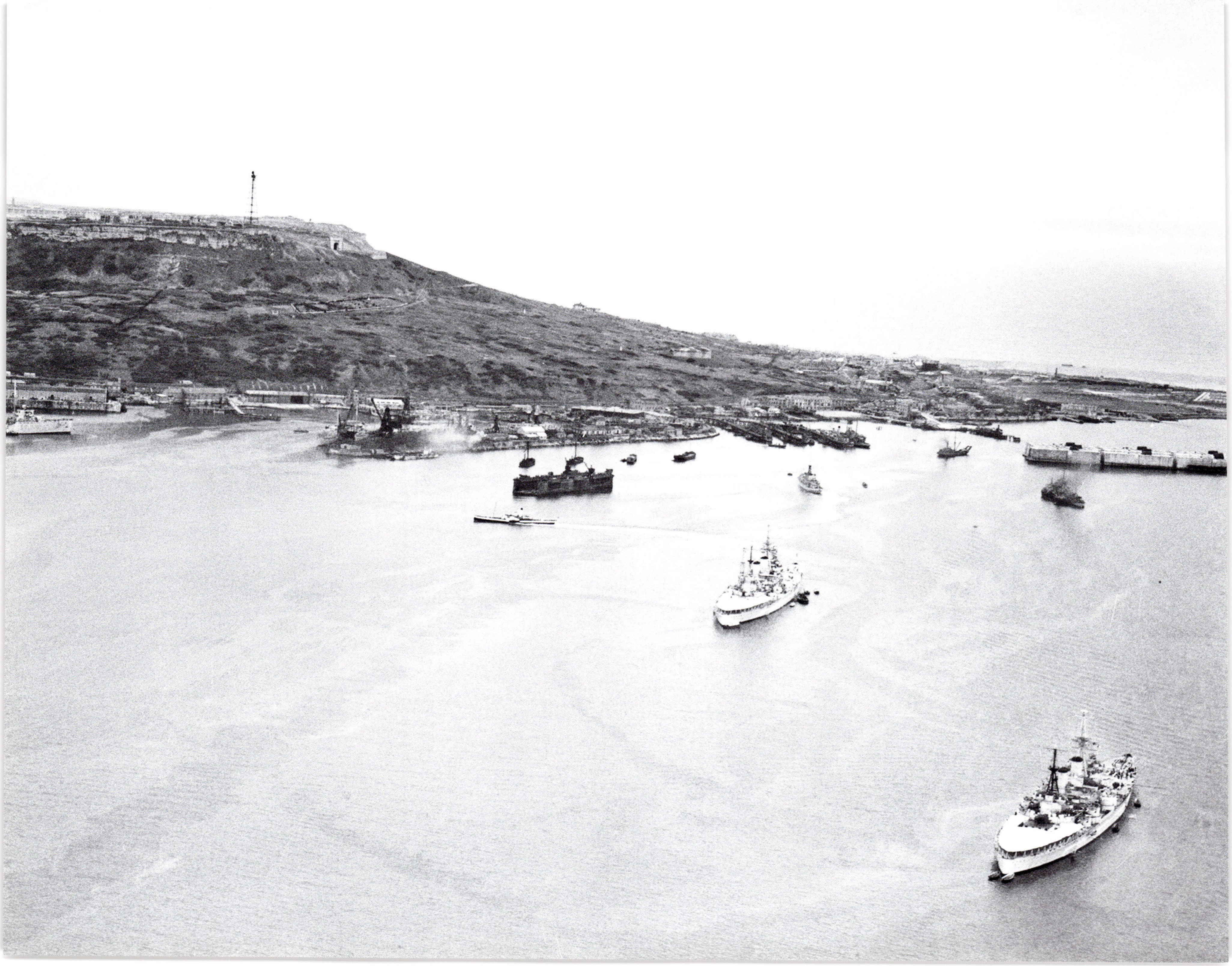

The port and harbour, Portland, Dorset
3 October 1946

In 1944, seaside resorts along the south coast of England were thrust into the headlines as ports of embarkation for Operation Overlord, the landing of Allied troops in Normandy. While some of the forces left from the small harbour at Weymouth, the vast majority of Allied forces in this area left via the harbour at nearby Portland. A bronze plaque inside Portland dockyard records the sheer scale of the logistics for the Normandy invasion. It was presented by the 14th Major Port, US Army, and bears the names of Colonel Sherman L Kiser, the port commander, and Major Harold G Miller, the sub port commander:

> The major part of the American assault force which landed on the shores of France 6 June 1944, was launched from the Weymouth and Portland Harbors. From 6 June 1944 to 7 May 1945, 517,816 troops and 144,093 vehicles embarked from these harbors. Many of these troops left Weymouth Pier. The remainder of the troops and all vehicles passed through Weymouth en route to Portland points of embarkation.

Portland Harbour lies to the south of Weymouth, beside the Isle of Portland, which is the backdrop to the harbour in this photograph (*see* p 235). This had long been a strategic location and during the later years of the reign of Henry VIII, Portland Castle and Sandsfoot Castle were constructed to defend it. Construction of the modern harbour began in 1849 and was completed in 1872, at which date it was the largest artificial harbour in the world, enclosing 520ha (2 square miles). To achieve this, there were breakwaters measuring 4.5km (2.8 miles) in length, constructed with stone quarried by convicts at the nearby prison on Portland. Today, there is a second prison on the island, which occupies the Verne Citadel (seen on the distant hilltop), built between 1860 and 1881 as part of the defences for the harbour.

Aerial photographs taken by the RAF at the end of the Second World War show that a large part of the Royal Navy and Britain's merchant fleet was docked in what appears to be a rather crowded harbour, an indication of the scale of Britain's naval effort during the war. This photograph in 1946 shows a rather quieter harbour with only a few naval vessels in the picture. To the right may be a number of the ten Phoenix caissons of the Mulberry Harbour that were towed back to Portland. In 1953, eight of these were donated to the Netherlands to repair breaches in their dykes caused by the highly damaging storm in 1953, which also flooded parts of eastern England (*see* p 213 and p 215).

Portland Harbour continued to serve as host to the Royal Navy, including as a training facility, a naval air station and a weapons research establishment. It ceased to operate as a naval facility in 1995 and in the subsequent quarter of a century has been used for a range of commercial and recreational activities. A new National Sailing Academy was established in 1999 and in 2005 a purpose-built clubhouse and training centre opened. Together with the excellent local sailing conditions, the existence of this facility was key to the selection of Portland as the site for the London 2012 Olympic and Paralympic Games sailing events.

EAW002986

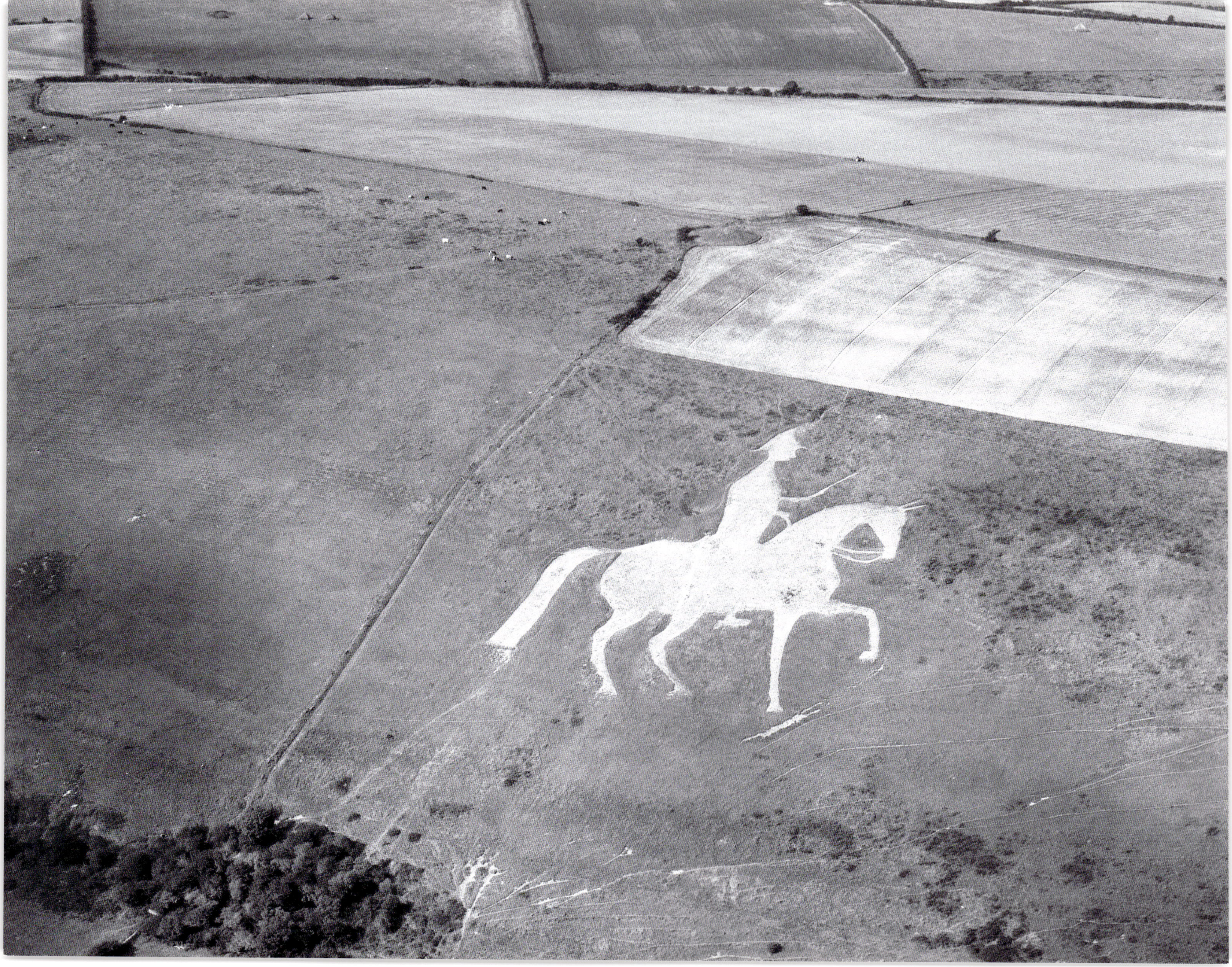

The Osmington White Horse, Osmington, Dorset
24 September 1947

In 1781, a large house was built at Cheltenham near the Old Well for Lord Fauconberg, creating what was then the most palatial building in the town. This would be a key event in the early development of the town as it proved to be a suitable place to accommodate the ailing King George III, his wife and three of his daughters when he came to Cheltenham in July 1788 to spend five weeks drinking the waters and riding out into the countryside. During his stay, Bath sent a delegation to try to lure him to their town, but in the following year he went instead to Weymouth where he became a regular visitor until 1805.

The reason for the king's visit to Cheltenham was that he had been struck down with porphyria, a disease affecting his nervous system, and after his health failed to improve, it was felt that a stay at the seaside would be beneficial. He arrived in Weymouth on 30 June 1789 and stayed for ten weeks. A week after his arrival he bathed in the sea, an event accompanied by great ceremonials, including fiddlers playing 'God Save the King' while he took the plunge. During this visit, and subsequent ones, the king and the royal family were at the heart of the social scene; they attended events at the assembly rooms and promenaded along the seafront, attracting significant crowds. The king also visited local aristocrats in their country seats; he regularly inspected regiments of troops in barracks or camps near Weymouth and he went on board naval ships moored offshore.

From 1791 to 1802, the king visited Weymouth every summer except 1793, and in 1801 he bought Gloucester Lodge from his brother. His last visit took place in 1805. In 1802 the town council decided to commemorate the king's visits, but it took until 1810 for his statue to be completed. Another belated commemoration of his visits was a white horse mounted by the king, carved into the hillside at Osmington in 1808. On a clear day, it can be seen from Weymouth, but what is unfortunate is that it shows the king riding away from the town rather than towards it.

EAW010928

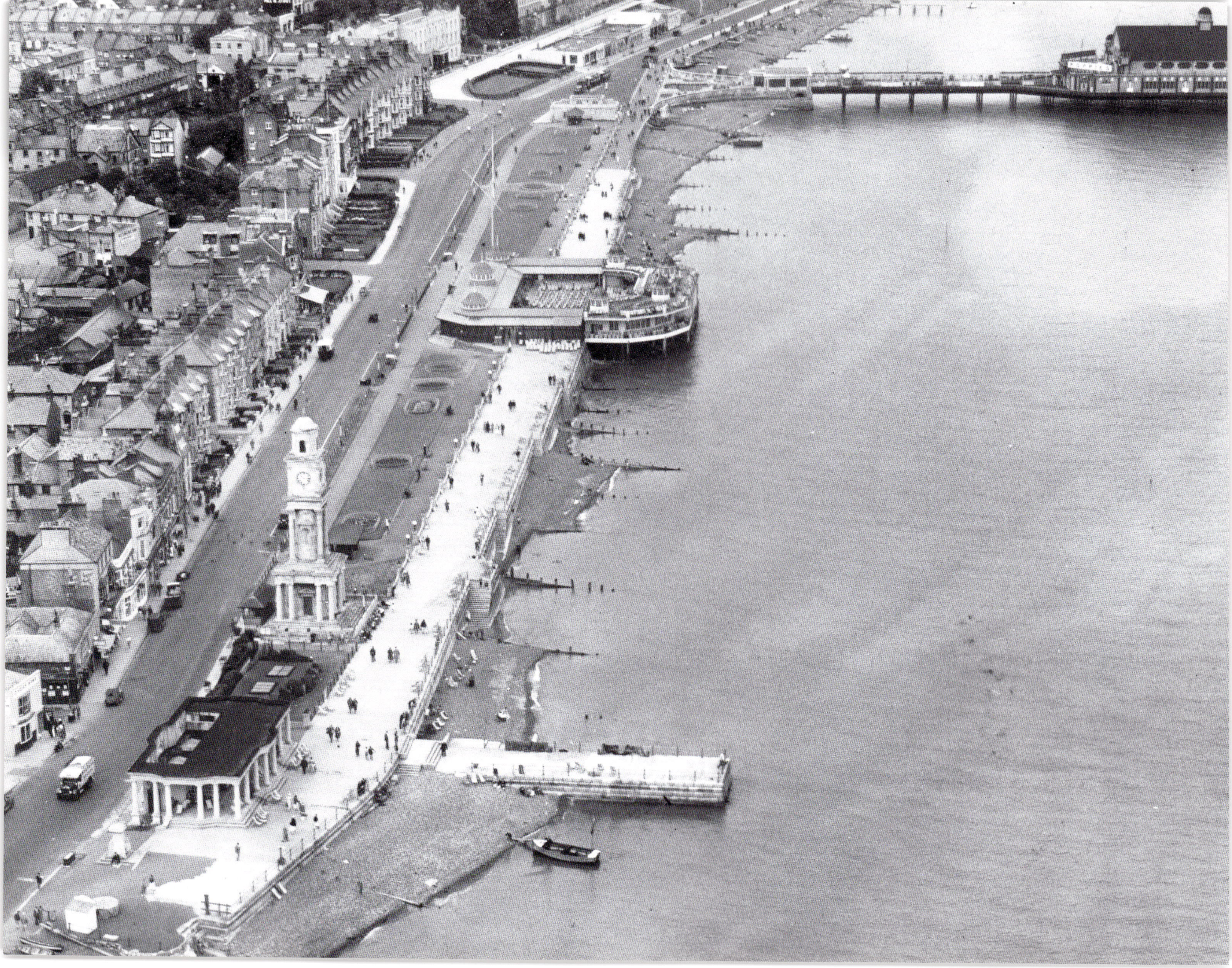

Tower Gardens, Herne Bay, Kent
July 1932

As well as statuary, other more practical forms of memorial were erected at seaside resorts. The earliest example is the clock tower that was erected at Herne Bay in 1836–7 by the architect Edwin J Dangerfield, who lived nearby at 5 Telford Terrace. An inscription reveals that it was 'The gift of Mrs Ann Thwaites to this town, 11 October, A.D. 1837'. This bizarre structure, which cost £4,000, uses a wholly incorrect combination of classical orders in its design. Its ground floor is square and decorated with Greek Doric Columns, while on the first floor there is a circular core surrounded by four Corinthian columns. The second storey is square with corner Corinthian pilasters, while the top storey is octagonal. The whole building is too tall for its width and looks like the work of a local architect unfamiliar with the use of classical orders. The ambition of the scheme, which was considerably beyond the ability of its architect, is almost a metaphor for the early failed development of the town. However, this quirky design predates other examples of commemorative seafront clocks by a generation, and other practical forms of memorial that normally belong to the last decades of the 19th century and the early 20th century.

Further up the seafront at Herne Bay, in the middle of the formal gardens, can be seen the new bandstand, which opened in 1924, and beyond it is the pier. The first pier was a timber structure, which welcomed its first steamer in May 1832, but its wood was soon succumbing to its location, and therefore a second, cast iron, pier was constructed, opening on 27 August 1873. It was only 98m (322ft) long, and therefore was too short to be used by steamers, but to remedy this situation a long extension was opened on 14 September 1899, stretching 1,155m (almost three-quarters of a mile) out to sea. The pier was taken over by the council in 1909 and they enlarged the entrance. On 3 August 1910 the Grand Pavilion opened about 100m (328ft) down the pier, a venue that seated 1,000.

EPW039302

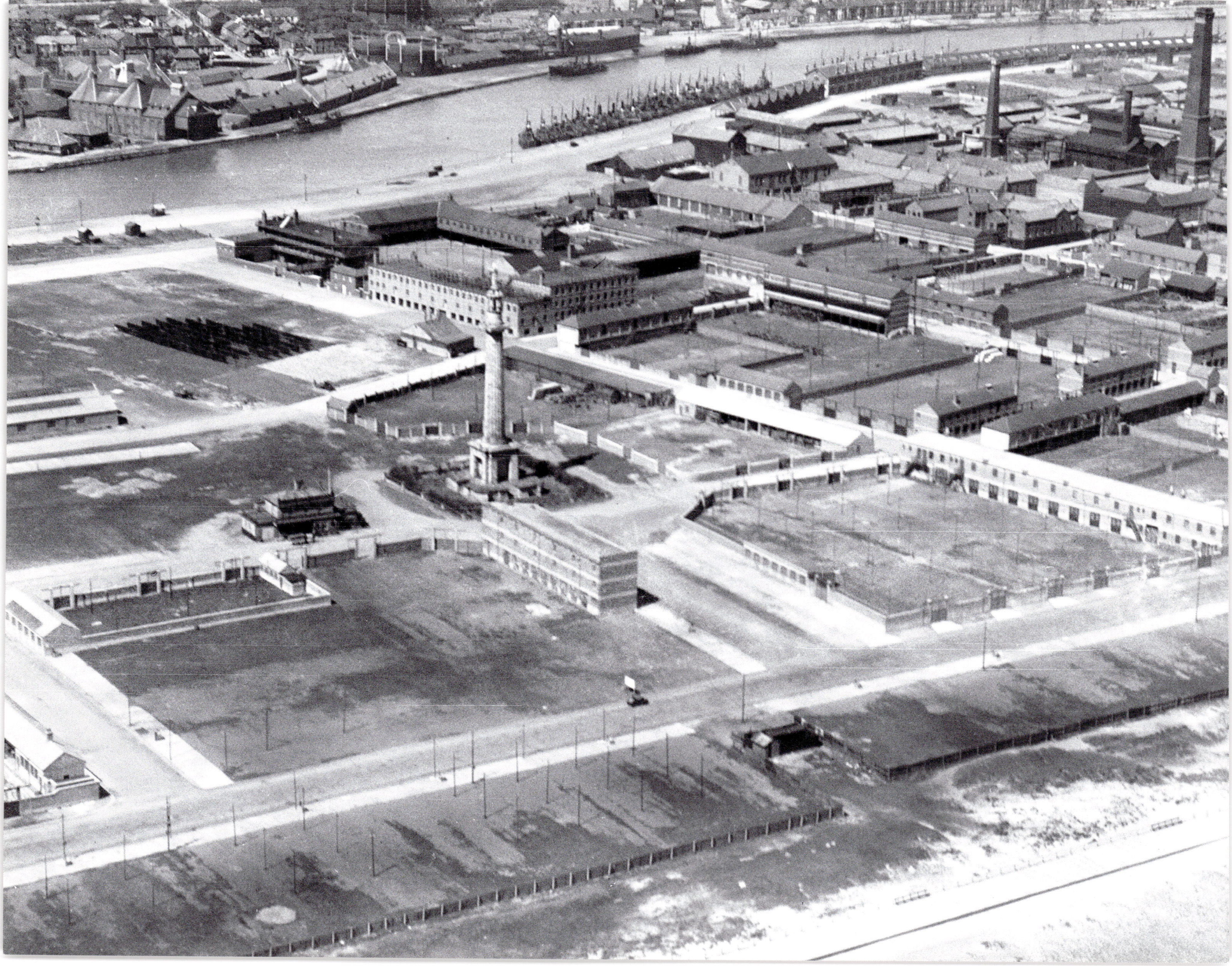

South Beach, Nelson's Monument and the River Yare, Great Yarmouth, Norfolk
May 1928

The seafront of a seaside resort is often a place to celebrate the lives and achievements of individuals, whether military, civilian or celebrity. Like towns and cities of all shapes and sizes, seaside resorts are also places to commemorate the lives of great monarchs. Queen Victoria's long reign and the country's great wealth at the end of the 19th century led to a spate of commemorative Golden and Diamond Jubilee monuments in 1887 and 1897.

As the seafront of the seaside resort often serves as the town's main civic space, there are often memorials commemorating specific wars or military events from the third quarter of the 19th century onwards. Their forms drew on a number of traditions. Obelisks can trace their origins back to ancient Egypt and columnar monuments reflect the Roman Empire, while a range of cruciform shapes, including Celtic crosses and variations on the Eleanor Cross were also employed. By the early 20th century, figures were also incorporated into the more ambitious memorials, either in the form of statues or depicted in low relief on plaques.

From the early 19th century, there were also memorials to national military heroes and the first of these was Admiral Lord Nelson. His death on 21 October 1805 was commemorated nationally on that day each year, though this event declined after the end of the First World War. A monument to Admiral Lord Nelson, the earliest in England, was erected in 1817–19 by another Norfolk man, William Wilkins, a short distance to the south of Great Yarmouth's developing resort. The monument, officially called the Norfolk Naval Pillar, is a Doric column topped by six caryatid figures supporting a statue of Britannia, rather than a figure of Nelson.

This part of the seafront at Great Yarmouth, the South Denes, was chosen as the location for the monument because this was where military activity was taking place and structures were being erected. As early as 1806 an armoury was being constructed along with a naval hospital on the South Denes; there was also a barracks and three forts. The first-edition one-inch Ordnance Survey map of 1837–8 shows this military infrastructure of the seafront still in place, a noticeable presence on a seafront that would have been busy with visitors during the summer months. A little further north, by the date of this photograph industrial activity was appearing in this area, including a gasometer, and today the monument stands among industrial units.

The monument in Great Yarmouth is considerably earlier than the more famous Nelson's Column in Trafalgar Square, which was constructed in 1840–3, but Nelson's Pillar in Dublin dated from 1808, but was blown up in 1966.

EPW021183

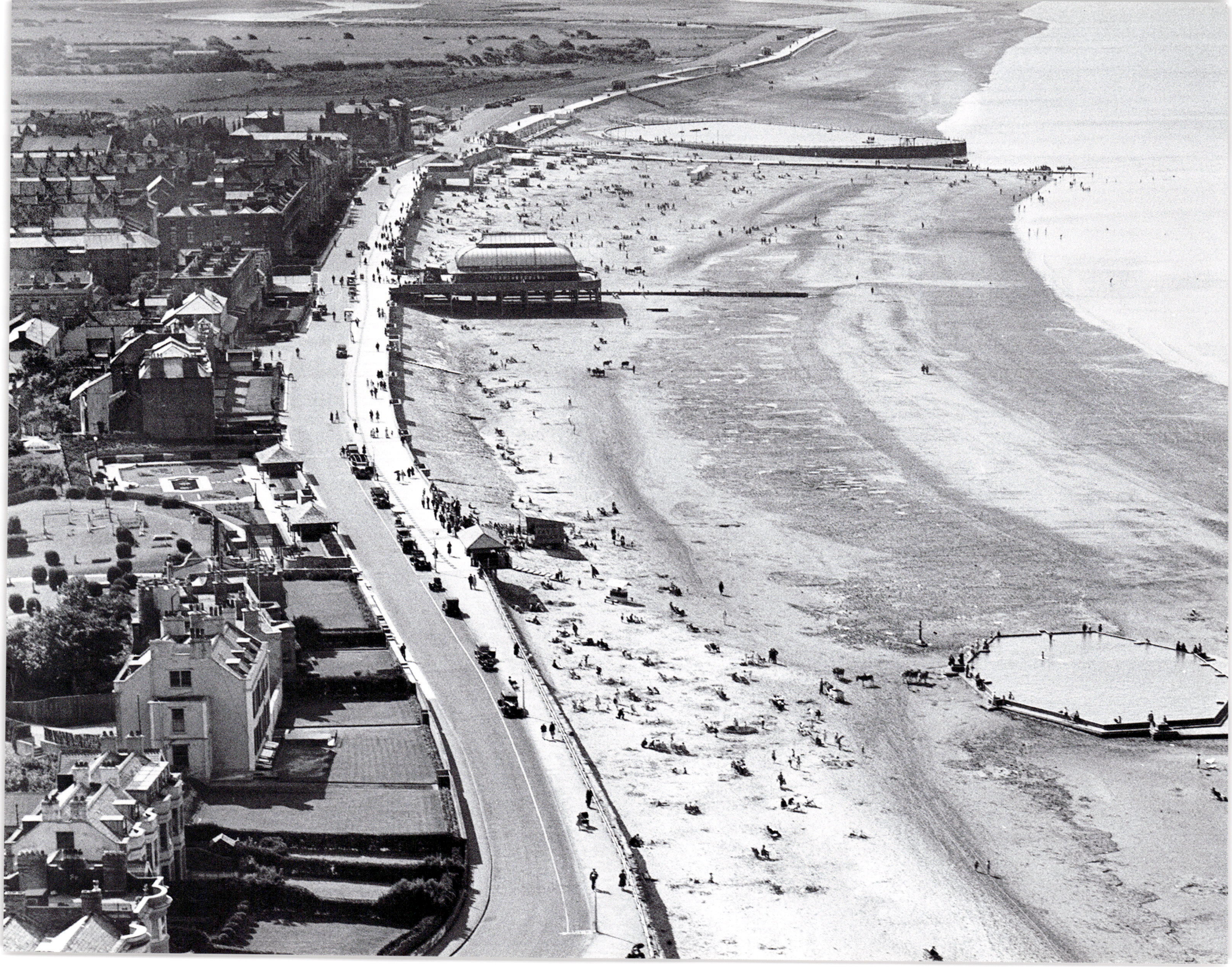

The Esplanade and the beach, Burnham-on-Sea, Somerset
August 1932

At seaside resorts there are many memorials to people and events, ranging from monumental statues of monarchs and war heroes to simple brass plaques on the back of a park bench. There is also a wide range of more practical types of monument such as a water fountain, a clock tower or a water trough for the hardy animals that work on seafronts.

One of the largest, and most unusual, commemorative structures found on a seafront is the elongated, octagonal paddling pool built on the beach at Burnham-on-Sea in 1921 by Mr and Mrs Joseph Bevan Braithwaite in thanks for the safe return of their five sons from the First World War. Joseph Bevan was a partner in a firm of stockbrokers and was a Quaker, as were his sons, yet they fought during the war. At high tide, the pool would fill with sea water and here at low tide, when the sea is some distance out, this is an ideal pool in which children can play. The site for the pool was chosen because it was near where the family lived. Due to cost and structural reasons, the pool was demolished in 2010.

Beyond the pool can be seen the pier at Burnham, which was the last to be built before the First World War. It is claimed to be the shortest pier in England, though this necessarily raises the question of the definition of a pier as it scarcely projects into the sea. The pier was constructed on the site of a bandstand that had been erected in 1901 to commemorate the coronation of Edward VII; it consists of an Edwardian Pavilion standing on concrete piles.

EPW039925

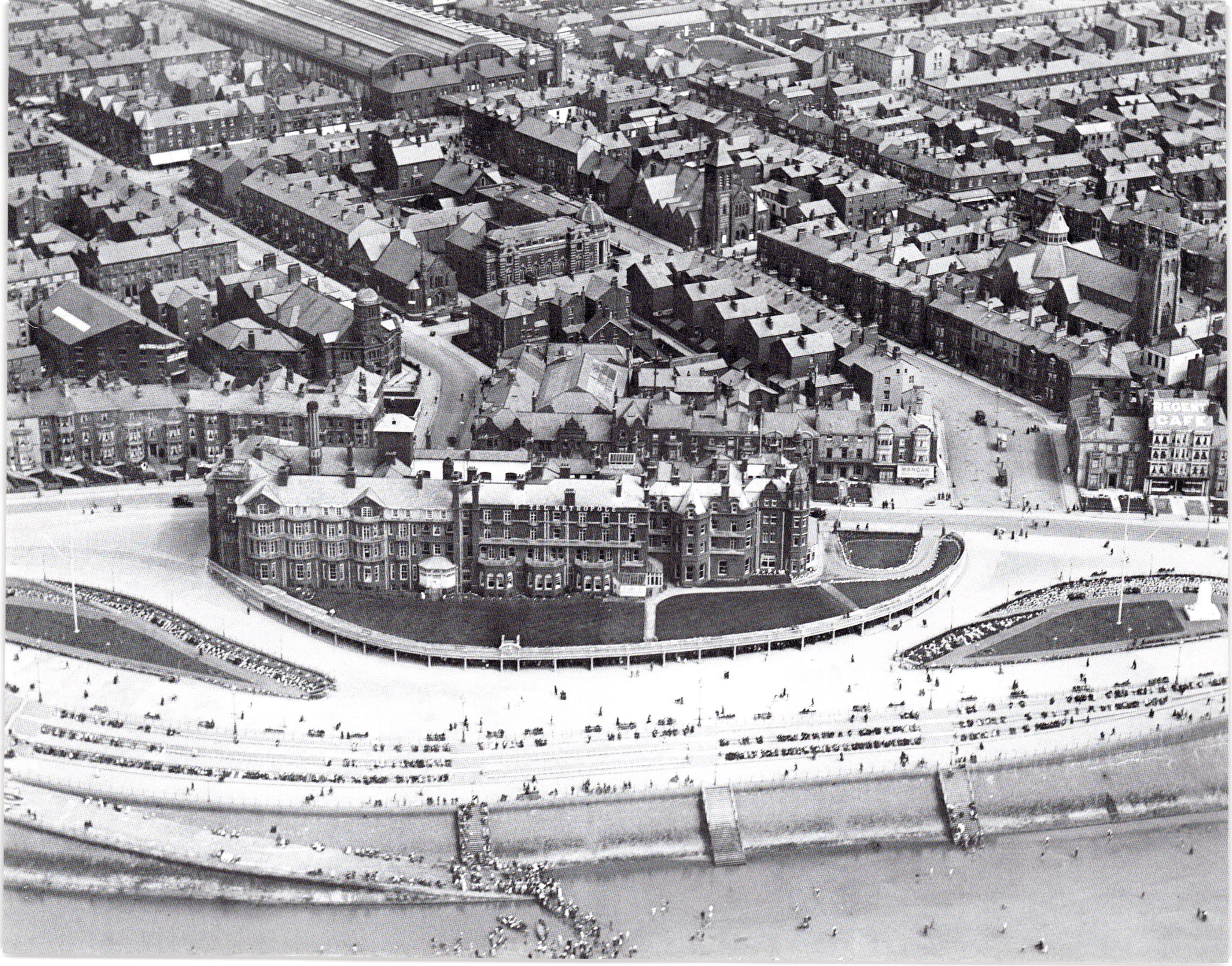
REGENT
CAFE

Hotel Metropole and the war memorial, Blackpool, Lancashire

July 1920

The First World War was a conflict that was experienced on the British mainland and involved every family in the country. During the war, the decision was taken not to repatriate the bodies of dead servicemen and instead the Imperial War Graves Commission (the Commonwealth War Graves Commission since 1960) was founded in 1917, initially, where possible, to care for the graves of the fallen. However, after the war, its primary function was to establish proper cemeteries, but, as many victims had no known grave, other appropriate means of commemoration needed to be found. Tributes were established in communities of all sizes, ranging from commemorative cottage hospitals or hospital wings to public baths, libraries, reading rooms, halls, and parks and gardens.

The most widespread form of commemoration was the war memorial, and to erect one a suitable site was required. At seaside resorts, often the largest public space available for development in the early 20th century was on the seafront. Fortunately, the Armistice, falling in mid-November, reduced the likelihood of any conflict between the solemn dignity of remembrance and the boisterous play of seaside holidaymakers.

The most spectacular seafront war memorial is located between North Pier and the Metropole Hotel at Blackpool. It consists of an obelisk almost 100ft (30.5m) high, designed by the Lancashire architect Ernest Prestwich, with carved reliefs by Gilbert Ledward. The Blackpool memorial, which was completed in 1923, has colossal reliefs cast in bronze entitled '1914 the outbreak of War' and '1918 the end of War'. There are also statues of two soldiers, an armed sailor, and an aviator in the four corners. However, as this elaborate memorial would take a number of years to create, the local community erected a temporary cenotaph immediately after the war and this is the white object that can be seen to the right-hand side of the hotel.

In the late 18th century, a number of large houses on the seafront at Blackpool served as hotels, the northernmost of which was known as Bailey's Hotel. This hotel was enlarged and rebuilt during the 19th century and underwent a lavish refurbishment and extension before reopening in 1900. As the revived Metropole Hotel, it provided guests with lavish facilities including a Moorish-style lounge, a Louis XV-style drawing room, and a main dining room in a Georgian style. The ground floor also contained a ballroom, a restaurant, and smoking and billiard rooms. As well as bedrooms on the upper floors, there were suites of apartments consisting of a sitting room, one or more bedrooms and a bathroom. Guests could enjoy hot and cold freshwater as well as seawater in their rooms and bathrooms.

The Metropole Hotel is unusual because it sits on the seaward side of the main road. Between it and the sea, the Princess Parade was completed in 1912 to link the new sea defences in central Blackpool to those created to protect the Claremont Park Estate to the north (left); it included elegant colonnades around the gardens of the Metropole Hotel.

EPW002073

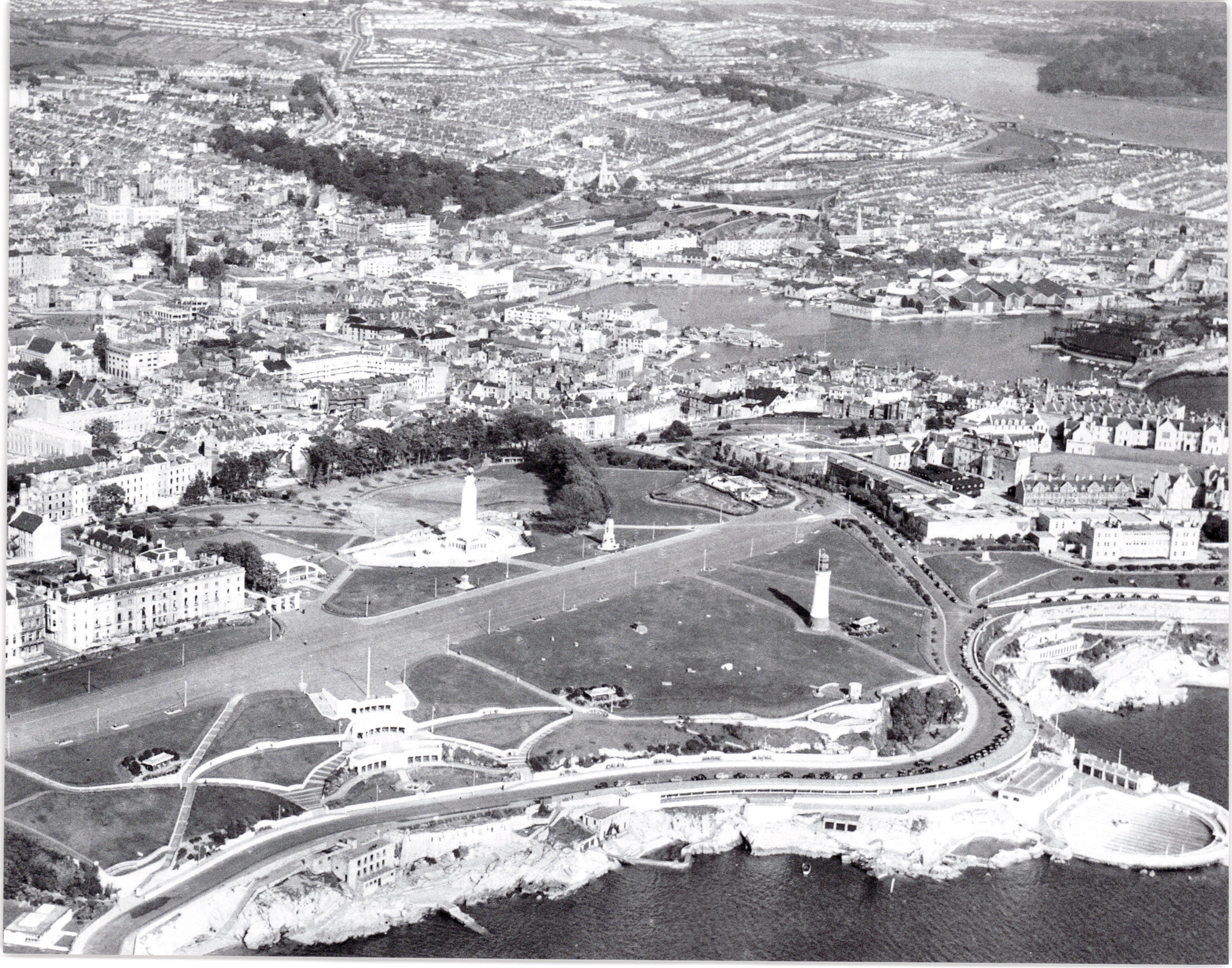

The Hoe and the city, Plymouth, Devon
19 November 1953

As well as local cenotaphs, some seaside resorts became the site for national memorials. The First World War Memorial at Plymouth, set at the heart of Plymouth Hoe, commemorates the action of the Royal Marines who fell during the war. The Royal Navy, and the navies of the Dominions, lost around 48,000 men, with over 25,000 being lost or buried at sea. Therefore, their sacrifice was not recorded in any cemetery or on any battlefield, and so it was decided that three national memorials of the same design should be established near the Royal Navy's home ports at Portsmouth, Plymouth and Chatham. The memorial at Plymouth, between the Armada Memorial and the Drake statue, was unveiled in July 1924. The three memorials were designed by the Scottish architect Sir Robert Lorimer, using, but adapting, the Navy's preferred obelisk design, with sculpture provided by Henry Poole. At Chatham, bronze panels were inscribed with 8,541 names; the memorial on Southsea Common commemorates 9,666 sailors; and the Plymouth Memorial initially had 7,256 names (*see* p 299).

After the Second World War, these Navy memorials were enlarged and updated by Sir Edward Maufe, principal architect for the Imperial War Graves Commission, with figurative sculpture by Sir Charles Wheeler and William McMillan. Plymouth's extension opened in 1954 and featured a sunken garden with statues of naval personnel and bronze plaques naming the 15,935 sailors lost from the port. This photograph taken in November 1953 seems to show the work of providing the new garden in progress.

Plymouth Hoe, most famously associated with the apocryphal story of Sir Francis Drake and his game of bowls before confronting the Spanish Armada, was the obvious place to construct the Armada Memorial. In 1888, the architect Herbert A Gribble and the sculptor W Charles May created the statue of Drake to celebrate the tercentenary of the victory over the Armada. This can be seen in front, and to the right, of the First World War Memorial.

The Hoe is also a location for part of the lighthouse originally built in 1759 by John Smeaton on the Eddystone Rocks; its upper floors were re-erected on Plymouth Hoe in 1882. While Plymouth is beside the seaside, its rocky shoreline makes accessing the sea difficult and therefore a number of structures were created, including in 1935 the Tinside Lido, which can be seen on the right of the photograph.

EAW053020

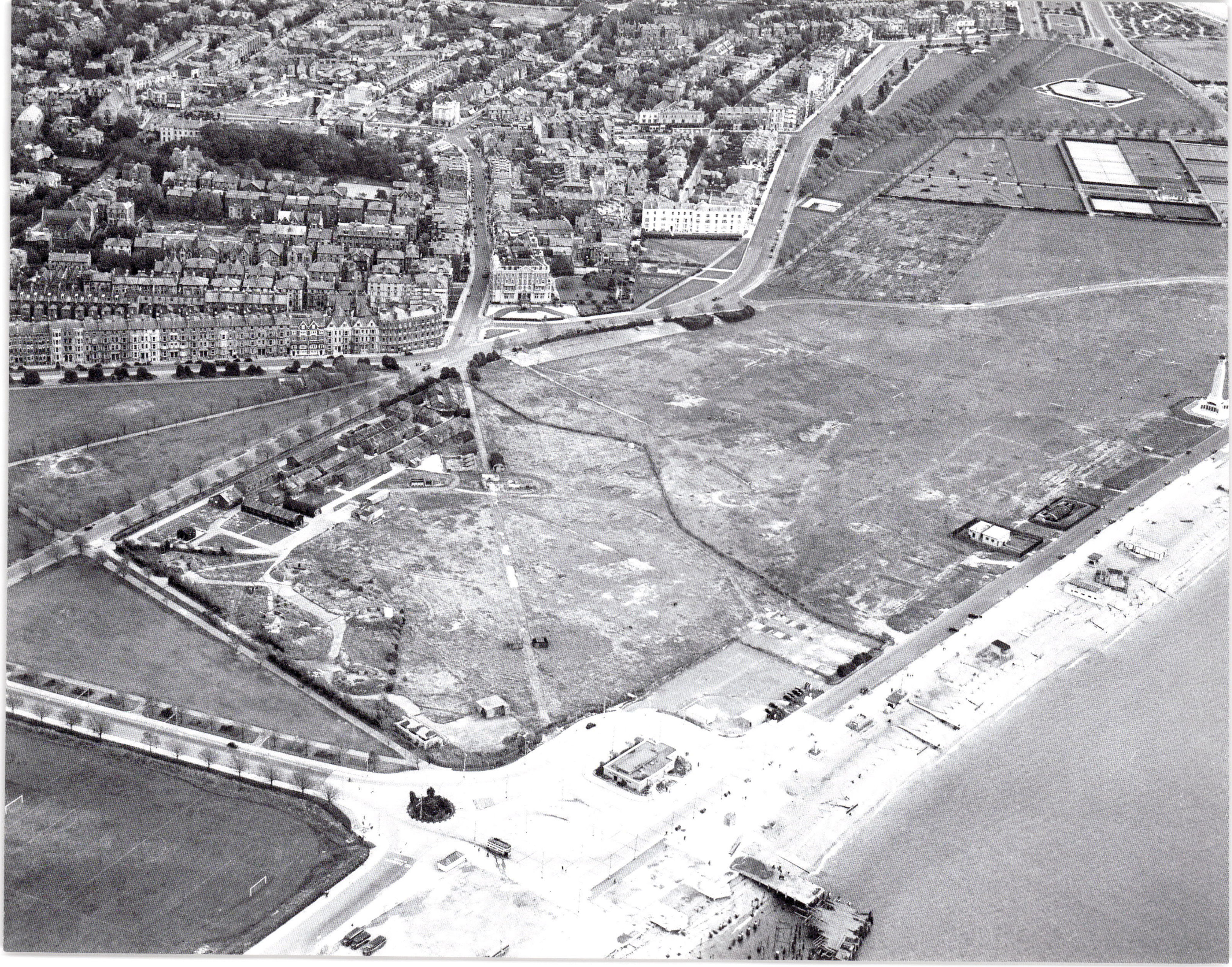

Southsea Common, Southsea, Hampshire

3 October 1946

The proximity of Southsea Common to the city of Portsmouth, with its large naval dockyard, means that this area serves as a pleasure ground for local residents and holidaymakers, as well as a place where the actions and the sacrifices of the Royal Navy are commemorated. Southsea has the earliest war memorials and the largest collection, the earliest being erected in 1857 commemorating the Crimean War. It was 'Erected by the Debating Society of Portsmouth aided by their fellow townsmen' to commemorate 'those brave soldiers and sailors who during the late war with Russia died of their wounds and are buried in this garrison'. In 1860, the Peel or Shannon Naval Brigade Monument was unveiled beside the Crimean Memorial, while the Trident Memorial was erected in *c* 1860 and re-erected in 1877. This was a memorial 'To the memory of forty-four Officers and Men of *H.M.S. Trident*' who died during a yellow fever epidemic in Sierra Leone in 1859. There are also memorials to other ships, including the HMS *Aboukir*, which lost 48 officers and men during an epidemic of yellow fever at Jamaica in 1873–4. To complete this unrivalled set of early war memorials, there is the Trafalgar Monument, which incorporates an anchor from HMS *Victory* set on a battered granite stone plinth. These memorials can be seen in a line at the top of the beach, in front of the seafront road.

The largest war memorial on Southsea Common is the First World War Memorial, seen at the top-right of this photograph. Like the monuments at Chatham and Plymouth (*see* p 297), it provides a memorial to men lost or buried at sea. It was inaugurated by the Duke of York in October 1924. Designed by the Scottish architect Sir Robert Lorimer (1864–1929), it commemorated 9,666 sailors, and after the Second World War it was enlarged by Sir Edward Maufe, principal architect for the Imperial War Graves Commission, with figurative sculpture by Sir Charles Wheeler and William McMillan. The extension took the form of a sunken garden with statues around it, mostly of naval personnel. On the walls are mounted 78 bronze panels bearing the names of 14,921 sailors from the port who died during the war. The extension was inaugurated by Queen Elizabeth, the Queen Mother, on 29 April 1953.

Amidst all the potential solemnity of these war memorials, Southsea Common is also a place of leisure. Today people swim in the sea from the shingle beach, while others fish, but most simply sit or lie down to enjoy warm summer sun. There is also now a range of leisure facilities including a swimming pool and an aquarium. The large open area of grass is the site of festivals, informal sporting events and picnics. Towards the western end of the seafront, at the bottom of the photograph, is the site of Southsea's second seaside pier. Named after the then Lieutenant Governor of Portsmouth, Clarence Pier was opened by the Prince of Wales (later Edward VII) on 1 June 1861 as a plain wooden jetty primarily for steamers sailing to the Isle of Wight, but also for people to walk along. The pier was extended in 1869, and in 1882 a two-storey circular pavilion was opened, offering music and refreshment. It was enlarged in 1907 and further improvements took place in 1932.

This photograph was taken on 3 October 1946 and shows the heavily damaged structure that remained after an air raid on Portsmouth Docks on 10 January 1941. A new pier was built on the site and opened on 1 June 1961. As this image dates from a year after the end of the Second World War, a range of military features can be seen. On the common there are a number of circular and rectangular earthwork features and to the left can be seen some concrete structures, including one that still had its camouflaged paint scheme.

EAW003001

Bibliography

Barker, Nigel *et al* 2007 *Margate's Seaside Heritage*. Swindon: English Heritage

Berry, Sue 2005 *Georgian Brighton*. Chichester: Phillimore & Co. Ltd

Braggs, Steven and Harris, Diane 2000 *Sun, Fun and Crowds: Seaside Holidays Between the Wars*. Stroud: Tempus

Brodie, Allan 2018 *The Seafront*. Swindon: Historic England

Brodie, Allan 2019 *Tourism and the Changing Face of the British Isles.* Swindon: Historic England

Brodie, Allan and Whitfield, Matthew 2014 *Blackpool's Seaside Heritage.* Swindon: English Heritage

Brodie, Allan and Winter, Gary 2007 *The English Seaside Resort*. Swindon: English Heritage

Brodie, Allan, Roethe, Johanna and Hudson-McAulay, Kate 2019 *Weston-super-Mare: The Town and its Seaside Heritage*. Swindon: Historic England

Brodie, Allan *et al* 2008 *Weymouth's Seaside Heritage.* Swindon: English Heritage

Easdown, Martin 2007 *Piers of Kent.* Stroud: Tempus

Easdown, Martin 2009 *Lancashire's Seaside Piers*. Barnsley: Wharncliffe Books

Ferry, Kathryn 2009 *Beach Huts and Bathing Machines*. Oxford: Shire

Ferry, Kathryn 2016 *The Nation's Host: Butlin's and the Story of the British Seaside*. London: Viking

Fischer, Richard and Walton, John K 1987 *British Piers*. London: Thames and Hudson

Gray, Fred 2006 *Designing the Seaside: Architecture, Society and Nature*. London: Reaktion

Gray, Fred 2020 *The Architecture of British Seaside Piers*. Ramsbury: The Crowood Press

Hardy, Dennis and Ward, Colin 1984 *Arcadia for All: The Legacy of a Makeshift Landscape*. London: Mansell

Kane, Josephine 2013 *The Architecture of Pleasure: British Amusement Parks and the Architecture of Pleasure 1900–1939*. Farnham: Ashgate

Morrison, Kathryn A and Minnis, John 2012 *Carscapes*. New Haven and London: Yale University Press

Pearson, Lynn 1991 *The People's Palaces: The Story of the Seaside Pleasure Buildings of 1870–1914*. Buckingham: Barracuda

Pearson, Lynn 2002 *Piers and Other Seaside Architecture*. Princes Risborough: Shire

Pimlott, John A R 1976 *The Englishman's Holiday*. Hassocks: Harvester Press

Simmons, Jack 1986 *The Railway in Town and Country, 1830–1914*. Newton Abbot: David & Charles

Simmons, Jack and Biddle, Gordon (eds) 1999 *The Oxford Companion to British Railway History, from 1603 to the 1990s*. Oxford: Oxford University Press

Smith, Janet 2005 *Liquid Assets: The Lidos and Open Air Swimming Pools of Britain*. Swindon: English Heritage

Walton, John K 1983 *The English Seaside Resort: A Social History, 1750–1914*. Leicester: Leicester University Press

Walton, John K 1998 *Blackpool*. Edinburgh: Edinburgh University Press

Walton, John K 2000 *The British Seaside: Holidays and Resorts in the Twentieth Century*. Manchester: Manchester University Press

Wills, Anthony and Phillips, Tim 2014 *British Seaside Piers.* Swindon: English Heritage

Location index